AQA

GCSE Science

ADDITIONAL HIGHER

Editor: Nigel Heslop

Nigel Heslop, Graham Hill,
Toby Houghton, Steve Witney
and Christine Woodward

Hodder Murray

A MEMBER OF THE HODDER HEADLINE GROUP

The Publishers would like to thank the following for permission to reproduce copyright material:

p.1 *tl* Science Photo Library/Andrew Syred, *tc* Science Photo Library/Susumu Nishinaga, *tr* Science Photo Library/Dr Torsten Wittmann, *bl* Science Photo Library/Manfred Kage, Peter Arnold INC., *br* Science Photo Library/Steve Gschmeissner; **p.2** *t* Science Photo Library/Adam Hart-Davis, *c* Science Photo Library/Omikron, *b* Science Photo Library/Dr Gopal Murti; **p.3** *t* Science Photo Library/Dr Jeremy Burgess, *b* Science Photo Library/Steve Gschmeissner; **p.13** *main photo* Corbis/Stefan Puchner/dpa, *inset* Science Photo Library/Eye of Science; **p.14** Science Photo Library/Biophoto Associates; **p.20** Alamy/Holt Studios; **p.22** *l* Alamy/Tom Mareachal, *tr* Corbis/Paul A Souders, *br* Corbis/Paul A. Souders; **p.23** *t* Alamy/Phil Degginger, *b* Courtesy Wadsworth Control Systems; **p.34** *main photo* Science Photo Library/CC Studio, *t inset* Grace/zefa/Corbis , *b inset* Science Photo Library/Prof.K.Seddon & Dr.T.Evans, Queen's University, Belfast; **p.38** Getty/Hulton Archive; **p.44** Alamy/Phototake, inc.; **p.45** *bl* Anthony Blake Photo Library/Tony Robins, *br* Getty/Gary Buss; **p.46** Lorna Ainger; **p.47** Lorna Ainger; **p.51** PYMCA/Manuela Zanotti; **p.55** Corbis/Bettmann; **p.58** Science Photo Library/L. Willatt, East Anglian Regional Genetics Service; **p.62** Science Photo Library/Professor Miodrag Stojkovic; **p.63** *tl* Science Photo Library/Professor Miodrag Stojkovic, *tc* Science Photo Library/Steve Gschmeissner, *tr* Science Photo Library/Susumu Nishinaga, *cl* Science Photo Library/Innerspace Imaging, *cr* Science Photo Library/Steve Gschmeissner, *bl* Science Photo Library/Steve Gschmeissner, *br* Science Photo Library/David McCarthy; **p.65** PureStockX; **p.66** Science Photo Library/CNRI; **p.72** *l* Science Photo Library/David Parker, *tr* Science & Society Picture Library/Science Museum, *br* Rex Features; **p.74** Corbis/Russell Boyce/Reuters; **p.78** University of Cambridge Cavendish Library; **p.80** Lorna Ainger; **p.81** *t* Alamy/Steve Atkins, *b* Alamy/Gunter Marx; **p.82** Rex Features/The Travel Library; **p.85** PureStock X; **p.87** PureStock X; **p.94** Corbis/Matthias Kulka; **p.95** *t* Alamy/Kevin Schafer/Peter Arnold Inc., *b* Science Photo Library/Sinclair Stammers; **p.96** *l* Science Photo Library/Philippe Plailly/Eurelios, *r* Science Photo Library/Kenneth Libbrecht; **p.97** *l* Corbis/Alan Goldsmith, *r* Corbis/David Samuel Robbins; **p.98** Science Photo Library/Charles D. Winters; **p.100** Corbis/Owaki – Kulla; **p.101** Corbis/Nik Wheeler; **p.104** *t* Hodder, *b* Corbis/Bruce Peebles; **p.105** Alamy/Frances Roberts; **p.107** *t* Still Pictures/Leonard Lessin, *b* Corbis/Paul McErlane/Reuters; **p.108** Wellcome Trust; **p.115** Rex Features/Woman's Weekly; **p.116** Science Photo Library/Andrew Lambert; **p.117** Science Photo Library/Colin Cuthbert; **p.120** *l* Alamy/David Hoffman, *r* Corbis/Jon Hicks; **p.121** Corbis/photocuisine; **p.124** Geoscience Features; **p.125** *t* PureStock X, *c* PureStock X, *b* Lorna Ainger; **p.126** Nigel Heslop; **p.131** Science Photo Library/Richard Folwell; **p.132** *l* Robert Opie, *c* Alamy/Dennis MacDonald, *r* Rex Features/Dan Talson; **p.133** Nigel Heslop; **p.135** Science Photo Library/Emilio Segre Visual Archives/American Institute of Physics; **p.141** Science Photo Library/Alan Sirulnikoff; **p.143** Science Photo Library/Andrew Lambert; **p.146** Science Photo Library/Gusto; **p.147** Science Photo Library/Martyn F. Chillmaid; **p.148** Nigel Heslop; **p.149** Science Photo Library/James Holmes, Hays Chemicals; **p.155** Science Photo Library/TRL Ltd.; **p.156** PureStock X; **p.157** *t* Corbis/Seguin Franck/Sygma, *b* Getty/Tony R. Tolley/U.S. Air Force; **p.161** PureStock X; **p.165** Getty/Bryn Lennon; **p.166** PureStock X; **p.169** *tr* Alamy/Andi Duff, *c* Science Photo Library/Peter Bowater; **p.173** Getty/Lester Lefkowitz; **p.174** *t* Rex Features/James Fraser, *c* Getty Images/Al Bello, *bl* Alamy/Sally & Richard Greenhill; **p.176** Rex Features; **p.178** Getty/Carlo Baroncini/AFP; **p.179** *t* Action Plus, *b* Alamy/Tim Graham; **p.180** *t* Empics/David Zalubowski/AP, *c* PureStock X, *b* Getty/Brian Bahr; **p.181** *tl* Alamy/David Crausby, *bl* PureStock X, *r* Getty/Romilly Lockyer; **p.183** Corbis/Gulliver/Zefa; **p.184** NASA; **p.187** Rex Features/Lewis Whyld; p.189 Science Photo Library/Hank Morgan; **p.190** Science Photo Library/Andrew Lambert; **p.192** Science Photo Library/David Parker; **p.195** Corbis/Armando Arorizo/epa; **p.197** Alamy/Tim Gartside; **p.199** Lorna Ainger; **p.200** *t* Science Photo Library/Andrew Lambert, *b* Science Photo Library/Andrew Lambert; **p.205** Alamy/Paul Bradforth; **p.208** Courtesy Peratech; **p. 211** *l* Science Photo Library/Cordelia Molloy, *c* Science Photo Library/Andrew Lambert, *r* Science Photo Library/Adam Hart-Davis; **p.212** *l* Alamy/Blue Shadows, *r* Science Photo Library/Sheila Terry; **p.213** Science Photo Library/Sheila Terry; **p.219** *l* Getty/Greg Mathieson/Time Life Pictures, *r* NASA; **p.226** Science Photo Library/Sheila Terry; **p.227** Science Photo Library/Emilio Segre Visual Archives/American Institute of Physics.

Every effort has been made to trace all copyright holders, but if any have been inadvertently overlooked the Publishers will be pleased to make the necessary arrangements at the first opportunity.

Although every effort has been made to ensure that website addresses are correct at time of going to press, Hodder Murray cannot be held responsible for the content of any website mentioned in this book. It is sometimes possible to find a relocated web page by typing in the address of the home page for a website in the URL window of your browser.

Risk Assessment

As a service to users, a risk assessment for this title has been carried out by CLEAPSS and is available on request to the publishers. However, the publishers accept no legal responsibility on any issue arising from this risk assessment: whilst every effort has been made to check the instructions of practical work in this book, it is still the duty and legal obligation of schools to carry out their own risk assessments.

Hodder Headline's policy is to use papers that are natural, renewable and recyclable products and made from wood grown in sustainable forests. The logging and manufacturing processes are expected to conform to the environmental regulations of the country of origin.

Orders: please contact Bookpoint Ltd, 130 Milton Park, Abingdon, Oxon OX14 4SB. Telephone: (44) 01235 827720. Fax: (44) 01235 400454. Lines are open 9.00–17.00, Monday to Saturday, with a 24-hour message answering service. Visit our website at www.hoddereducation.co.uk.

First published in 2006 by
Hodder Murray, an imprint of Hodder Education,
a member of the Hodder Headline Group
338 Euston Road
London NW1 3BH

Impression number 10 9 8 7 6 5 4 3 2 1
Year 2011 2010 2009 2008 2007 2006

Cover photos Science Photo Library: salt crystals, Andrew Syred; lightning, Keith Kent; pollen grain, Andrew Syred
Illustrations by Barking Dog Art
Typeset in Times 11.5pt by Fakenham Photosetting Limited, Fakenham, Norfolk
Printed in Italy

A catalogue record for this title is available from the British Library

ISBN-10: 0 340 90711 8
ISBN-13: 978 0340 90711 5

Contents

Introduction

AQA GCSE Science Additional Higher Student's Book

Welcome to the AQA GCSE Science Additional Student's Book for the Higher Tier. This book has been written to support you through your Additional Science GCSE with AQA. The book covers all the Biology, Chemistry and Physics material as well as the key 'How science works' elements of the new specification.

Each chapter begins with a list of **learning objectives**. Don't forget to refer back to these when checking whether you have understood the material covered in a particular chapter. **Questions** appear throughout each chapter, which will help to test your knowledge and understanding of the subject, as you go along. They will also enable you to develop key skills and understand how science works.

Activities are found throughout the book. These will take you longer to complete than the questions but will show you many of the real-life applications and implications of science. At the end of each chapter a **summary** evaluates the important points and key words. You will find the summaries useful in reviewing the work you have completed and in revising for your examinations. Don't forget to use the **index** to help you find the topic you are working on.

You will find **exam questions** at the end of each chapter, to help you prepare for your exams. These include similar questions to those in the structured questions for the exam.

You will take three written papers, one for Biology (chapters 1 to 4), one for Chemistry (chapters 5 to 8) and one for Physics (chapters 9 to 12).

This book is written for the **Higher-tier** examination. It will push you so that you get the best possible result at GCSE. If you are planning to take the **Foundation-tier** examination, you may wish to use the Foundation Student's Book instead.

Good luck with your studies!

Nigel Heslop, Graham Hill, Toby Houghton, Steve Witney and Christine Woodward

Chapter 1
How do substances get into and out of cells?

By the end of this chapter you should:

- ✓ know the names and be able to explain the function of the different parts of animal and plant cells;
- ✓ be able to describe the differences between animal and plant cells;
- ✓ be able to identify a range of specialised cells;
- ✓ be able to relate the structure of a specialised cell to its function;
- ✓ be able to explain how substances move in and out of cells by diffusion;
- ✓ know how water moves in and out of cells by osmosis;
- ✓ understand how osmosis is affected by the concentrations of the solutions inside and outside a cell.

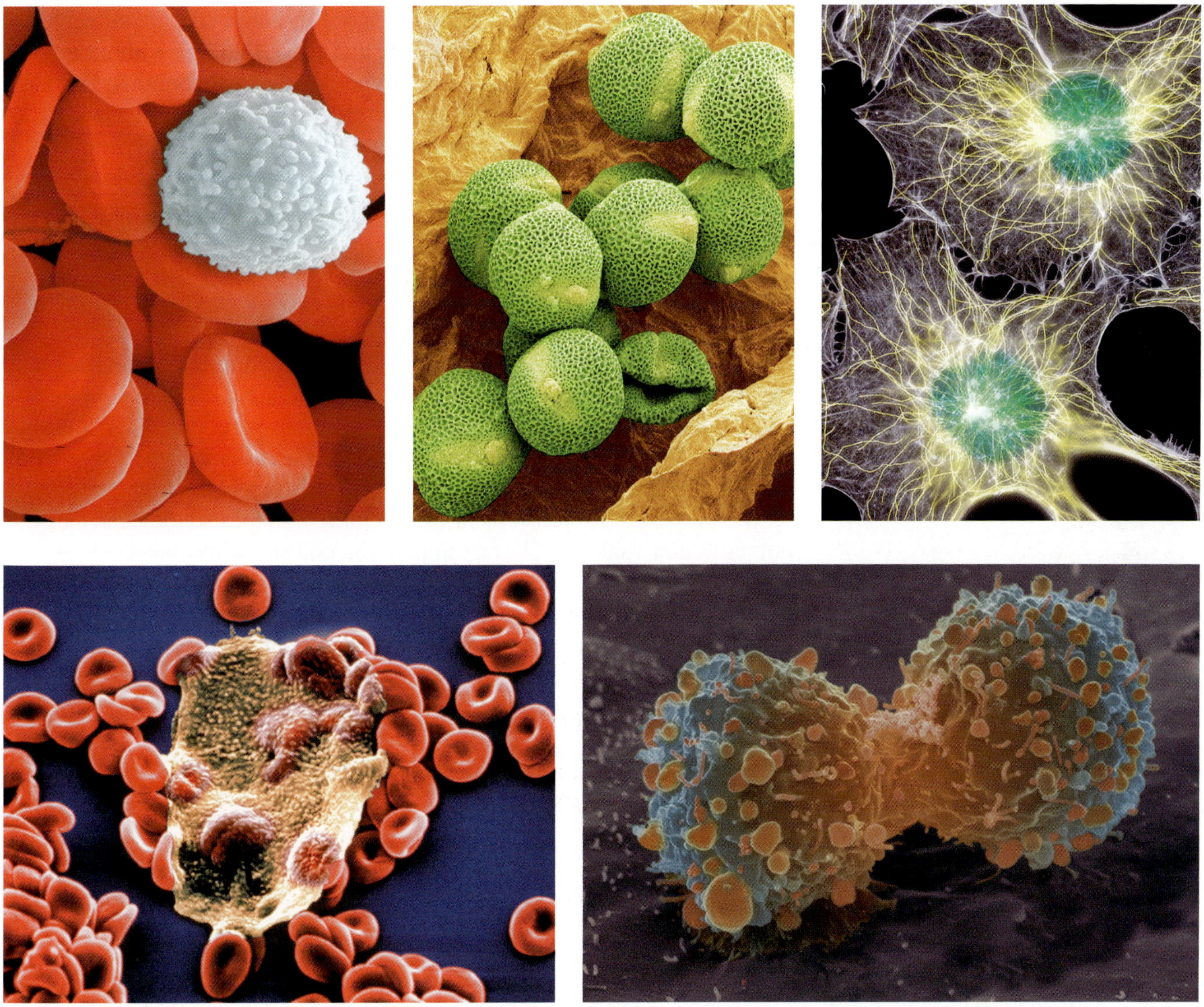

Figure 1.1 Cells are essential for life. They control all the processes in your body that keep you alive and are responsible for reproduction. The cells in the pictures are all very different. How does this allow them to do different jobs?
Top: Red and white blood cells; pollen cells, fibroblast making new connective tissue. Bottom: macrophage killing red blood cells, cancer cells.

1.1 How do cells perform different functions?

Figure 1.2 Robert Hooke and the drawing he made of the cork cells he could see with his microscope

We now understand that all living things are made up of cells, but this was not always the case. In 1665 a scientist called Robert Hooke used a primitive microscope to discover that samples from a cork tree were made up from repeating structures. He called these **cells**.

Hooke's discovery was only the start of what is now known as cell theory. Although he observed cells in one type of plant, he did not link cells to other species and had no idea what was inside cells. In 1831 improvements in microscope technology allowed a scientist called Robert Brown to observe nuclei inside a number of different cells. Later in the same decade two German biologists, Theodor Schwann and Matthias Jakob Schleiden, carried out more research and linked cells to all plants and animals. Schwann published these findings without any acknowledgment of Schleiden's or anyone else's contributions. He was correct to suggest that cells are the unit that make up all living things. However, he also suggested that new cells formed out of nothing. This was proved to be wrong by Rudolph Virchow in 1858. Virchow proposed the theory, still in place today, that all cells are formed from other cells.

What are the functions of different parts of a cell?

Modern microscopes now let us see an incredible amount of detail about the structure of cells, details that Robert Hooke's microscope simply could not display. We can now identify different parts of cells that each carry out different functions. From our observations we have discovered that all cells have some parts in common, such as a cell membrane. However, parts of some cells have specialised shapes so they can carry out particular functions. For example, you can see a fibroblast cell in Figure 1.1, making new connective tissue. This process is essential for the body to heal after an injury. There are also some fundamental differences between the cells that make up animals and those found in plants.

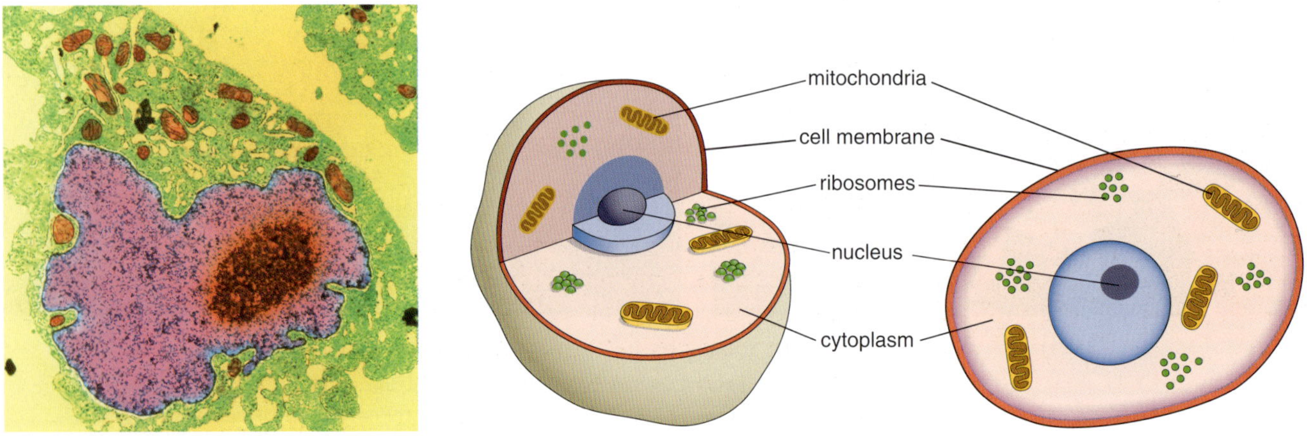

Figure 1.3 An animal cell shown as it is seen with a microscope (magnified × 4800) and as three- and two-dimensional diagrams

1. Cells are often described as the 'building blocks of life'. What does this mean?
2. Robert Hooke observed cells but did not identify anything inside them. What was limiting his research?
3. Why do you think that Robert Brown's discovery was important in developing a better understanding of cells?
4. No one scientist can claim that they came up with cell theory. However, Schwann did not acknowledge anybody's contributions when he published his findings. What reasons do you think he had for doing this?

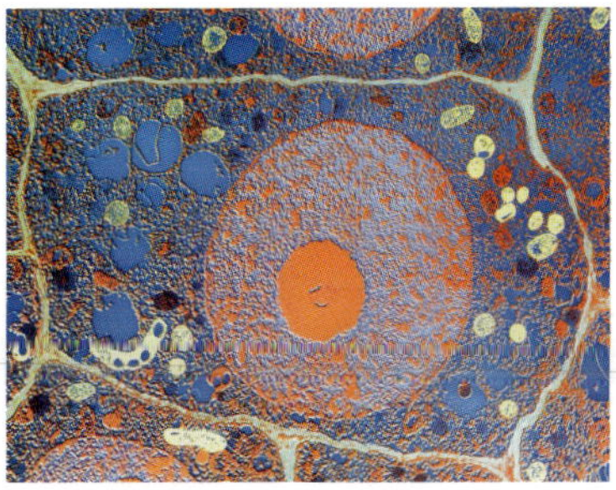

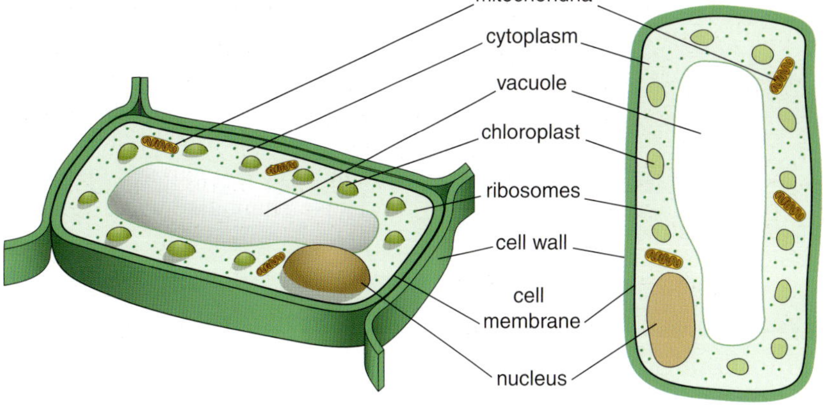

Figure 1.4 A plant cell shown as it is seen with a microscope (magnified × 2800) and as three- and two-dimensional diagrams. Note the cell wall, vacuole and chloroplasts that are not found in animal cells.

Proteins are long chains of amino acids that form the basis of most body structures such as skin, muscle and hair. They also form chemicals in the body such as enzymes.

Similar cells group together to form body tissue. For example, your skin is made up of layers of skin cells and your muscle is formed from muscle cells packed together. New tissue forms when cells divide. The cells make exact copies of themselves. This includes making copies of all the cell parts you can see in Figures 1.3 and 1.4. Each of these parts carries out a job. This enables the cell to contribute to the function of the tissue it is part of. Now you need to look at the function carried out by each part of a cell.

Nucleus

The nucleus of a cell contains an individual's genes. These carry out two functions:

1. They can make copies of themselves when the cell divides to make a new cell.
2. They synthesise (make) **proteins**, such as enzymes.

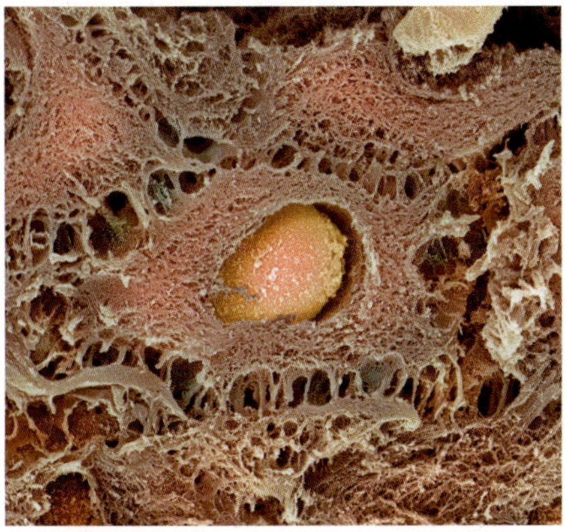

Figure 1.5 The nucleus of a human skin cell

Enzymes control all the reactions that take place in the cell. These reactions include respiration, photosynthesis and protein synthesis. Enzymes even control cell division when it takes place. Some of these enzymes pass out of the cell membrane to control reactions outside the cell. For example, amylase is an enzyme produced by cells in your salivary glands. Amylase passes out of the cells and digests starch into sugar in your mouth and oesophagus. Ideas about enzymes are developed in Chapter 3.

Cytoplasm

The cytoplasm is mostly water and fills the cell membrane. It is where most of the cell's chemical reactions take place. When a cell is making an enzyme, this happens in the cytoplasm. The cytoplasm also stores the dissolved raw materials, such as amino acids and glucose, needed for all these reactions.

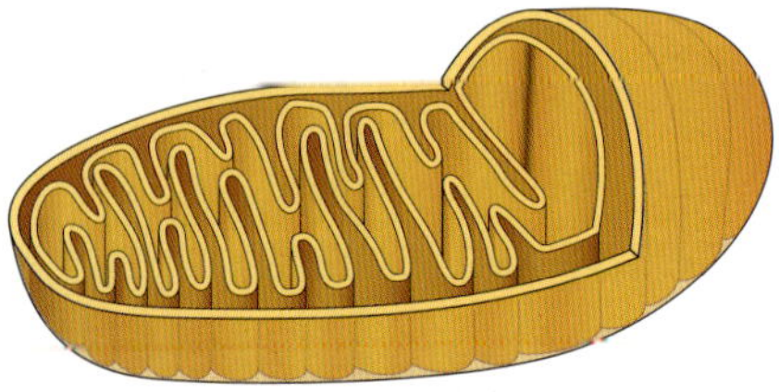

Figure 1.6 A human mitochondrion

Mitochondria

Your whole body needs energy to keep warm, grow and move around. This energy gets into your body in your food where it is stored in the chemical bonds in the food. **Mitochondria** release the energy from glucose molecules during a process called respiration. Respiration is a series of chemical reactions that take place on the surface of the channels you can see inside the mitochondrion shown in Figure 1.6. These channels have a large surface area so that respiration can take place at a fast rate.

Mitochondria are the parts of a cell responsible for releasing energy from glucose by respiration.

Ribosomes put amino acids into the correct order to make a specific protein.

Ribosomes

You have already seen that the genes in the nucleus make proteins in the cytoplasm, such as enzymes which control all the chemical reactions in your body. **Ribosomes** are structures that control the making of proteins. They join together the amino acids into the long chains that become proteins.

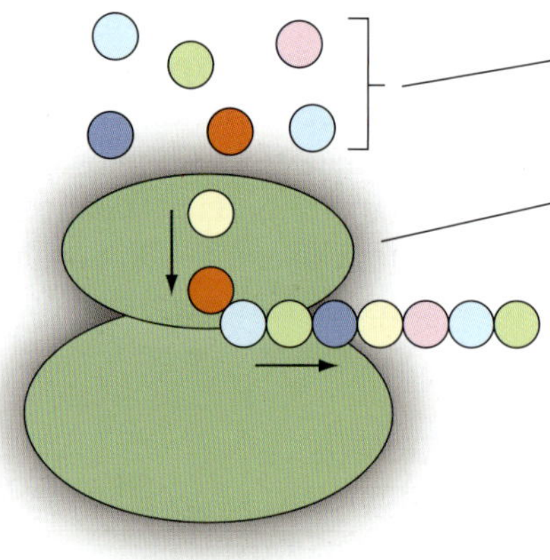

Figure 1.7 A ribosome forming a protein chain from amino acids in the cytoplasm

Cell membrane

The cell membrane surrounds the cytoplasm. Anything that has to get in or out of the cell has to pass through the cell membrane. For example, the glucose used in the mitochondria for respiration enters the cell through the membrane, and insulin produced in pancreas cells leaves the cell through the membrane. The cell membrane actually controls the movement of many of these substances in and out of the cell.

Cell wall – found only in plant cells

Plant cells have a rigid cell wall around the cell membrane that strengthens the cell and keeps its shape. It is made from a chemical called cellulose. Without cell walls plants would not be able to stay upright. Most animals have an internal or external skeleton to give them structure and so do not need cell walls.

Chloroplasts use light energy to make glucose and oxygen from carbon dioxide and water by photosynthesis. They are found only in some plant cells.

Chloroplasts – found only in some plant cells

Chloroplasts are structures that contain a chemical called chlorophyll which absorbs light energy to make food for the plant by a process called photosynthesis. Photosynthesis is actually a series of chemical reactions that are all controlled by enzymes.

Permanent vacuole – found only in plant cells

The vacuole in a plant cell contains water and some dissolved chemicals. This mixture is called cell sap. The vacuole acts a bit like a reservoir for the cell.

5. Copy and complete Table 1.1 to summarise the functions of the different cell parts.

6. A cell could be compared to a factory with the different parts working together so that the cell can function. Compare each part of a cell to part of a factory. For example:

   The mitochondria are like the generators in a factory because they release the energy from fuel.

7. The nucleus is sometimes called the 'brain' of a cell. Explain how much you agree with this statement.

8. People sometimes say they have a 'high metabolic rate' if they release energy from their food quickly. Use the information about the different cell parts to suggest why some people release energy from their food more quickly than others. Explain your answer.

9. Where in a plant would you expect to find cells with the most chloroplasts? Give a reason for your answer.

Cell part	Function	Found in...
Nucleus	Controls the chemical reactions in the cell.	Animal and plant cells.
Cytoplasm		
Cell membrane		
Mitochondria		
Ribosomes		
Cell wall		
Chloroplasts		
Vacuole		

Table 1.1

Most cells have a specific function to carry out. For example, nerve cells transmit electrical impulses around the body and cells in the pancreas produce insulin. Once these cells have specialised they keep producing these specialised cells. However, there are some cells, called stem cells, that can produce a range of different cells. Stem cells are found in embryos, adult bone marrow and some other body tissue such as liver tissue. Stem cells will be covered in Section 4.3.

1.2 How do dissolved substances move into and out of cells?

So far this chapter has referred to a range of processes, such as respiration and photosynthesis, that take place inside cells. These processes take place as a series of chemical reactions and therefore need chemicals that can get into a cell. They also produce chemicals that need to leave the cell. In this section you will consider how these substances move into or out of a cell.

In this chapter we are going to concentrate on the movement of oxygen and water into and out of cells. Both of these substances will, at times, enter or leave cells.

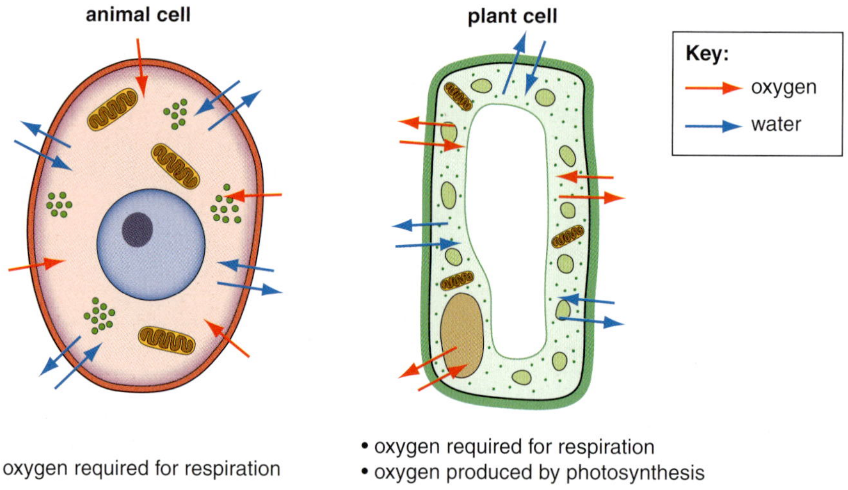

Figure 1.8 The movement of oxygen and water in and out of animal and plant cells

10. Make a list of substances that you think need to:
    a) get into a cell;
    b) leave a cell.

11. What do these substances need to pass through in order to enter or leave a cell?

Diffusion

Concentration is the amount of one substance in a given volume of another.

Diffusion is the movement of particles in a gas or any dissolved substance from a region of higher concentration to a region of lower concentration.

A **partially permeable membrane** is a membrane, such as a cell membrane, that has tiny gaps and will only allow some substances pass through it.

If you spray air freshener in one corner of a room it is not long before it can be smelt throughout the room. This happens because the particles that make up the air freshener move around. To start with there are lots of particles in the space where you sprayed the air freshener, but quickly they spread out to where there are fewer particles. They move from a region where there is a higher **concentration** of particles to a region where there is a lower concentration. This process is called **diffusion** and it explains why gases spread out. Imagine if your class started huddled in the corner of the room and then ran about until they were evenly spread around the room. This gives a 'picture' or a model of how the particles behave when diffusion takes place.

Particles of a substance that is dissolved in a liquid will also diffuse. If you put a drop of ink in a glass of water you can see the ink gradually spread throughout the water. This happens because the particles in the ink are diffusing amongst the water particles. They are moving from where there is a higher concentration of 'ink' particles.

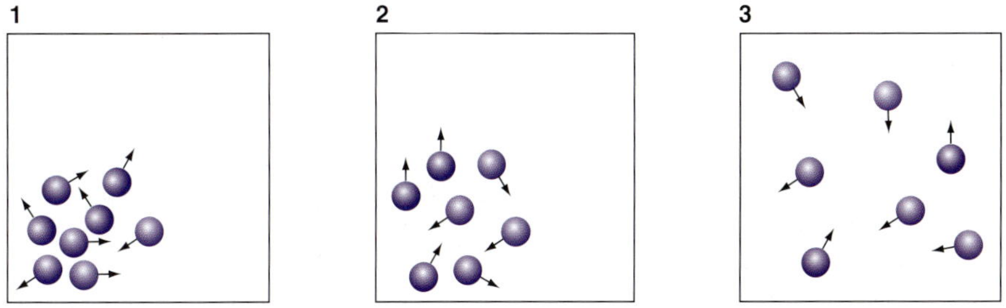

Figure 1.9 How particles in a gas spread out by diffusion

Oxygen will dissolve in water and so can diffuse when in solution. This is how it moves into cells when it is used for respiration. Since oxygen is used up quickly in the mitochondria for respiration, there will always be a lower concentration of oxygen inside the cell than in the liquid outside the cell. This ensures that the oxygen will always diffuse into the cell. The greater the difference in concentration, the faster the rate of diffusion.

Of course oxygen, or anything else trying to get into a cell, has to get through the cell membrane. Oxygen can do this by passing through tiny channels, a bit like holes, in the cell membrane. These channels are too small to let through larger molecules such as starch. Therefore the cell membrane is referred to as a **partially permeable membrane**.

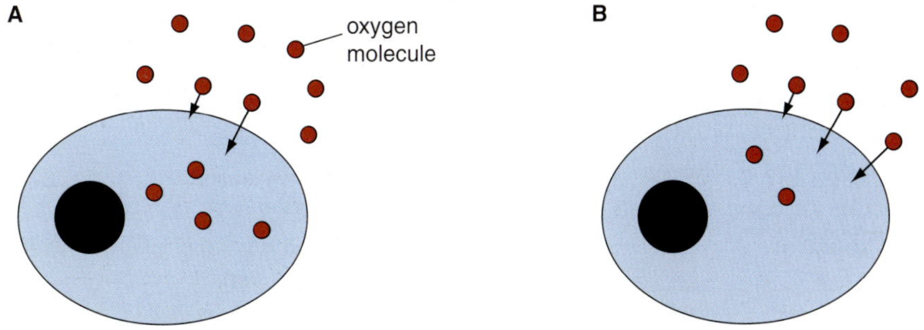

Figure 1.10 Diffusion of oxygen in cell B will take place faster than in cell A because there is a bigger difference between the concentration of oxygen inside and outside cell B.

⓬ If a slice of lemon is left in a glass of cranberry juice it turns red, even if it is taken out of the glass and rinsed under a tap. Explain why this happens. Try to use the words in the definition box, on p. 7, in your answer.

⓭ 'Stabilised liquid oxygen' (Figure 1.11) is a new product that claims to be able to increase your energy levels by raising the concentration of oxygen in the blood.
   a) What effect would increasing the concentration of oxygen in the blood have on the rate of oxygen diffusion into a cell?
   b) Explain your answer to part a). Use diagrams if they will help explain your ideas.
   c) Explain how increasing the oxygen concentration of the blood could boost your energy levels.
   d) There are a lot of people who do not agree that stabilised liquid oxygen actually works. What scientific ideas could they use to back up their point of view? Remember, this product is a dietary supplement.

Figure 1.11 Stabilised liquid oxygen – a new dietary supplement.

Osmosis is the diffusion of water, through a partially permeable membrane, from a region of higher water concentration to a region of lower water concentration.

⓮ Explain, in terms of water movement, what has happened to the red blood cells in each solution in Figure 1.12.

Osmosis

Having the correct amount of water in your blood is crucial, and this is controlled by your kidneys. You may remember learning about this in Core Science. If the concentration of water in your blood changes it will affect the cells in your body because water can diffuse into and out of cells. The diffusion of water into or out of cells is called **osmosis**. This is illustrated very clearly by red blood cells.

Red blood cells are specialised cells with a large surface area and no nucleus, a structure that makes them very good at carrying oxygen around the body. When they are in a solution with the correct concentration of water they have a recognisable 'bi-concave' shape. If the concentration of water around them is too low they shrivel up and if it is too high they swell up and can even burst. You can see a similar effect if you put a tomato in a glass of water and one in a glass of water with lots of salt dissolved in it.

Figure 1.12 This is what happens to red blood cells in solutions with different concentrations of water.

What can affect osmosis?

To fully understand osmosis you have to consider the water molecules and any substances dissolved in the water inside and outside the cell. Look at Figure 1.13 and think about the number of water and glucose molecules in each solution.

In Figure 1.13 a) water moves from left to right, from a region of higher water concentration to a region of lower water concentration. However, some people will explain this by referring to the concentration of glucose in each solution. In this case you would say that water has moved from a less concentrated (dilute) glucose solution to a more concentrated glucose solution through a partially permeable membrane. In Figure 1.13 b) the water moves from right to left because the concentration of glucose is higher on the left than on the right. So, you can alter the movement of water by osmosis by adding more water or by adding more solute to the water.

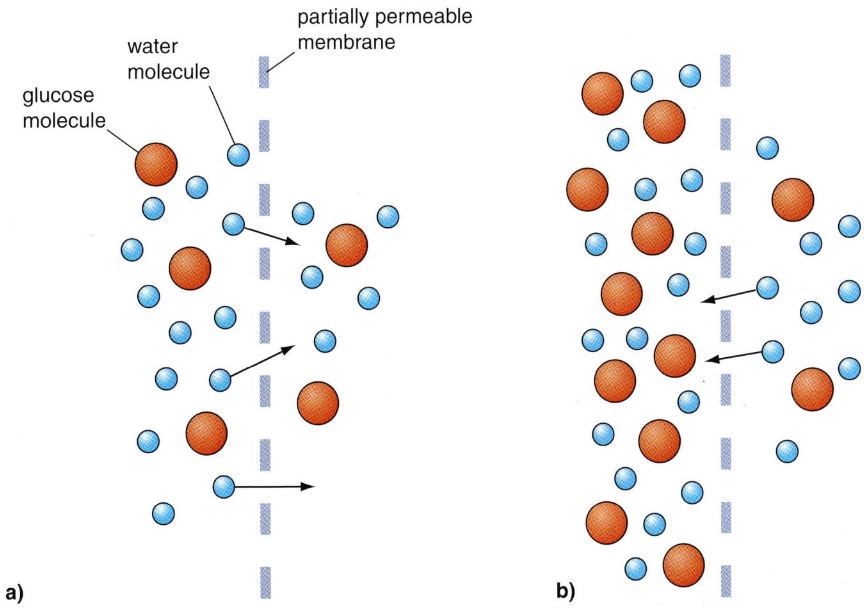

Figure 1.13 Two partially permeable membranes. Both membranes have the same concentration of solution on the right-hand side. However, water moves in opposite directions through the membranes.

15 Why is it important to avoid getting dehydrated when you are exercising?

16 Very occasionally marathon runners can in fact drink too much water and become over-hydrated. This is more likely to happen when they have been sweating heavily and have lost a lot of salt from their body.

a) What effect will over-hydration have on the cells in the body?

b) Why does losing a lot of salt from the body increase the effect of over-hydration on body cells?

⓱ For each diagram in Figure 1.14, state which way the water will move and explain why this will happen in terms of water and solute concentration.

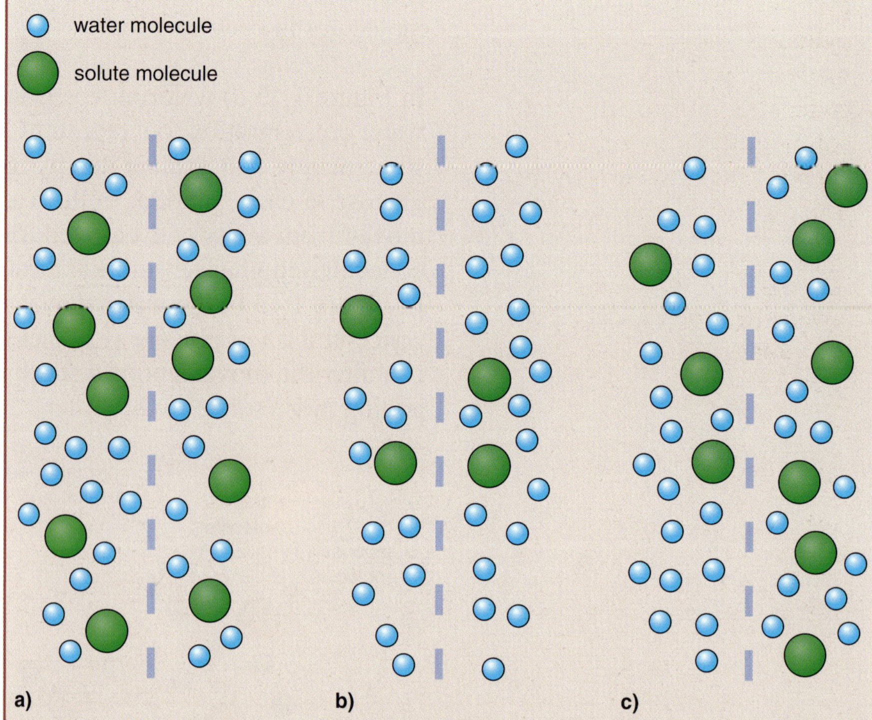

Figure 1.14 These partially permeable membranes have a different concentration of solution on each side.

⓲ Sports drinks can be divided into three types. Hypotonic drinks have a sugar concentration lower than your body fluid, isotonic drinks have the same concentration of sugar as your body fluid and hypertonic drinks have a higher sugar concentration than your body fluid.

a) Which type of sports drink would be best to drink if you wanted to re-hydrate your cells quickly?
b) Explain your answer to part a).
c) What are the benefits and drawbacks of drinking hypertonic drinks if you go for a long bike ride on a hot day?

Activity – Changing the rate of osmosis

Two students carried out an investigation using cylinders of potato. They cut out five potato cylinders and measured the mass of each one. They made up five glucose solutions with a different concentration and left a potato cylinder in each solution for 24 hours. After 24 hours they dried each potato cylinder and measured its mass again. The results are shown in Table 1.2.

Glucose concentration in moles per litre	Starting mass of potato cylinder in grams	Mass of potato after 24 hours in grams
0	7.76	9.38
0.2	8.01	8.04
0.4	7.96	7.21
0.6	7.92	7.78
0.8	7.93	6.65

Table 1.2 The results from the five potato cylinders left in different glucose solutions for 24 hours

1. Why did the students dry each potato cylinder before measuring its mass after each experiment?
2. What possible variables should be kept the same to make this investigation a fair test?
3. Work out the change in mass of each cylinder. These mass changes will be positive for cylinders that got heavier and negative for those that got lighter.
4. Now plot a graph for this data showing glucose concentration on the *x*-axis and change in mass on the *y*-axis. Think carefully about how you set this out so that you can plot positive and negative values on the same graph.
5. One of the results appears to be anomalous. Which one is it and what may have caused this?
6. Write a conclusion for this investigation. You will need to describe the pattern shown by the graph and use scientific ideas to explain what happened.
7. Use the graph to predict the concentration of glucose that you would use that would cause no change in mass of the potato. Explain, in terms of osmosis, why this would happen.

Summary

- ✓ All living things are made up of cells.
- ✓ Most animal cells have a nucleus, a cytoplasm, a cell membrane, **mitochondria** and **ribosomes**.
- ✓ In addition to these parts, plant cells often have **chloroplasts** and a permanent vacuole.
- ✓ Each cell part has a specific function.
- ✓ The chemical reactions that take place inside a cell are controlled by enzymes.
- ✓ Some cells are specialised to carry out a particular function.
- ✓ The structure of a specialised cell relates to its particular function.
- ✓ **Diffusion** is the spreading out of particles of a gas or a substance dissolved in a liquid.
- ✓ Particles move by diffusion from a region of higher **concentration** to a region where there is a lower concentration.
- ✓ Oxygen diffuses into and out of cells through a **partially permeable membrane**.
- ✓ Water moves through a partially permeable membrane by **osmosis** from dilute solutions to more concentrated solutions.

EXAMQUESTIONS

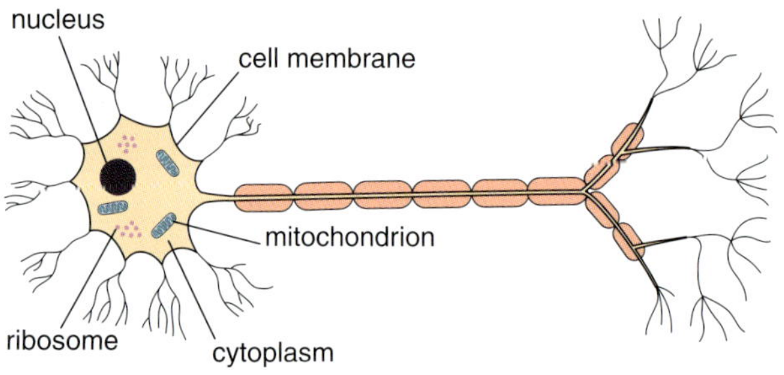

Figure 1.15 A nerve cell with some cell parts labelled

1 a) Name the labelled part of the cell in Figure 1.15 that releases energy from glucose. *(1 mark)*

b) Name the part of the cell that synthesises enzymes. *(1 mark)*

c) A nerve cell is a specialised cell that carries electrical nerve impulses throughout the body.

i) Describe one feature of a nerve cell that allows it to carry out this function. *(1 mark)*

ii) Explain how this feature allows a nerve cell to carry out this function. *(1 mark)*

2 a) Red blood cells (Figure 1.16) are specialised to carry oxygen around the body. Explain how the structure of a red blood cell relates to its function. *(2 marks)*

Figure 1.16 A red blood cell

b) Explain how oxygen enters a red blood cell. *(3 marks)*

c) When mountaineers climb high mountains the concentration of oxygen in the air they are breathing decreases. Explain how this will affect the uptake of oxygen by their red blood cells. *(2 marks)*

3 A chip shop owner claimed that if he soaked his potato chips in water before he fried them they were firmer than if they were cut up and fried without soaking them.

a) Explain how scientific ideas can be used to back up his claim. Use correct scientific words in your explanation. *(4 marks)*

When some uncooked chips were soaking, a worker in the shop poured some salt into the water and left the chips soaking in salty water.

b) Suggest how this may have affected the potato chips. *(2 marks)*

A student carried out an experiment to see if adding salt to the water that potato chips were soaking in affected the amount they changed in mass while soaking. She soaked one potato chip in pure water and one in a concentrated salt solution. She measured their masses before and after they had been soaked.

c) i) State the dependent variable in this investigation. *(1 mark)*

ii) State the independent variable in the investigation. *(1 mark)*

d) Do you think that the results from this investigation would provide enough information to draw a firm conclusion about the effect of salt concentration on the change in mass of potato chips? Explain the reasons for your answer. *(3 marks)*

Chapter 2
What are the energy inputs and energy losses in a food chain?

By the end of this chapter you should:

- ✓ understand the process of photosynthesis;
- ✓ know the factors that affect the rate of photosynthesis;
- ✓ know how plants use the products of photosynthesis;
- ✓ be able to apply knowledge of the factors affecting photosynthesis in a range of habitats and agricultural situations;
- ✓ understand why plants need minerals and the effects of a deficiency;
- ✓ understand the construction of pyramids of biomass;
- ✓ be able to apply biomass and energy principles to the efficiency of food production;
- ✓ be able to evaluate the conflicts and compromises between feeding the population and damaging the environment;
- ✓ understand the role of microorganisms in decomposition and recycling carbon and plant nutrients.

Figure 2.1 The start of the food chain in biodiverse rough pasture. Inset shows the stomata through which the carbon dioxide diffuses into the leaf for photosynthesis.

2.1 Photosynthesis

The word **photosynthesis** can be split into two parts, 'photo' meaning light and 'synthesis' meaning to make.

Remember you should always write **light energy**, not light or sun.

Green plants use light energy to convert the simple molecules carbon dioxide and water into larger glucose molecules using enzymes in chloroplasts. This process is called photosynthesis.

We can break down the summary equation for photosynthesis into three parts, as shown below:

Raw materials	Conditions	Products
carbon dioxide + water $6CO_2 + 6H_2O$	light energy → enzymes chlorophyll	glucose + oxygen $C_6H_{12}O_6 + 6O_6$

How is the light energy captured?

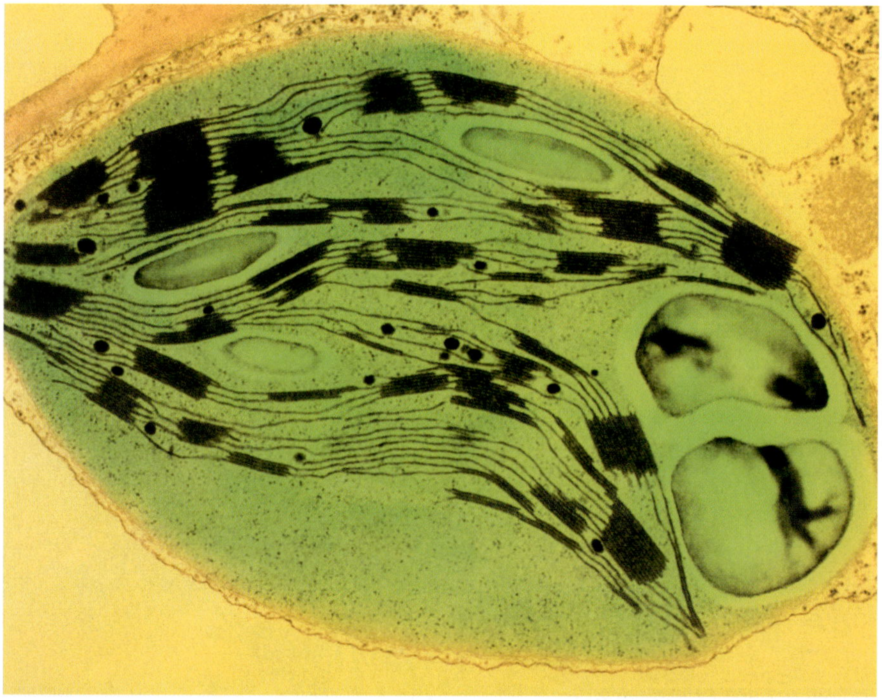

Figure 2.2 The structure of a chloroplast (magnification about 50,000)

You studied plant cell structure in Section 1.1 and will recall that some plant cells have chloroplasts to absorb light energy. Figure 2.2 shows that the chloroplast has many membranes inside it. These membranes contain chlorophyll, which makes the leaves appear green. When light energy reaches the chlorophyll, enzymes in the chloroplasts use this energy to catalyse reactions that produce glucose. Glucose is quickly converted to starch that can be stored in the leaf, and oxygen is released as a waste product.

How is the raw material, carbon dioxide, obtained?

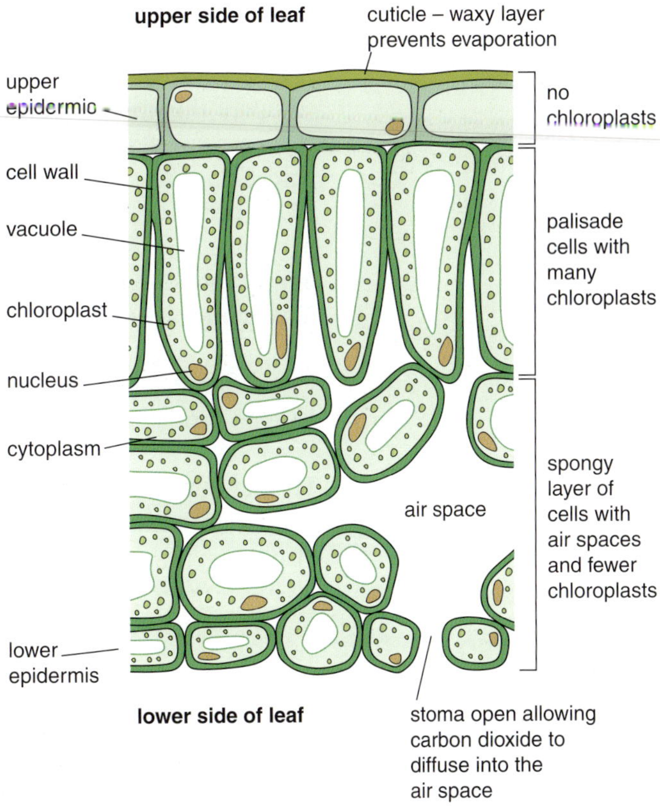

Figure 2.3 A section of a leaf showing the open stomata on the lower surface

The carbon dioxide concentration of the atmosphere can be written as a percentage or as ppm (parts per million). Atmospheric carbon dioxide levels are changing, and in 2006 a record high level of 381 ppm was recorded.

Stomata are the tiny openings in the surface of a leaf through which gases can pass by diffusion.

1. What materials are needed for photosynthesis?
2. What is the energy input for photosynthesis?
3. A variegated plant has many white leaves.
   a) What essential condition for photosynthesis is missing from these leaves?
   b) Explain why this plant would not grow as rapidly as a normal green-leaved plant.
4. What are the products of photosynthesis?

During the day, the leaf is photosynthesising and using carbon dioxide. The **stomata** (small pores) are open and the carbon dioxide diffuses into the leaf from the air. Diffusion always takes place from a region of higher concentration to a lower concentration. Although the concentration of carbon dioxide in the air is on average only about 0.037% (or 370 ppm), when the leaf is photosynthesising it will be using up the carbon dioxide inside the leaf and so maintaining the concentration difference needed for diffusion.

How is the raw material, water, obtained?

Roots take up water from the soil by osmosis (see Section 1.2). The water is then transported up the stem to the leaves. Water is essential for support of the leaf cells; if there is a shortage of water, the stomata will close to reduce water loss and photosynthesis will stop. This may happen around midday on a hot sunny day when there is a high water loss from the leaves, or during drought conditions when the soil is very dry.

2.2 What factors affect the rate of photosynthesis?

> **Rate of photosynthesis** is the speed at which the photosynthesis reaction takes place. It can be measured as the rate of formation of oxygen.

A **rate** is the quantity produced or used per unit time. You might compare this to a model with which you are familiar such as the money you earn for washing cars for a Saturday job. For example, if you get paid £2 per wash and you wash two cars an hour, your hourly rate is £4.00 per hour. If you wash five cars an hour, your hourly rate is £10 per hour. The more cars you can wash in an hour, the greater your hourly rate of pay. Five cars an hour is about the limit – so the maximum rate of pay is £10 per hour.

You can measure the rate of photosynthesis by finding the volume of oxygen produced per hour using a range of input values.

To find out how the input of carbon dioxide, light intensity and temperature limit the rate of photosynthesis, we need to measure the rate of photosynthesis.

Activity – Analysing the effect of carbon dioxide concentration on rate of photosynthesis

A group of students decided to investigate the effect of carbon dioxide concentration on the rate of photosynthesis. They decided to calculate the rate of photosynthesis by measuring the volume of oxygen produced from an aquatic plant, *Elodea* (see Figure 2.4).

To investigate the effect of carbon dioxide concentration, the students made a **series dilution** of sodium hydrogen carbonate solution. They started with a 5.0% solution. They followed these instructions to make solutions with different concentrations.

> A **series dilution** is a range of concentrations. A minimum of five dilutions from concentrated to weak would give the input variable for the carbon dioxide concentration. The students planned the dilutions to give sensibly spaced points on the x-axis of their graph.

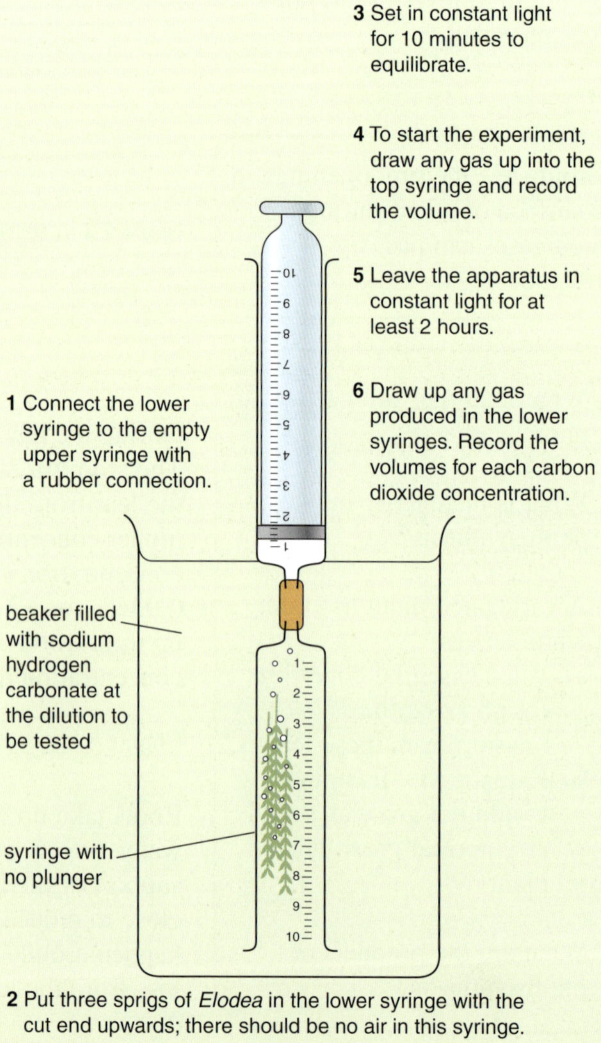

Figure 2.4 The apparatus and method used to measure rate of photosynthesis

1 Take six 1000 cm^3 beakers. Label them A to F.
2 Fill beaker A with 5% solution.
3 Use a measuring cylinder to add 900 cm^3 of water into beaker B.
4 Using a second measuring cylinder transfer 100 cm^3 sodium hydrogen carbonate solution from A to beaker B.
5 Stir beaker B with a glass rod to mix. This gives a 0.5% sodium hydrogen carbonate solution.
6 Use the 0.5% solution to make up the solutions in the proportions shown in Table 2.1.

❶ Copy and complete the final column of Table 2.1.

Beaker	Starting concentration of $NaHCO_3$	Volume of $NaHCO_3$ in cm^3	Volume of H_2O in cm^3	Final concentration
B	5%	100	900	0.5%
C	0.5%	800	200	
D	0.5%	600	400	
E	0.5%	400	600	
F	0.5%	200	800	

Table 2.1 A summary of the series dilution

The students used the apparatus and method shown in Figure 2.4 to investigate rates of photosynthesis. The students knew that they should only change one input variable in each investigation. The input variable was the range of concentrations of sodium hydrogen carbonate solution. They knew that the light intensity and temperature should be kept constant.

❷ What factor were the students controlling in this experiment?
❸ This experiment was completed outside on a hot June day. What factors may not have been controlled?

To develop the experiment further the students decided to calculate the rate of photosynthesis in each experiment as the rate per gram dry mass per hour. They measured the total dry mass of the *Elodea* used each time by placing it into a folded filter paper in a drying cupboard set at 100 °C. The samples were dried and weighed every hour until the mass of dried *Elodea* remained constant for two successive weighings.

Here is the set of results they obtained.

4 Copy the table and complete the calculations. Use the following equation to complete the final column:

$$\frac{\text{volume of oxygen in cm}^3}{\text{mass of } Elodea \text{ in g}} \times \frac{1}{\text{time (h)}}$$

5 Use the results in the table to construct a graph with volume of oxygen in $cm^3/g/h$ on the y-axis and concentration of sodium hydrogen carbonate solution on the x-axis.

6 Suggest a suitable title for this graph, which links the output variable with the input variable.

7 Describe the pattern shown by your graph.

8 Suggest how you would modify this experiment to investigate the effect of light intensity on the rate of photosynthesis.

Concentration of $NaHCO_3$ as %	Starting volume in cm^3	Final volume in cm^3	Volume of oxygen in cm^3	Mass of *Elodea* in g	Time in h	Volume of oxygen in $cm^3/g/h$
0.5	0.2	9.6	9.4	1.341	2	
0.4	0.4	8.6	8.2	1.399	2	
0.3	0.3	7.1	6.8	1.439	2	
0.2	0.5	5.9	5.4	1.510	2	
0.1	0.4	4.8	4.4	1.522	2	

Table 2.2

A **limiting factor** is the one that controls the rate of the product formation. This is usually the factor that is present at the lowest value.

From the equation for photosynthesis given in Section 2.1 you can see that carbon dioxide is one of the raw materials. Although leaf cells respire 24 hours of the day, carbon dioxide cannot leave the leaf at night, since the stomata are closed (light intensity controls when the stomata open). By daybreak there will be a build-up of carbon dioxide in the leaf from the respiration which has taken place overnight. Initially light intensity will be a **limiting factor** for photosynthesis, but as the day gets brighter there will be more rapid photosynthesis, using up the carbon dioxide.

Carbon dioxide forms a small percentage of atmospheric gases and can be a limiting factor when the light intensity is high.

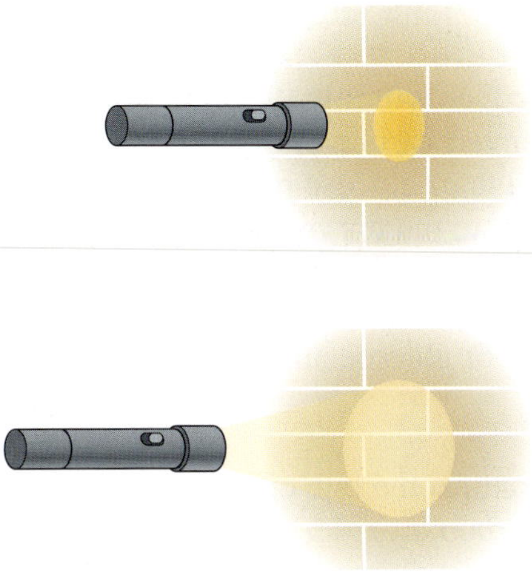

Figure 2.5 The light energy from the torch remains the same. As the torch get further away the light spreads over a larger area, so the light energy per unit area is less.

Light intensity is the amount of light energy per unit area of the surface. Light intensity decreases with the square of the distance from the light source.

How does light intensity affect the rate of photosynthesis?

First, work through this simple model to make sure you understand what light intensity means. If you switch on a torch, hold it close to a wall and shine the beam at the wall, you get a small circle of light. As you move the torch further from the wall the circle of light gets larger and dimmer. The light energy given out by the torch is the same, but the light energy falling on each square centimetre of wall (the **light intensity**) is less when the torch is at a greater distance.

The decrease in light intensity is proportional to $1/d^2$, where d is the distance from the light source. This relationship shows that as the distance from a light source is increased, the light intensity reduces very rapidly (see Figure 2.6). You could use this graph of light intensity against distance if you were to plan an experiment to find how light intensity affected the rate of photosynthesis. Unfortunately, normal light bulbs are very inefficient and give off heat as well as light. Could this introduce another variable when the lamp is very close to the apparatus? Energy-efficient fluorescent bulbs give off less heat.

Light intensity generally increases towards midday and then decreases towards evening, but can change quite quickly on a cloudy day. Light is the energy input and will have a significant effect on the rate of photosynthesis. The light-energy capture stage of photosynthesis depends on the light intensity and is independent of temperature.

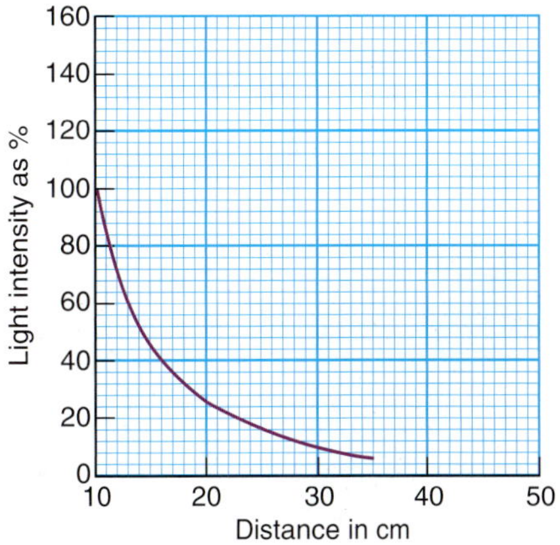

Figure 2.6 How light intensity decreases with increase in distance. For this graph the light intensity was taken as 100% at 10 cm distance.

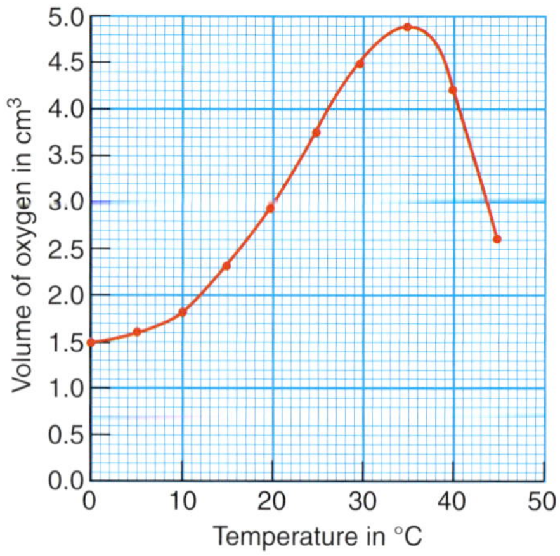

Figure 2.7 Effect of temperature on the rate of photosynthesis at a fixed light intensity and fixed carbon dioxide concentration.

How does temperature affect the rate of photosynthesis?

After the light energy has been captured, enzymes in the chloroplasts catalyse the chemical reactions that convert carbon dioxide to glucose. Therefore, you would predict that the rate of glucose production would increase with increase in temperature up to the optimum temperature of the enzymes (enzymes are covered in Sections 3.1 and 3.2). The rate of photosynthesis increases on a warm day since the enzyme reactions are temperature-dependent. The production of glucose and hence starch will be slower on a cold day.

Figure 2.7 shows that at higher temperatures the rate of photosynthesis is faster, for a fixed concentration of carbon dioxide. Above the optimum temperature, photosynthesis slows down.

Having worked through this section, you can see that the rate of photosynthesis at any time is a result of the interaction of several factors. Any one factor of low temperature, low light intensity or low levels of carbon dioxide could limit the rate of photosynthesis.

2.3 How does the plant use glucose, the end product of photosynthesis?

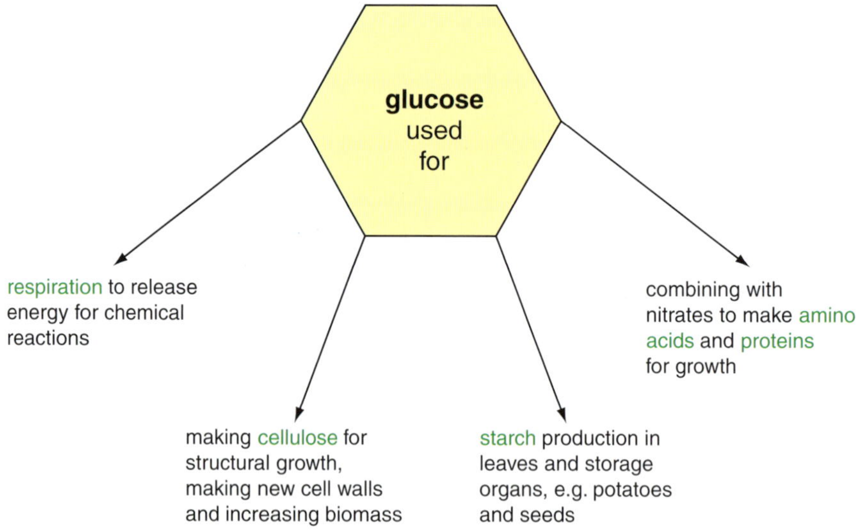

Figure 2.8 How the plant makes use of the glucose produced

Figure 2.9 A shortage of magnesium ions makes a plant's leaves turn yellow.

After glucose is produced, it is converted to starch in the leaf. We can test for starch to find out whether a leaf has been photosynthesising (Figure 2.10). Materials can only be carried when dissolved in water, so the insoluble starch is converted to soluble sugar for transport to other parts of the plant.

All parts of the plant need a supply of glucose for respiration. The growing shoots of the plant need glucose for respiration, to release chemical energy for making new cells. Just as you need minerals to

1 Dip
Take a leaf from a plant standing in sunlight and dip in boiling water for 10 seconds to denature enzymes and make the membrane permeable.

THEN TURN OFF BUNSEN because alcohol vapour is inflammable.

2 Decolorise
Put tube of alcohol into the water bath and allow to warm up. Add leaf and shake gently until alcohol becomes green.

3 Soften
Soften the leaf by rinsing in the hot water.

4 Flatten
Flatten the leaf underside up on a white tile and add a few drops of iodine. Where starch is present it will give a blue black colour.

This method can be used with a leaf which has been partly covered with a stencil, photonegative or a variegated leaf.

Figure 2.10 Testing a leaf for starch

keep healthy, so do plants. Nitrates are required for making amino acids and therefore for building proteins to make the cytoplasm and enzymes in the new cells. Magnesium ions are needed to produce chlorophyll molecules. The mineral ions are taken up from the soil into the roots. If plants are unable to produce sufficient protein, they will grow very slowly and remain small. If they are unable to obtain enough magnesium they will not be able to make chlorophyll, so their lower leaves will become yellow and not photosynthesise efficiently.

5. A plant was put into a black plastic bag and left for 24 hours. The leaves were then tested for starch. Explain why you would not expect to find starch in the leaves even during the day.

6. Where are the enzymes located that control the conversion of carbon dioxide to glucose?

7. When testing a leaf for starch it is dipped into boiling water to stop enzyme reactions.
   a) Suggest which enzyme reactions these are.
   b) Why does the alcohol become green?
   c) If parts of the leaf become blue-black when tested with iodine solution, it indicates that starch is present. What could you conclude if the iodine solution stayed brown?

8. Draw sketch graphs to compare the rate of oxygen produced on a bright winter day and on a bright summer day. Assume the light intensity is the same on both days.

9. A student grew a tomato plant in sand. After a month he compared it with his friend's that had been grown in potting compost. Both plants had been watered regularly but the plant in sand was shorter, had much smaller leaves and the lower leaves were yellow. Suggest reasons for these differences.

2.4 What factors limit the rate of photosynthesis in the environment?

We have seen that under laboratory conditions light intensity, carbon dioxide concentration and temperature can all affect the rate of photosynthesis.

Activity – From laboratory to outdoors

Use the information gained from laboratory examples to consider photosynthesis in the different environments shown below.

A field crop on a hot, sunny day

Figure 2.11

1. Will light intensity be a limiting factor?
2. By 9 am the rate of photosynthesis has reached a constant level and does not increase even though the light intensity is increasing. What could be the limiting factor?
3. At night the stomata are closed and the plant continues to respire resulting in a build up of carbon dioxide inside the leaf. What effect would you expect this to have on the rate of photosynthesis when it first gets light in the morning?

A forest in Iceland

It has been said that you can't get lost in a forest in Iceland because the birch trees only grow to about 1.5 m high (see Figure 2.12). Iceland has periods of 24 hours darkness in winter and 24 hours light in summer, although the light intensity is not the same during that 24 hours.

4. What factors limit the growth of the trees?
5. Is carbon dioxide concentration likely to be a limiting factor?

Figure 2.12

A pond

Figure 2.13

Geese use the pond and their waste has resulted in extra nitrates (plant food) in the water. As a result there is dense weed growth and many snails feeding on the weeds.

6. What do you think will happen to the carbon dioxide concentration in the water overnight? Explain your answer.
7. During mid-morning streams of tiny bubbles can be seen rising to the surface. What gas do you think these bubbles contain, and where does it come from?
8. What do you think happens to the carbon dioxide content of the water during the day? Explain your answer.

2.5 Can understanding of photosynthesis be used to increase greenhouse crop production?

Figure 2.14 A large commercial greenhouse

Figure 2.15 A computer control panel that controls conditions within a greenhouse

For maximum profit, greenhouse crops must have a high yield and good quality, and the producers need to raise the crops to maturity in the minimum possible time. You saw in the activity in Section 2.2 that carbon dioxide could be a limiting factor for photosynthesis. Many experiments have been carried out to find the optimum light intensity and carbon dioxide concentrations that will increase the rate of photosynthesis for crop plants.

Activity – Greenhouse crop production

Use the graph in Figure 2.16 to answer the following questions.

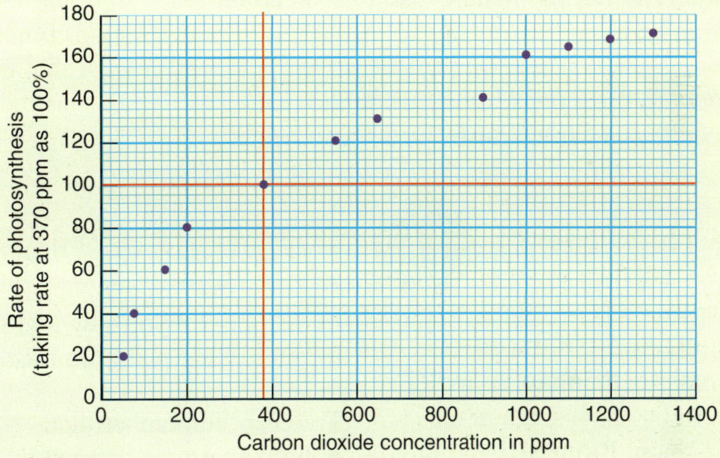

Figure 2.16

In a closed greenhouse in winter with artificial lighting and no ventilation, the levels of carbon dioxide can drop during the day to 200 ppm. (The rate of photosynthesis at 370 ppm carbon dioxide, atmospheric level, is taken as 100%. This is shown in red on the graph in Figure 2.16.)

1. Use the graph to find the effect on the rate of photosynthesis of reducing carbon dioxide levels from 370 ppm to 200 ppm.

Increased carbon dioxide concentration results in larger leaves, which increases the size and quality of lettuces. Colorado State University found that increasing carbon dioxide levels to 550 ppm meant that they could only fit 16 instead of 22 lettuces into a box.

2. Use your knowledge of photosynthesis to explain why the lettuces were bigger.

3 From the graph, by what percentage was the rate of photosynthesis increased by changing from 370 to 550 ppm carbon dioxide?

If the carbon dioxide concentration is raised to 1000 ppm, for salad crops such as tomatoes, peppers and cucumbers, they flower earlier producing more flowers and more fruits.

4 What shape is the curve above a concentration of 1000 ppm?

5 Suggest why the grower does not usually increase the concentration above 1000 ppm.

Victorian greenhouses were heated by manure. The decomposition produced sufficient heat for fruits such as peaches to be produced early in the season. The rotting manure also raised carbon dioxide levels.

In modern greenhouses the carbon dioxide concentration can be raised by using a heater burning oil. This will increase the temperature as well as carbon dioxide levels. However, there are problems:

- the water produced during combustion increases the growth of mildew;
- if impure fuel is burnt, sulfur dioxide and oxides of nitrogen are given off; these cause acid rain-type damage to leaves, thus reducing photosynthesis.

The best, but not the cheapest, way of supplementing the carbon dioxide is to use storage cylinders of liquid carbon dioxide and computer control to regulate carbon dioxide gas concentration within the greenhouse.

6 Sensors linked to a computer measure the carbon dioxide concentration. Suggest why the computer is programmed to activate a valve that increases the carbon dioxide concentration as the light intensity increases.

2.6 Pyramids of biomass

Biomass is the mass of living material at each stage in the food chain. Biomass is measured as dry mass. A practical method of finding dry mass was given in the activity in Section 2.2.

In Section 2.3 you saw that the products of photosynthesis can be used for increasing plant **biomass**.

To recap, remember that:

- light energy is trapped by the chlorophyll;
- this energy is used to 'fix' carbon dioxide into a carbohydrate form (glucose); and
- carbohydrate is converted in the plant to cellulose cell walls, plant protein or stored as starch.

Plants (primary producers) are at the start of the food chain and are eaten by herbivores (primary consumers). The plant material eaten is used by the herbivore for respiration, to release the energy needed for maintaining body temperature, for movement and for growth of new tissues. The herbivore can be eaten by a carnivore, and once again some energy is used for movement and maintaining body temperature and some energy is transferred to new carnivore tissue.

To draw a **pyramid of biomass** (Figure 2.17) you need to:

- sample all the organisms to estimate the size of the population;
- examine the size distribution of organisms and find the dry mass of a representative sample (dry mass figures are often available on field centre websites);

A **pyramid of biomass** is a diagram that illustrates quantitatively the decrease in mass of living material in each level of a food chain.

The **trophic level** is the feeding level in a food chain. There can be more than one organism at each trophic level.

Figure 2.17 A pyramid of biomass

- calculate the biomass of each species;
- group the organisms into **trophic** (feeding) **levels** in a food web and calculate the biomass for each level;
- construct a pyramid on graph paper with the area of each rectangle proportional to the biomass.

Gaining all this information is not easy. Some problems are:
- Obtaining dry mass of an animal means killing it, and you would certainly have problems obtaining dry mass if your herbivore were a cow! Hence, we use calculated data.
- The pyramid shows the biomass of what is growing at that moment. A tree for instance may have accumulated its biomass over 30 years, in contrast with green algae that grow quickly, reproduce and die within a few weeks.
- There are seasonal variations with some plants growing quickly in spring, seeding and dying by mid-summer.
- Anyone who mows a lawn knows that the productivity of a regularly mown lawn is greater than one that is neglected to seed in summer. This also applies to grazed meadows.

If you construct a pyramid of biomass to scale you will see a reduction in the biomass at each trophic level. If you examine the organisms in the food web that you used to construct the pyramid, you will see that there are large numbers of small organisms at the lowest feeding level and that the numbers decrease, but the size of organism increases, as you move up the feeding levels.

Pyramids of energy

A **pyramid of energy** is a diagram that illustrates quantitatively the decrease in the energy contained in biomass in each level of a food chain.

Efficiency of energy transfer is the percentage of the energy that is passed on to the next organism in the chain and is not lost.

For a **pyramid of energy**, if there is less biomass at each successive level there must also be less energy contained in the biomass. It is easier to examine energy loss in a food chain for animals. At each link, energy is released from the food by respiration and used for the chemical reactions taking place in the cytoplasm, for nerve impulse conduction, for muscle contraction, for movement and for keeping the body temperature constant and above that of the environment. When the body temperature is higher than the environment, energy will be lost as heat. Chemical energy is lost from the food chain in faeces and urine. This energy passes to the decomposers, which are not part of the food chain.

Taking the light energy input as 1000 units, the food chain in Figure 2.19 shows how little of that energy input reaches the secondary consumer, the fox. However, the percentage energy transfer is different in each ecosystem.

Can the biomass and energy principles be applied to food production?

Food production must be managed if the population is to be fed. Reducing the number of links in the food chain increases the efficiency

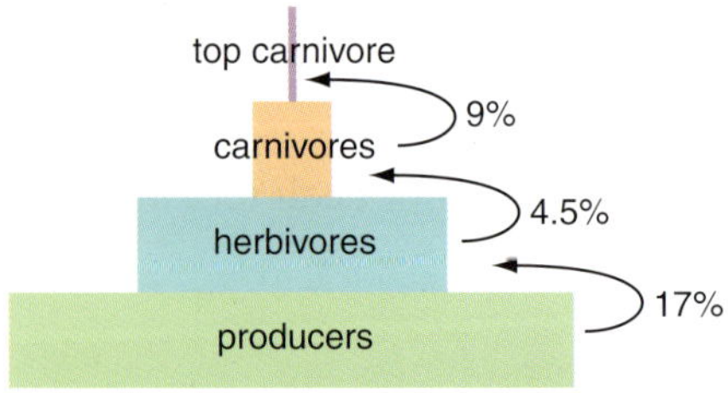

Figure 2.18 A pyramid of energy shows the **efficiency of energy transfer** from one trophic level to the next.

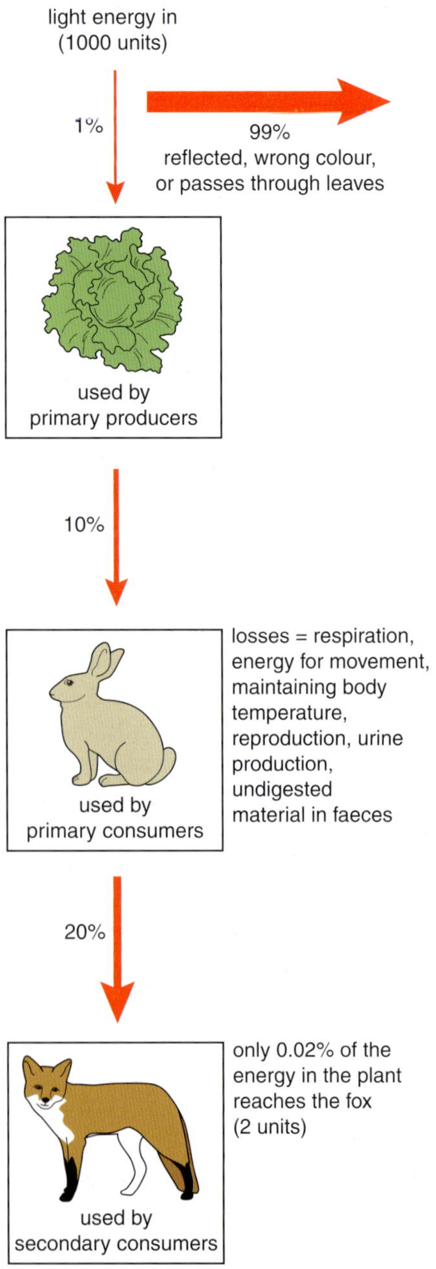

Figure 2.19 Food chain for a fox, showing energy losses at each stage

of food production, so that a greater amount of food is available to feed more consumers. By examining the pyramid of energy in Figure 2.18 we can see that if humans are the secondary consumer (meat eater) they receive less of the energy input than if they were the primary consumer (eating as a herbivore).

By looking at the energy conversion for a cow (Figure 2.20) you can see just how little energy is converted to increased biomass (muscle tissue) over the period of time that the animal is growing, typically 30 months.

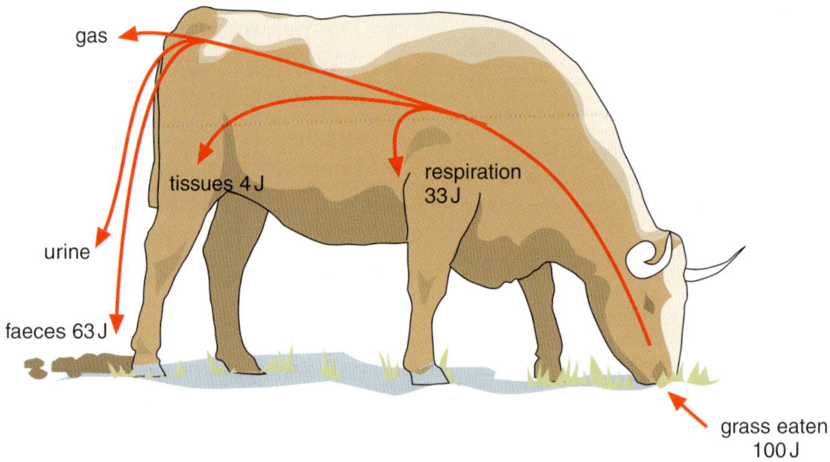

Figure 2.20 For every 100 J of energy available in the grass, only 4 J gets into the animal's tissues

This gives us some points to think about.

- Would less energy be lost in producing animals for human consumption with a shorter 'age to slaughter', for example, rabbits, chickens or ostriches?
- Could we reduce the amount of energy used by beef cattle?
- Would it be more energy-efficient for humans to consume more at the herbivore level (i.e. eat more vegetarian food)?
- Should we use biotechnology to produce more non-animal foods such as mycoprotein, frequently marketed as Quorn™?

The answer to all these questions is probably 'yes,' but in each case, traditions in society can result in a pre-determined pattern of behaviour. Scientific evidence is not generally taken into account when making decisions about what to eat. Here are some examples of human responses that you could use as discussion points.

- Beef is a traditional food and people would be slow to convert to eating rabbit meat. How quickly are people likely to change their established patterns of eating?
- The energy used by beef cattle could be reduced by restricting their movement and keeping them in an insulated barn to maintain a warm temperature. However, cattle are herbivores and grazing on grass

Food miles give a measure of the distance a food travels from field to plate. This includes distance travelled in a plane and transport from distribution depots.

Foot and mouth disease is an infectious disease affecting cattle, sheep, pigs, goats and deer. The sale of livestock is severely restricted by an outbreak of the disease.

BSE is a neurological disease that affects cattle. On 8 March 2006 the export restrictions against export of British beef to Europe were lifted, as the feed controls and inspections had been effective in controlling the disease.

Herbicides are chemicals that are used to kill weeds so the weeds do not compete with the crop for water, light or nutrients.

Insecticides are used to kill insect pest species that eat and damage the crop plants, but insecticides can also kill beneficial insects, such as bees.

Biodiversity is the number of different types of plants and animals living and feeding in the ecosystem. These will include pollinators and biological control species that are beneficial to crops.

rather than being fed with concentrates or silage produces the best lean meat. Following scares such as BSE ('mad cow disease'), more people are concerned about intensive farming and are supporting organic and natural farming.

- Having fewer links in the food chain would increase the efficiency of food production. Humans could consume more plant proteins such as beans and eat less red meat. However, not all land used for grazing, for example hill pastures and marsh areas, is suitable for growing crops.
- Novel foods such as Quorn™ are slow to be taken up by consumers unless the foods have a niche appeal such as being low-fat or cholesterol-reducing, or are advertised by celebrities.

The costs of food production and distribution

The following points highlight some of the conflicts between the demands of the shopper for a good quality product at the lowest possible price, and the needs of the producer to increase productivity and reduce costs.

- Crops sold in supermarkets are intensively produced using fertilisers, pesticides and irrigation.
- Where greenhouses are used, there will be extra costs for the input of heat, light and carbon dioxide.
- Exotic or out-of-season crops that are grown abroad have to be flown or shipped to the UK, incurring 'food miles'. People living in rural areas have the benefit of being able to purchase local produce direct from farm shops.
- Meat production costs include costs of rearing, feed material, housing, waste disposal, distribution transport to market, veterinary bills and labour.

Food distribution could also help the spread of infection. The serious outbreaks of foot and mouth disease informed the public of the distance travelled by livestock from rearing locations to fattening locations, often hundreds of miles away. It also informed them of the problems associated with live export of lambs and calves. BSE made the public aware of the risks of intensive rearing which, in the 1980s, used animal carcass protein as a protein supplement in food: this practice is now banned. Currently, we are concerned about the spread of bird flu in intensive poultry units, and poultry imports to the UK from certain countries are banned.

There are also conflicts between agricultural production methods such as use of fertilisers, herbicides and insecticides and damage to the environment, for example excess weed growth in rivers and streams and loss of biodiversity. In addition to increasing the cost of food distribution, 'food miles' use up non-renewable fuels.

Activity – Are shoppers becoming more aware of food production issues?

In a small group, take a large piece of paper (A3). Using a pencil and ruler measure and mark the paper into four sections, as shown below.

Write down the positive and negative effects of managing food production. For example, you might say that the use of an insecticide made sure that there were no holes in the cabbage leaves and no caterpillars lurking between the leaves!

You might like to include other topics such as selling only seasonal or local produce, genetically modified (GM) crops, organic farming, free-range chicken or pigs, set-aside, problems faced by families on very low incomes and any issues relevant to your local area. Do a web search for 'sustainable farming'; the following website might be useful: www.sustainweb.org .

Food production	
Positive aspects	Negative aspects
Food distribution	
Positive aspects	Negative aspects

2.7 What happens to the waste material produced by plants and animals?

Ask yourself what happens to all the dead leaves, dead plants and animals, piles of faeces and other natural debris? What causes them to decay?

In Core Science you saw that in a rainforest there was rapid recycling of nutrients. If the trees, which were the source of the leaf litter, were removed the cycle stopped. Here we will look in detail at the nutrient cycling process.

Dead leaves, other dead organic matter and animal waste products are broken down or decomposed by bacteria and fungi (**microorganisms** called **decomposers**). If you turn over a damp leaf on the ground in autumn you might see fine cotton-wool like threads on the underside. These are the fungal hyphae (feeding structures of the fungus), which are chemically breaking down, or digesting, the dead leaf cells (enzymes and digestion are described in Sections 3.4 and 3.5). The cellulose of plant cell walls is very difficult to break down and so the enzyme cellulase secreted by the fungi is very important in starting the decay process.

Bacteria and fungi are examples of **microorganisms**.

Microorganisms involved in the process of decay are called **decomposers**.

⑩ Dead leaves have cellulose cell walls. Name the types of enzymes that will be required to break the leaves down.

⑪ Name the nutrient that is taken up and combined with sugars to make amino acids, which can then be assembled into proteins.

⑫ Name the mineral ion which is taken up from soil and used to make chlorophyll.

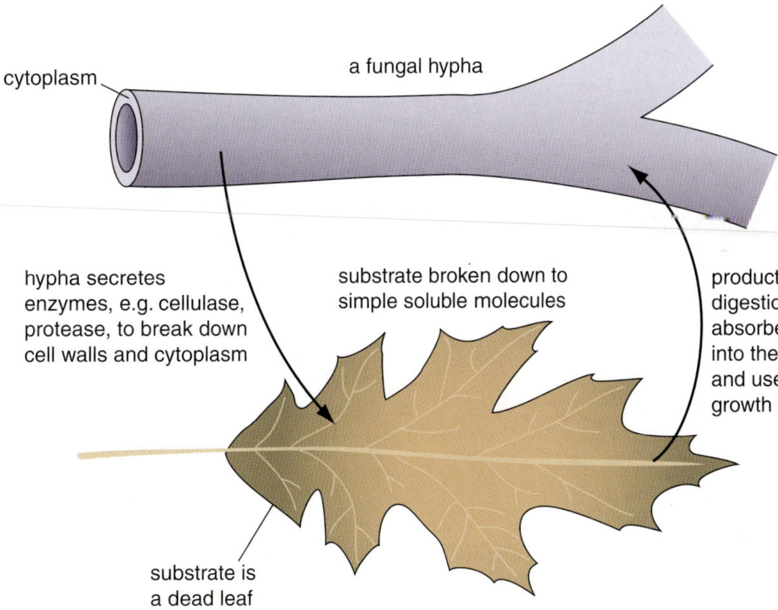

Figure 2.21 Fungi carry out extracellular digestion to break down dead leaves.

Water – **O**xygen – **W**armth

Microorganisms require some of the same conditions that you do – water, oxygen, warmth and nutrients.

The digestion reactions take place faster if there is warmth and oxygen. These are the conditions you will find in a garden compost bin or a municipal waste composter.

The breakdown of waste materials by microorganisms produces simpler, soluble materials that can be used as nutrients by plants. In a stable ecosystem, some nutrients released by the decay process are used for bacteria or fungal growth and some are taken up by the trees to be used again to make more leaves – the nutrients are cycled.

2.8 How do carbon atoms move around in the carbon cycle?

The **carbon cycle** is a description of how carbon atoms circulate through carbon compounds in living organisms to carbon dioxide in the air and back again.

Carbon dioxide makes up 0.037% of the atmosphere by volume and is the raw material for photosynthesis for plants (see Section 2.1). Let's examine the possible route taken by a carbon atom in a carbon dioxide molecule.

- Carbon dioxide is combined with hydrogen from water, using energy from sunlight, in the process of photosynthesis.
- The glucose formed by photosynthesis can be used for the synthesis of structural and storage materials in the plant (see Figure 2.8). In this way the carbon atoms from carbon dioxide become incorporated into oils, starch, cellulose and proteins in the plant biomass.
- If the plant is eaten by a herbivore, the carbon atoms can become incorporated into the fat, glycogen or proteins in the animal, and may pass to the next animal in the food chain, a carnivore. This chain – plant to herbivore to carnivore – can be thought of as the 'light chain' because it starts with the capture of light energy.

13 In the carbon cycle, what is the only process that removes carbon dioxide from the atmosphere?

14 What three groups of living organisms are shown respiring in the carbon cycle diagram?

15 What is the additional source of carbon dioxide that is increasing atmospheric carbon dioxide?

16 Complete the cycle for a carbon atom as it passes from the atmosphere to its eventual release back into the atmosphere by respiration in a rabbit. Name the processes and structures in which it will be involved.
- Diffuses as carbon dioxide through open stomata into leaf.
- _______ in leaf.
- Stored as _______ and used to make a structural material, _______.
- Eaten by rabbit and _______ in rabbit's gut by enzymes.
- Taken up as _______ into the rabbit's bloodstream.
- _______ in rabbit muscle cells.

17 a) Name the two types of decomposer organisms in the carbon cycle.
b) Decomposers break down the dead organic matter into small soluble molecules. Give two different uses for these molecules.

- Dead plant or animal remains and waste material pass to decomposers, the bacteria and fungi in the soil or leaf litter. This part of the cycle can be considered as the 'dark chain' and is very important in terms of cycling nutrients and energy flow. The bacteria and fungi secrete enzymes onto the dead organic matter to break it down (digest it). Some of the soluble products of digestion are taken up by the bacteria and fungi for their growth or respiration; the remainder stay in the soil and can be taken up by plants. The nutrients have been cycled.
- Respiration of plants, animals and decomposers returns the carbon atoms to the atmosphere as carbon dioxide.
- There can be an extra input of carbon dioxide into the atmosphere by the burning of fossil fuels such as methane, diesel, petrol, coal, oil and gas and by burning wood.

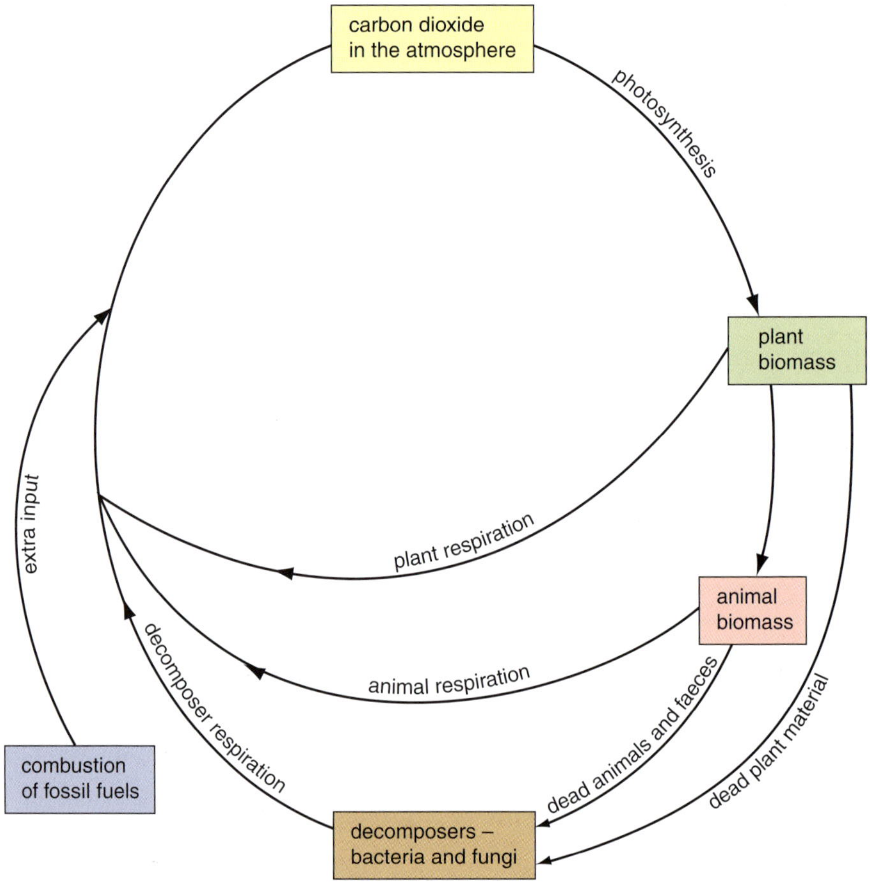

Figure 2.22 The carbon cycle

We have looked at the cycling of carbon atoms and at how nutrients are released and cycled by microorganisms. In the **carbon cycle** diagram the arrows go around in a circle, showing the route of the carbon. However, energy flows through an ecosystem in a straight line. Energy enters the ecosystem, is converted and used, and some passes out of the ecosystem – it cannot be cycled.

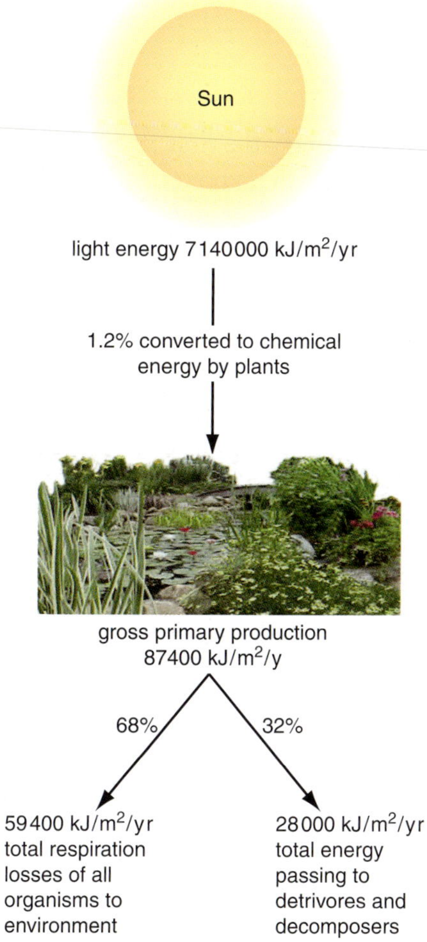

Figure 2.23 Energy flow in an ecosystem

In the process of photosynthesis, the energy from sunlight is used by plants to convert carbon dioxide and water into chemical potential energy in sugar. In the plant, or the animal that eats the plant, respiration releases the chemical energy in the sugar molecules and heat is lost from the organism. This energy flow is summarised in Figure 2.23.

This can also be written as:

light energy → chemical potential energy in food → heat energy which is lost to the environment

Summary

- ✓ **Photosynthesis** is the process in green plants that converts light energy into chemical potential energy.
- ✓ **Chlorophyll** in chloroplasts absorbs light energy.
- ✓ The raw materials for photosynthesis are carbon dioxide and water.
- ✓ The products of photosynthesis are oxygen and glucose.
- ✓ The glucose can be used for energy, combined with nitrates to make plant proteins, converted to starch for storage, or used as a structural material such as cellulose.
- ✓ If carbon dioxide is in short supply or if the temperature or **light intensity** is low, the rate of photosynthesis will be reduced. Any one of these factors could be a **limiting factor**.
- ✓ Plant roots absorb mineral ions, including nitrates (needed to form amino acids) and magnesium (needed to form chlorophyll). Mineral deficiency can cause stunted growth and yellow leaves.
- ✓ To maximise greenhouse crop production, light intensity, carbon dioxide concentration and temperature are artificially controlled at optimum levels.
- ✓ A **pyramid of biomass** shows the mass of organisms at each **trophic** (feeding) **level**. It measures the material present at the time.
- ✓ In a pyramid of biomass there are generally large numbers of small organisms at the base, but size of organisms increases and numbers of organisms decrease at each trophic level.
- ✓ In a **pyramid of energy** there is less energy in each successive level.
- ✓ Energy transferred from one level to the next is reduced because some energy is used for movement or is lost in waste materials, and in mammals and birds heat is lost in maintaining body temperature above that of the environment.
- ✓ Food production would be more energy efficient if humans fed as herbivores, because this reduces the number of stages in the food chain.
- ✓ The efficiency of food production is increased by restricting movement and heat loss in food animals.
- ✓ Bacteria and fungi play an essential role in decomposing dead organic matter and in recycling mineral ions to the plants.
- ✓ Bacteria and fungi (**decomposers**) break down dead organic matter by extracellular digestion.
- ✓ Nutrients cycle within and are reused in an ecosystem – there is a finite supply of nutrients.

- ✓ The carbon cycle shows how carbon atoms circulate through carbon compounds in living organisms to carbon dioxide in the air and back again.
- ✓ Energy flows through an ecosystem – the light energy input is available every day.

EXAMQUESTIONS

1 A glasshouse owner wishes to grow many successive crops of lettuce and harvest the crops all year round.

a) Examine the computer control panel in Figure 2.24 and decide which factors are limiting the productivity. *(3 marks)*

b) Suggest suitable new settings. *(3 marks)*

c) The grower decides to install a paraffin heater. What problems might this cause? *(2 marks)*

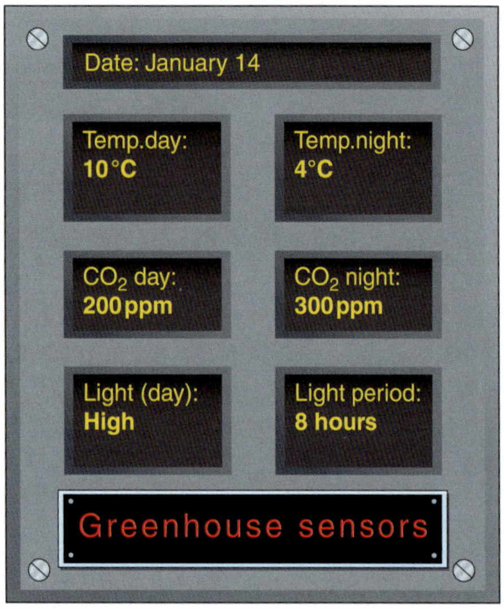

Figure 2.24

2 A student is planning a trial to find the best concentration at which to apply a liquid fertiliser. The recommended strength is 20 cm^3 per 10 dm^3 – which the student calls 100% strength. He decides to try the first concentration at double the recommended strength, i.e. 200%, and then a range of other concentrations. He records the dilutions in Table 2.3. (1 dm^3 = 1000 cm^3)

Volume concentrated solution in cm^3	Volume water in cm^3	Final concentration in %
40	9 960	200
20	9 980	100
10	9 990	
5	9 995	
2.5	9 997.5	
0	10 000	

Table 2.3

a) Complete the table to find his dilutions. *(4 marks)*

b) Do you think the range of percentage concentrations chosen was suitable? Give a reason for your answer. *(2 marks)*

c) The student's idea was to harvest the plants at the end of the experiment by cutting them off at soil level to find the fresh biomass. His friend suggested that he should harvest the plants and then find the dry biomass. What is the difference between fresh and dry biomass? Which do you think would give the most accurate result, and why? *(3 marks)*

3 Look at the carbon cycle in Figure 2.25.

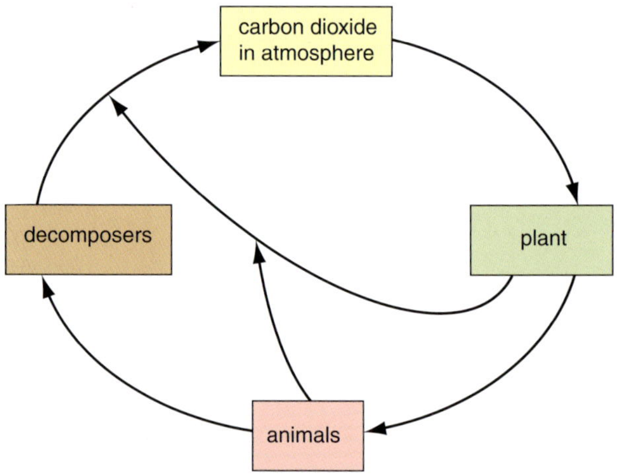

Figure 2.25 Carbon cycle

a) i) Name the only type of organism shown which removes carbon dioxide from the atmosphere. *(1 mark)*

ii) For what process is the carbon dioxide used? *(1 mark)*

b) Name i) a structural material and ii) a storage product in a plant, which contain carbon. *(2 marks)*

c) If the cow eats grass it assimilates the carbon atoms into compounds in its body. Name i) a structural material and ii) a storage product in a cow, which contain carbon. *(2 marks)*

d) The manure (cow pat) of the cow contains the remains of the grass. What is the general name given to organisms that help in the chemical breakdown of the manure? *(1 mark)*

4 A student turns over a dead log and finds fine cotton-like threads on the underside. Complete the sentences below to explain what is happening at a), b) and c) in Figure 2.26.

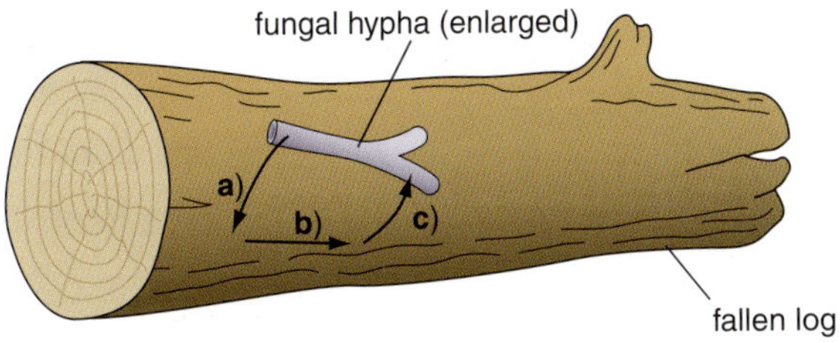

Figure 2.26

a) Enzymes are secreted to ______ the wood. These enzymes will include ______.
b) Soluble ______ and ______ produced by the enzymes will be taken up by plants.
c) The soluble products will be used by the plant for ______. *(5 marks)*

5 The mangrove swamps in the Gulf of Mexico support five trophic levels.

The main producer in this ecosystem is the seagrass, which grows underwater and is consumed by small herbivorous fish.

Unicellular algae make up a smaller biomass but they are the main food of the zooplankton (microscopic animals).

The zooplankton provide the food source for the invertebrates such as shrimp and for small carnivorous fish.

Puffer fish eat mainly the invertebrates. Together with the larger fish they make up the fourth trophic level.

The top carnivore is the snapper fish.

Table 2.4 shows the biomass at each trophic level.

	Biomass in kg/km^2
Primary producers	3700
Primary consumers	39
Secondary consumers	18
Third consumers	6
Top carnivore	1

Table 2.4

a) Use the data in Table 2.4 to construct a pyramid of biomass for this ecosystem on graph paper. Use a square 1 cm × 1 cm (25 small squares on 2 mm graph paper) to represent a biomass of 50 kg/km^2; one small square 2 mm × 2 mm therefore represents a biomass of 2 kg/km^2.
b) Label the organisms at each trophic level beside your diagram. *(6 marks)*
c) What do you notice about the area representing the primary producers? *(1 mark)*
d) What can you say about the change in biomass at each trophic level? *(1 mark)*
e) The biomass given is what is growing at a given time. The algae reproduce every few days. How would this contribute to the food available to the zooplankton? *(1 mark)*
f) The list of species takes no account of bird predators flying in to catch and eat the fish. Suggest which trophic level might be most reduced by these predators. *(1 mark)*

Chapter 3
Enzymes: how do they function and how can their properties be used industrially?

At the end of this chapter you should:

- ✓ know that enzymes are proteins which act as biological catalysts that increase the rate of reactions in living organisms;
- ✓ understand that protein molecules and enzymes are made of chains of amino acids coiled together;
- ✓ be able to explain why the shape of an enzyme is vital for its function;
- ✓ be able to explain that heat affects enzyme function;
- ✓ know that enzymes have an optimum temperature and optimum pH;
- ✓ know that enzymes catalyse the reactions in processes such as respiration, photosynthesis and protein synthesis;
- ✓ be able to summarise aerobic respiration and explain how energy is released by a chemical reaction inside mitochondria;
- ✓ explain how amino acids and proteins are made (synthesised) in reactions catalysed by enzymes;
- ✓ be able to describe the digestive enzymes that catalyse the breakdown of different foods, and where this happens;
- ✓ be able to describe how enzymes produced by microorganisms are used in detergents to remove food stains;
- ✓ be able to describe applications of enzymes used in industry including pre-digested baby food and products containing sugar or fructose syrup, and
- ✓ be able to evaluate the advantages and disadvantages of using enzymes in the home and in industry.

Figure 3.1 a) Why is biological washing powder called biological when it's full of chemicals? b) All detergents contain hydrocarbon molecules that help remove dirt and grease. c) Biological detergents work really well on food stains by literally digesting the food with enzymes just like the enzymes in your digestive system.

3.1 What are enzymes and what are some of their functions?

Enzymes are the biological molecules that catalyse reactions in living organisms.

A **substrate** is the substance acted on by an enzyme.

1. What is the benefit of enzyme-controlled reactions inside living cells?
2. Give three advantages of using enzymes in biotechnology applications.
3. Give two similarities and two differences between enzymes and catalysts. (You might want to look at Section 7.3 in the chemistry part of this book.)

Enzymes are called biological catalysts because they control most of the reactions that take place in living organisms. All catalysts change the rate of chemical reactions but are not themselves changed by the reaction. Enzymes catalyse essential reactions such as respiration and photosynthesis that take place inside cells. The enzyme is not used up so it can catalyse the same reaction many times.

The function of enzymes is to enable reactions to take place at lower temperatures. At low temperatures, such as the temperature of the human body, the chemical reactions inside cells would take place very slowly without enzymes.

Enzymes are used in many processes in the food and biotechnology industries so that the industrial reaction temperature can be kept low. This saves energy used to heat the container and so saves money (see Section 3.5). Enzymes also increase the reaction rate so that large amounts of product can be made quickly.

Enzymes differ from chemical catalysts because enzymes are protein molecules. Therefore, they have some properties of both catalysts and proteins. As catalysts, enzymes change the rate of reactions and as proteins they have a complex 3-D structure that allows other molecules to fit into the enzyme.

3.2 How do enzymes work?

Cracking the name code. The ending *-ase* tells you that the substance is an enzyme. The first part of the name tells you the substrate. For example, protease is the enzyme that breaks down protein, and amylase breaks down amylose. Think of some compounds with names ending in *-ose*. What type of substance are these?

Amino acids are molecules that can be combined in long chains to form proteins.

Each type of enzyme only works on one particular reaction, to produce certain products from one **substrate**. You probably know that when your body digests food, different enzymes work on different food types. Protease enzymes speed up digestion of protein and amylase breaks down the substrate amylose (commonly called starch) to give the products glucose and fructose.

Why does an enzyme only work on one substrate? Let us look at the structure of enzymes in more detail. You will need to think at the level of the three-dimensional structure of the molecule. Remember that enzymes are protein molecules.

Amino acids are the building blocks of proteins. They are joined end to end to form a long chain. This molecular chain is stabilised when it is folded into a three-dimensional shape and cross-bonds form between the amino acids (rather as a girl might twist up her hair and put in slides). All enzymes have this same basic structure, but they have a different sequence of amino acids to form different protein molecules. The order

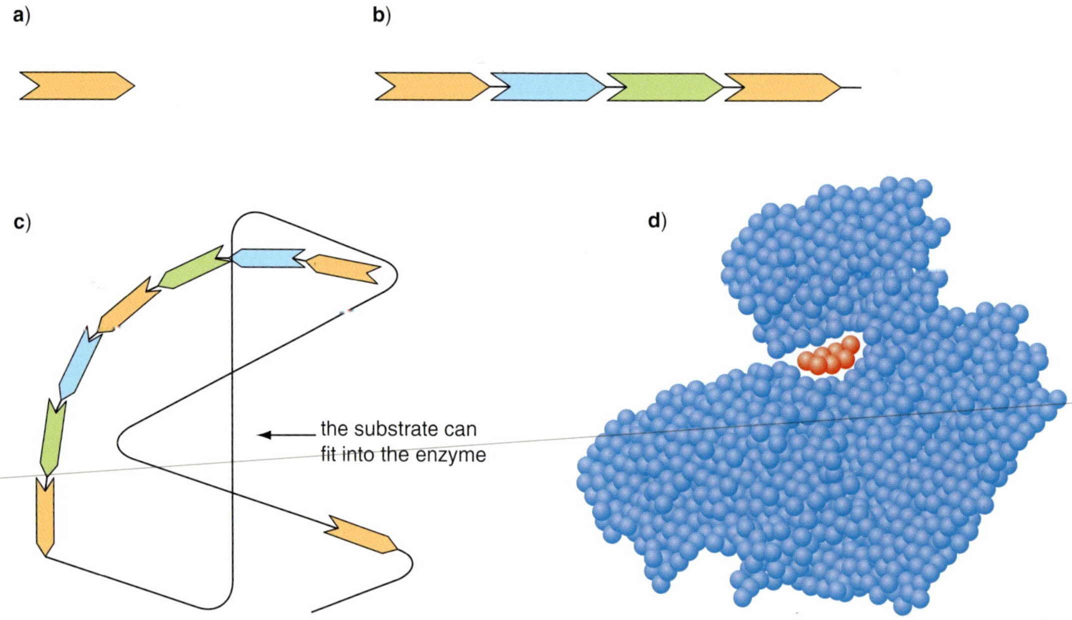

Figure 3.2 a) A single amino acid. b) A long chain of amino acids joined together. c) The chain folds to become more stable. d) The complete three-dimensional enzyme with substrate.

A **model** is a simplified picture that scientists construct to fit observed data to a theory.

The **lock and key model** suggests that each enzyme has a special shape, which means that only one substrate can fit into each enzyme.

in which amino acids are joined together is controlled by the DNA code in the nucleus. Each tightly folded protein molecule or enzyme has ridges and grooves, giving it a unique shape. This means that each enzyme fits only one type of substrate.

This idea of the substrate fitting into the enzyme is called the **'lock and key' model** for enzyme structure. Enzymes unlock a particular reactant molecule so that a chemical reaction can take place and the molecular bonds can be broken. This is why each enzyme is specific to one type of chemical reaction.

What conditions affect enzymes?

The **activation energy** is the energy that must be provided to the reactants to start a chemical reaction.

Rates of enzyme reactions increase with increase in temperature. To understand why, you can apply your understanding of what is happening at the molecular level (see also Chapter 7). First, the enzyme and substrate molecules must collide with enough energy for the substrate to fit into the enzyme structure. This is called the **activation energy** (more about this in Chemistry, Section 7.3). This is a bit like putting a missing piece into a jigsaw puzzle: you can place a missing piece over a gap, but it needs a little push (energy) to fit it in.

An increase in temperature will cause the particles to move faster, that is to increase their kinetic energy. As a result enzyme molecules and substrate molecules will collide more often. The enzyme can catalyse more reactions so the reaction rate is increased.

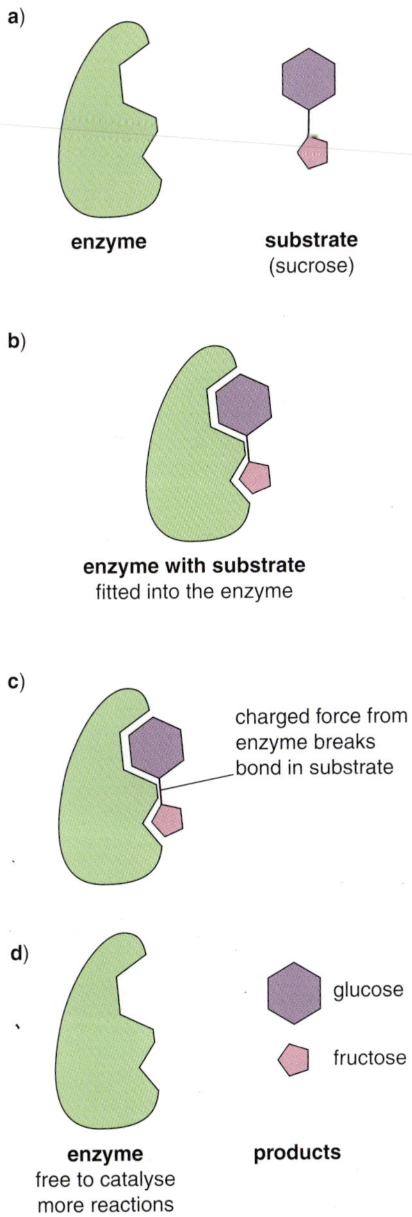

Figure 3.3 This sequence of diagrams shows how an enzyme breaks down a substrate. Here, the substrate is sucrose and the products are glucose and fructose.

When temperature destroys the three-dimensional shape of a protein molecule or enzyme, it is **denatured**.

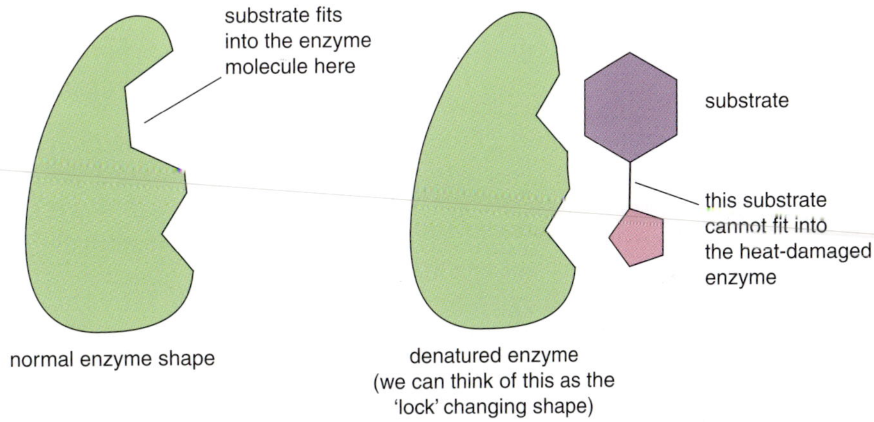

Figure 3.4 The effect of heat (denaturation) on an enzyme molecule. Heat changes the bonds and changes the three-dimensional shape.

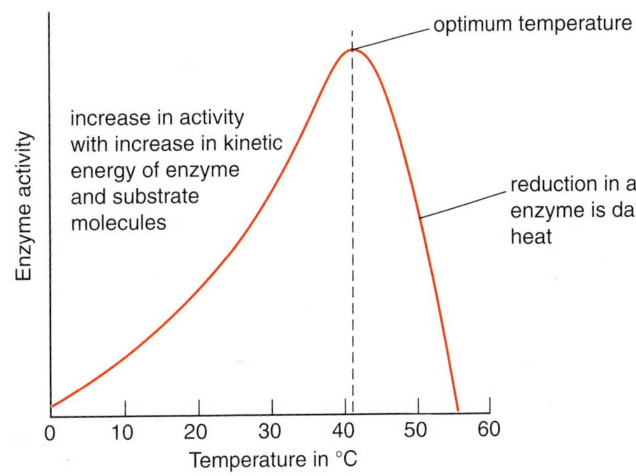

Figure 3.5 Sketch graph to show the effect of heat on an enzyme reaction

But this is where enzymes differ from catalysts: enzymes function best at an **optimum temperature**. An increase in temperature above this changes the shape of the protein molecule. You can see the effect of change in the protein structure when you cook an egg white. When the enzyme molecule shape has been changed, the substrate can no longer fit into the enzyme – we say that the enzyme has been **denatured** and it can no longer function as a catalyst.

Living organisms are adapted to exist in a range of habitats, so the enzymes inside bacteria which live in hot springs will be able to function within a different temperature range from those enzymes in plants in the Arctic. There are also differences in pH levels at which enzymes work. Each enzyme has an optimum pH, which is the pH at which it functions best or most effectively. These differences have been used in industrial applications such as those discussed in Section 3.5.

4. Why are enzyme reactions slow at low temperatures?
5. Why does the rate of product formation increase as the temperature increases between 5 °C and 30 °C?
6. A student was carrying out an experiment using the enzyme protease on egg white. He found that the white solution became colourless for all temperatures up to 45 °C, but above this temperature the solution remained cloudy. Can you explain this?
7. What word is given to the temperature at which enzymes function most efficiently?
8. The mouth is slightly alkaline but the stomach has a low pH. Why do you think salivary amylase stops working when the food it is mixed with enters the stomach?
9. Why can protease break down protein but not starch?

Activity – Who was Emil Fischer?

Emil Fischer was born in Germany in 1852. His father, who said that Emil was too stupid to be a businessman and had better be a student, sent Emil to the University of Bonn in 1871 to study chemistry. Emil Fischer won a Nobel prize in 1902. This was the first prize awarded for organic chemistry. He was famous for rigorous teaching and making links between science and industry. Six of his students later went on to become Nobel prize winners.

Emil Fischer first suggested the 'lock and key' model in 1894. The amazing thing about Fischer's model was that he suggested this before scientists had discovered that enzymes were protein molecules.

Figure 3.6 Emil Fischer

The lock and key model is used today to develop computer simulations that investigate possible new drugs. The computer programs design and test thousands of different molecules with different shapes, to see how they could 'fix' onto receptors on the surface of target disease cells.

1. Write and illustrate a newspaper report about Fischer's great award. Find out about him by searching for his name and biography. Include how long after his discoveries he was rewarded.
2. Find the answers to the following questions.
   a) In Emil Fischer's model, what does the lock represent?
   b) After the 'lock and key' model was suggested, how long was it before the nature of enzymes was worked out, and how long before a three-dimensional model of a protein was first made?
3. Draw a diagram to show the 'lock and key model' as a lock and key, and a more modern diagram showing an enzyme and substrate.

3.3

What reactions do enzymes control inside cells?

Most chemical reactions in the cell take place in the cytoplasm. Different enzymes catalyse each of the many chemical reactions in the cell. Enzymes working inside cells have a constant temperature and pH.

Building protein for growth

Growing cells need to build new structures inside the cell or more organelles such as mitochondria; to do this they make proteins. Amino acids can be joined together to form structural protein molecules or more enzymes. Enzymes catalyse the reactions that make proteins inside the cell. This called **protein synthesis** – different enzymes control which proteins can be built. Different cells do different jobs, and so there are thousands of different proteins.

Protein synthesis is the building of protein molecules from a chain of amino acid molecules, using enzymes to catalyse the reaction.

Respiration to release energy

Making larger molecules from smaller molecules needs energy. All cells in living organisms release energy from food by respiring. **Aerobic respiration** is a reaction in cells that uses glucose and oxygen to release energy. Aerobic respiration occurs as a series of reactions, each controlled by an enzyme.

Aerobic respiration occurs when oxygen reacts with glucose and releases energy. Carbon dioxide and water are the products of the reaction.

The reactions in aerobic respiration are summarised by the equation:

$$\text{glucose} + \text{oxygen} \rightarrow \text{carbon dioxide} + \text{water } (+ \text{ energy})$$
$$C_6H_{12}O_6 + 6O_2 \rightarrow 6CO_2 + 6H_2O \ (+ \text{ energy})$$

First, glucose is broken down in the cytoplasm to form smaller molecules that can enter the mitochondrion. In the mitochondrion a sequence of reactions takes place. In the final stage hydrogen atoms removed from the glucose are combined with oxygen to form water and energy is released.

So why is respiration a series of reactions and not a single reaction? If you oxidise glucose by setting fire to it you end up with the same overall reaction and the same products, but a great deal of energy is released rapidly causing heating – we call this combustion. This type of reaction within cells would damage the proteins. Instead, in respiration the energy is released bit by bit at each reaction, in small units that have sufficient energy to power the other reactions in the cell. You could think of it as being like arriving at a holiday destination with all your money as large value notes – it's best if you have smaller values and coins for buying drinks and chocolates.

10. Name two large molecules made in plant cells by joining together smaller molecules.
11. In which part of the cell is most of the energy in respiration released?
12. Combustion is one reaction but respiration takes place as a series of small reactions. What points are the same about these reactions and how do they differ?

What do cells do with these small units of energy?

Remember that energy is needed for building up small molecules into large molecules, such as amino acids into large protein molecules. Other chemical reactions in the cytoplasm also need energy. For example, plants need energy to add nitrates to the sugars produced by photosynthesis to form amino acids. Plants also build up glucose molecules into cellulose for their cell walls.

Photosynthesis itself is a chemical reaction, and without plant enzymes this reaction could not take place. In photosynthesis the enzyme systems in chlorophyll convert light energy into chemical energy in the form of glucose. The majority of food webs are based upon this reaction (see Chapter 2).

Energy released by respiration is used by warm-blooded animals to maintain their body temperature, and for muscle fibre contractions so that the animal or bird can move.

13 Examine the following statements and identify which are correct.
a) Plants respire at night and photosynthesise in daylight.
b) Plants respire for 24 hours a day.
c) Plants photosynthesise for 24 hours a day.
d) For plants to grow, the rate of photosynthesis must be greater than the rate of respiration over the year.
e) For growing plants the rate of photosynthesis equals the rate of respiration over the year.
f) Plants can photosynthesise for longer each day in spring than in winter.

14 Give three uses that animals make of the energy released in respiration.

3.4 Are enzymes used outside cells in the body?

Digestive enzymes catalyse the breakdown of food as it passes down the intestine from the mouth. The digestive system can be thought of as a tube through the body carrying food.

A **gland** is an organ that produces and releases or secretes a substance used by other cells.

Digestive enzymes are produced by specialised cells in **glands**, such as the salivary gland or the pancreas, or by cells in the lining of the stomach and intestine. These enzymes pass out of the cells and are released into the intestine.

The purpose of digestion is to break down large insoluble molecules into small soluble molecules. For example, amylase breaks down the substrate amylose (starch) to give glucose and fructose. Smaller

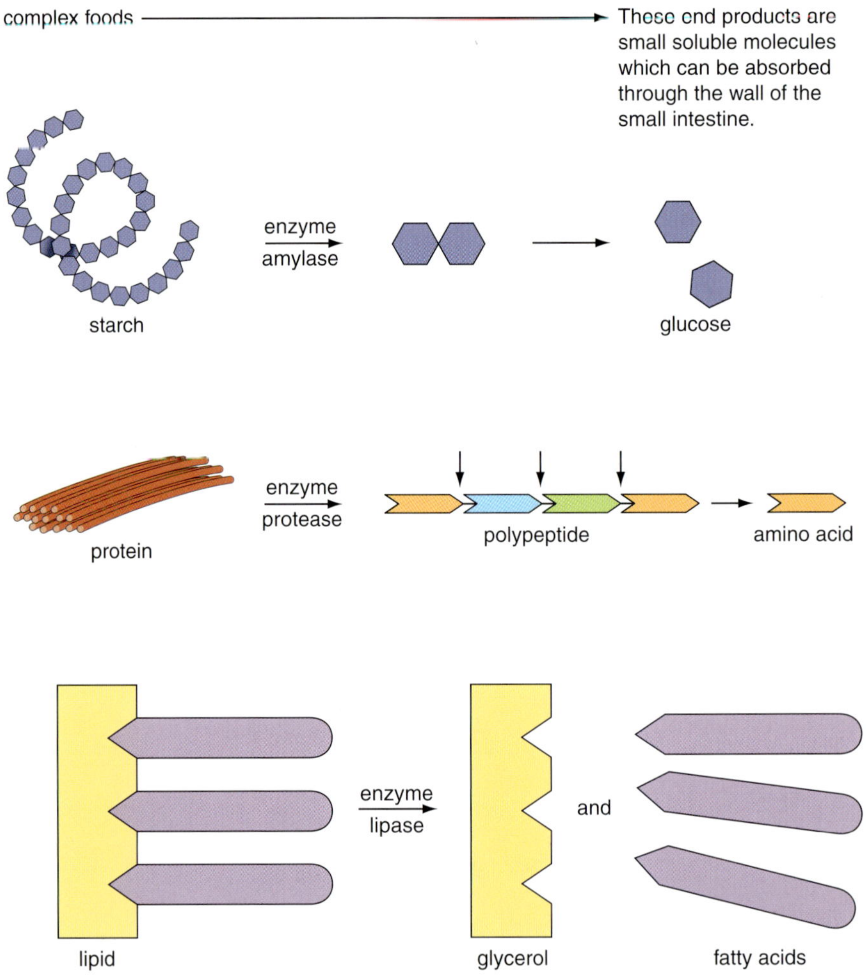

Figure 3.7 The breakdown of the complex food molecules into small, soluble, useable molecules

molecules are needed because they are soluble and can pass (diffuse) from the small intestine into the blood plasma for transport to body cells. Smaller molecules, like glucose and amino acids, are also in a form that cells can use.

Protease enzymes that break down proteins are produced by cells in the stomach lining, so protein digestion begins in the stomach. However, different proteases are produced by the pancreas and secreted into the small intestine where proteins continue to be broken down into amino acids. The stomach protease and the pancreatic protease function at different pH levels as you can see in Table 3.1.

Other substances are released that help the enzymes function by providing the optimum pH. Hydrochloric acid is released into the stomach to provide the low pH required by the protein-digesting enzyme called protease. **Bile** produced in the liver cells is stored in the gall bladder and added to the small intestine via a small duct (tube); bile neutralises the acidic food, leaving the stomach to provide the higher pH needed by enzymes which work in the small intestine.

Bile is a substance produced by the liver and released during digestion into the small intestine to provide alkaline conditions. Bile also reduces the size of the fatty droplets, making them easier to digest.

Amylase is the digestive enzyme that breaks down starch into glucose and fructose.

Lipase is the digestive enzyme that breaks down lipids (fats and oils) into fatty acids and glycerol.

Protease is the digestive enzyme that breaks down proteins into amino acids.

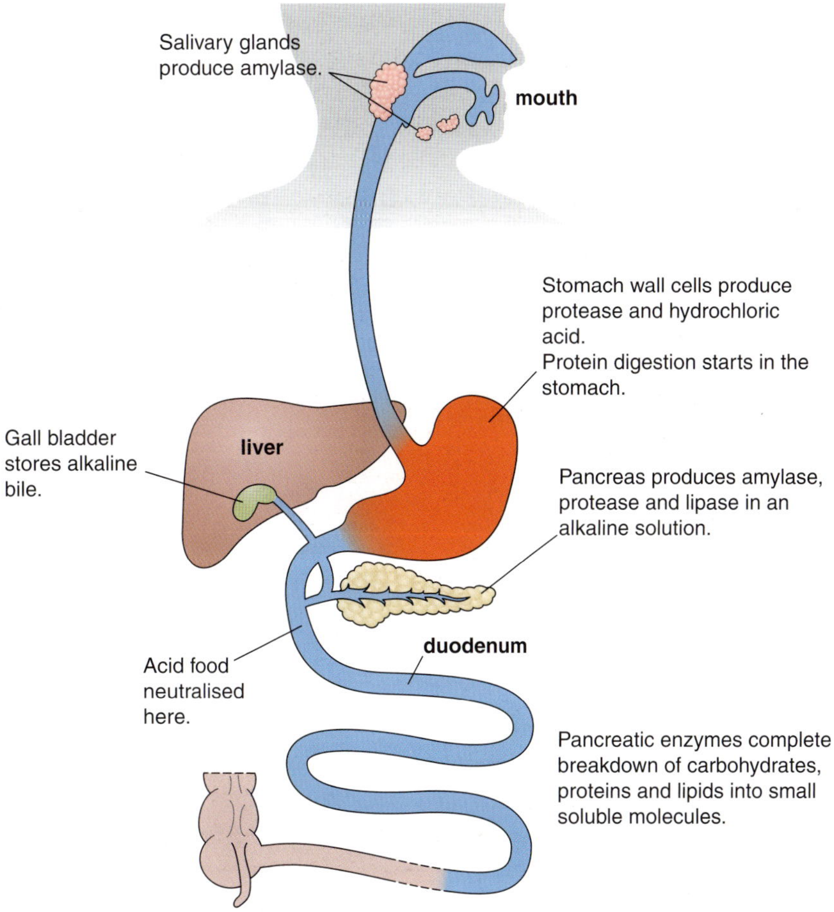

Figure 3.8 Digestive enzymes control reactions that take place in the digestive system.

Enzyme	Site of production	Site of action	pH	Substrate	Products
Salivary amylase	Salivary glands	Mouth	8	Starch	Sugars
Pancreatic amylase	Pancreas	Small intestine	8	Starch	Sugars
Protease	Cells in stomach wall	Stomach	2 (hydrochloric acid produced by the stomach acidifies food)	Protein	Polypeptides and amino acids
Protease	Pancreas	Small intestine	8 (bile from the liver neutralises the acid food leaving the stomach)	Protein	Polypeptides and amino acids
Protease	Small intestine wall	Small intestine	8	Peptides	Amino acids
Lipase	Pancreas and cells in small intestine wall	Small intestine	8	Lipids	Fatty acids and glycerol

Table 3.1 Enzymes of the digestive system

15 a) The food leaving the mouth is slightly alkaline. How is the pH lowered in the stomach?
b) What is the optimum pH for the enzyme amylase?
c) The food leaving the stomach is strongly acidic. How is the pH raised?
d) What is the optimum pH for all the pancreatic enzymes?
e) What is the optimum pH for stomach protease?

16 At the start of the chapter, in question 1, 'What is the benefit of enzyme-controlled reactions inside living cells?', you considered temperature. Now think about rate of energy production and give a second answer. Suggest how very slow uncatalysed reactions would affect life.

17 Copy and complete the four blanks in the table.

Enzyme	Large complex molecules	Small soluble end products of digestion
Amylase	Starch	a) _______
Protease	b) _______	Amino acids
c) _______	Lipids (fats and oils)	d) _______ and glycerol

Table 3.2

18 a) Name the two places where amylase is produced.
b) Name the two sites of protein digestion.
c) Describe where fats and oils are digested.

19 a) Where is bile produced?
b) Where is bile stored?
c) What is the function of bile?

3.5 Industrial production and use of enzymes

Many industrial enzymes come from soil microorganisms. One of the best sources of industrial proteases used in laundry detergents is the *Bacillus* species, a common soil bacterium.

The list of industrial applications for enzymes is amazing and includes food, wine and beer production, making fructose sweeteners for soft drinks, laundry detergents, producing the 'stone-washed' jeans effect and manufacturing pharmaceuticals. The food industry uses many enzymes, which can be 'tailor-made' to give an exact product for the development of a new food.

Like all living organisms, bacteria and fungi produce and secrete enzymes. The enzymes pass out of their cells into the environment. The enzyme products, small soluble molecules, are then taken into the organism's cytoplasm (see Section 2.7, Figure 2.21). Microorganisms are collected from different locations around the world and the enzymes they produce are tested. Biotechnologists look for enzymes that could be used for particular processes, and that work at the temperature of the industrial plant.

As bacteria and fungi normally live in cool environments, their enzymes usually function at low temperatures. However, if an enzyme is required in industry to work at high temperature or extremes of pH, then enzymes have to be found from microorganisms living in those environmental conditions. Enzymes that act on the right substrates but at the wrong temperature may need to be modified by gene transfer.

A **fermenter** is a large steel process vessel that is used for biochemical reactions. Sensors monitor the conditions inside. The sensors send information to a computer, which then controls input valves to maintain the temperature, pH, nutrient and oxygen levels at the optimum value.

To produce the enzymes, the microorganisms are cultured in a fermentation process. At the end of the batch process, the **fermenter** is emptied and the enzymes are collected from the solution in which the bacteria have grown.

Figure 3.9 An industrial fermenter for producing enzymes. The raw material is converted by the enzymes as it flows slowly over the surface of the beads.

Carbohydrase enzymes break down complex carbohydrate molecules such as starch into simple sugars.

Isomerase is an enzyme that converts glucose into fructose.

Enzymes in the food industry

An early application of enzymes in the food industry was the production of sweet syrups by breaking down starch. This process can be done chemically by boiling starch with acid, but the reactions using the enzyme method give a pure and reliable product, with no other by-products. Another advantage is that energy costs are lower as the enzyme process can be carried out at a lower temperature.

Glucose syrup is widely used as an ingredient and food additive. Most glucose syrup is produced from maize (corn) using enzymes. Maize processing results in a large amount of starch waste products. Using a common and cheap (waste) material as the raw material for glucose syrup is cost effective.

Many **carbohydrase** enzymes are used in sequence to produce a variety of syrups of different sweetness. For example:

- maize starch is treated with one form of amylase to convert it to a thick starch paste;
- this paste is then reacted with different amylase enzymes to form sugars such as maltose or glucose. The reaction can be stopped here; or
- the final stage is the conversion of glucose syrup to fructose syrup, using the enzyme **isomerase**.

In the early 1970s a continuous flow system was developed in which glucose solution was added through the top and fructose solution was delivered from the bottom. The continuous process can run for about 6 months non-stop. As enzymes are proteins, their structure eventually breaks down and the enzyme needs replacing. The old enzymes are biodegradable in the environment so do not result in toxic waste. Fructose syrup is much sweeter than sucrose or glucose syrup so it can be used in smaller quantities as a sweetener. This saves food manufacturers money, but another result was that in the 1970s fructose syrup began to be used in slimming foods to give sweetness with fewer calories.

Although there are clear economic advantages of using enzymes in industrial processes, there are some disadvantages:

- development and production of new enzymes is costly;
- enzyme action is highly specific, so they have only one use;
- enzymes require exact conditions of temperature and pH in which to work;
- as enzymes are proteins, they can cause allergic reactions, and so must be encapsulated to minimise the risk of skin contact or inhalation; and
- some people may object to genetically modified (GM) enzymes being used to produce food.

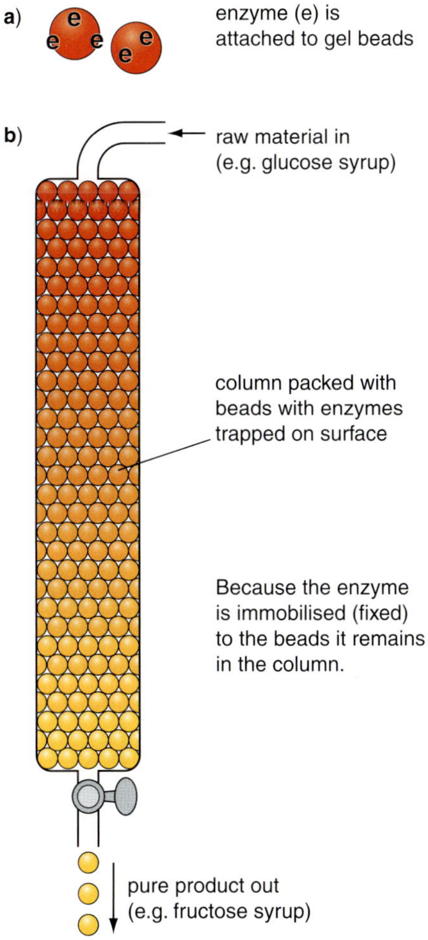

Figure 3.10 In a continuous flow column the substrate (glucose) is added through the top and reacts as it flows slowly over beads, which have the enzyme attached to the surface. The product can be collected from the bottom of the column.

20 List the economic advantages of using enzymes in the food industry.

21 a) In a continuous flow column, what is the advantage of having the enzymes immobilised on beads?

b) In a batch process, the raw materials and the enzymes are reacted together in a reactor vessel until an economic concentration of products has been formed. The remaining raw materials and the enzymes are then separated from the products. What are the advantages of 'continuous-flow' rather than 'batch' processes?

22 Complete the following table showing the use of enzymes in common food production.

Food product	Enzyme used in manufacture	Substrate	Product	Advantage of the product
Baby food	Protease		Amino acid	Readily available amino acids for baby growth
Slimming products	Invertase	Glucose syrup		Sweetens without adding calories
Soft drinks	Carbohydrase	(Maize) starch		
Baby food		Fats	Fatty acids	No digestion needed

Table 3.3

Other food products made from enzymes

Figure 3.11 What is the connection between these two?

Figure 3.12 An enzyme product loved by many people

You would not expect anything in common between babies and bodybuilders, but there is. Some baby food is pre-digested using proteases so that the baby can use the amino acids without digestion. Baby-milk powders are manufactured from cows' milk and are treated with enzymes to break down the proteins. This has the advantage that they are less likely to cause allergic reactions. The protein supplements taken by body builders are also pre-digested into amino acids, which can be quickly taken up for building and repairing muscles if consumed straight after training.

Soft-centred chocolates start with the centre as a hard sugar paste, which can be easily handled for chocolate coating. The addition of invertase enzyme converts the sucrose to glucose and fructose syrup within 1 to 2 days. In other words, by the time the chocolates reach the shop the hard centre has become soft. This has other advantages in that fructose retains water within the centre and prevents the sugar crystallising out.

Laundry detergents

Washing used to be carried out at high temperatures with a great deal of agitation to break down dirt. This was costly in terms of electricity used to heat the water. Modern detergents use enzymes that function efficiently at low temperatures, reducing fuel costs.

Food or biological stains on clothes can include fats and oils from fried items, butter or oily dressings, proteins such as eggs, grass or blood and starches from sauces made with flour. Biological washing powders have the following enzymes added: lipase to break down fats, proteases to digest proteins and carbohydrases to remove starch stains. Similar enzymes are used in dishwasher detergents.

Figure 3.13 What stains might be on the toddler's T-shirt? How could these be removed in a cool wash?

Although using 'biological detergents' improves stain removal and reduces costs, so much washing detergent is used in industrial production, the hotel and catering industry and in the home that environmental factors must also be considered. Biological detergents are biodegradable, because enzymes are proteins and breakdown naturally in the environment. They also have other environmental advantages in energy efficiency and water efficiency.

23. Figure 3.13 shows a typical toddler's T-shirt. Explain how biological washing powder will solve the problem for each stain, for example the egg, butter and tomato sauce.

24. What are the environmental advantages of using enzymes in detergents?

25. The instructions on the box state that biological wash powders are not effective when used at temperatures above 40 °C.
    a) Explain why this is so.
    b) If you had dropped fruit and cream down the front of your best silk shirt, what would be the advantage of using biological washing powder?

Activity – Stone-washed jeans

Figure 3.14

Denim fabric is made by weaving. The cross threads are unbleached cotton and the warp (vertical threads) are dyed with indigo. Indigo is a very stable dye and strong hypochlorite bleach (high pH and high temperature) is needed to remove it chemically.

Stone-washed jeans were originally produced literally with stones, in an enormous machine that shook 150 kg of pumice stone with 150 pairs of jeans for up to 6 hours. The stones damaged the cellulose fibres and released the indigo dye. This process was damaging to the seams of the jeans, the machines, the operators, because of the pumice dust in the air, and took a lot of water to rinse off all the grit particles from the jeans.

The new method uses an enzyme called DeniMax, which produces the stone-wash effect faster without damage to the fabric and uses a minimum quantity of water.

The new enzyme process removes the need for pumice stones, the final look is the same and the jeans last longer.

1. List four problems with the old stone-wash system.
2. A new enzyme has been developed which is specific to indigo and which works under such mild conditions that it can also be used on stretch denim. The result of using the enzyme is to reduce the depth of the colour and produce an aged effect.
   What is meant by the term 'the enzyme is specific to indigo'?
3. What are the environmental advantages of the enzyme process used in the manufacturing of jeans?

What do the homemaker, laundry and hotel industry want from a detergent?	What are the environmental requirements for a detergent?
A good clean wash	No foam in water-treatment works
Low temperatures to reduce the cost of heating the water	Reduced amount of energy used, to reduce air pollution and greenhouse gas emissions from electricity generation
Less water used, as many house and businesses now have water meters	Reduced amount of water used, to avoid water shortages particularly in the south of England
Less agitation to reduce wear on fabrics	Biodegradable materials
All stains removed	
Fabrics to feel soft after washing	
Shorter washing time	

Table 3.4 The requirements for a good washing powder

Summary

- ✓ Enzymes are biological catalysts that enable reactions to take place at a lower temperature.
- ✓ Enzymes are **protein molecules** with a three-dimensional structure and are **denatured** by high temperatures.
- ✓ Enzymes function most effectively at an **optimum temperature** and **optimum pH**.
- ✓ Enzymes inside living cells catalyse respiration, photosynthesis and **protein synthesis** reactions.
- ✓ **Aerobic respiration** reactions release energy from glucose, this energy is needed for movement, building new molecules and maintaining body temperature.
- ✓ Some enzymes are secreted from cells and function outside cells, for example in the digestive system
- ✓ Digestive enzymes catalyse the breakdown of food molecules into smaller molecules. **Amylase** breaks down starch into sugars, **proteases** break down proteins into amino acids, **lipases** break down lipids (fats and oils) into fatty acids and glycerol.
- ✓ Microorganisms that secrete enzymes outside their cells are used in industry for enzyme production.
- ✓ Enzymes are used in industry because they save time, money and environmental pollution.
- ✓ Enzymes are used in the food industry to produce sugar syrup from starch, fructose syrup used in slimming products, and pre-digested baby food.
- ✓ Enzymes are used in domestic detergents to improve stain removal by digesting protein and fat in foods.

EXAMQUESTIONS

1. Pectin in fruit holds the cellulose fibres in the cell wall together. The enzyme pectinase breaks down the pectin and cell walls releasing the juice.

A student did a laboratory experiment to extract apple juice. She grated the apple to form pulp and weighed out 50.0 g into five separate beakers. The pulp was warmed in water baths and then the pectinase added and left for 15 minutes to react. Juice was collected by straining through fine mesh lining a filter funnel into a measuring cylinder.

The results are shown in Table 3.5.

a) Plot the results on a graph. *(3 marks)*
b) From your graph, suggest the optimum temperature for this enzyme. *(1 mark)*
c) Describe and explain the trend shown by the results. *(3 marks)*

Water bath temperature in °C	Volume of juice collected in cm^3
10	12
25	25
35	50
45	78
60	45
70	12
85	12

Table 3.5

d) Do you think there are enough results to make an accurate prediction of the volume of juice you would expect at 50 °C? How could you improve the experiment? *(3 marks)*

EXAMQUESTIONS

2 A student was investigating two protease enzymes labelled A and B. Table 3.6 shows a copy of his practical record.

Tube number	Boiled egg white solution in cm^3	Enzyme	Other solutions added (2 cm^3)	Result after 10 minutes
1	5	A	Water	No change
2	5	A	Dilute HCl	Clear
3	5	A	$NaCO_3$	No change
4	5	B	Water	Less cloudy
5	5	B	Dilute HCl	No change
6	5	B	$NaCO_3$	Clear

Table 3.6

a) Where in the human intestine would:
   i) enzyme A be produced (*1 mark*)
   ii) enzyme B be produced (*1 mark*)
   iii) enzyme B react? (*1 mark*)

b) What is the role of the hydrochloric acid (*1 mark*)

c) Explain why enzyme B did not break down the egg white when dilute hydrochloric acid was present. (*2 marks*)

d) What substances in the intestine produce the optimum conditions for enzyme B to react? (*2 marks*)

3 Quorn is produced in a continuous flow process in a 150 000 dm^3 reactor vessel. The filamentous fungus *Fusarium* is cultured in a medium based on glucose, ammonium compounds and vitamin B (biotin). Cultures are maintained at 28–30 °C and pH 6.0.

a) Examine the diagram. Is this an aerobic or anaerobic process? (*1 mark*)

b) What gas is extracted from the top of the vessel? (*1 mark*)

c) Why are ammonium compounds added? (*1 mark*)

d) What is meant by a continuous flow process? (*1 mark*)

e) Biotin is a B group vitamin. Suggest how the fungus might use this. (*1 mark*)

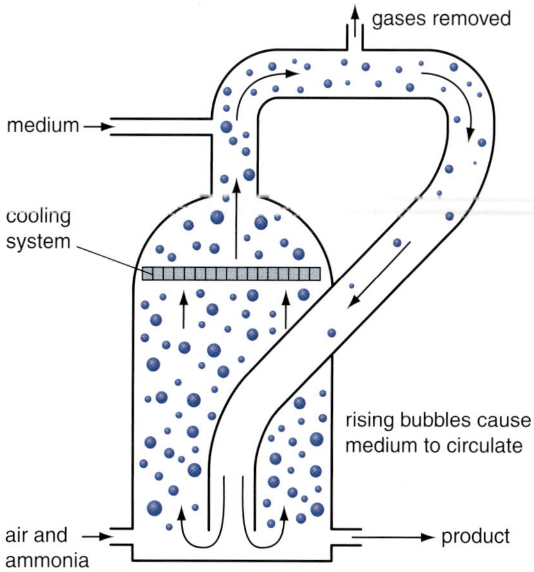

Figure 3.15

f) Why do you think the temperature is maintained closely between 28 and 30° C? (*1 mark*)

g) What do you predict would happen to the production rate if the system became more acidic? (*1 mark*)

4 A student decided to carry out investigations with a low temperature biological washing powder, which had a banner on the box stating 'suitable for delicate coloureds – no bleach added'. He produced a standard dirty piece of material with egg yolk and mayonnaise stains on white cotton. He investigated a range of temperatures between 5 °C and 75 °C at 10-degree intervals. He found that the washed material was whitest in the range 25 °C to 35 °C.

a) Name two types of enzymes would you expect to find in biological washing powder. (*2 marks*)

b) Why was the result for the higher temperatures not so good? (*1 mark*)

c) Why do you think that the result at 5 °C was rather poor? (*2 marks*)

d) What are the environmental advantages of using a low temperature biological washing powder? (*2 marks*)

e) The instructions on the packet stated that gloves should be worn if clothes were hand-washed. Suggest why. (*1 mark*)

Chapter 4
How do our bodies control internal conditions and pass on characteristics?

By the end of this chapter you should:

- ✓ understand how the water and ion content of the body are controlled;
- ✓ know that ADH secreted by the pituitary gland controls the water content of urine;
- ✓ be able to explain how body temperature is maintained;
- ✓ know that the pancreas controls blood glucose concentration through the production of insulin;
- ✓ be able to explain how diabetes affects the body and how it can be treated;
- ✓ know how carbon dioxide and urea are removed from the body;
- ✓ understand the importance of DNA in living organisms;
- ✓ understand that mitosis and meiosis are different types of cell division and understand the role these two processes play in the living organisms;
- ✓ be able to describe how a person's sex is determined;
- ✓ be able to explain how simple characteristics and some diseases are inherited;
- ✓ be able to complete genetic diagrams to illustrate inheritance;
- ✓ be able to make judgements about the applications of embryo screening.

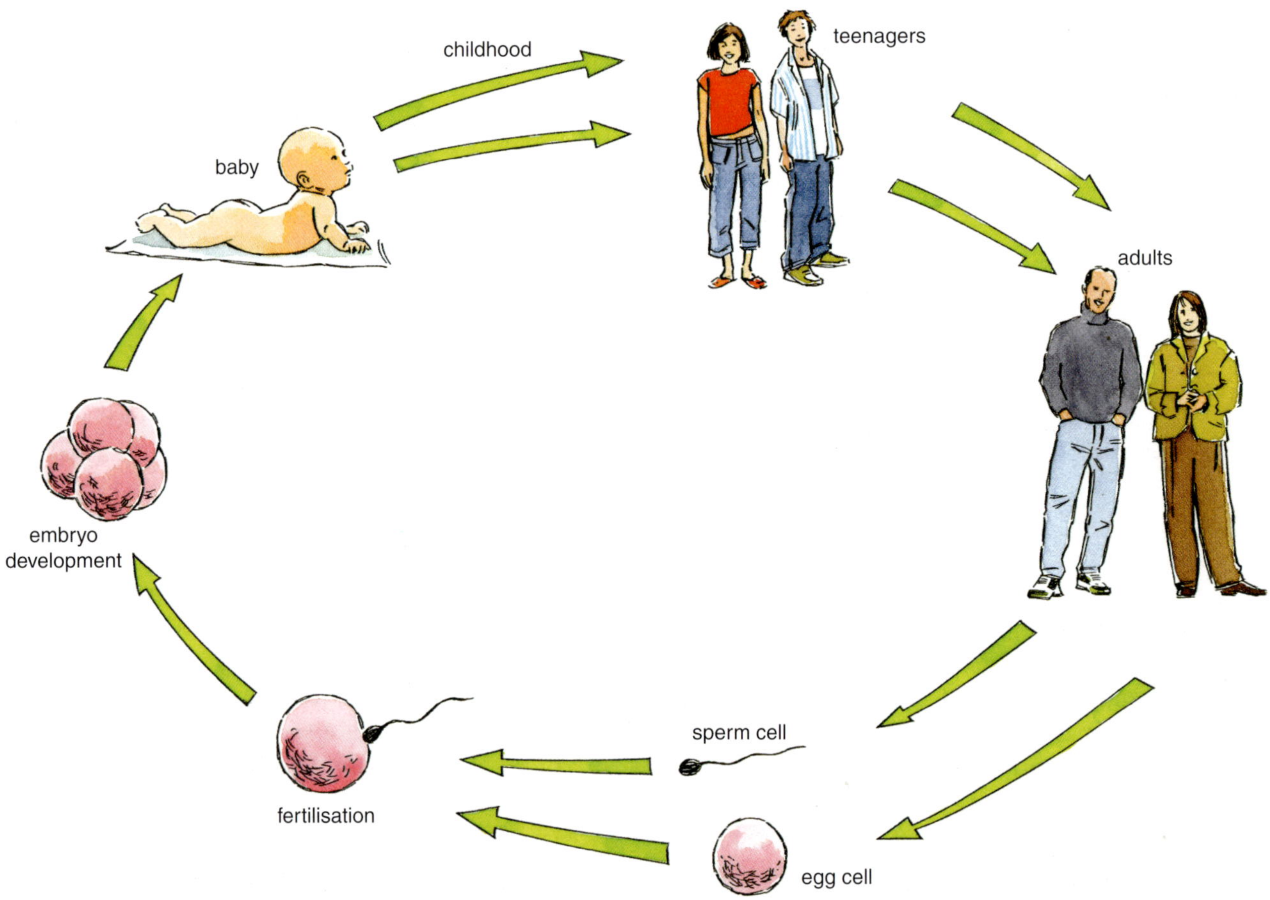

Figure 4.1 The human life cycle. At every stage the body monitors and controls the changes that are taking place. All the information that allows you to do this is inherited from your parents and can be passed onto your children. How can all this develop from just one cell?

4.1 How does your body control its internal conditions?

Homeostasis is the maintenance of steady conditions within the body, including water content, blood glucose concentration and body temperature.

Your body is constantly monitoring its internal conditions and making changes to try and control them. This means the body is controlling conditions in the cells, blood and body tissue. You will have been introduced to this idea whilst studying Core Science when you learnt about how hormones control the water and blood sugar levels in the body. The internal conditions which are controlled include the water and ion content of the body. Your temperature, oxygen, carbon dioxide and blood sugar levels are also controlled. **Homeostasis** is the name given to mechanisms in the body that regulate its internal conditions.

Figure 4.2 The girl is sweating to control her body temperature, which leads to water loss from the body. What else is lost from her body, in sweat?

Controlling the water and ion content of the body.

When you get too hot you sweat to reduce your body temperature. The water in the sweat evaporates from your skin, cooling you down. But sweat doesn't only contain water. Ions, such as sodium and potassium, which are dissolved in your sweat, are also lost. Both water and ions are essential for health and we can obtain both when we eat and drink at mealtimes. You will remember the effects of dehydration and over-hydration from Chapter 1. Too much water in the blood can cause body cells to swell up or even burst. Too little water causes cells to shrivel. Too much or too little water in our cells means that they stop functioning properly. Body tissues, such as muscle can stop working and cells can become permanently damaged.

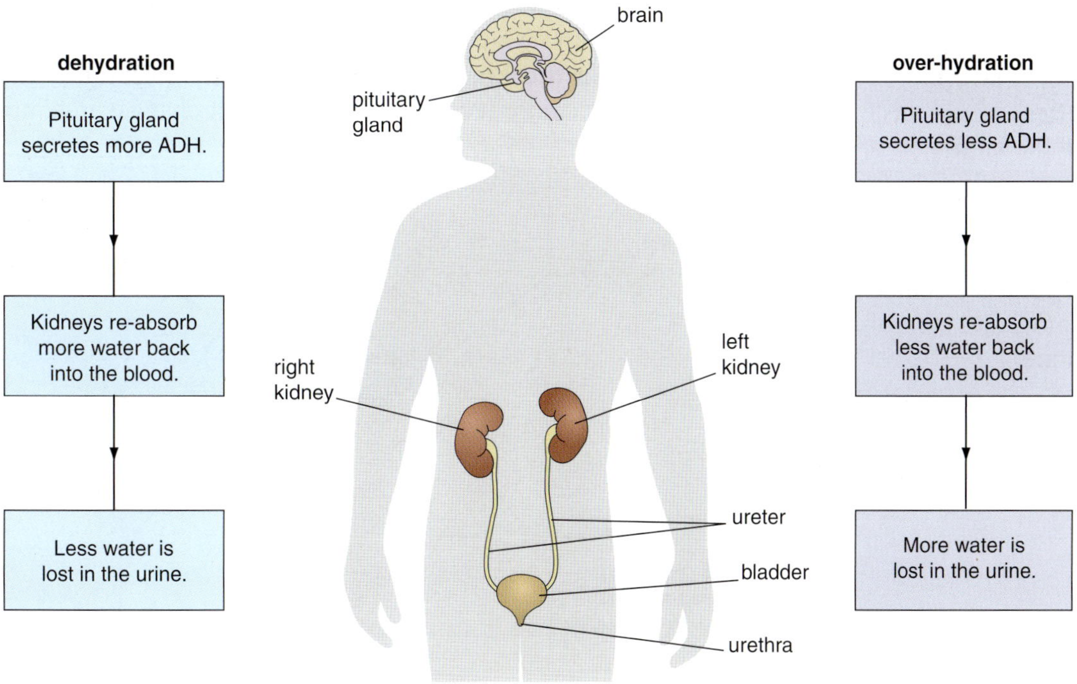

Figure 4.3 The pituitary gland and the kidney control the level of water in the blood. The kidney can adjust the amount of water in the urine.

1. Look at Figure 4.2 on page 51. The girl in the picture is losing water by sweating. How else may she lose water from her body?
2. She is also losing dissolved ions in her sweat. Explain how this will affect the water uptake by her cells. You may need to look back over the section on osmosis in Chapter 1.
3. How does sweating help her body to maintain the correct body temperature?
4. You can see that she is drinking to replace the water lost from her body. What would she have to do to replace the ions she has lost?
5. Imagine that the girl has only just started to dance.
   a) How would the pituitary gland respond when the girl initially starts losing water in her sweat?
   b) What effect would this have on the kidney?

The **thermoregulatory centre** in the brain monitors and controls body temperature.

In severe cases, dehydration or over-hydration can lead to unconsciousness or even death. Altering the concentration of ions dissolved in the blood also interferes with water uptake by the cells.

Controlling the water content of the blood is the job of the kidney. The kidney responds to a hormone called anti-diuretic hormone (ADH) which is secreted from the pituitary gland at the base of the brain. When a person becomes dehydrated, the pituitary gland secretes ADH which is transported in the blood to the kidneys. The kidneys respond by absorbing more water back into the blood and putting less water in urine. When a person becomes over-hydrated, less ADH is secreted, which causes the kidney to re-absorb less water into the blood. This results in more water going into urine and then being lost from the bladder when the person goes to the toilet.

Controlling body temperature

Birds and mammals have the ability to control their own body temperature. Other animals, such as reptiles, rely on the sun to warm up their blood. Humans usually maintain a body temperature of between 36.5 °C and 37.5 °C. If body temperature drops below 30 °C, sleepiness can set in, followed by unconsciousness. This can lead to death if the condition is not treated. Fortunately the body has a very effective way of monitoring and controlling its temperature.

Body temperature is monitored by a part of the brain called the **thermoregulatory centre**. The centre receives impulses from receptors in the surrounding area that monitor the temperature of blood flowing through the brain. The centre also receives impulses from temperature receptors in the skin. You will remember from Core Science how receptors send electrical impulses to the brain along neurones. If the thermoregulatory centre receives impulses about changes in temperature

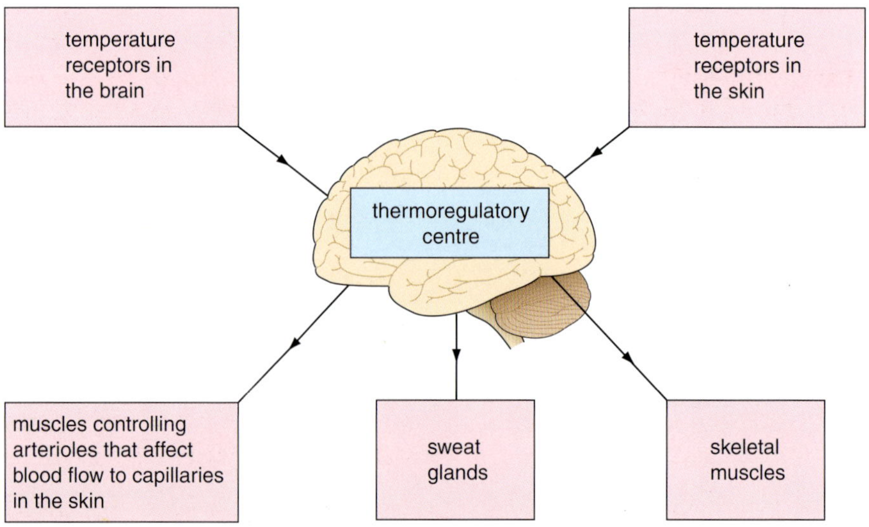

Figure 4.4 The thermoregulatory centre monitors and controls body temperature by co-ordinating a response to impulses received from receptors.

it will send impulses out to other parts of the body. Various parts of the body make changes to adjust the temperature. All of these responses are automatic or reflex responses. Figure 4.4 summarises this system.

Sweat glands release sweat onto the surface of the skin, which evaporates to decrease body temperature.

So, how do these effectors change the body temperature? If the temperature in the body increases, the body can reduce the amount of heat it generates and increase the amount of heat it loses. If the temperature drops, the body can try to generate more heat and lose less heat. These changes are achieved by a combination of responses by the **sweat glands**, the skeletal muscles and muscles controlling blood flow through the arterioles to the skin capillaries. (Arterioles are small arteries that connect your main arteries to capillaries. Arteriole muscles relax and contract to increase or decrease blood flow to the skin capillaries to control body temperature. The blood vessels dilate (get wider).) Table 4.1 shows the three mechanisms for controlling body temperature.

	Increase in body temperature	Decrease in body temperature
Muscles controlling arterioles in the skin	Relax to allow more blood to flow into capillaries near the surface of the skin.	Contract to reduce the amount of blood flowing in capillaries near the surface of the skin.
Sweat glands	Secrete more sweat onto the surface of the skin.	Secrete less sweat on the surface of the skin.
Skeletal muscles	Do not cause shivering.	Contract and relax quickly to cause shivering.

Table 4.1 How the body responds to changes in temperature

Vasodilation decreases body temperature by allowing more blood to flow through capillaries near the surface of the skin.

Vasoconstriction reduces the amount of blood flowing near the surface of the skin to retain heat inside the body.

Your skin plays a crucial role in controlling body temperature. When body temperature increases, muscles that control blood flow through arterioles relax. This allows more blood to flow through the arterioles and into capillaries near the surface of the skin. Heat from the blood is then lost to the air surrounding the skin. This response is called **vasodilation**. The opposite happens when body temperature drops. Blood flow near the surface of the skin is reduced so that less heat is lost. This response is called **vasoconstriction**.

Skin is also involved in the sweating response. When the body heats up sweat glands in your skin start to release sweat onto the skin's surface. Some of the heat near the surface of the skin causes the sweat to evaporate. As the particles in the sweat evaporate away from the skin they transfer heat energy with them, which causes the body temperature to drop. More water is lost from the body through sweating when it is hot than when it is cooler. We must always make sure that we drink enough water or eat enough food that contains a high percentage of water, such as fruit, to replace this water that has been lost.

When the body cools down, the muscles contract and relax rapidly – this is know as shivering. As the cells in the muscles respire they use up energy and release heat, which warms us up.

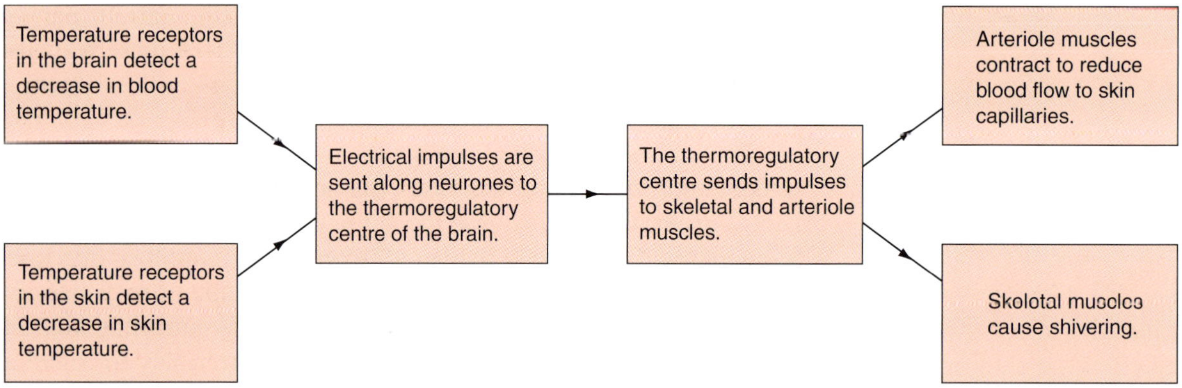

Figure 4.5 A flow diagram showing the body's response to a decrease in temperature

6 Figure 4.5 shows how the body responds to a decrease in temperature. Draw a similar flow diagram to show how the body responds to an increase in temperature.

7 Shivering is caused by your skeletal muscles contracting and relaxing repeatedly. Explain how this increases body temperature.

8 Look at Figure 4.6. It shows how the skin responds to changes in temperature.

a) Which diagram shows the skin on a hot day?
b) What changes can you see in this diagram that will decrease body temperature?
c) Explain how each of these changes will decrease body temperature.

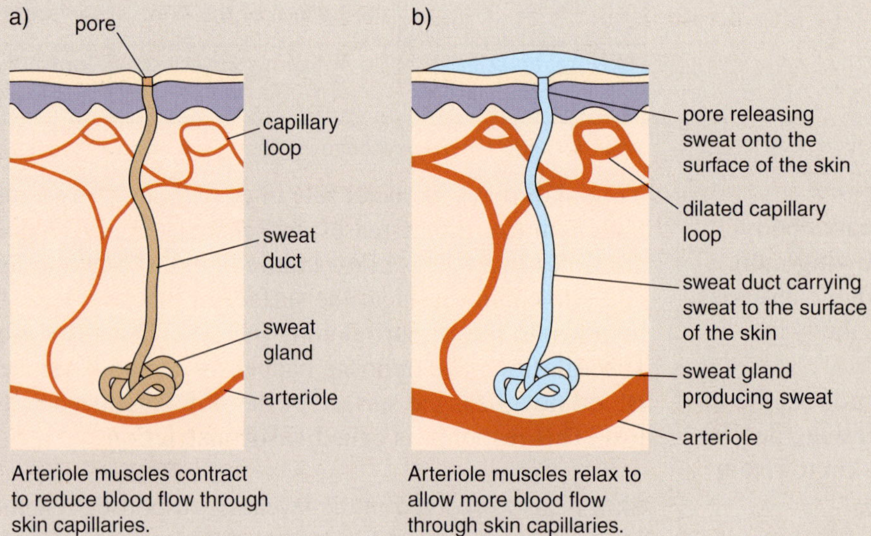

Figure 4.6 A cross-section of the skin on a) a cold and b) a hot day

Controlling blood sugar levels

The **pancreas** is an organ that monitors and controls blood glucose concentration. It produces the hormone **insulin**.

The **pancreas** is an organ that produces insulin. **Insulin** causes glucose to move out of the blood into cells. The production of insulin allows glucose to be stored in the liver and muscles and also to be used by body cells for respiration. Too much glucose in the blood can damage blood vessels and cells, so it is essential to have a mechanism to remove it. When blood glucose concentration is high, glucose is lost in the urine.

Insulin is a hormone that causes glucose to be moved from the blood into liver and muscle cells.

People who suffer from **diabetes** do not produce enough insulin in their pancreas, which leads to dangerously high blood glucose levels.

You will remember from Core Science that insulin controls blood glucose levels. **Diabetes** is a disease that occurs when the pancreas does not produce enough insulin. This means that the amount of glucose in the blood rises to levels that are dangerously high and can be fatal. Before 1922, nothing was known about insulin and the effect it had on the body, so people with diabetes almost always died prematurely.

Fortunately, diabetes can now be treated because sufferers can inject insulin to reduce blood glucose levels. People with diabetes can also control their illness by being very careful about what foods they eat.

Activity – Discovering insulin

A doctor called Fredrick Banting had studied diabetes and thought that the condition was linked to the pancreas. With an assistant called Charles Best, he carried out a set of experiments using dogs. Best first tied up the tube connecting the dog's pancreas to its blood system. He then measured the dog's blood glucose levels and noted that these rose dramatically over an eight-week period. He deduced from his observations that the pancreas must produce something that controlled the amount of glucose in the blood.

He then removed the pancreas of the dog, along with the pancreas from another dog. He ground up the pancreas from the second dog with salt water, and injected this mixture into the first dog. Best observed that the dog's blood glucose levels were temporarily reduced. However the levels soon rose and the dog died the following day. Banting used these findings to conclude that the pancreas produced a substance that controlled blood glucose level. He called this substance insulin. Banting went on to show that insulin obtained from healthy dogs could be used to treat diabetic dogs and won the Nobel Prize for his work.

Figure 4.7 Fredrick Banting and Charles Best with the dog they used in their experiment

1. Draw a flow diagram summarising the work of Banting and Best.
2. The first set of experiments were carried out using just two dogs. Bearing this in mind, do you think Banting was right to be so confident of his conclusion? Give reasons for your answer.
3. Suggest some improvements that Banting could have made to his experiment to collect more reliable results.
4. People often refer to Banting's work when they argue for the use of animals in experiments to develop new medical treatments. Do you think that referring back to experiments carried out in 1922 is a strong enough argument to justify animal experiments today? Explain your opinion.

Once people realised that Banting's discovery could lead to a treatment for diabetes, further research into insulin was quickly carried out. It was found that insulin could be extracted from the pancreases of cows and pigs and used successfully to treat diabetes. Many thousands of lives were saved in this way but a huge amount of insulin was needed, which meant that lots of pancreases had to be collected from abattoirs. Nowadays insulin is manufactured using genetically modified bacteria. This removes the need to use the pancreases from slaughtered animals.

5 Some people objected to using insulin from animals' pancreases. What reasons do you think they had for this viewpoint?
6 Produce an information sheet that could be included on a website or in a leaflet aimed at people who have just been diagnosed with diabetes. You should include a summary describing the disease and information about the different ways of treating it.

A search for diabetes at www.bbc.co.uk is an excellent starting point. You may find that www.diabetes.org.uk is also useful.

4.2 How does your body get rid of waste products?

Some of the chemical reactions that take place in your body produce useful products such as proteins. Respiration is essential because it releases energy from glucose. However, these reactions also produce waste products that can be toxic to the body. Fortunately your body has ways of removing these waste products so that they do not reach harmful levels in the blood.

How is carbon dioxide removed from the body?

Respiration is a series of chemical reactions that take place in cells. It is summarised by the equation:

glucose + oxygen → carbon dioxide + water + energy

The carbon dioxide produced moves from the cell into the blood by diffusion (see Chapter 1). Too much carbon dioxide in the blood can be dangerous because it lowers the blood pH and inhibits enzyme action. When the blood flows through the lungs, carbon dioxide diffuses out of the blood and into the air in the lungs. At the same time oxygen diffuses from the air into the blood. This takes place across the walls of tiny structures called alveoli and is called gas exchange. Once the carbon dioxide is in the air in the lungs it is breathed out of the body.

How are other types of waste removed from the body?

Proteins are digested by enzymes, called proteases, and broken down into amino acids (enzymes are described in Section 3.1). These amino acids are used by the body to make other useful proteins that are needed for growth and to control body processes. You often have more amino acids in your blood than your body can use. The liver converts these excess amino acids into a chemical called urea. Urea can harm the body, so it must be removed. Figure 4.8 shows how this happens.

9 Explain why oxygen diffuses from the alveoli in the lungs to the blood, and why carbon dioxide diffuses from the blood into the alveoli.

10 Why does your breathing rate increase when you go for a run? Refer to oxygen and carbon dioxide in your answer.

11 What is the difference between urea and urine?

12 People who suffer from liver damage are sometimes asked to reduce the amount of protein in their diet. Explain the scientific reason behind this advice.

13 Urine can be tested for the presence of amino acids. What possible medical problems do you think somebody might have if amino acids are detected in their urine?

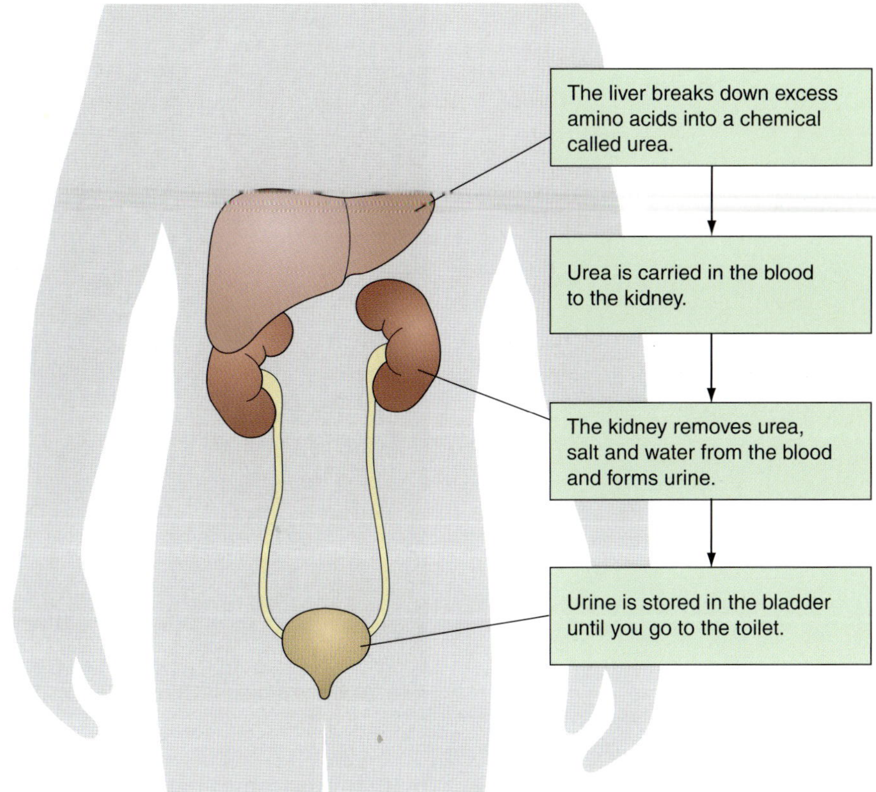

Figure 4.8 How excess amino acids are removed from the body

As you can see in Figure 4.8, the liver and the kidney work together to remove amino acids from the body. The liver breaks down excess amino acids by a series of chemical reactions. This produces urea, which dissolves in the blood plasma and is then transported to the kidneys. Since it is dissolved in the plasma it is removed from the blood along with some of the water it is dissolved in. This mixture, along with some salt, makes up the urine that is stored in the bladder until you go to the toilet.

4.3 Why is cell division so important?

You will remember from Core Science that chromosomes are structures found in the nucleus of cells. When cells divide they form new cells with copies of these chromosomes. Without cell division people would not grow, reproduce or be able to repair damaged body tissue.

Chromosomes are molecules of DNA found in cells. A single chromosome is made up of a single strand of DNA.

DNA (deoxyribonucleic acid) is a long-chain molecule, made up from a series of bases.

What are chromosomes and genes?

In humans, there are 23 pairs of chromosomes inside the nucleus of a normal cell, or 46 in total. This number is different in other species. **Chromosomes** are each made up of a long molecule of **DNA** (deoxyribonucleic acid). A single chromosome is made up from a molecule of DNA about 5 cm long. This is amazing when you consider

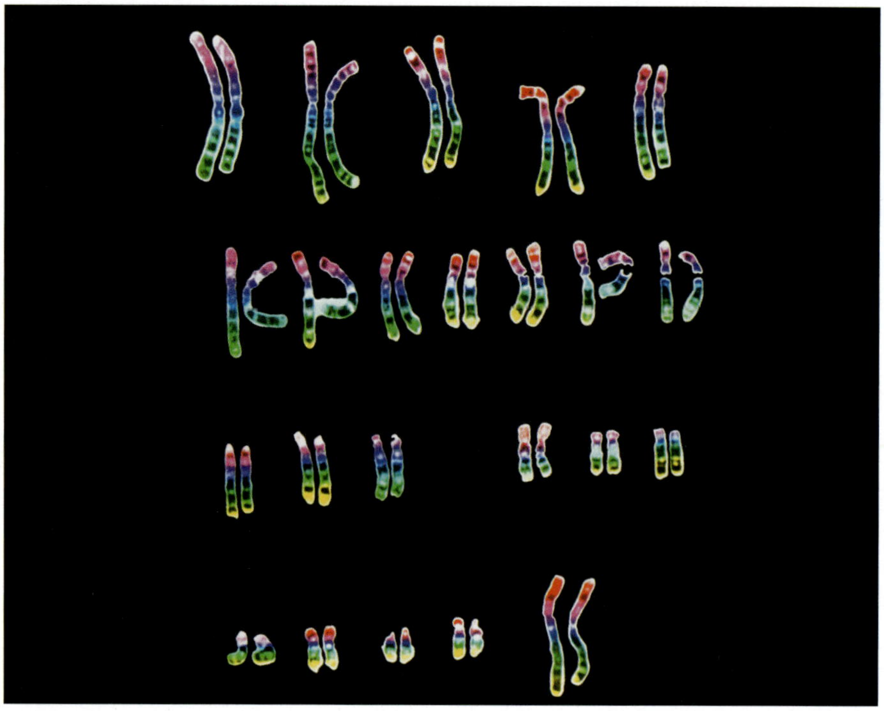

Figure 4.9 The chromosomes from one human cell

that chromosomes can be seen only under very powerful microscopes. To achieve this each DNA molecule is very thin and has to be coiled up very tightly to form a chromosome.

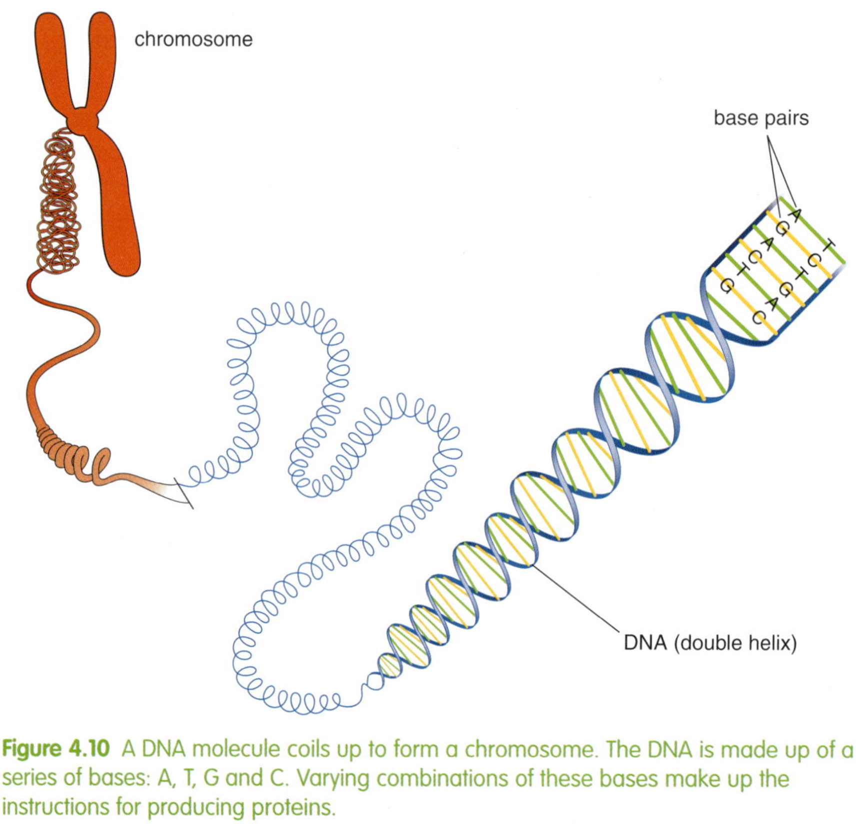

Figure 4.10 A DNA molecule coils up to form a chromosome. The DNA is made up of a series of bases: A, T, G and C. Varying combinations of these bases make up the instructions for producing proteins.

A **gene** is a length of DNA that codes for a specific protein.

DNA fingerprinting is a technique that uses the non-coding pieces of our DNA to provide a unique identification DNA sequence.

14 The DNA in one chromosome is far longer than the chromosome itself. Why is this? Think about how the shortening of DNA to a chromosome is achieved.

15 a) Why do there have to be so many genes in a human cell?
b) Sometimes a gene mutates. This means that the sequence of bases on that gene is altered. What effect will this have on the protein that the gene is responsible for making? Explain your answer.

A **gene** is a small section of a DNA molecule. There are between 20 000 and 25 000 genes in each human nucleus. You can see in Figure 4.10 that a DNA molecule contains a series of bases that are represented by the letters G, C, A and T. Bases are molecules that form part of DNA. A gene is therefore really a sequence of these bases. The sequence of bases in a gene acts as a code (instructions) for making a protein.

All humans have the same types of genes, so what makes us unique? Some areas of DNA, called non-coding sequences, don't contain any genes. These areas are different for each person in the world, unless you have an identical twin. This means that a person can be identified from the non-coding DNA obtained from a swab of their cells. This technique, called **DNA fingerprinting**, can be used to link people to a crime scene. If, for example, skin cells are found at a crime scene, then the DNA inside them can be removed and identified. If the non-coding DNA matches the DNA collected from a suspect then it places the suspect at the scene.

Section 4.2 referred to amino acids that are obtained when proteins are digested. A gene's job is to take these amino acids and put them together in a specific order to make new proteins that the body needs. This order of amino acids is controlled by the order of the DNA bases. Since each gene is a unique sequence of bases, each gene puts the amino acids in a different order and makes a different protein. This takes place in a ribosome (see Chapter 1). The proteins made can be enzymes or hormones, but they may also be used to form new body tissue, such as muscle, or even to produce the colour in your eyes.

What happens to chromosomes when cells divide?

You will remember from Chapter 1 that a cell can make a genetically identical copy of itself. This takes place when you grow and also when cells need to be replaced if a body tissue becomes damaged. For example, if you were to cut yourself, the new skin that would form over the cut would be made by skin cells dividing to make new skin cells. When a cell divides in this way it forms two cells that are both genetically identical to the original cell. This can happen because chromosomes have the amazing ability to make identical copies of themselves. This type of cell division that produces genetically identical cells is called **mitosis**. Figure 4.11 overleaf shows how it takes place.

A cell divides by **mitosis** to produce two genetically identical cells with a full set of chromosomes.

Mitosis also takes place in some plants and in single-celled organisms such as bacteria and yeast during asexual reproduction. Offspring produced by this means have exactly the same genes as their parents, because they contain an exact copy of their chromosomes. They are often referred to as a clone.

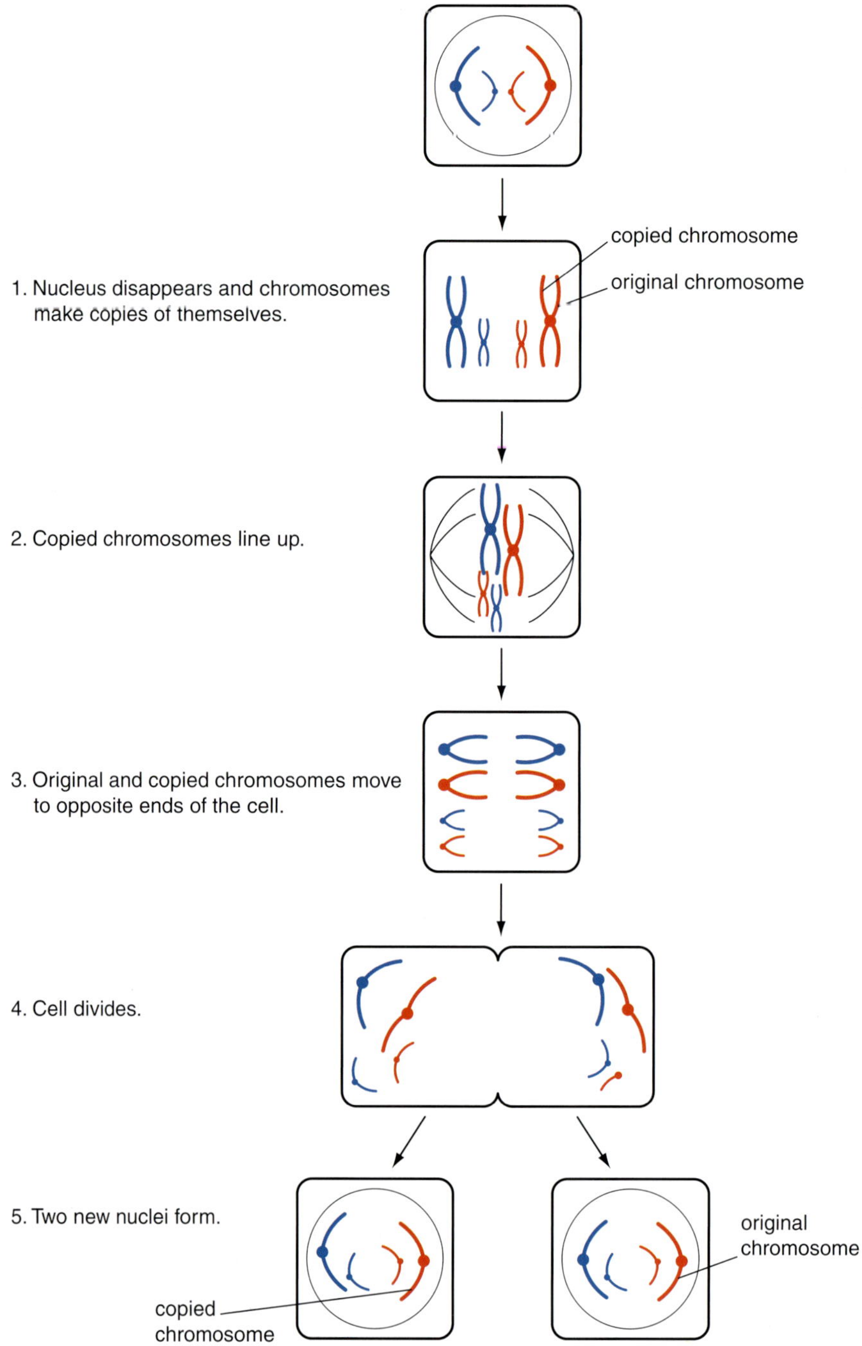

Figure 4.11 The diagram shows the main stages in mitosis for a cell with just two pairs of chromosomes. The original and the copied chromosomes are labelled so you can see that the new cell is an exact copy of the original cell.

> **Gametes** are sex cells. These include sperm cells, egg cells and pollen cells.
>
> A cell divides by **meiosis** to produce four genetically non-identical cells, each with half the original number of chromosomes. Meiosis forms cells called gametes.

A second type of cell division, found in most animals and plants, has only one function – to make sex cells. In animals the sex cells, or **gametes**, are sperm cells and egg cells. In plants the male gametes are pollen cells. In humans, this type of cell division only takes place in the reproductive organs, the testes and ovaries. Cell division that forms gametes is called **meiosis**. The cells that are formed by meiosis are not

16 What are the differences between mitosis and meiosis?

17 Look back at Figure 4.1 on page 50, which shows a human life cycle. At what stages in the life cycle would you find a) mitosis and b) meiosis taking place?

18 Why do gametes have only half the number of chromosomes found in a normal body cell?

19 It is almost impossible for two human egg cells produced from one person to be identical. Explain why this is the case.

identical to the original cell. They only have half the number of chromosomes. This means that in humans a gamete has 23 chromosomes. Figure 4.9 on page 58 shows a full set of human chromosomes. A gamete will only contain one chromosome from each pair.

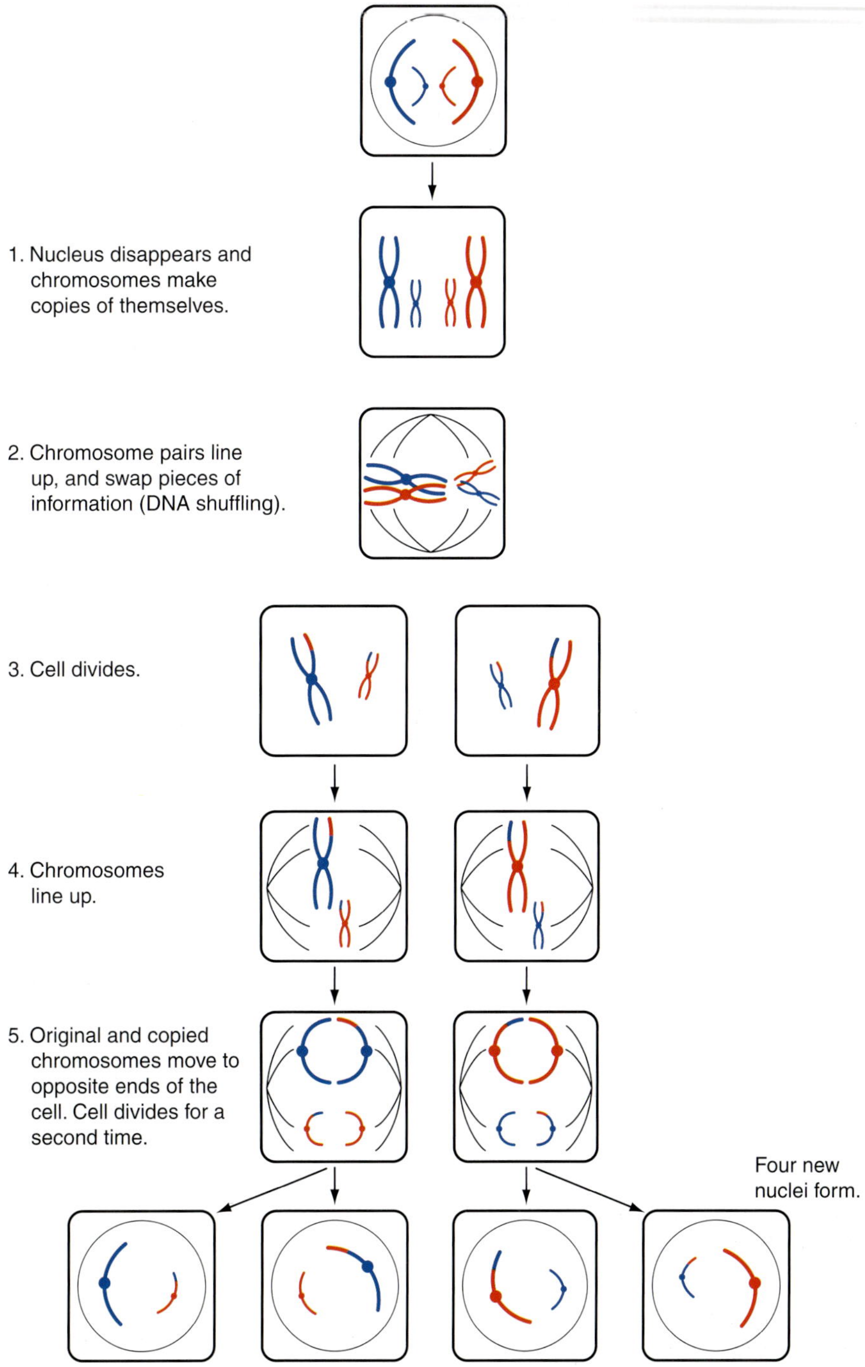

Figure 4.12 The diagram shows the main stages in meiosis for a cell with just two pairs of chromosomes. Once the matching chromosomes have paired up, they swap pieces of information between them. This is called DNA shuffling. The cell then divides twice and ends up with four cells (gametes), each with a single set of chromosomes (half the original number).

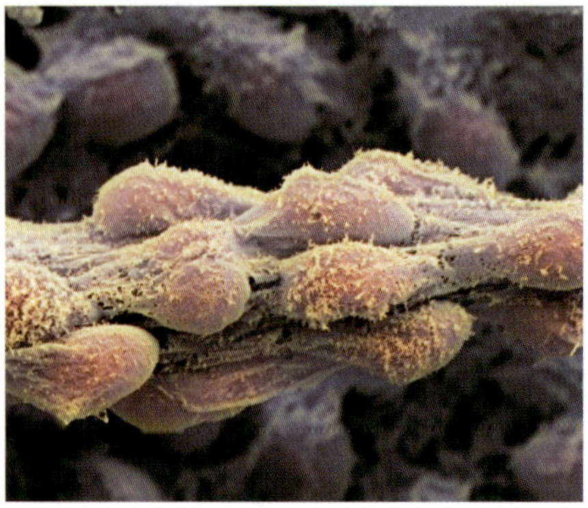

Figure 4.13 Embryonic stem cells, like those shown here, can differentiate into completely different types of cell. Do these cells have any specialised features?

Differentiation is the process by which an unspecialised early embryonic cell acquires the features of a specialised cell.

Stem cells and specialised cells

Figure 4.13 shows some human stem cells. They look like normal cells, so why are they so important? Stem cells can carry out one function that other cells cannot. When stem cells divide they can make specialised cells.

Compare these with the nerve cells studied in Core Science. Nerve cells have a specialised structure that allows them to carry electrical impulses around the body. Chapter 1 describes some other specialised cells. Nerve cells and most types of animal cell **differentiate** at an early stage of embryo development and then divide to produce only that type of specialised cell. However, many plant cells retain the ability to produce different differentiated cells throughout their life.

Stem cells are **undifferentiated**, which means that they have no specialised features to carry out a specific function. It is still not understood exactly how they do this but, under the right conditions, stem cells can develop into other types of cells such as liver, brain or heart muscle cells.

There are two groups of stem cells: embryonic stem cells and adult stem cells. Embryonic stem cells are found in the embryo soon after an egg cell has been fertilised. Embryonic stem cells differentiate into all the different specialised cells that eventually form a fetus and then a baby. Adult stem cells are found inside some body tissue, such as bone marrow. Adult stem cells make the type of specialised cells in the tissue where they are found. For example, stem cells in the pancreas produce cells that are specialised to make insulin.

Activity – Stem cells and medical research

'Stem cell promise lures patients'

'Stem cells treat blood disorder'

'Stem cell heart cure to be tested'

'MS sufferer in stem cell gamble'

'Winston warns of stem cell "hype" '

These are just a few recent headlines from articles about research that focuses on human stem cells. Of all the current biomedical research, stem cell research has probably attracted more attention than any other from the media. But why is this?

To understand the level of interest and range of views expressed, it is crucial to know exactly what happens when stem cells divide (see above) and the potential medical benefits these cells could bring.

1. Explain why stem cells are essential in human development.
2. Figure 4.14 shows some of the specialised cells that stem cells produce. Each one has a specific structure that allows it to carry out its function. Carry out research to find out the function of each of these specialised cells. Explain how each cell's structure enables it to carry out its function.

3 Stem cells can be collected and kept alive outside the body. With this in mind, suggest two possible uses scientists could make of stem cells. For each suggestion explain how you think scientists would carry out the procedure. Try to put the main points into a flow diagram.

Current stem cell research involves manipulating embryonic stem cells to try to produce specialised cells. Hypothetically, these new specialised cells could replace cells that have been damaged either by disease or by an accident. Currently only small amounts of embryonic stem cells can be created using this technique, and scientists have not yet been able to create specialised cells. However, scientists believe that one day it may be possible to grow entire organs using this process.

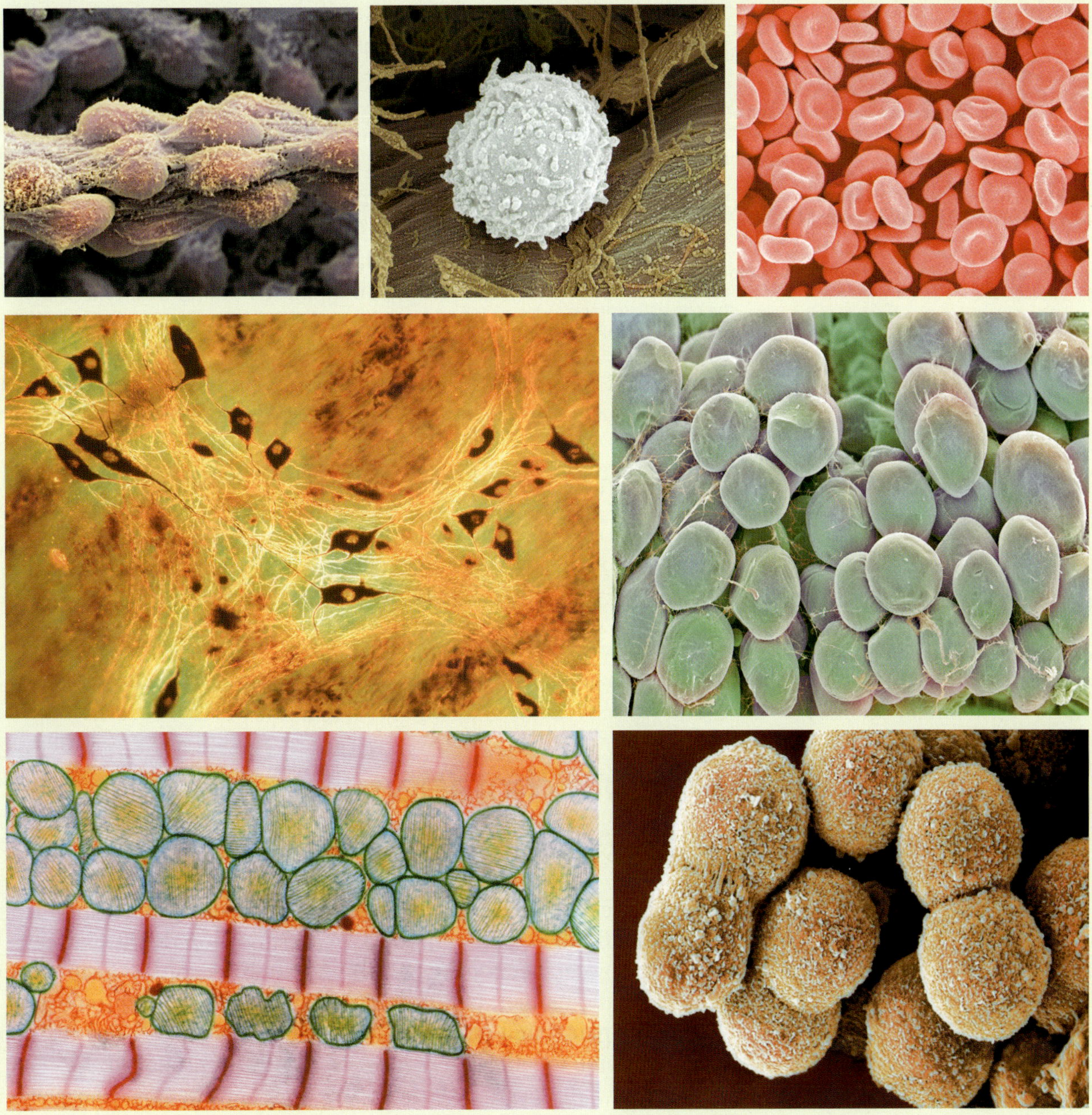

Figure 4.14 Some of the specialised cells that can develop from stem cells

Stem cell scientists take an unfertilised egg cell from a donor and insert the patient's DNA into its nucleus. The cell then divides in a laboratory until a clump of cells is formed. This clump of cells is effectively a tiny embryo, which if implanted into the womb of a woman could develop into a baby. Like all embryos, it contains embryonic stem cells, which are removed and then manipulated to try to produce the specialised cells required.

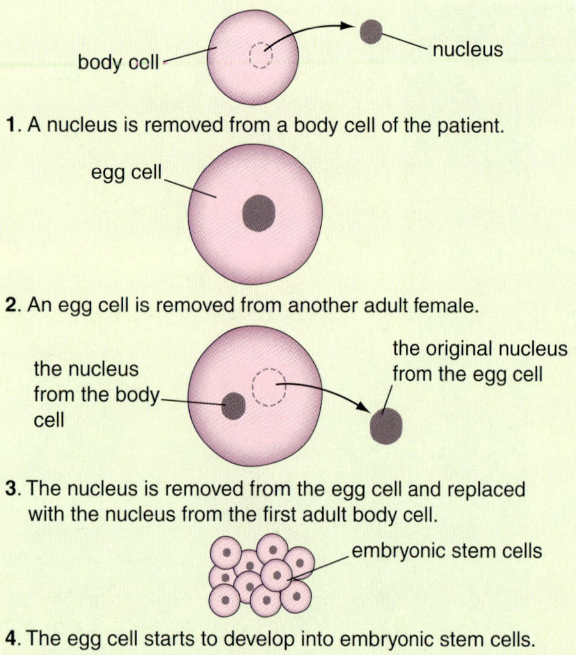

Figure 4.15 The procedure used to produce stem cells that match the DNA of a patient. This means the new cells or tissue produced will not be rejected by the patient's body.

Stem cells produced like this may one day be used to treat diseases such as Parkinson's disease. Patients with Parkinson's disease have nerve cells that are damaged. As more and more nerve cells become damaged, the patient suffers from progressive paralysis. Stem cells could be manipulated in the laboratory to produce healthy nerve cells to replace those that are damaged in the Parkinson's patient.

Opinions on stem cell research are mixed. Some people support stem cell research as they feel it gives patients with previously incurable diseases a better quality of life. Other people argue against the use of stem cell research. They insist that researchers should not be allowed to experiment on embryos since these balls of cells have the capacity to develop into a complete human being.

4. In small groups, debate reasons that people may have to support or oppose embryonic stem cell research. Write these down as a list of reasons for and a list against the research.
5. Now put the reasons in each list into order based upon which ones present the strongest arguments for and against stem cell research.
6. Finally, write a paragraph expressing your views about this issue. Support your views with reasons.

4.4 How are characteristics passed on from one generation to the next?

When a sperm cell fertilises an egg cell the genetic information from the mother and father is brought together. Fertilisation produces a cell, called a zygote, that contains a full set of chromosomes. Each gamete (one from the mother, one from the father) carries one chromosome from each pair found in a normal human body cell, so when the two gametes come together the full set of 23 pairs is produced. At fertilisation, all the characteristics that are controlled by your genes are determined, for example, your eye colour and hair colour. After fertilisation, the zygote divides by mitosis and develops into an embryo.

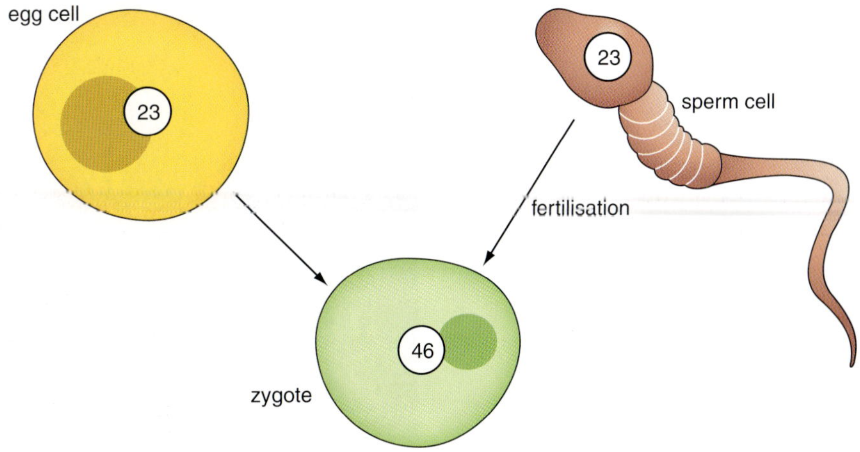

Figure 4.16 During fertilisation in humans the sperm and the egg cell bring together 23 chromosomes from each parent to form the first cell that goes on to produce a new human being. After fertilisation, this cell has the full number of chromosomes – 46.

Children in a family are never genetically identical unless they are identical twins. This is because each child has different chromosomes. Each sperm cell their father produces and egg cell their mother produces contains only one chromosome each from the 23 pairs in a normal body cell. If gametes contained the usual 23 pairs found in all other body cells, fertilisation would produce a cell with 46 pairs of chromosomes! This is why gametes contain only 23 chromosomes.

Figure 4.17 Each child in this family inherited half their chromosomes from their mother and half from their father. The differences between them exist because each gamete carries different chromosomes.

The one chromosome from each pair is selected randomly when gametes are formed by meiosis. If you consider that there are 23 pairs, it is incredibly unlikely that any two gametes will have exactly the same 23 chromosomes. Imagine you had two sets of 23 numbered cards. The 46 cards represent the 23 pairs of chromosomes in a normal human cell. The two sets are numbered 1–23 but one set is coloured red and the other blue. The red set represent 23 chromosomes (one from each chromosome pair) and the blue set represents the remaining 23 chromosomes from each pair. If you were to randomly pick 23 cards out of the 46, and then do it again, there is only a tiny chance that you would end up with the same 23 cards both times. This is a bit like the way in which random chromosomes are selected from each chromosome pair, when gametes are produced by meiosis.

How is the sex of a person determined?

One of the most obvious differences between children in a family is their sex, whether they are a boy or a girl. A person's sex is determined at fertilisation because it is controlled by the genes found on a pair of chromosomes. All the differences between males and females are actually controlled by just one chromosome.

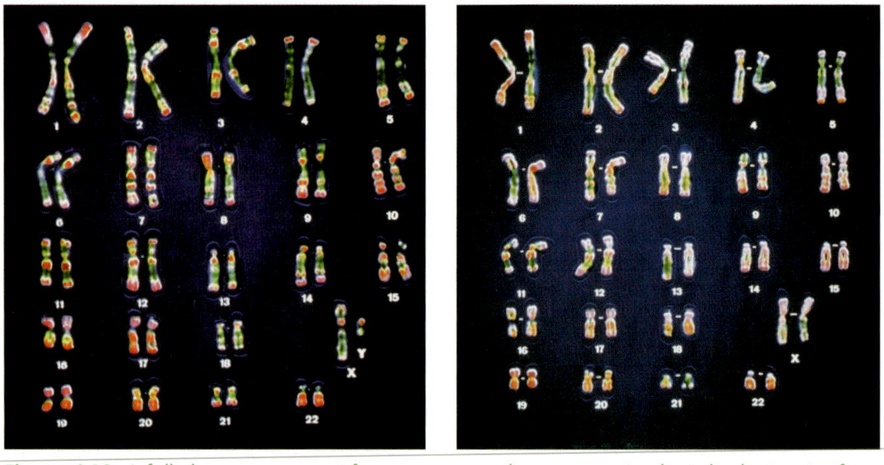

Figure 4.18 A full chromosome set from a man and a woman. Look at the last pair of chromosomes (marked X, Y) in each set.

The 23rd pair of chromosomes in each cell are the **sex chromosomes** and they determine a person's sex. XX = female; XY = male.

A **genetic diagram** shows all the possible combinations of chromosomes or genes that could be passed on during fertilisation.

You can see in Figure 4.18 that both chromosomes in the last pair of 23 are the same in females, but different in males. These chromosomes are called the **sex chromosomes** and are the 23rd pair in each cell. In females both of the sex chromosomes are called X chromosomes. Males have one X and one Y sex chromosome. Every egg cell that a woman produces carries an X chromosome. Half the sperm cells that a man produces carry an X and half carry a Y chromosome. Remember that each gamete gets one randomly selected chromosome from each pair during meiosis. So if an X-carrying sperm cell fertilises an egg, then a baby girl will be born. If a Y-carrying sperm cell fertilises an egg, then a boy will be born.

The genetic diagram in Figure 4.19 shows how sex chromosomes are passed on from parents to their children.

20. Explain how sexual reproduction leads to variation between children in the same family.

21. Why is it essential that gametes in humans are produced by meiosis and not mitosis?

22. 'The sex of a baby is determined entirely by the father.' Do you consider this statement to be correct? Explain your answer by referring to how sex is inherited.

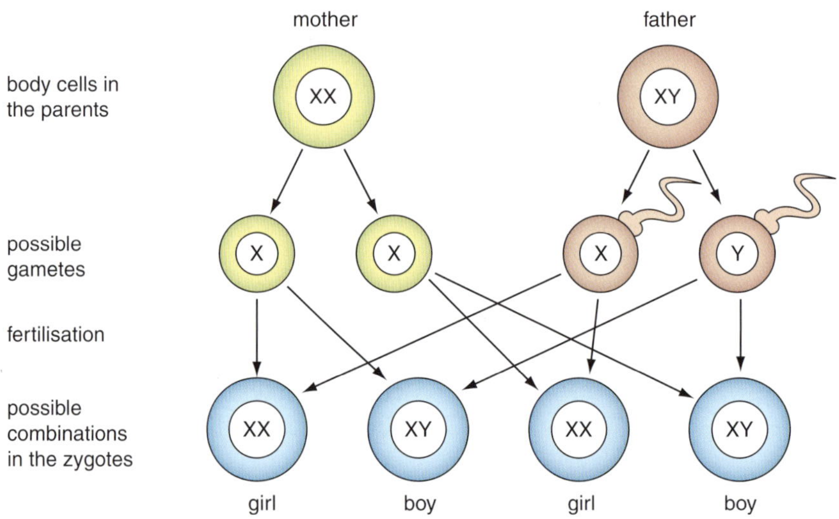

Figure 4.19 This genetic diagram shows how sex chromosomes are inherited.

How are some characteristics controlled by a single gene?

23 There are now two methods available to parents which enable them to select the sex of their baby. The first is called the 'sperm cell selection method' and the second is known as the 'embryo selection method'. Both of these methods are based on being able to detect the X and Y chromosomes in cells.

a) Explain how you think each of these methods works.

b) Give two reasons for and two reasons against giving people the chance to select the sex of their baby.

You will remember the history of ideas about inheritance from Core Science. An Austrian monk called Gregor Mendel did not agree with the explanation of inheritance held in the 1800s, known as the 'blending theory', which suggested that all your characteristics were simply a mixture of your parents' characteristics. As Mendel was working in the monastery gardens he noticed that pea plants had either red or white flowers. When they were bred together an individual new plant still produced red or white flowers, but never pink or a mixture of red and white flowers. To him this made it clear that inherited characteristics were not just a mixture of parental characteristics.

To test this idea he carried out many repeated experiments and collected reliable evidence. This evidence supported his idea that individual characteristics, such as flower colour, were inherited separately from other characteristics, such as stem length, and not simply a mixture of the parents' characteristics. However, his discovery was not widely accepted until after his death when scientists carried out similar experiments that led to the same conclusions. Mendel's reports were later translated into English, which meant that they had a far wider audience. This undoubtedly helped persuade more people that Mendel's idea was a far better explanation of inheritance than the blending theory.

Alleles are alternative forms of a single gene.

A **dominant** allele will lead to a dominant characteristic when only one dominant allele is present.

A **recessive** allele will lead to a recessive characteristic only when no dominant allele is present. This usually means that it is present on both chromosomes in a pair.

It is now understood that many characteristics are controlled by a pair of alleles for a single gene – found on a pair of chromosomes. The flower colour in Mendel's pea plants was controlled by a single gene. This gene had two possible forms called **alleles**, known as the **dominant** allele and the **recessive** allele. In pea plants the dominant allele produces a protein that forms red flowers. The recessive allele cannot produce this enzyme. So if one or both of the genes in the pair is the dominant allele the plant will have red flowers. It is only when there is no dominant allele (i.e. both recessive alleles) that the flowers will be white because there is no protein produced to turn them red. You often use a capital letter (e.g. R) to represent the dominant allele and a lower case letter (e.g. r) to represent the recessive allele.

A **recessive** allele will lead to a recessive characteristic only when no dominant allele is present. This usually means that it is present on both chromosomes in a pair.

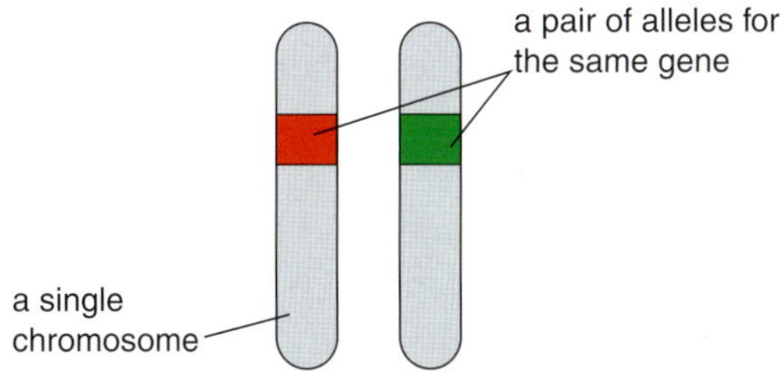

Figure 4.20 The red and the green section on the chromosomes represents a pair of alleles for the same gene.

24 Even though Mendel did not know about the nature of genes he helped to develop our current understanding of inheritance. Explain how he did this.

25 a) Use both types of genetic diagrams shown in Figure 4.21 to show the possible offspring when two Rr pea plants are crossed together.
b) Use your diagrams to explain how two red flowering pea plants can produce a seed that grows into a white flowering plant.

26 Humans may produce two types of earwax: a wet, sticky type or a dry, hard type. The wet type is caused by a dominant allele, E, and the dry type is caused by a recessive allele, e.
a) Write down the pairs of alleles that somebody with wet, sticky ear wax may have.
b) Explain why it is impossible to say what alleles a person who produces wet ear wax will have.
Rob and Jo are married. Rob has wet ear wax and Jo has dry ear wax. They have a child who produces wet ear wax.
c) What pair of alleles for ear wax will their child have?
d) Rob and Jo are planning on having another child. Draw a genetic diagram to show what possible pairs of alleles for ear wax their next child could inherit.

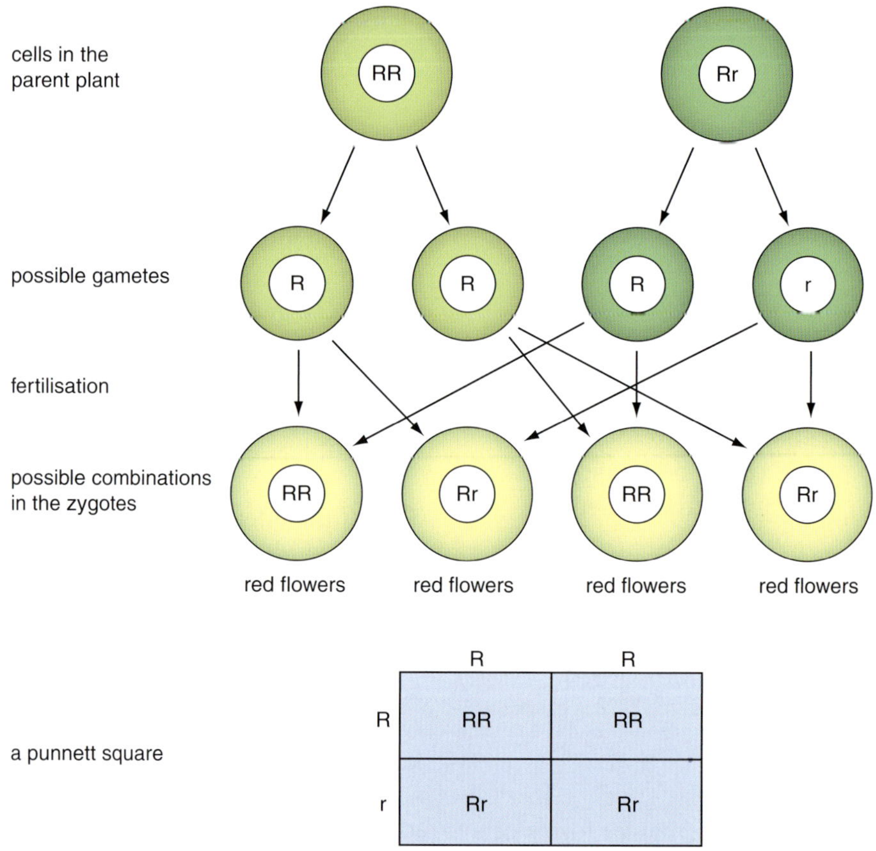

Figure 4.21 Two ways of drawing genetic diagrams to explain inheritance. Each shows all the possible combinations of alleles that could be passed on for a single gene.

How are some diseases inherited?

Some diseases are inherited because a defective gene from the parent is passed to their offspring. A defective gene is one that usually codes for a protein but no longer works because the order of bases has changed in one of the 46 chromosomes. This means that the instructions for making a specific protein no longer work. The lack of this protein causes the symptoms of the disease. **Huntington's disease** affects the nervous system. It causes gradual loss of co-ordination, jerky involuntary movements and often affects sufferers' sight and speech. People affected also develop dementia. Symptoms do not usually start to develop until people are in their 30s or 40s. Huntington's disease is caused by a dominant allele. A person will develop the disease if they inherit one dominant allele for this condition.

Cystic fibrosis is also inherited. It affects cell membranes and makes it difficult for a sufferer to absorb enough oxygen in the lungs. It is caused by a recessive allele. This means that a person needs to inherit two recessive alleles and no dominant alleles for this condition.

Huntington's disease

If you use an H to represent the dominant allele and an h for the recessive allele, the possible pairs of alleles are:

HH – this is a lethal combination. A fetus with this genotype would not develop.
Hh – this pair will also cause the disease.
hh – this pair will not cause the disease.

Cystic fibrosis

Cystic fibrosis is caused by a recessive allele. This means that a person can have the allele for this disease without actually suffering from the disease. In this case they would have one dominant and one recessive allele. A person with this pair of alleles is called a symptomless carrier. Figure 4.22 shows a family tree that has the cystic fibrosis allele in it. It is shown by cf.

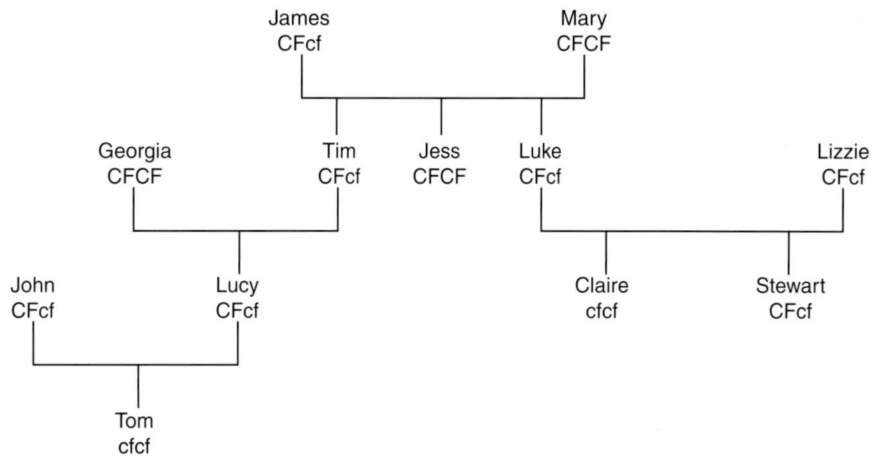

Figure 4.22 In this family the cystic fibrosis allele, cf, has passed through the generations.

Embryo screening

Embryo screening is a technique that can be used to identify some inherited diseases, such as Huntington's and cystic fibrosis. An embryo can be tested for these disorders and then only embryos that are free of the faulty allele are implanted into the woman's womb. You will remember from Core Science that IVF (*in vitro* fertilisation) is often used when a couple cannot have children naturally. Embryo screening is only used as part of IVF and only offered to parents with a family history of inherited disorders.

Embryo screening is regulated by an organisation called the Human Fertilisation and Embryology Authority (HFEA). The HFEA receives many requests to extend the embryo screening technique to other disorders. Some genes are linked to various cancers. These genes do not cause these cancers directly. They only increase the chance of

Huntington's disease is an inherited disease that affects the nervous system. It is caused by a dominant allele.

Cystic fibrosis is a disease that affects membranes of cells that line the lungs, gut and reproductive tract. It is caused by a recessive allele and therefore has symptomless carriers.

A **carrier** has one allele for an inherited disease caused by a recessive allele but does not have the disease. Two carriers can have children who inherit the disease.

27 A father had Huntington's disease and was Hh but his wife did not have the disease.
a) What is the probability that their child would inherit the disease? Use a genetic diagram to work out your answer.
b) If you were in this couple's situation, would you try to have children? Give reasons for your answers.

28 a) Name three people in the family tree in Figure 4.22 who were cystic fibrosis carriers.
b) Name one person who suffered from the disease.
c) Explain why Jess is unaffected by the disease.
d) Draw a genetic diagram to show the possible outcomes of Claire having children with somebody who is a carrier of cystic fibrosis.

developing cancer; however, not all people with the gene will get the disease. Embryo screening for genes linked to an increased cancer risk is permitted. However some people are concerned that in future the technique may be extended to allow parents to screen embryos for non-medical reasons.

29 It costs about £2000 to carry out IVF with embryo screening, which is twice as much as it costs without screening. With this in mind do you think that the use of embryo screening should be extended to include all births conceived by IVF? Give reasons for your answer.

30 Can you suggest any other reasons why some people object to embryo screening, apart from financial reasons?

Summary

- ✓ The body controls its water and ion content to avoid cells becoming damaged.
- ✓ Body temperature is controlled by changes made to; the amount of sweat being produced by the **sweat glands**, the amount of blood flowing through the arterioles to the **skin capillaries** (**vasodilation and vasoconstriction**) and shivering.
- ✓ Body temperature is monitored and controlled by the **thermoregulatory centre** in the brain.
- ✓ Blood glucose concentration is monitored and controlled by the **pancreas**. The pancreas produces **insulin** to move glucose from the blood into cells.
- ✓ **Diabetes** is a disease where the pancreas does not produce enough insulin. It is treated by controlling a person's diet and injecting with insulin.
- ✓ Urea and carbon dioxide are waste products of chemical reactions in the body.
- ✓ Carbon dioxide is removed from the body by the lungs and urea is removed by the kidneys.
- ✓ **Chromosomes** are molecules of **DNA** and are normally found in pairs.
- ✓ **Genes** are lengths of DNA responsible for making a specific protein.
- ✓ Body cells divide by **mitosis** to produce genetically identical cells used for growth and for replacement of older cells.
- ✓ Cells in the reproductive organs divide by **meiosis** to produce genetically non-identical sex cells (**gametes**) with a single set of chromosomes.
- ✓ Gametes join at fertilisation to form a single body cell with a full set of chromosomes that divides by mitosis to form a new individual.
- ✓ Most types of animal cell remain **undifferentiated**. **Stem cells** can divide to produce a range of different types of specialised cells.
- ✓ Asexual reproduction by mitosis produces genetically identical offspring.
- ✓ Sexual reproduction leads to genetic variation because an individual inherits one allele in each pair from each parent.
- ✓ A person's sex is controlled by the **sex chromosomes**: XX is female and XY is male.
- ✓ **Alleles** are alternative forms of a gene for a specific characteristic.
- ✓ Some characteristics are controlled by a single pair of alleles which may be **dominant** or **recessive**. The effects of dominant and recessive genes can be demonstrated by **genetic diagrams**.

- ✓ Some disorders, such as **Huntington's disease** and **cystic fibrosis**, are inherited. Huntington's disease is controlled by a dominant gene. Cystic fibrosis is controlled by a recessive gene so there can be **carriers**. **Embryo screening** can be used to test for the faulty allele.
- ✓ There are ethical issues surrounding the use of stem cells from embryos, and in the use of embryo screening in IVF treatment.

EXAMQUESTIONS

1 a) Which part of the body monitors and controls body temperature? *(1 mark)*
b) Describe, in as much detail as you can, how the body responds to an increase in body temperature. *(2 marks)*
c) On a cold day people often appear to have very pale skin. Explain the scientific reason behind this observation. *(2 marks)*

2 a) Which organ in the body does not function properly in somebody who suffers from diabetes? *(1 mark)*
b) Explain how diabetes affects the body. *(3 marks)*
c) Describe two ways in which diabetes may be treated. *(2 marks)*

3 When a body builder trains, his muscles get bigger because more muscle cells are produced.
a) What type of cell division produces the new muscle cells? *(1 mark)*
b) What type of cell division produces his sperm cells? *(1 mark)*
c) Explain, in as much detail as you can, why the body needs two different types of cell division. *(4 marks)*

4 Fur length in rabbits is controlled by a single gene which has two alleles, L and l. A pair of rabbits bred together. The mother had long fur and the father had short fur. All their babies had long fur.
a) Give the alleles for fur length present in the body cells of:
i) the mother; ii) the father. *(1 mark)*
b) One of the offspring bred with a rabbit with short fur. Use a genetic diagram to show how some of their babies had long fur and some had short fur. *(3 marks)*

5 Medical researchers hope that human stem cells could be transplanted into patients to make new cells in patients with diseased or damaged body tissue. This could lead to treatments for diseases such as Alzheimer's and Parkinson's, or for spinal cord injuries.

Most human stem cells used in research came from embryos created but not used at *in-vitro* fertilisation clinics. The cells are taken from embryos a few days old and the embryo is destroyed. The cells are then grown in the lab. At the moment no-one is quite sure how to make the stem cells form particular types of tissue – such as nerve rather than brain.

Because the cells come from embryos, the research is controversial. To some people, an embryo is a human and has a right to life. Those who support the use of stem cells from embryos say that a four-day-old embryo has not yet developed to a stage where a human life has begun.

Stem cells are also found in adult bone marrow and in a baby's umbilical cord blood. Some people say that embryonic stem cells are not the only hope of a treatment for, say, Parkinson's disease. Unfortunately, those stem cells may be limited in the cell types they can develop into. Embryonic stem cells can grow into 200 different types of specialised cell.
a) Explain why researchers think stem cells collected from embryos could lead to medical treatments. *(1 mark)*
b) Use the information in the passage to suggest why people may be concerned about the source of stem cells used in medical research. *(1 mark)*
c) A patient who is paralysed says that whatever the ethical concerns, they think the research should continue so that a cure can be found. Explain the difficulties researchers have to overcome for this therapy to become available to patients in the future. *(2 marks)*

Chapter 5
How do sub-atomic particles explain the structure and reactions of substances?

At the end of this chapter you should:

- ✓ know the relative masses and relative charges of protons, neutrons and electrons;
- ✓ understand the terms atomic number and mass number and how they relate to isotopes and relative atomic masses;
- ✓ appreciate that elements are arranged in the modern Periodic Table in order of their atomic number;
- ✓ be able to calculate relative formula masses, the percentages of elements in compounds and formulae;
- ✓ be able to calculate the amount of product obtained from a given amount of reactant;
- ✓ understand how chemical bonding involves either transferring or sharing electrons in the outer shells (highest occupied energy levels) in atoms;
- ✓ understand how electron transfer results in the formation of positive and negative ions held together by ionic bonds;
- ✓ understand how electron sharing results in the formation of uncharged molecules in which atoms are held together by covalent bonds;
- ✓ be able to represent the electronic structures of the atoms and ions of the first 20 elements in the Periodic Table;
- ✓ be able to represent the covalent bonds in simple molecules.

Figure 5.1 The work of scientists with sub-atomic particles has changed dramatically since J. J. Thomson first discovered electrons in 1897 (top right) and Rutherford and Geiger (bottom right) found evidence for protons. Today, scientists working with sub-atomic particles use much more sophisticated and complex equipment like the detector in the particle accelerator (above) at the European Centre for Nuclear Research (CERN) in Geneva. Particle accelerators can accelerate sub-atomic particles almost to the speed of light.

5.1 What's inside atoms?

Just over a century ago, scientists thought that atoms were solid, indestructible particles like tiny snooker balls. Then, between 1897 and 1932, experiments showed that atoms contained three smaller particles – electrons, protons and neutrons. You should already know something about these three sub-atomic particles. But how were they discovered and how did this change our ideas about atoms?

Activity – Thomson's big surprise

In 1897, J. J. Thomson was investigating the way that gases conduct electricity. When he connected 15 000 volts across the terminals of a tube containing air, he observed rays travelling in straight lines from the negative terminal (Figure 5.2). Further study of a narrow beam of the rays surprised Thomson. He found that the rays consisted of tiny negative particles about 2000 times lighter than hydrogen atoms. Thomson called these tiny negative particles electrons.

1. Why was Thomson surprised by his discovery of electrons? (Hint: In 1897, scientists thought that atoms were indivisible.)
2. How did the narrow beam move after the parallel plates were charged?
3. Why did Thomson conclude that particles in the beam were negatively charged? (Hint: Why was the beam deflected when the plates were charged?)
4. Before his experiment, Thomson removed most of the air from the tube using a vacuum pump. Why do you think he did this?
5. Thomson obtained electrons even with different gases in the tube and when the terminals were made of different substances. What could he conclude from this?
6. Our TV screens today work like the one used by Thomson. Why do you think the material on the screen fluoresces when the beam of electrons hits it?

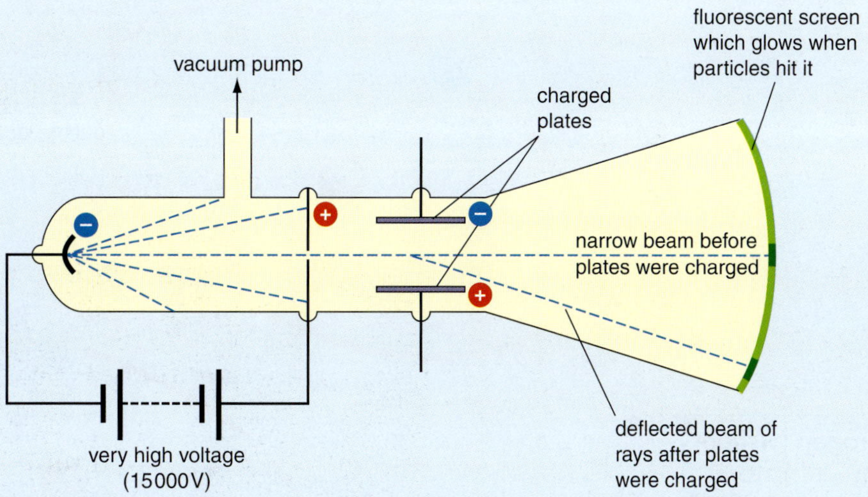

Figure 5.2 The effect of charged plates on a beam of electrons

Electrons, protons and neutrons

Thomson's experiments led scientists to conclude that all atoms contained electrons. So, as atoms are neutral, they must contain sufficient positive charge to cancel the negative charge on their electrons.

Figure 5.3 If the nucleus of a hydrogen atom is enlarged to the size of a marble and put in the centre of Westminster Abbey, the atom's one electron would be whizzing around well outside the walls of the Abbey.

In the early twentieth century, Ernest Rutherford and his colleagues found a way of probing inside atoms, using a form of radioactivity that had just been discovered – alpha particles from radioactive substances. Chapter 12 describes how these experiments led to the discovery of the atomic nucleus.

Through Rutherford's work we know that:

- atoms have a small positive nucleus surrounded by a much larger region of empty space in which there are tiny negative electrons;
- the positive charge of the nucleus is due to positive particles which Rutherford called protons;
- protons are about 2000 times heavier than electrons;
- atoms have equal numbers of protons and electrons, so the positive charges on the protons cancel the negative charges on the electrons;
- the smallest atoms are those of hydrogen with one proton and one electron. The next smallest atoms are those of helium with two protons and two electrons, then lithium atoms with three protons and three electrons, and so on.

Although Rutherford was successful in explaining many aspects of atomic structure, one big problem remained. If hydrogen atoms contain one proton and helium atoms contain two protons, then the relative masses of hydrogen and helium atoms should be 1 and 2 respectively. But the mass of helium atoms relative to hydrogen atoms is four and not two.

In 1932, James Chadwick, one of Rutherford's colleagues, discovered where the extra mass in helium came from. Chadwick showed that the

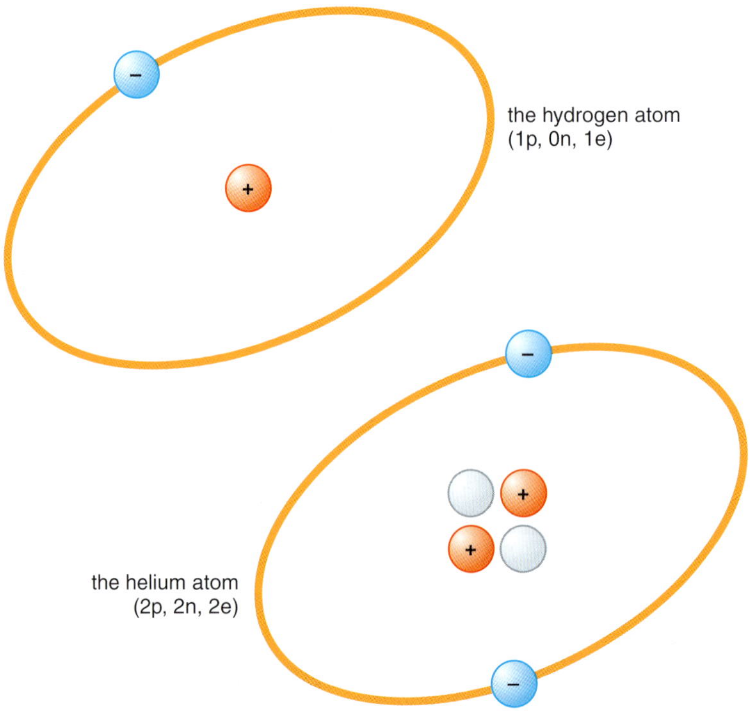

Figure 5.4 Protons, neutrons and electrons in a hydrogen atom and a helium atom

	Hydrogen atom	Helium atom
Number of protons	1	2
Number of neutrons	0	2
Relative mass	1	4

Table 5.1 The relative masses of hydrogen and helium atoms

nuclei of atoms contain uncharged particles as well as positively charged protons. Chadwick called these uncharged particles neutrons. Experiments showed that neutrons have the same mass as protons. This helped Chadwick to explain the problem concerning the relative masses of hydrogen and helium atoms (Table 5.1).

Hydrogen atoms have one proton and no neutrons, so a hydrogen atom has a relative mass of one unit. Helium atoms have two protons and two neutrons, so a helium atom has a relative mass of four units. This makes a helium atom four times as heavy as a hydrogen atom (Figure 5.4).

We now know that all atoms are made up from protons, neutrons and electrons. The relative masses, relative charges and positions within atoms of these sub-atomic particles are summarised in Table 5.2.

Particle	Relative mass (atomic mass units)	Relative charge	Position within atoms
Proton	1	+1	Nucleus
Neutron	1	0	Nucleus
Electron	$\frac{1}{2000}$	−1	In space outside the nucleus

Table 5.2 The relative masses, charges and positions within atoms of protons, neutrons and electrons

Atoms and ions

From the structure of atoms, we can understand how ions form from atoms by the loss or gain of electrons. A helium atom (He) has two protons each with one positive charge, two neutrons, and two electrons each with one negative charge. If an electron is removed from a helium atom, it leaves an ion (charged particle) with two positive charges and only one negative charge. This gives an overall charge on the ion of one positive charge. So, we can write the symbol He^+ for this particle.

If two electrons are removed from a helium atom, the remaining particle has two positive charges and no negative charges. This can be represented by the symbol He^{2+} (Figure 5.5).

1. Lithium atoms have three protons and a relative mass of 7 compared to hydrogen atoms.
   a) How many electrons are there in one lithium atom?
   b) How many neutrons are there in one lithium atom?
   c) How many protons, neutrons and electrons are there in one lithium ion, Li^+?

2. Oxygen atoms have eight protons. How many protons and how many electrons are there in:
   a) one O atom;
   b) one O^{2-} ion;
   c) one O_2 molecule;
   d) one H_2O molecule?

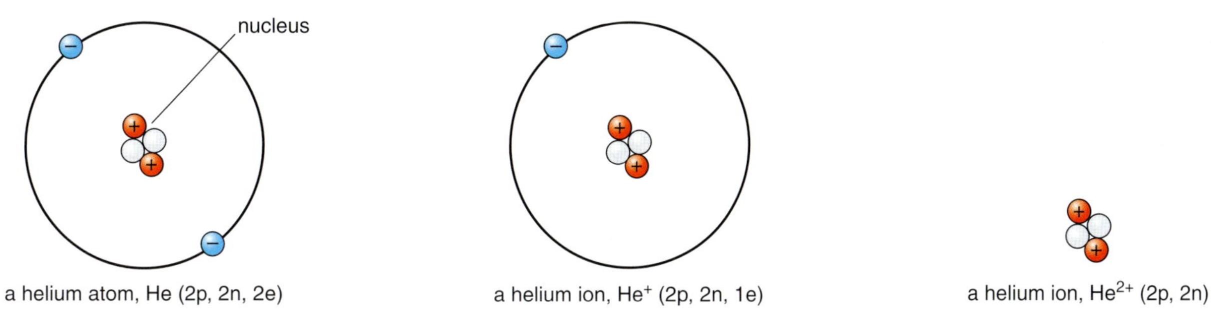

Figure 5.5 Protons, neutrons and electrons in a helium atom and helium ions

Atomic number and mass number

The **atomic number** is the number of protons in an atom.

The **mass number** is the total number of protons plus neutrons in an atom.

Atoms of different elements have different numbers of protons. Hydrogen atoms are the only atoms with one proton. Helium atoms are the only atoms with two protons. Lithium atoms are the only atoms with three protons, and so on. This means that the number of protons in an atom determines which element it is. Scientists call this the **atomic number** or proton number. So, hydrogen has an atomic number of 1, helium has an atomic number of 2, lithium has an atomic number of 3, and so on.

Notice that hydrogen, the first element in the Periodic Table, has atoms with one proton. Helium, the second element in the Periodic Table, has atoms with two protons. Lithium, the third element in the Periodic Table, has atoms with three protons, and so on. So, the position of an element in the Periodic Table tells us how many protons it has.

Aluminium is the thirteenth element in the Periodic Table. This means it has13 protons and its atomic number (proton number) is therefore 13. The number of protons in an atom can tell you which element it is, but it cannot tell you its mass. The mass of an atom depends on the number of protons plus the number of neutrons. This number is called the **mass number** of the atom.

mass number = 23

Na

atomic number = 11

Figure 5.6 The mass number and atomic number shown with the symbol for sodium

Hydrogen atoms (with one proton and no neutrons) have a mass number of 1. Helium atoms (two protons and two neutrons) have a mass number of 4, and sodium atoms (11 protons and 12 neutrons) have a mass number of 23.

We can write the symbol ${}^{23}_{11}Na$ (Figure 5.6) to show the mass number and the atomic number of a sodium atom. The mass number is written at the top left and the atomic number at the bottom left of the symbol.

3 Look at Figure 5.6.

a) How many protons, neutrons and electrons are there in:
   i) one Na atom;
   ii) one Na^+ ion?

b) What do 27, 13, 3+ and Al mean with reference to the symbol ${}^{27}_{13}Al^{3+}$?

5.2 Comparing the masses of atoms

A single atom is so small that it cannot be weighed on a balance. However, the mass of one atom can be compared with that of another atom using an instrument called a mass spectrometer (Figure 5.7).

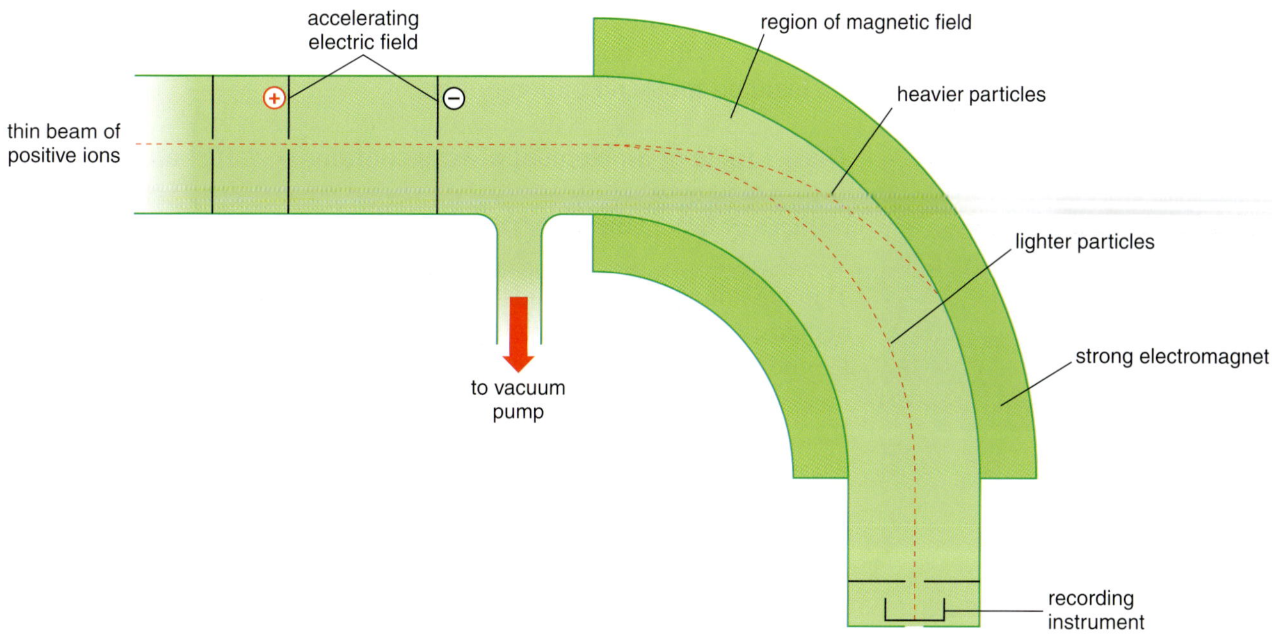

Figure 5.7 A mass spectrometer produces positive ions of the elements being analysed. A thin beam of these ions passes through an electric field, which accelerates the ions. The ions then pass through a magnetic field, which deflects them. How much they are deflected depends on the mass of the particles – lighter particles are deflected more than heavier particles. From the amount of deflection, we can compare the masses of different atoms and make a list of their relative masses.

Relative atomic masses

Relative atomic masses tell us the relative masses of the atoms of different elements.

One **mole** of an element has a mass equal to its relative atomic mass in grams.

❹ Why is the relative atomic mass of helium four and that of hydrogen one?

The relative masses of different atoms are called **relative atomic masses** (symbol A_r). As you might expect, the relative atomic mass of hydrogen is 1.0, the relative atomic mass of helium is 4.0 and the relative atomic mass of carbon is 12.

The relative atomic mass of an element in grams is sometimes called one **mole**.

So, 12 g of carbon = 1 mole
1 g of hydrogen = 1 mole
and 24 g of carbon = 2 moles

Notice that: $\text{number of moles} = \dfrac{\text{mass}}{\text{relative atomic mass}}$

Relative atomic masses show that one atom of carbon is 12 times as heavy as one atom of hydrogen. This means that 12 g of carbon will contain the same number of atoms as 1 g of hydrogen. An atom of oxygen is 16 times as heavy as an atom of hydrogen, so 16 g of oxygen will also contain the same number of atoms as 1 g of hydrogen.

The relative atomic mass in grams (i.e. one mole) of every element (1 g of hydrogen, 12 g carbon, 16 g oxygen, etc.) will contain the same number of atoms. This number is called Avogadro's constant. The term 'Avogadro's constant' was chosen in honour of the Italian scientist,

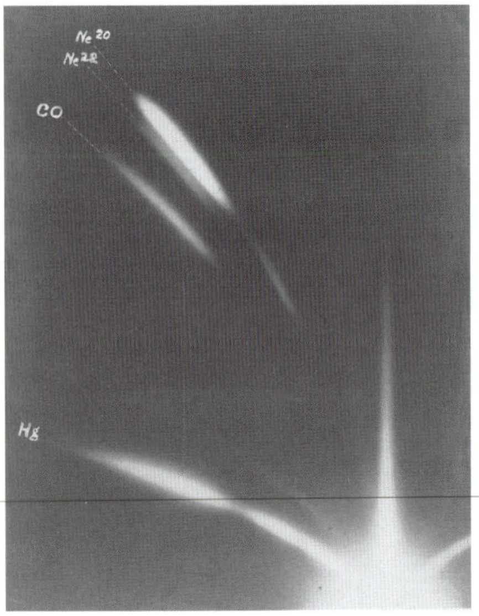

Figure 5.8 This photo shows evidence for the two isotopes in neon, neon-20 and neon-22.

Isotopes are atoms of an element with the same atomic number, but different mass numbers.

Isotopes have the same:
• number of protons; • number of electrons; • atomic number; • chemical properties.
Isotopes have different:
• numbers of neutrons; • mass numbers; • physical properties.

Table 5.3

5 Look closely at Figure 5.8.

a) The trace from neon-20 is much stronger than that from neon-22. What does this tell you about the two isotopes?

b) A beam of CO has been deflected less than the neon isotopes. What substance is CO? Why is CO deflected less than the neon isotopes?

Amedeo Avogadro. Experiments show that Avogadro's constant is 6×10^{23}. Written out in full this is 600 000 000 000 000 000 000 000 or six hundred thousand billion billion.

Thus, **1 mole of an element always contains 6×10^{23} atoms**.

Isotopes and atomic mass

The mass of an atom depends on the number of protons and neutrons in its nucleus. As both these particles have a relative mass of 1.00, the relative atomic masses of many elements are very close to whole numbers.

But, some elements have relative atomic masses that are nowhere near whole numbers. For example, the relative atomic mass of chlorine is 35.5 and that of copper is 63.5. At one time, scientists could not understand why the relative atomic masses of these elements were not close to whole numbers. The answer soon became clear when the first mass spectrometer was built in 1919. When atoms of elements such as chlorine or copper were ionised and passed through a mass spectrometer, the beam of ions separated into two or more paths (Figure 5.8). This suggested that one element could have atoms with different masses. These atoms of the same element with different masses are called **isotopes**.

All the isotopes of one element have the same number of protons. So, they have the same atomic number and the same number of electrons. This gives them the same chemical properties because chemical properties depend upon the number of electrons in an atom.

Isotopes do, however, have different numbers of neutrons, and this gives them different masses. This means that isotopes have the same atomic number but different mass numbers (Table 5.3).

For example, neon has two isotopes (Figure 5.9). Each isotope has 10 protons and 10 electrons and therefore an atomic number of 10. But one of these isotopes has 10 neutrons and the other has 12 neutrons. Their mass numbers are therefore 20 and 22. They are sometimes called neon-20 and neon-22.

These two isotopes of neon have the same chemical properties because they have the same number of electrons. But they have different physical properties because they have different masses. So, $^{20}_{10}Ne$ and $^{22}_{10}Ne$ have different densities, different melting points and different boiling points.

At one time, the standard for relative atomic masses was hydrogen. Because of the existence of isotopes, it became necessary to choose one particular isotope as the standard. Today, the isotope carbon-12 ($^{12}_{6}C$) is chosen as the standard and given a relative mass of exactly 12.

Element	Symbol	Relative atomic mass
Carbon	C	12.0
Hydrogen	H	1.0
Helium	He	40
Oxygen	O	16.0
Magnesium	Mg	24.0
Sulfur	S	32.1
Iron	Fe	55.8
Copper	Cu	63.59
Gold	Au	197.0

Table 5.4 The relative atomic masses of a few elements

	neon-20	neon-22
	$^{20}_{10}\mathrm{Ne}$	$^{22}_{10}\mathrm{Ne}$
number of protons	10	10
number of electrons	10	10
atomic number	10	10
number of neutrons	10	12
mass number	20	22

Figure 5.9 The two isotopes of neon

6 Look at Table 5.4.
a) How many times heavier are carbon atoms than hydrogen atoms?
b) How many times heavier are magnesium atoms than carbon atoms?
c) Which element has atoms almost four times as heavy as oxygen atoms?
d) Write the following elements in order of increasing deflection in a mass spectrometer – helium, iron, gold.

The relative masses of other atoms are then obtained by comparison with carbon-12. On this scale, the relative atomic mass of hydrogen is still 1.0 and that of helium is 4.0. A few relative atomic masses are listed in Table 5.4.

The symbol for relative atomic mass is A_r. So, we can write A_r (C) = 12.0, A_r (H) = 1.0 and so on, or simply C = 12.0 and H = 1.0 for short.

Measuring relative atomic masses

Most elements contain a mixture of isotopes. This explains why their relative atomic masses are not whole numbers. Using modern mass spectrometers, it is possible to obtain print-outs showing the relative amounts of the different isotopes in a sample of an element and the relative atomic masses of each isotope. One of these print-outs is shown in Figure 5.10. The print-out shows that chlorine consists of two isotopes, $^{35}_{17}\mathrm{Cl}$ and $^{37}_{17}\mathrm{Cl}$, with relative atomic masses of 35 and 37.

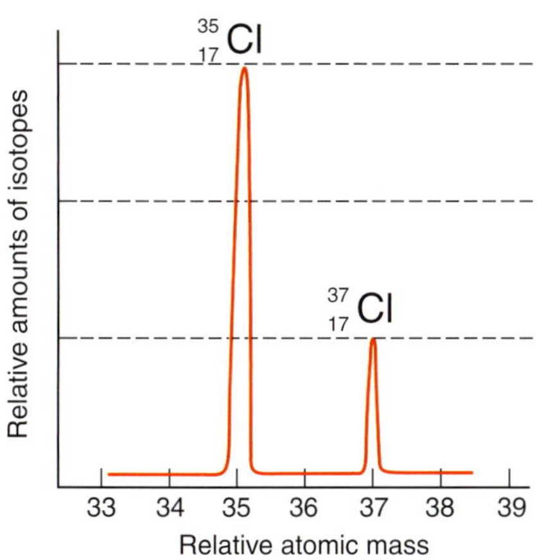

Figure 5.10 A mass spectrometer print-out for chlorine

The relative atomic mass of an element is the average mass of one atom of the element. This average must take into account the relative amounts of the different isotopes. For example, if chlorine contained 100% $^{35}_{17}\mathrm{Cl}$, its relative atomic mass would be 35.0. If it contained 100% $^{37}_{17}\mathrm{Cl}$, then its relative atomic mass would be 37.0. A 50 : 50 mixture of $^{35}_{17}\mathrm{Cl}$ and $^{37}_{17}\mathrm{Cl}$ would have a relative atomic mass of 36.0

Figure 5.10 shows that naturally occurring chlorine contains three times as much $^{35}_{17}\mathrm{Cl}$ as $^{37}_{17}\mathrm{Cl}$, i.e. ¾ or 75% of chlorine is $^{35}_{17}\mathrm{Cl}$ and ¼ or 25% is $^{37}_{17}\mathrm{Cl}$.

So, the relative atomic mass can be calculated as:

75% chlorine-35 + 25% chlorine-37

$$= \frac{75}{100} \times 35.0 + \frac{25}{100} \times 37.0 = 26.25 + 9.25 = 35.5$$

5.3

Using relative atomic masses to find out about compounds

Comparing the masses of molecules

Relative formula masses can be used to compare the masses of different compounds.

In the last section, we learned that relative atomic masses can be used to compare the masses of different atoms. Relative atomic masses can also be used to compare the masses of molecules in different compounds. The relative masses of compounds are called **relative formula masses** (symbol M_r). The relative formula mass of a compound is the sum of the relative atomic masses of all the atoms in its formula.

For example, the relative formula mass of water, M_r (H_2O)

= 2 × relative atomic mass of hydrogen + relative atomic mass of oxygen

$= (2 \times 1.0) + 16.0$

$= 18.0$

The relative formula mass of red iron oxide, M_r (Fe_2O_3)

= 2 × relative atomic mass of iron+ 3 × relative atomic mass of oxygen

$= 2 \times 55.8 + 3 \times 16.0 = 159.6$

The relative formula mass of a compound in grams is known as one mole of that substance.

So, 1 mole of water is 18.0 g and

0.1 mole of water $= 0.1 \times 18.0 = 1.8$ g

One mole of red iron oxide is 159.6 g, and so

5 moles of red iron oxide $= 5 \times 159.6 = 798.0$ g

7 What is the relative formula mass of:
a) carbon dioxide, CO_2;
b) sulfuric acid, H_2SO_4?

8 Calculate the mass of
a) 3 moles of carbon dioxide;
b) 0.6 moles of carbon dioxide;
c) 5 moles of sulfuric acid;
d) 0.2 moles of sulfuric acid.

Finding the percentage composition of compounds

Relative atomic masses can be used to calculate the percentage of different elements in a compound. First, you work out the relative amounts of each element in the relative formula mass of the compound. For example, carbon dioxide (CO_2) contains 12.0 g of carbon and 2 × 16.0 g (32.0 g) of oxygen in 44.0 g of carbon dioxide.

So, it contains 12/44 parts carbon and 32/44 parts oxygen. Changing to percentages, this is:

$$\frac{12}{44} \times 100 = 27\% \text{ carbon and } \frac{32}{44} \times 100 = 73\% \text{ oxygen}$$

Figure 5.11 The chemical formula for table sugar is $C_{12}H_{22}O_{11}$. The relative formula mass of sugar, M_r ($C_{12}H_{22}O_{11}$):
$= 12 \times A_r(C) + 22 \times A_r(H) + 11 \times A_r(O)$
$= 12 \times 12.0 + 22 \times 1.0 + 11 \times 16$
$= 144 + 22 + 176$
$= 342$

Figure 5.12 The yellow substance in 'no parking' double lines is lead chromate, $PbCrO_4$.

Figure 5.13 This sulfur is being stored after mining. 32.1 g of sulfur can be reacted with oxygen and water to manufacture 98.1 g of sulfuric acid.

Finding the masses of reactants and products in a reaction

In industry, it is vitally important to know the amounts of reactants that are needed for a chemical process and the amount of product that can be obtained. Industrial chemists need to know how much product they can obtain from a given amount of starting material. To do this, they use relative formula masses and equations.

As an example, let's calculate how much iron we could obtain by reducing 1 kg (1000 g) of pure iron ore (red iron oxide) with carbon monoxide in a blast furnace.

The equation for the reaction is:

$$Fe_2O_3 + 3CO \rightarrow 2Fe + 3CO_2$$

From this equation:

$$1 \text{ mole } Fe_2O_3 \rightarrow 2 \text{ moles Fe}$$

Using relative formula masses for Fe_2O_3 and 2Fe:

$$(2 \times 55.8 + 3 \times 16) \text{ g } Fe_2O_3 \rightarrow 2 \times 55.8 \text{ g Fe}$$

$$159.6 \text{ g } Fe_2O_3 \rightarrow 111.6 \text{ g Fe}$$

$$1.0 \text{ g } Fe_2O_3 \rightarrow \frac{111.6}{159.6} \text{ g Fe} = 0.7 \text{ g Fe}$$

$$\Rightarrow 1.0 \text{ kg } Fe_2O_3 \rightarrow 0.7 \text{ kg Fe}$$

So, 1 kg of pure red iron oxide produces 0.7 kg of iron.

The amount of product that we actually make in a chemical process doesn't always match the theoretical (calculated) amount. You will learn more about this in Section 7.1.

9 a) Look at Figure 5.12. What elements are present in lead chromate besides lead?
b) What is the relative formula mass of lead chromate?
c) What is the percentage of lead in lead chromate? (Pb = 207, Cr = 52, O = 16)

10 Copy and complete the following calculation to find how much lime (calcium oxide) can be obtained by heating 1 kg of pure limestone (calcium carbonate). (Ca = 40, C = 12, O = 16.)

The equation for the reaction is:

calcium carbonate → _____ + _____

$CaCO_3 \rightarrow$ _____ + CO_2

∴ 1 mole $CaCO_3 \rightarrow$ ___ mole CaO

∴ ___ g $CaCO_3 \rightarrow$ ___ g CaO

∴ 1000 g $CaCO_3 \rightarrow$ ___ g CaO

Activity – Extracting tin from tinstone

The production manager at a tin smelter has to meet certain production targets. The smelter must produce 595 tonnes of tin every month. In order to achieve this, the manager must calculate how much purified tinstone (tin oxide) he must buy to produce 595 tonnes of tin. To do this he uses the equation:

tin oxide + carbon (coke) → tin + carbon monoxide

SnO_2 + 2C → Sn + 2CO

The equation shows that 1 mole of SnO_2 produces 1 mole of Sn. (The relative atomic masses of tin, carbon and oxygen are Sn = 119, C = 12, O = 16.)

1. Now complete the following statement.
   __ g SnO_2 produces __ g Sn.
2. What mass of tinstone is needed to meet the production target of 595 tonnes of tin per month?
3. What mass of carbon (coke) is needed each month?
4. What concerns should the production manager have about the emissions from the smelter?
5. The smelter normally operates all through the day and night. It can produce a maximum of 1 tonne of tin per hour. Is the production target possible? Explain your answer.
6. In the first six months of 2006, the amount of tin produced each month, to the nearest five tonnes, was: 650, 630, 575, 585, 560 and 600.
   a) What is the range in production over the six months?
   b) What is the mean (average) production per month?
   c) Has the monthly target been achieved on average over the first six months of 2006?
   d) What should the production manager do to get a more reliable value for the average production per month?
   e) What should the production manager do to get a more accurate value for the average production per month?
7. In 2006, tin from the smelter was sold at £3500 per tonne. What is the value of the tin produced by the smelter in the first six months of 2006?
8. Why did the smelters have tall chimneys?
9. Why is tin no longer mined and produced in Cornwall?

Figure 5.14 A disused tin smelting building in Cornwall

An **empirical formula** shows the simplest whole number ratio for the atoms of different elements in a compound.

Finding formulae using relative atomic masses

We have used some formulae already such as H_2O for water and CO_2 for carbon dioxide. But, how do we know, for example, that the formula of water is H_2O?

All formulae of compounds are obtained by doing experiments to find the number of moles of the different elements that react to form a given mass of compound. This is called the **empirical formula**. When water is decomposed into hydrogen and oxygen, results show that:

18.0 g of water give 2.0 g of hydrogen + 16.0 g of oxygen

= 2 moles of hydrogen + 1 mole of oxygen

= $2 \times 6 \times 10^{23}$ atoms of hydrogen + 6×10^{23} atoms of oxygen

	H	O
Masses reacting	2.0 g	16.0 g
Mass of 1 mole	1 g	16 g
∴ moles reacting	2	1
Ratio of atoms	2	1
⇒ formula = H_2O		

Table 5.5 Finding the formula of water

This shows that 12×10^{23} hydrogen atoms combine with 6×10^{23} oxygen atoms, so two hydrogen atoms combine with one oxygen atom. Therefore, the formula of water is H_2O. These results are set out in Table 5.5.

Activity – Finding the formula of red copper oxide

After finding that the formula of black copper oxide was CuO, George and Meera decided to investigate the formula of red copper oxide.

They took a weighed amount of red copper oxide and reduced it to copper (Figure 5.15). They carried out the experiment five times, starting with different amounts of red copper oxide. Their results are shown in Table 5.6.

Experiment number	Mass of red copper oxide in g	Mass of copper in the oxide in g
1	1.43	1.27
2	2.10	1.87
3	2.72	2.54
4	3.55	3.15
5	4.29	3.81

Table 5.6

1. Look at Figure 5.15. What safety precautions should George and Meera take during the experiment?
2. Write a word equation for the reduction of copper oxide to copper using methane (CH_4) in natural gas. (Hint: The only solid product is copper.)
3. What steps could George and Meera take to ensure that all the copper oxide is reduced to copper?
4. Make a table similar to Table 5.6 but with three extra columns.
   a) In the first of these extra columns, write the mass of oxygen in each of the samples of red copper oxide.
   b) In the second extra column, calculate the number of moles of copper in the oxide (Cu = 63.5).
   c) In the third extra column, calculate the number of moles of oxygen in the oxide (O = 16.0).
5. Use the results in the last two columns of your table to plot a graph of moles of copper (*y*-axis) against moles of oxygen (*x*-axis). Draw the line of best fit through the points on your graph.
6. Which of the points is anomalous and should be disregarded in drawing the line of best fit?
7. Look at your graph.
   a) Find the average value for
   $$\frac{\text{moles of copper}}{\text{moles of oxygen}}$$
   in red copper oxide.
   b) How many moles of copper combine with one mole of oxygen in red copper oxide?
   c) What is the formula for red copper oxide?
8. How did George and Meera improve the reliability of their results?
9. Is their result for the formula of red copper oxide valid? State 'Yes' or 'No' and explain your opinion.
10. Use the results in Table 5.6 to explain why a balance reading to only one decimal place would have been useless for this investigation.
11. a) What was i) the independent variable and ii) the dependent variable in this investigation?
    b) Are these categoric, continuous or ordered variables?

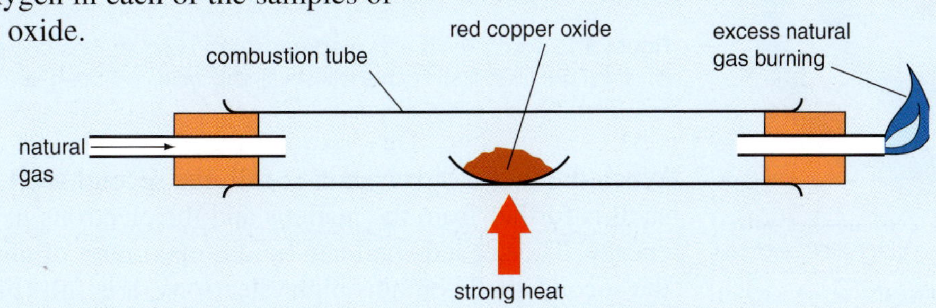

Figure 5.15 Reducing red copper oxide by heating in natural gas

5.4 How are the electrons arranged in atoms?

In science, ideas change all the time. New evidence is used to improve theories so that they give a better explanation of what we observe.

In 1911, Rutherford put forward some key ideas about atomic structure (see Section 5.1). He said that atoms had a small positive nucleus containing protons surrounded by lots of empty space. Rutherford compared atoms to the Solar System and said that electrons orbited the nucleus like planets orbiting the Sun.

In 1913, the Danish scientist Niels Bohr suggested a more detailed model for the arrangement of electrons in atoms. Bohr said that electrons were grouped together in layers or shells at particular energy levels. Bohr's ideas about electrons in layers or shells helped us to understand what happens when elements react.

Electron shells are the regions occupied by electrons around the nucleus of an atom.

Electron structures show the number of electrons in each shell (energy level). The structures can be drawn as shell diagrams, or written as numbers of electrons in each shell, for example 2, 8.

Filling the shells

Different atoms have different **electron structures**. Atoms with larger atomic numbers have more electrons as the number of electrons is the same as the number of protons. The electrons in an atom always occupy the lowest energy levels first, starting with the **electron shell** nearest the nucleus.

The electrons in the first shell are strongly attracted to the nucleus. The first shell can hold only two electrons. When it contains two electrons, it is full and the electrons in it are stable (Figure 5.16).

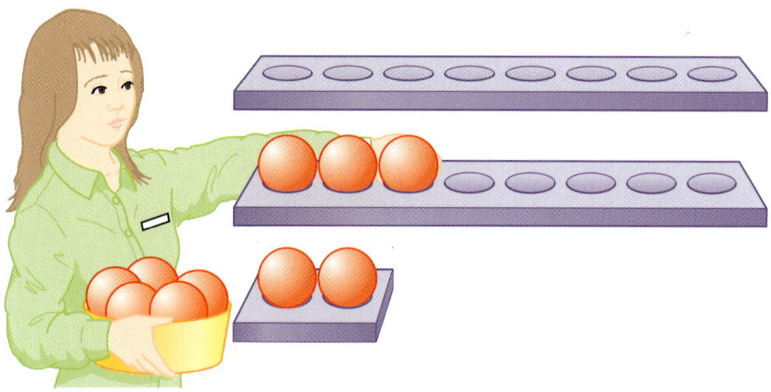

Figure 5.16 Filling shells with electrons is like filling shelves in a shop. The lowest shells (shelves) are filled first. Each shell (shelf) only holds a limited number of electrons (items).

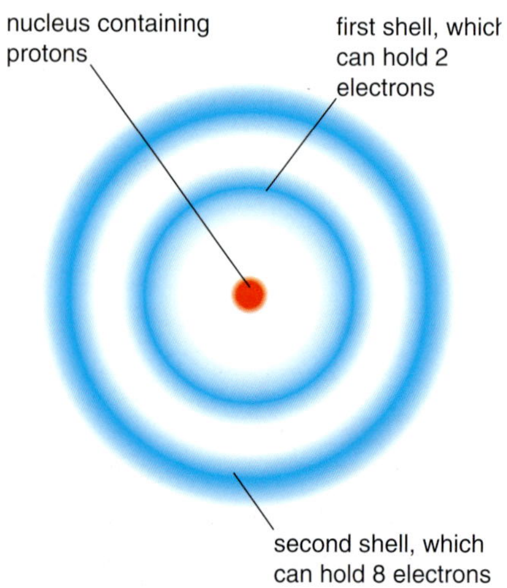

Figure 5.17 A model for the arrangement of electrons in the first and second shells

When the first electron shell is full, the second shell starts to fill. This shell is further from the nucleus and the electrons in it have more energy. The second shell can hold a maximum of eight electrons. When the second shell contains eight electrons, it is full (Figure 5.17). This electron structure is very stable.

Once the second shell is full, the third shell starts filling. This shell is further from the nucleus than the second shell and at a higher energy level. The third shell is also very stable when it contains eight electrons.

The noble gases
Helium He 2
Neon Ne 2, 8
Argon Ar 2, 8, 8

Figure 5.18 The electron structures of the noble gases

Electron structures and the noble gases

Bohr's ideas about electrons in shells or energy levels have helped us to understand why the noble gases are so unreactive. The first shell is full and the electrons in it are stable when the shell contains two electrons. This corresponds exactly with the structure of helium. Helium has two electrons. They both go into the first shell, which is then full and stable.

The second shell is full and the electrons in it are stable when the shell contains eight electrons. So, the next element to be unreactive like helium will have two electrons filling the first shell and then eight electrons filling the second shell. This corresponds to neon, the tenth element in the Periodic Table. Because neon has two electrons in the first shell and eight electrons in the second shell, we say its electron structure is 2, 8 (Figure 5.18).

The third shell is also stable when it contains eight electrons. So, the next very unreactive element will have two electrons filling the first shell, eight filling the second shell and eight in the third shell. This corresponds exactly with the electron structure of argon, which we can write as 2, 8, 8 (Figure 5.18).

Figure 5.19 Electric light bulbs are filled with argon or krypton. These noble gases are so unreactive and their electrons are so stable that the metal filament can be white hot at 1000 °C without reacting with them.

5.5 Electron structures and chemical reactivity

Figure 5.20 shows the first 20 elements in their order in the Periodic Table. The atomic number and electron structure of each element are written below its symbol. When the first shell is full at helium, further electrons go into the second shell. So, the electron structure of lithium is 2, 1, beryllium is 2, 2, boron is 2, 3 and so on. When the second shell is full at neon, electrons start to fill the third shell.

Period 1			H					He
Atomic no.			1					2
Electron structure			1					2
Period 2	Li	Be	B	C	N	O	F	Ne
Atomic no.	3	4	5	6	7	8	9	10
Electron structure	2, 1	2, 2	2, 3	2, 4	2, 5	2, 6	2, 7	2, 8
Period 3	Na	Mg	Al	Si	P	S	Cl	Ar
Atomic no.	11	12	13	14	15	16	17	18
Electron structure	2, 8, 1	2, 8, 2	2, 8, 3	2, 8, 4	2, 8, 5	2, 8, 6	2, 8, 7	2, 8, 8
Period 4	K	Ca						
Atomic no.	19	20						
Electron structure	2, 8, 8, 1	2, 8, 8, 2						

Figure 5.20 The electron structures of the first 20 elements in the Periodic Table

The alkali metals	The halogens
Lithium Li 2, 1	Fluorine F 2, 7
Sodium Na 2, 8, 1	Chlorine Cl 2, 8, 7
Potassium K 2, 8, 8, 1	Bromine Br 2, 8, 18, 7

Figure 5.21 The electron structures of some of the alkali metals and some of the halogens

Group 1 – the alkali metals

Electron structures help us to explain why elements in the same group of the Periodic Table, like the alkali metals, have similar chemical properties.

All the alkali metals in Group 1 react with non-metal elements to form compounds containing ions (ionic compounds). In these ionic compounds, each alkali metal ion has one positive charge.

Look at Figure 5.21. Notice that each of the alkali metals has one electron in its outermost shell. Alkali metals can lose this outer electron very easily to form ions with one positive charge (Li^+, Na^+, K^+). These ions are very stable because they have an electron structure like a noble gas. For example, the electron structure of Na^+ is 2, 8, which is like neon. The electron structure of K^+ is 2, 8, 8 like argon. So, alkali metals have similar properties because they have similar electron structures.

Group 7 – the halogens

The elements in Group 7 of the Periodic Table, called the halogens (Figure 5.21), have similar chemical properties. They react with alkali metals to form ionic compounds in which the halide ions, such as chloride, Cl^- and fluoride F^-, have one negative charge.

All the halogen atoms have seven electrons in their outermost shell. By gaining one electron, they form negative ions such as F^-, Cl^- and Br^-.

These ions have stable electron structures like the next noble gas. Halogens have similar properties because they have the same number of

⓫ Why are the noble gases so unreactive?

⓬ How many protons, neutrons and electrons are there in
a) one $^{14}_{7}N$ atom;
b) one $^{14}_{7}N^{3-}$ ion?

⓭ Write the electron structure for:
a) Li; b) Li^+; c) O;
d) O^{2-}.

⓮ a) Write down the electron structures of magnesium and calcium.
b) How many electrons are there in the outer shell of an atom of an element in Group 2?
c) What charge will the stable ions of Group 2 elements have?

electrons in the highest occupied energy level (outermost shell). The halogens are so reactive because they gain one electron very easily.

In general, elements in the same group of the Periodic Table have similar chemical properties because they have the same number of electrons in their outer shell (highest energy level).

Figure 5.22 Chlorine is the most useful and most common halogen. It is added in very small quantities to the water in swimming pools, to kill bacteria and other microorganisms.

Activity – Atoms, ions and the Periodic Table

Look carefully at Table 5.7. This shows the electron structures of the atoms and ions of the elements in period 3 of the Periodic Table.

❶ What pattern can you see in the ions formed by elements in Groups 1, 2 and 3?

❷ Predict the ions formed by the following atoms:
a) Li; b) Be; c) K; d) Ca.
(If you need help, look at Figure 5.20.)

❸ We can write an equation for the formation of a sodium ion (Na^+) when a sodium atom (Na) loses an electron as:

$$Na \rightarrow Na^+ + e^-$$
$$(2, 8, 1) \quad (2, 8)^+ + \text{electron}$$

Now write a similar equation for the formation of a magnesium ion (Mg^{2+}) from a magnesium atom (Mg).

❹ What pattern can you see in the ions formed by elements in Groups 5, 6 and 7?

❺ Predict the ions formed by the following atoms:
a) N; b) O; c) F.

Elements in period 3	Na	Mg	Al	Si	P	S	Cl	Ar
Group	1	2	3	4	5	6	7	0
Electron structure	2, 8, 1	2, 8, 2	2, 8, 3	2, 8, 4	2, 8, 5	2, 8, 6	2, 8, 7	2, 8, 8
No. of electrons in outer shell	1	2	3	4	5	6	7	8
Common ion	Na^+	Mg^{2+}	Al^{3+}	No ion	P^{3-}	S^{2-}	Cl^-	No ion
Electron structure of ion	2, 8	2, 8	2, 8	–	2, 8, 8	2, 8, 8	2, 8, 8	–

Table 5.7 Electron structures of the atoms and ions of elements in period 3

6 We can write an equation for the formation of a chloride ion (Cl^-) when a chlorine atom (Cl) gains an electron as:

Cl	+	e^-	→	Cl^-
(2, 8, 7)		electron		$(2, 8, 8)^-$

Now write a similar equation for the formation of a sulfide ion (S^{2-}) from a sulfur atom (S).

7 Why does argon not form an ion?

8 Use your answer to question 7 to explain why argon is used to fill electric light bulbs.

9 Suggest a reason why silicon does not usually form Si^{4+} or Si^{4-} ions.

5.6 What happens to the electrons when elements react?

In Section 5.5, you learned that:

- metal atoms, like sodium and magnesium, lose electrons and form positive ions when they react to form compounds;
- non-metal atoms, like chlorine and sulfur, gain electrons and form negative ions when they react to form compounds;
- non-metals can also share electrons when they react to form compounds.

The **electronic theory of chemical bonding** says that when atoms react, they lose, gain or share electrons in order to get a more stable electron structure.

An **ionic bond** results from the electrical attraction between oppositely charged ions.

A **covalent bond** is formed by the sharing of a pair of electrons between two atoms. Each atom contributes one electron to the bond.

These ideas form the basis of the **electronic theory of chemical bonding**. When elements react to produce compounds, chemical bonds are formed. These chemical bonds involve either the transfer or the sharing of electrons in the outer shell (highest occupied energy level) of atoms. When the atoms react, they lose, gain or share electrons in order to get a more stable electron structure. Their more stable electron structures are often like those of the noble gases.

Two kinds of bond are formed when atoms react – ionic bonds and covalent bonds.

Ionic bonds are formed when metals react with non-metals. Metals lose electrons and form positive ions. The electrons are transferred to non-metals which gain the electrons and form negative ions. The attraction of the opposite charges on the ions forms the ionic bond.

Covalent bonds are formed when non-metals react with each other. The non-metals share one or more pairs of electrons. The positive nucleus of each non-metal attracts the shared negative electrons and this forms the covalent bond.

Ionic bonds – transfer of electrons

Figure 5.23 shows what happens when sodium chloride (Na^+Cl^-) is formed. Full electron structures are shown with crosses for the electrons in all the shells of the sodium and chlorine atoms and their respective ions.

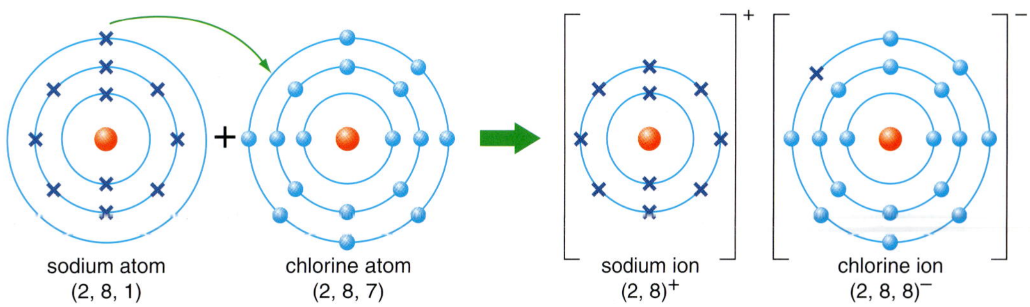

Figure 5.23 Electron transfer during the formation of sodium chloride

The sodium atom has one electron in its outer shell and chlorine has seven. During the reaction, the sodium transfers its one electron into the outer shell of the chlorine atom. This produces:

- a sodium ion (Na^+) with the same stable electron structure as the noble gas neon and
- a chloride ion (Cl^-) with the same stable electron structure as the noble gas argon.

So, the formation of sodium chloride involves the complete transfer of an electron from a sodium atom to a chlorine atom forming Na^+ and Cl^- ions.

The formation of sodium chloride in Figure 5.23 can be summarised by showing only the outer electrons, as in Figure 5.24.

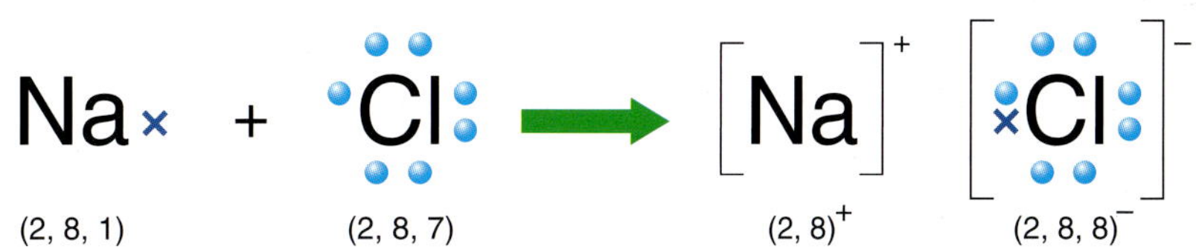

Figure 5.24 A 'dot-cross' diagram for the formation of sodium chloride

This is called a 'dot-cross' diagram because the electrons of the different atoms are shown as either dots or crosses. The electrons are not really different. They have only been shown as dots or crosses to help us understand what happens when the elements react.

Compounds containing ions are called ionic compounds. Ionic compounds have a giant, repeating structure of ions held together by strong forces of attraction between the oppositely charged ions. These forces act in all directions and this is called ionic bonding. The giant structure, bonding and properties of ionic compounds are discussed further in Section 6.7.

Figure 5.25 shows two more examples of electron transfer between a metal and a non-metal forming ionic compounds.

15 Look at the formation of magnesium oxide in Figure 5.25.

a) How many electrons do magnesium and oxygen atoms gain or lose in forming magnesium oxide?

b) What is the charge on:
   i) a magnesium ion;
   ii) an oxide ion?

c) What is the formula of magnesium oxide?

d) Which noble gas has an electron structure like the ions in magnesium oxide?

16 Look at the formation of calcium chloride in Figure 5.25.

a) How many electrons do calcium and chlorine atoms gain or lose in forming calcium chloride?

b) What is the charge on:
   i) a calcium ion;
   ii) a chloride ion?

c) What is the formula of calcium chloride?

d) Why does one calcium atom react with two chlorine atoms in forming calcium chloride?

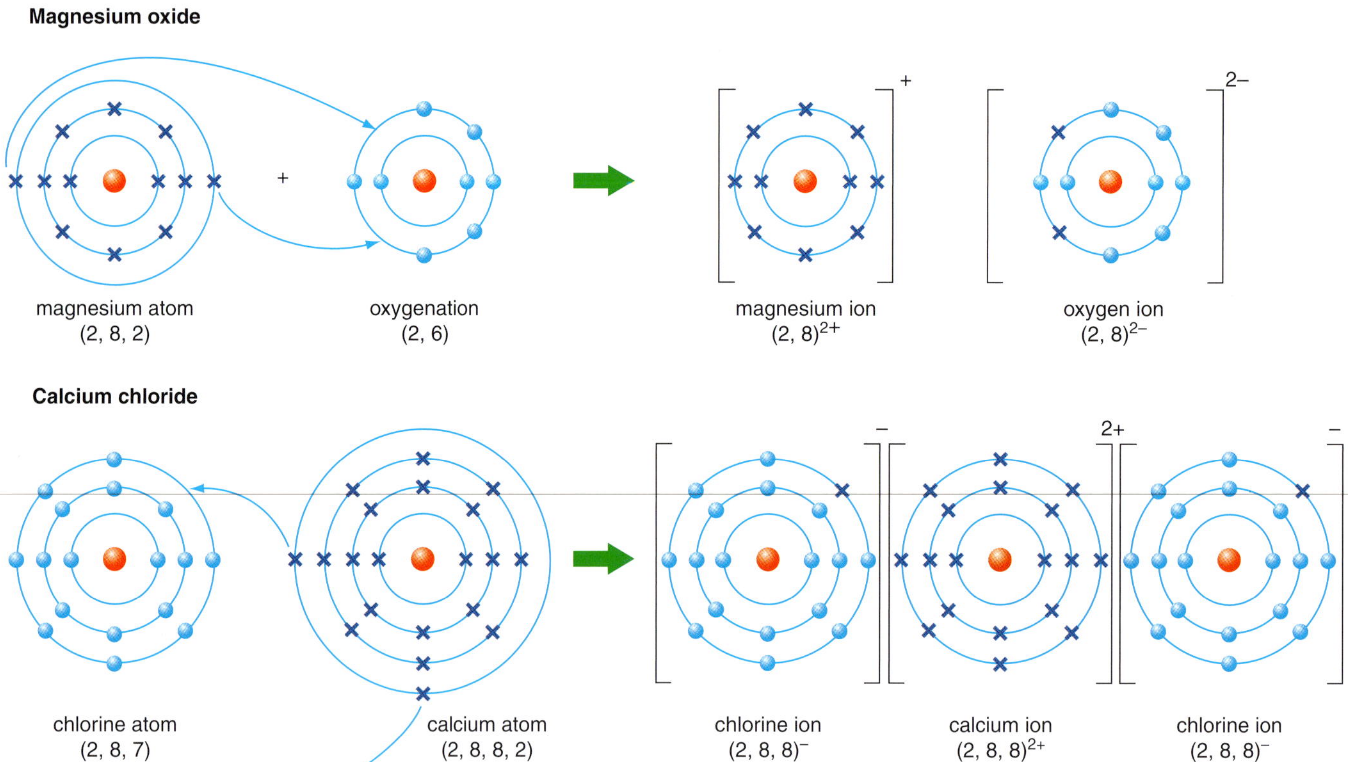

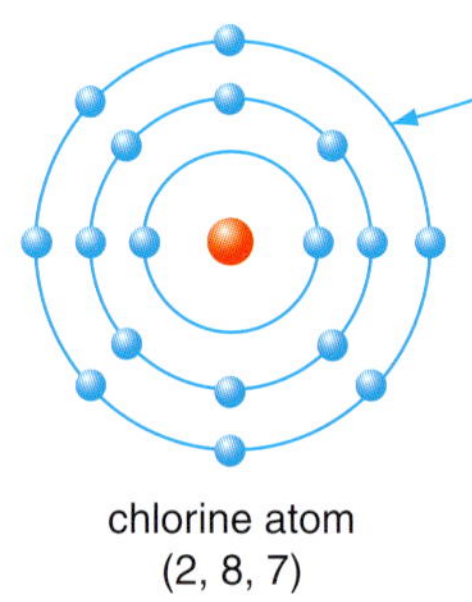

Figure 5.25 Electron transfers in the formation of magnesium oxide and calcium chloride

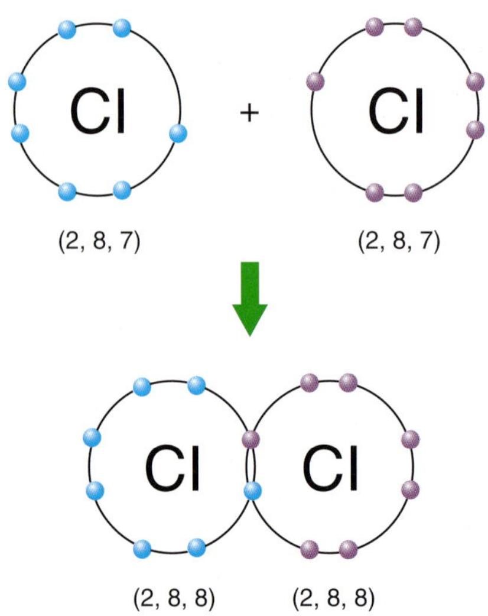

Figure 5.26 Electron sharing in the covalent bond in a chlorine molecule

Covalent bonds – sharing electrons

A chlorine atom is very unstable. Its outer shell contains seven electrons. At normal temperatures, chlorine atoms join up in pairs to form Cl_2 molecules by sharing electrons (Figure 5.26).

If the two chlorine atoms come close together, the electrons in their outer shells can overlap. Each chlorine atom can share one of its electrons with the other atom (Figure 5.26). The two chlorine atoms share a pair of electrons and get a stable electron structure like argon.

The positive nuclei of both atoms attract the shared electrons and this holds the atoms together. This attraction forms a covalent bond.

Notice in Figure 5.26 that:

- the shared pair of electrons form part of the outer shell of both chlorine atoms;
- circles are used to join up the electrons in the outer shell of each chlorine atom;
- the chlorine atoms are bonded together forming an uncharged molecule.

Covalent bonds between atoms are strong bonds. Some covalently bonded substances, such as chlorine (Cl_2), hydrogen (H_2), oxygen (O_2), hydrogen chloride (HCl), water (H_2O), ammonia (NH_3) and methane (CH_4), consist of simple molecules containing a small number of atoms. Other covalently bonded substances, such as diamond, silicon dioxide and many polymers, have giant structures (giant molecules) containing thousands and sometimes millions of atoms. The structure and properties of these giant structures are discussed further in Section 6.5. The covalent bonding and electron structures in some of the simple molecules are shown in Figure 5.27.

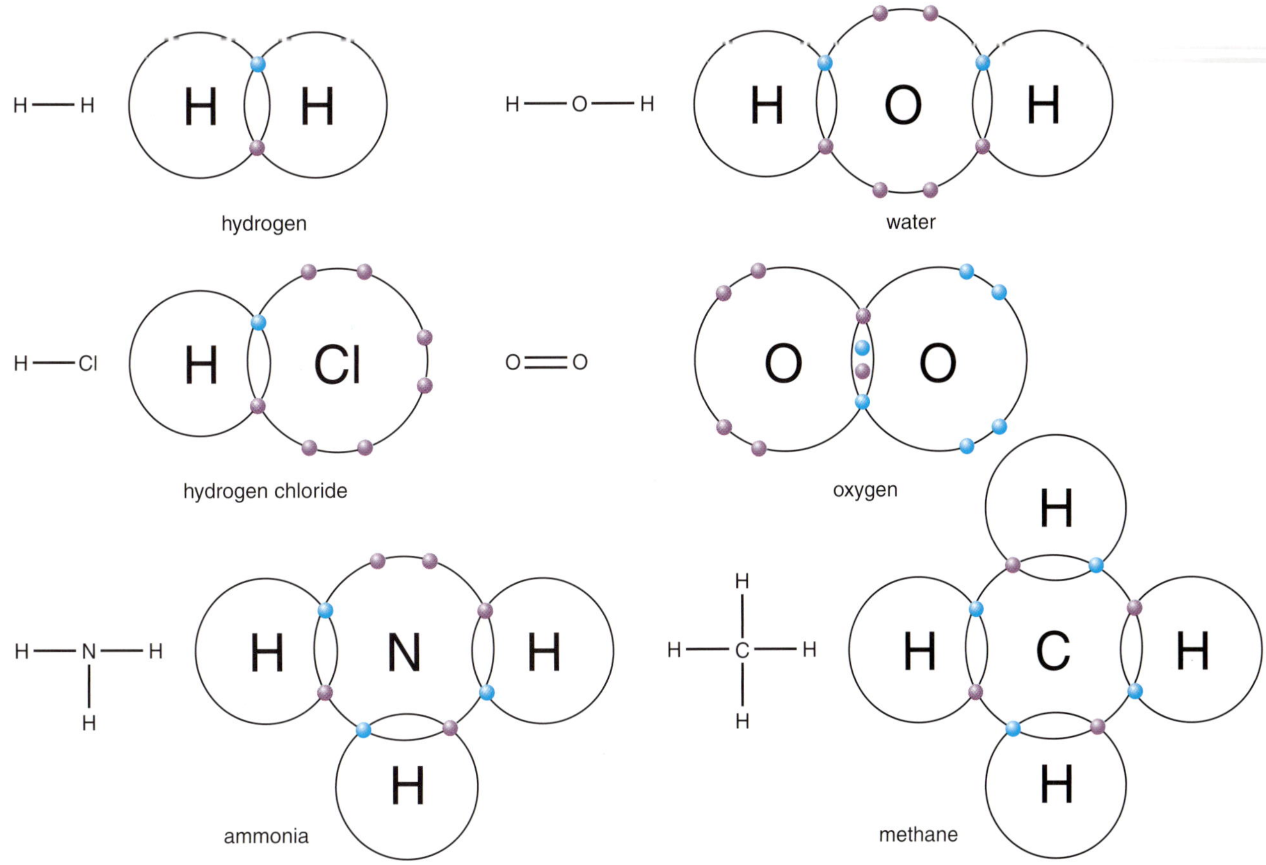

Figure 5.27 The covalent bonding and electron structures in some simple molecules

The **structural formula** of a compound shows which atoms are bonded to each other in a molecule of the compound.

In Figure 5.27 notice that:

- The electron structures of the simple molecules can be related to their **structural formulae** shown on the left hand side of each dot-cross diagram. In the structural formulae, each covalent bond is shown as a line between atoms. For example, H–O–H for water.
- Hydrogen atoms (H) always have one bond. Chlorine atoms (Cl) always have one bond. Oxygen atoms (O) always have two bonds, nitrogen atoms (N) have three bonds and carbon atoms (C) have four bonds.

17 Copy and complete the following statement.
A covalent bond is formed by the s _____ of a p_____ of electrons between t_____ atoms. Each atom contributes one e_____ to the b_____.

18 Look at Figure 5.27.

a) Which noble gas has an electron structure like the hydrogen atoms in H_2?

b) In oxygen, O_2, there is a double covalent bond between the two oxygen atoms. How many electrons are shared in a double covalent bond?

c) The structural formula for carbon dioxide is O=C=O. Draw the dot-cross diagram for carbon dioxide.

Summary

- ✓ Atoms have a small nucleus containing positive protons and uncharged neutrons around which there are tiny negative electrons.
- ✓ In all atoms, the positive charges on the protons are exactly cancelled by the negative charges on an equal number of electrons.
- ✓ **Ions** are formed from atoms by the loss or gain of one or more electrons.
- ✓ The **atomic number** is the number of protons in an atom.
- ✓ The **mass number** is the total number of protons plus neutrons in an atom.
- ✓ **Isotopes** are atoms of the same element with the same atomic number, but different mass numbers.
- ✓ **Relative atomic masses** are used to compare the relative masses of atoms. Atoms of the isotope carbon-12 are given a relative atomic mass of exactly 12. The relative atomic masses of other atoms are obtained by comparison with carbon-12.
- ✓ The **relative formula mass** of a compound is the sum of the relative atomic masses of all the atoms in its formula.
- ✓ The relative atomic mass of an element is the average mass of one atom, taking into account the relative amounts of its different isotopes.
- ✓ Using relative atomic masses and equations for reactions, it is possible to calculate the masses of reactants and products.
- ✓ The relative atomic mass of an element in grams and the relative formula mass of a compound in grams are sometimes called one **mole**.
- ✓ An **empirical formula** shows the simplest whole number ratio for the atoms of different elements in a compound.
- ✓ The electrons in an atom determine its chemical properties. Electrons are grouped together in **electron shells** at different distances from the nucleus and at particular **energy levels**. When the shells are full, the atoms or ions are stable. **Electron structures** show the number of electrons in each shell.
- ✓ Elements in the same group of the Periodic Table have the same number of electrons in their outermost shell (highest energy level). This gives them similar chemical properties.
- ✓ When atoms react, they lose, gain or share electrons in order to get a more stable electron structure. This idea is called the **electronic theory of chemical bonding**.
- ✓ **Ionic bonds** are formed when metals react with non-metals. Electron transfer occurs. Metals lose electrons to form positive ions. Non-metals gain electrons to form negative ions. The ionic bond results from the electrical attraction between ions with opposite charges.
- ✓ **Covalent bonds** are formed when non-metals react with each other. The non-metal atoms share electrons. The positive nucleus of each atom attracts the shared negative electrons and this forms the covalent bond.

EXAMQUESTIONS

1 Many processed foods contain chemicals as additives.

a) Sodium carbonate is used as an acidity regulator in some tinned foods. Sodium carbonate contains sodium ions (Na^+) and carbonate ions (CO_3^{2-}). Which one of the following is the formula of sodium carbonate?

A $NaCO_3$ B Na_2CO_3 C $Na(CO_3)_2$ D $Na_3(CO_3)_2$ *(1 mark)*

b) The electron structure of a sodium atom can be written as 2, 8, 1. Which one of the following is the electron structure of a sodium ion? *(1 mark)*

A 2, 2 B 2, 8, 2 C 2, 8 D 2, 8, 8

c) Calcium chloride is used as a firming agent in some tinned foods. Calcium chloride contains calcium ions (Ca^{2+}) and chloride ions (Cl^-). Which one of the following is the formula of calcium chloride? *(1 mark)*

A CaCl B Ca_2Cl C Ca_2Cl_2 D $CaCl_2$

d) Copy and complete the following sentence. A calcium ion (Ca^{2+}) is formed when a calcium atom ______ two ______. *(2 marks)*

2 If a person is anaemic and has a low red blood cell count, he or she may be prescribed iron tablets (Figure 5.28). These contain iron sulfate.

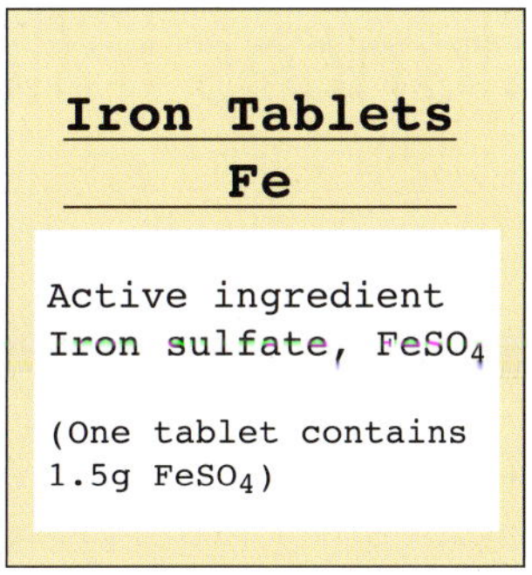

Figure 5.28

a) What elements are present in iron sulfate? *(3 marks)*

b) Iron sulfate contains iron ions (Fe^{2+}) and sulfate ions. Write the symbol and charge for a sulfate ion. *(2 marks)*

c) Calculate the relative formula mass (M_r) of iron sulfate. *(2 marks)*
(Fe = 55.8, S = 32.1, O = 16.0)

d) Calculate the percentage of iron in iron sulfate. *(2 marks)*

e) Calculate the mass of iron in one tablet. *(1 mark)*

f) Why do some people need to take iron tablets? *(1 mark)*

3 Toothpaste sometimes contains calcium fluoride, CaF_2, which helps to produce strong teeth and bones.

a) A fluoride ion can be written as ${}^{19}_{9}F^-$. How many protons, neutrons and electrons are there in one ${}^{19}_{9}F^-$ ion? *(3 marks)*

b) Why does one calcium ion combine with two fluoride ions in calcium fluoride? *(2 marks)*

c) Figure 5.29 shows the outer shell electrons and the full electron structures in brackets for a calcium atom and two fluorine atoms before reacting to form calcium fluoride. Copy and complete the diagram showing the outer shell electrons, charges and electron structures of the calcium and fluoride ions which form. *(8 marks)*

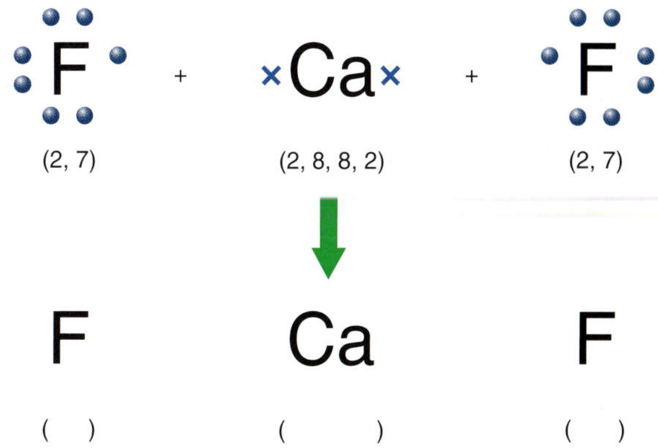

Figure 5.29

d) Why does children's toothpaste often contain calcium fluoride? *(2 marks)*

4 Read the newspaper cutting below and then answer the following questions.

> **Toxic gas scare at local factory**
>
> Workers were forced to flee from the 'Cupromets' factory in Woodside Avenue last Tuesday. The factory was evacuated when fumes of highly toxic nitrogen dioxide filled the building. The gas was produced when concentrated nitric acid spilled onto thin copper pipes.

a) What does 'toxic' mean? *(1 mark)*

b) Explain why the reaction in the factory was more dangerous because the acid spilled onto thin copper pipes rather than thick copper bars. *(2 marks)*

c) Water was sprayed onto the copper and nitric acid to slow down the reaction. Why would this slow down the reaction? *(2 marks)*

d) Copy and balance the following equation for the reaction: *(2 marks)*

$$Cu + \_\_ HNO_3 \rightarrow Cu(NO_3)_2 + \_\_ H_2O + 2NO_2$$

e) Calculate the mass of nitrogen dioxide produced when 254 g of copper reacts completely with concentrated nitric acid.
(Cu = 63.5, N = 14.0, O = 16.0) *(2 marks)*

Chapter 6
How do the structures of substances influence their properties and uses?

At the end of this chapter you should:

- ✓ know that the arrangement of particles in a substance determines its structure and the forces between particles determine its bonding;
- ✓ understand how the structure and bonding of a substance determine its properties and that these properties determine its uses;
- ✓ know that the particles in substances may be atoms, ions or molecules;
- ✓ understand how these three different particles give rise to four different structures (giant metallic, giant covalent, giant ionic and simple molecular) with very different properties;
- ✓ appreciate that the bonds between atoms in metals, between atoms in molecules and between ions in ionic compounds are strong, but the forces between molecules are much weaker;
- ✓ be able to relate the properties of substances to their uses;
- ✓ be able to identify the structure of a substance from its properties;
- ✓ understand that nanomaterials have different properties from normal-sized chunks of the same material because of their very small size;
- ✓ be able to evaluate the benefits and risks of using nanomaterials.

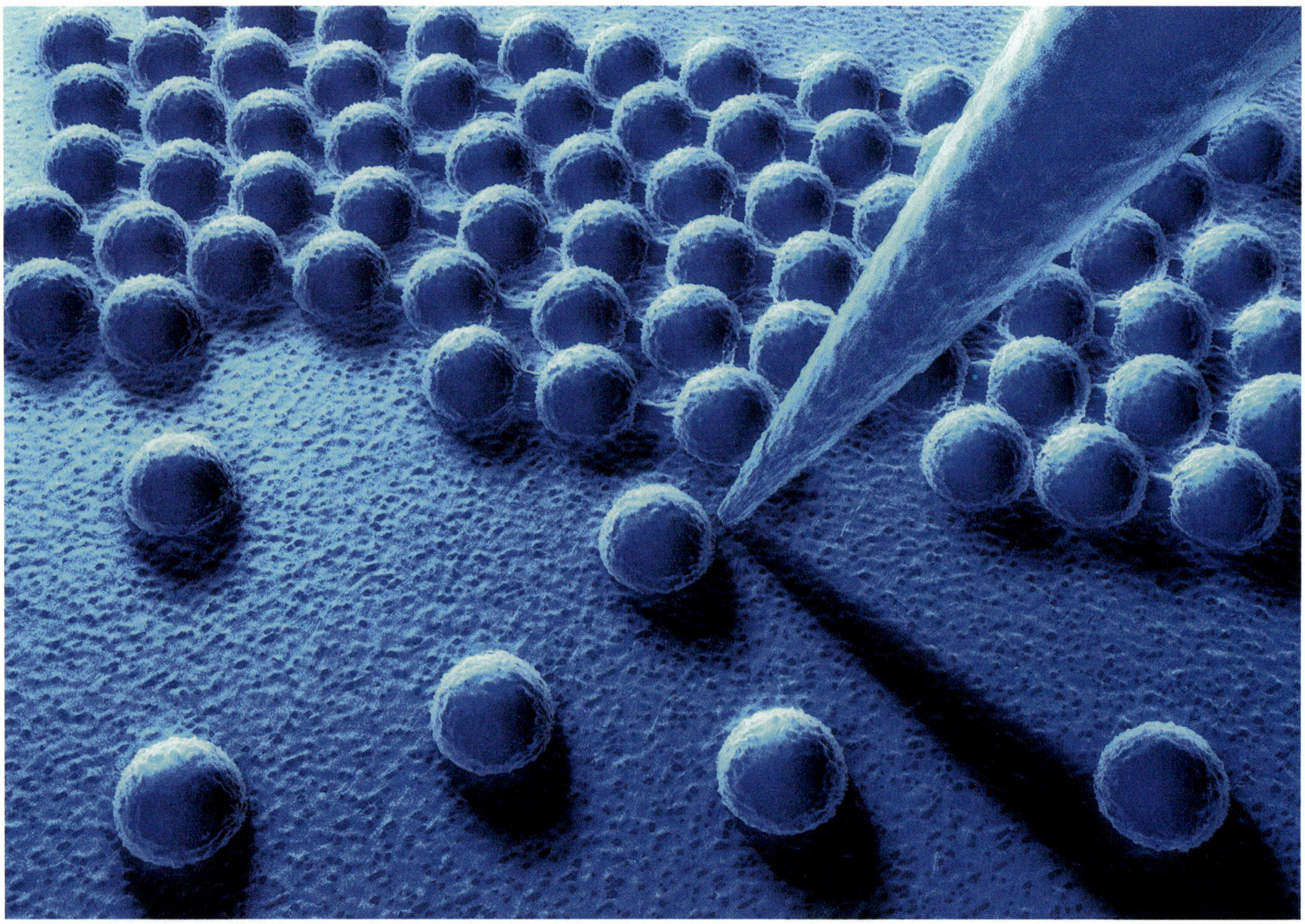

Figure 6.1 In recent years, scientists have developed new substances called nanomaterials with special properties because of the ultra-small size of their particles. This photo shows individual nanoparticles being moved around.

6.1 Studying the structures of materials

Figure 6.2 Crystals of rock salt (sodium chloride, NaCl)

Figure 6.3 Crystals of quartz. Quartz is silicon dioxide (SiO_2).

All substances are made up of particles – atoms, ions or molecules. If we know how these particles are arranged in materials, we can begin to understand their structure and properties.

The study of crystals and their shapes has helped scientists to understand the structures and properties of materials. Sometimes crystals grow unevenly and their shapes are not perfect. Even so, it is usually easy to see their general shape.

Careful study shows that all the crystals of a substance have similar shapes. For example, if you look carefully at Figure 6.2, you will see that individual crystals of rock salt are cubic even though they interlock with each other.

The similar shapes suggest that particles in the crystals of a substance always pack in the same way to give the same overall shape. A similar thing happens with piles of apples and oranges, which tend to form pyramid shapes.

Figure 6.4 shows how cubic crystals and hexagonal crystals can form. If the particles are always in parallel lines or at 90° to each other, the crystals will be cubic. If the particles are arranged in hexagons, the final crystal will be hexagonal.

The shape of a crystal only gives a clue to the way in which the particles are arranged. Using X-rays, it is possible to get much better evidence for the arrangement of particles.

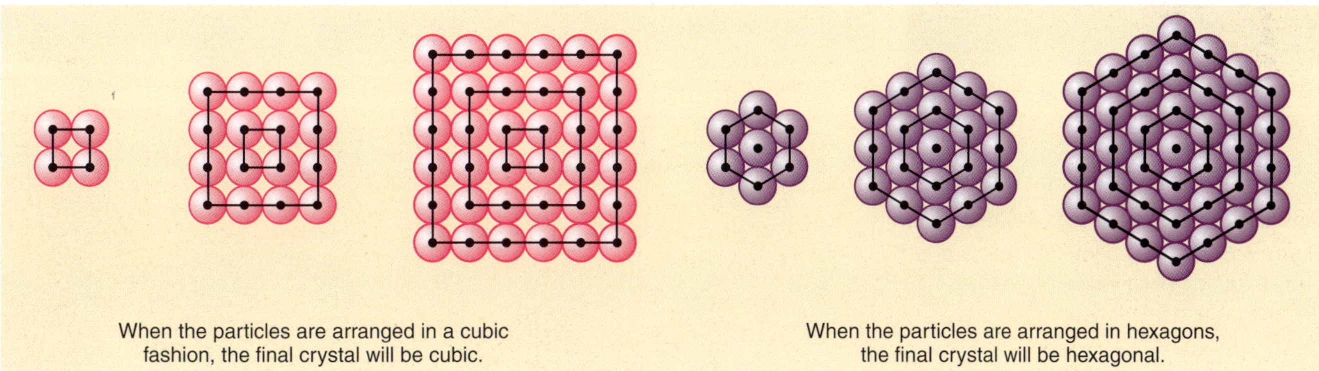

Figure 6.4

Using X-rays to study structures

Look through a piece of thin stretched cloth at a small bright light. You will see a pattern of bright dots. The pattern forms because the light gets deflected as it passes through the tightly spaced threads of the fabric.

From the pattern of bright dots which you can see, it is possible to work out the pattern of threads in the fabric which you cannot see.

Look at the crystals of rock salt and quartz in Figures 6.2 and 6.3.

1. Do most of the rock salt crystals have roughly the same shape?
2. Do most of the quartz crystals have roughly the same shape?
3. Describe the shape of:
   a) the rock salt crystals;
   b) the quartz crystals.

The same idea is used to find out how particles are arranged in substances. A thin beam of X-rays is directed at a crystal of the substance being studied (Figure 6.5).

The X-rays are deflected by particles in the crystal onto X-ray film. When the film is developed, a regular pattern of spots appears. From the pattern of spots which we can see, it is possible to work out the pattern of particles in the crystal which we cannot see. A regular arrangement of spots on the film indicates a regular arrangement of particles in the crystal.

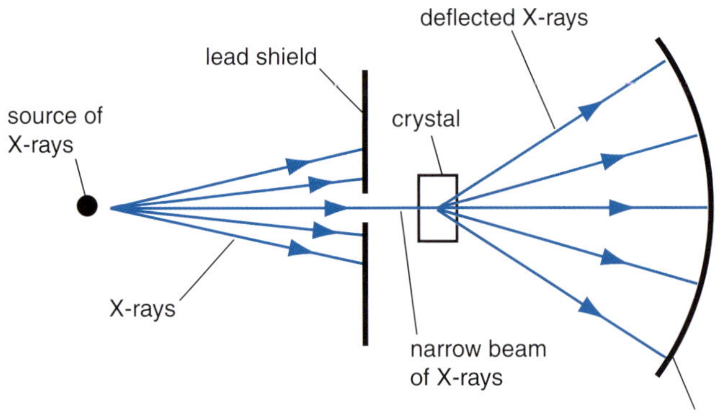

Figure 6.5 Using X-rays to study the particles in a crystal

A **lattice** is a regular arrangement of particles in a three-dimensional structure, such as a crystal or an ionic compound.

The regular arrangement of particles in a crystal is called a **lattice**. X-rays have been used in this way to study the structures of thousands of different solids. An X-ray photo is shown in Figure 6.6. Photos like this give accurate information about the structure of different substances.

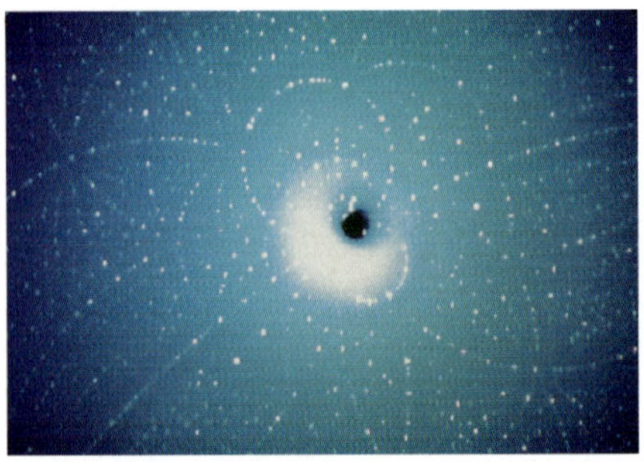

Figure 6.6 An X-ray photo of crystals of a protein found in egg white. Notice the general pattern in the dots.

4. Look at the photo of a snowflake in Figure 6.7.
   a) What substance makes up snowflakes?
   b) What are the particles in snowflakes?
   c) What is (are) the angle(s) between branches on the snowflake?
   d) How do you think the particles are arranged in snowflake crystals?

Figure 6.7 Crystals of a snowflake

5. Explain the following words:
   a) crystal;
   b) lattice.
6. Why do all crystals of one substance have roughly the same shape?

6.2 From structure to properties and uses

If we know how the particles in a substance are arranged (the structure) and how they are held together (the bonding), we can explain the properties of the substance.

For example, copper is composed of close-packed atoms with freely moving outer electrons. These electrons move through the structure when copper is connected to a battery, so it is a good conductor of electricity. Atoms in the close-packed structure of copper can slide over each other and because of this copper can be drawn into wires. These properties of copper lead to its use in electrical wires and cables.

Notice how:
- the structure and bonding of a substance determine its properties;
- the properties of a substance determine its uses.

Figure 6.8 Wet clay is soft and easily moulded by the potter. After she has moulded the clay, it is heated (fired) in a furnace. This makes it hard and rigid and it can be used for pots and crockery.

7 Use the words given below to complete the sentences.

bond hard molecules moulded three two water

Wet clay is soft and easily _____ because _____ molecules can get between its flat _____-dimensional particles. When the clay is fired, all the water _____ are driven out. Atoms in one layer _____ to those in the layers above and below. This gives the clay a _____-dimensional structure making it _____ and rigid.

The links from structure and bonding to properties help us to explain the uses of substances and materials. They explain why metals are used as conductors, why graphite is used in pencils and why clay is used to make pots.

From Chapter 5 we know that all substances are made up from only three kinds of particle – atoms, ions and molecules.

These three particles give rise to four different solid structures:
- giant metallic;
- simple molecular;
- giant covalent (macromolecular);
- giant ionic.

Table 6.1 shows the particles in these four structures, the types of substances they form and examples of these substances. In the following sections, we will look at each of these structures in more detail.

Type of structure	Particles in the structure	Types of substance	Examples
Giant metallic	Atoms	Metals and alloys	sodium, iron, copper, steel, brass
Simple molecular	Small molecules containing a few atoms	Non-metals or non-metal compounds	iodine (I_2), oxygen (O_2), water (H_2O), carbon dioxide (CO_2)
Giant covalent (macromolecular)	Very large molecules containing thousands or millions of atoms	Non-metals or non-metal compounds	Diamond, graphite, polythene, sand (silicon dioxide, SiO_2)
Giant ionic	Ions	Compounds of metals with non-metals	sodium chloride (salt, Na^+Cl^-), calcium oxide (quicklime, $Ca^{2+}O^{2-}$), magnesium chloride ($Mg^{2+}(Cl^-)_2$).

Table 6.1 The four types of solid structures and the particles they contain

8 Match each of the following substances to one of the solid structures in Table 6.1:
a) chlorine (Cl_2);
b) limestone (calcium carbonate, $CaCO_3$);
c) gold (Au);
d) PVC (polyvinylchloride);
e) copper sulfate ($CuSO_4$);
f) methane in natural gas (CH_4).

9 Look at the photo of a lead sulfide crystal in Figure 6.9.

Figure 6.9 A natural crystal of lead sulfide

a) What elements does lead sulfide contain?
b) Is each of these elements a metal or a non-metal?
c) What particles does lead sulfide contain – atoms, ions or molecules?
d) How do you think the particles are arranged in lead sulfide? Explain your answer.

6.3 Giant metallic structures

Metals are very important and useful materials. Just look around you and notice the uses of different metals – vehicles, girders, bridges, pipes, taps, radiators, cutlery, pans, jewellery and ornaments.

X-ray studies show that the atoms in most metals are packed together as close as possible. This arrangement is called close packing, which you probably met in your study of alloys.

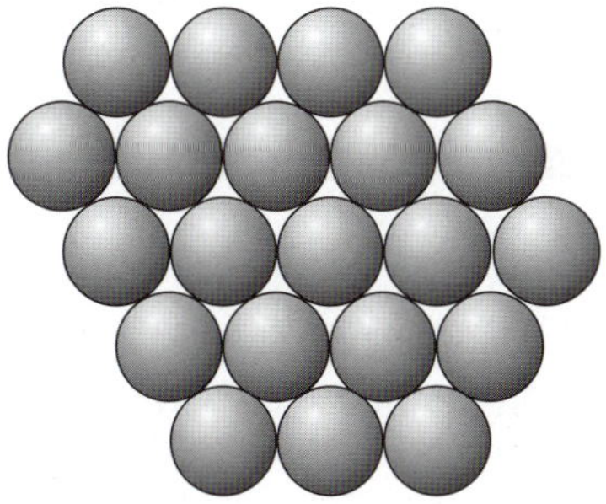

Figure 6.10 The close packing of atoms in one layer of a metal

Figure 6.10 shows a model of a few atoms in one layer of a metal crystal.

Notice that each atom in the middle of the layer 'touches' six other atoms in the same layer. When a second layer is placed on top of the first, atoms in the second layer sink into the dips between atoms in the first layer (Figure 6.11).

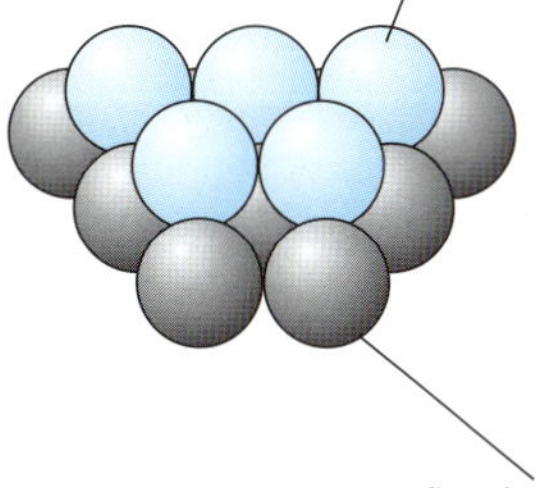

Figure 6.11 Atoms in two layers of a metal crystal

This close packing allows atoms in one layer to get as close as possible to those in the next layer. So, metals consist of **giant metallic structures** of closely packed atoms in a regular pattern. In this giant lattice structure, electrons in the outer shell of each metal atom are free to move through the whole structure. These electrons are described as 'delocalised'. The metal consists of a structure of positive ions with negative electrons moving around and between them (Figure 6.12). The electrostatic attractions between the 'sea' of delocalised electrons and the positive ions result in strong forces between the metal atoms.

In **giant metallic structures**, metal atoms are close-packed in a giant lattice through which the outer shell electrons can move freely.

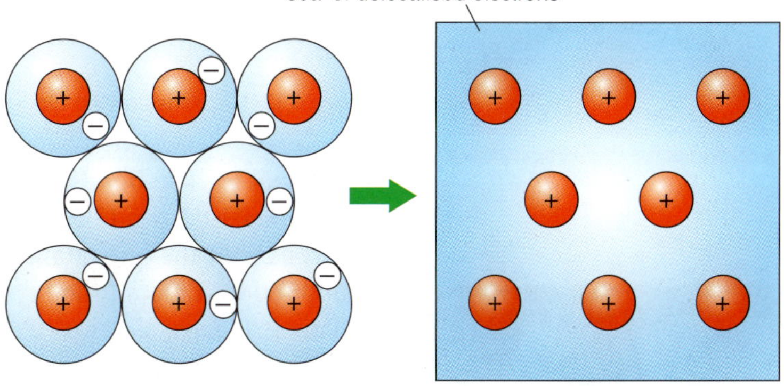

Figure 6.12 The attractions between negative delocalised electrons and positive ions result in strong forces between metal atoms.

In general, metals:
- have high densities,
- have high melting points and high boiling points,
- are good conductors of heat and electricity,
- are malleable (can be bent or hammered into different shapes).

The properties of metals

All the properties of metals can be explained by their close-packed structure.

- High density. The close packing means that all the atoms get as close as possible to atoms in their own layer and to atoms in the layers above and below them, resulting in a high density.
- High melting points and high boiling points. The atoms are closely packed with strong forces between delocalised electrons and positive ions. So, it takes a lot of energy to separate the particles and change state.
- Good conductors of heat. When a metal is heated, energy is transferred to the electrons. The delocalised electrons move around faster and conduct the heat (energy) rapidly to other parts of the metal.
- Good conductors of electricity. When a metal is connected in a circuit, the delocalised electrons move towards the positive terminal (Figure 6.13). This flow of electrons through the metal forms an electric current.

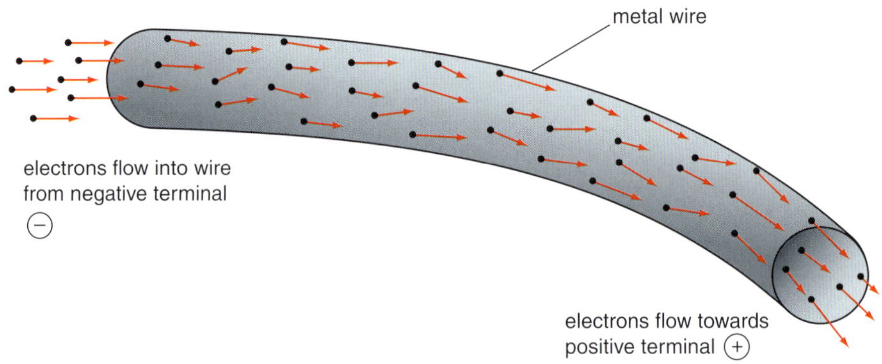

Figure 6.13 Electrons flowing along a metal wire form an electric current.

- Malleable. The bonds between metal atoms are strong but they are not fixed and rigid because the delocalised electrons are shared throughout the lattice and attract all the positive ions. When a force is applied to a metal, the layers of atoms can 'slide' over each other. This is known as 'slip'. After slipping, the atoms settle into close-packed positions again. Figure 6.15 shows the positions of atoms before and after slip. This is what happens when a metal is bent or hammered into different shapes.

Figure 6.14 Blacksmiths rely on the malleability of metals to hammer and bend them into useful shapes.

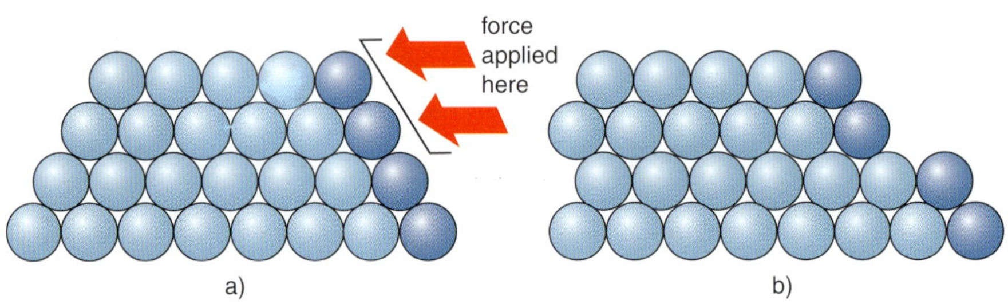

Figure 6.15 The positions of atoms in a metal a) before and b) after 'slip' has occurred

Figure 6.16 Steel was used to make suits of armour in the Middle Ages.

⑩ Why are the electrons in the outermost shell of metal atoms described as 'delocalised'?

⑪ Explain in terms of atoms why blacksmiths usually get metals red hot before hammering them into the shapes they want.

⑫ Which of the following statements provide evidence for classifying copper as a metal? Copper:
A burns to form an oxide.
B reacts with non-metals.
C reacts only with non-metals.
D is non-magnetic.
E conducts electricity.
F has two common isotopes.

⑬ Look at the suit of armour in Figure 6.16.
a) What particles make up the structure of steel in the armour?
b) How are these particles arranged in steel?
c) What properties of steel are important for its use in the armour?
d) Explain, in terms of particles, why steel has one of the properties you gave in answer to part c).

Activity – Choosing metals for different uses

Various properties of five metals are shown in Table 6.2.

Metal	Density in g/cm³	Relative strength compared with iron	Melting point in °C	Relative electrical conductivity compared with iron	Relative thermal conductivity compared with iron	Rate of corrosion	Cost per tonne in £
Aluminium	2.7	0.33	660	3.7	3.0	Very slow	950
Copper	8.9	0.62	1083	5.8	4.8	Very slow	1100
Iron	7.9	1.00	1535	1.0	1.0	Quick	130
Silver	10.5	0.39	962	6.1	5.2	Very slight	250 000
Zinc	7.1	0.51	420	1.6	1.4	Very slow	730

Table 6.2 The properties of five commonly used metals

❶ Use the information in Table 6.2 to explain the following statements.
a) The frames and poles of tents are made from aluminium.
b) Electrical cables in the National Grid are made of aluminium although copper is a better conductor.
c) Bridges are built from steel which is mainly iron, even though it corrodes (rusts) faster than the other metals.
d) Metal gates and dustbins are made from iron coated (galvanised) with zinc.

e) Silver is no longer used to make our coins.
f) High-quality saucepans have copper bottoms rather than steel (iron).

2 a) What is the range in values for i) densities, ii) melting points in Table 6.2?
b) Do you think any of the values for density or melting point are anomalous (unusual or irregular)? Explain your answer.

3 Luke and Kathy were working together on a metals project. Luke said, 'If the atoms in a metal pack closer, the density should be higher, the bonds between atoms should be stronger and so the melting point should be higher.' Kathy agreed with Luke and predicted that there could be a pattern (relationship) between the densities and melting points of metals.
a) Use the data in Table 6.2 to plot a graph of density against melting point for the five metals.
b) Is there a pattern or relationship between the densities and melting points of the metals in Table 6.2? State 'Yes' or 'No' and explain your answer.

4 The explanation of both electrical and thermal conductivity in metals relies on the idea of delocalised electrons. This suggests that there should be a pattern (relationship) between electrical and thermal conductivities for metals. Use the relative electrical and thermal conductivities in Table 6.2 to check whether there is a pattern.
a) Describe briefly what you did to investigate whether there is a pattern.
b) Is there a pattern? State 'Yes' or 'No' and explain your answer.

6.4 Simple molecular substances

Simple molecular substances are small molecules with just a few atoms, compared to polymers or giant molecules.

Intermolecular forces are weak forces between one molecule and another.

Most non-metals and compounds of non-metals are **simple molecular substances**. Oxygen, hydrogen, chlorine, water, hydrogen chloride and methane are good examples of simple molecular substances. They have simple molecules containing a few atoms. Their formulae and structures are shown in Figure 6.17. Sugar ($C_{12}H_{22}O_{11}$) has much larger molecules than the substances in Figure 6.17, but it still counts as a simple molecule.

In these simple molecular substances, the atoms are held together in each molecule by strong covalent bonds (Figure 6.18). But there are only weak forces between the separate molecules (Figure 6.19). These weak forces between the separate molecules are called **intermolecular forces** ('inter' means between).

The properties of simple molecular substances

The properties of simple molecular substances can be explained in terms of their simple structures and the weak forces between their molecules. In simple molecular substances, there are no ions (like ionic compounds) or delocalised electrons (as in metals). These substances consist of simple molecules with no overall charge. So, there are no obvious electrical forces holding the molecules together. However, some simple molecular substances, such as sugar, water and iodine, do exist as solids and liquids, so there must be some forces holding their molecules together.

Name and formula	Structural formula	Model of structure
Hydrogen, H_2	H—H	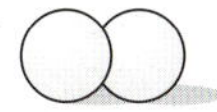
Oxygen, O_2	O=O	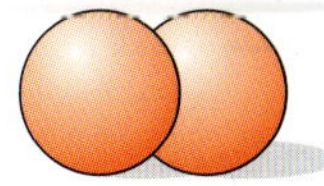
Water, H_2O	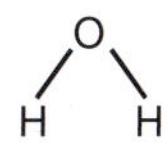	
Methane, CH_4	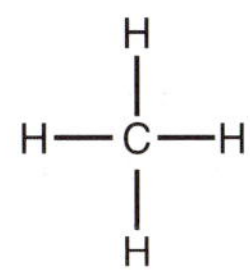	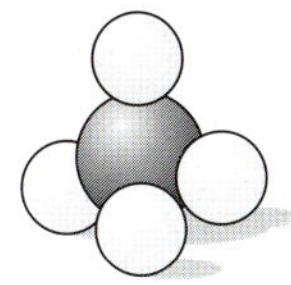
Hydrogen chloride, HCl	H—Cl	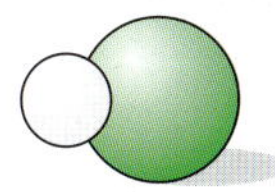
Chlorine, Cl_2	Cl—Cl	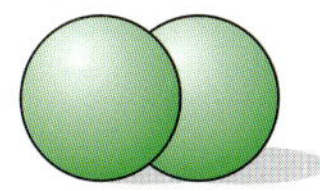
Carbon dioxide, CO_2	O=C=O	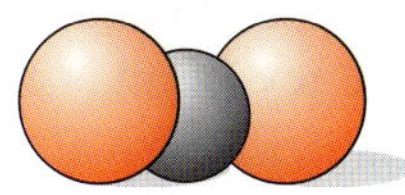
Iodine, I_2	I—I	

Figure 6.17 The formulae and structures of some simple molecular substances

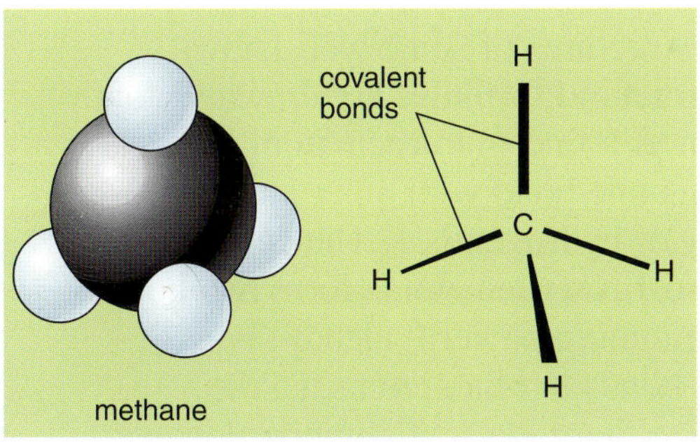

Figure 6.18 Methane (CH_4) is a simple molecular substance. In methane, the carbon atom and four hydrogen atoms are held together by strong covalent bonds.

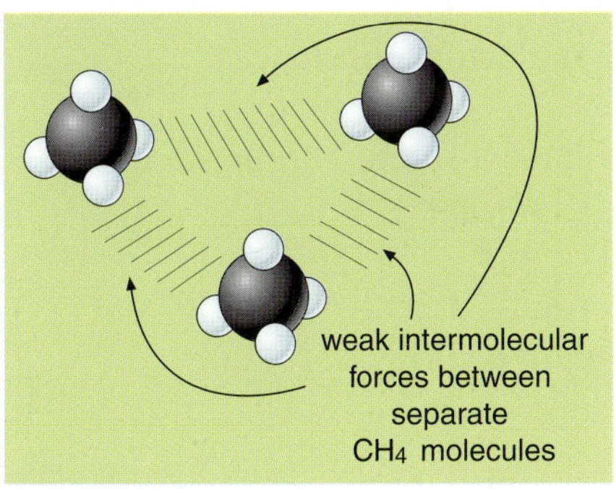

Figure 6.19 Intermolecular forces between molecules of methane

- Low melting points and low boiling points. There are only weak forces between the molecules in simple molecular substances. These weak intermolecular forces are overcome when simple molecular substances melt or boil on heating. It takes much less energy to separate the simple molecules than to separate the oppositely charged ions in ionic compounds or the atoms in metals.
- Soft. The separate molecules in simple molecular substances are usually further apart than atoms in metals and ions in ionic structures. The forces between the molecules are weak and the molecules are easy to separate. Because of this, simple molecular solids, such as iodine and sugar, are softer than other materials.
- Non-conductors of electricity. Simple molecules have no overall electric charge. They have no mobile (delocalised) electrons like metals and no ions like ionic compounds. This means they cannot conduct electricity.

Figure 6.20 This butcher is using 'dry ice' (solid carbon dioxide) to keep meat cool during mincing. 'Dry ice' is a simple molecular substance. After mincing, the 'dry ice' sublimes (changing directly from solid to gas) without spoiling the meat.

The formulae of molecular compounds

The **combining power** or **valency** of an atom is the number of covalent bonds that it forms with other atoms.

Figure 6.17 shows the formulae and structures of some well-known simple molecular compounds. The structural formulae are drawn so that the number of covalent bonds (drawn as a line –) to each atom are clear. Notice that each hydrogen atom forms one bond with other atoms (H –). So, the **combining power** or **valency** of hydrogen is 1. The combining powers of chlorine and iodine are also 1. Oxygen atoms form two bonds to other atoms (– O – or O=). Its combining power (valency) is therefore 2. Carbon atoms form four bonds to other atoms, so the combining power of carbon is 4. Using these ideas of combining power (the number of bonds which the atoms form), we can predict the formulae of most (but not all) molecular compounds.

Figure 6.21 Butter contains a mixture of simple molecular substances.

14 Look at the photo in Figure 6.21. What properties does butter have which show that it contains simple molecular substances?

15 Simple molecular substances often have a smell, but metals never have a smell. Why is this?

16 Solid X is a poor conductor of electricity. It melts at 150°C and boils at 350°C. Which of the following could X be?
A a metal
B a non-metal
C a compound of a metal with a non-metal
D a compound of non-metals
E an ionic compound
F a simple molecular compound

17 Assuming the usual combining power (valency) of the elements, draw structural formulae for the following compounds (show each bond as a line –):
a) dichlorine oxide (Cl_2O);
b) tetrachloromethane (CCl_4);
c) hydrogen peroxide (H_2O_2);
d) ethane (C_2H_6).

6.5 Giant covalent structures

Giant covalent structures contain very large numbers of atoms joined to each other by strong covalent bonds.

Atoms that share electrons in covalent bonds can also form **giant covalent structures** or macromolecules. One important group of compounds with giant covalent structures are polymers, such as polythene and polyvinylchloride (PVC). Polythene and PVC consist of long, thin molecules made by addition reactions between smaller monomer molecules. The polymers consist of hundreds and often thousands of atoms joined by strong covalent bonds.

Figure 6.22 This artist is using a soft graphite pencil.

Diamond, graphite and silicon dioxide are other examples of giant covalent structures, but these form three-dimensional lattices with billions of atoms.

Diamond and graphite are both made of pure carbon, but the two solids have very different properties and uses. Diamond is hard and clear, whereas graphite is soft and black. Diamonds are used to cut stone and engrave glass whereas graphite is used by artists to achieve a soft, shaded effect for their sketches.

Diamond and graphite have different properties and different uses because they have different structures. They both contain carbon, but the carbon atoms are packed in different ways. The arrangements of carbon atoms in diamond and graphite have been studied by X-ray analysis.

Diamond

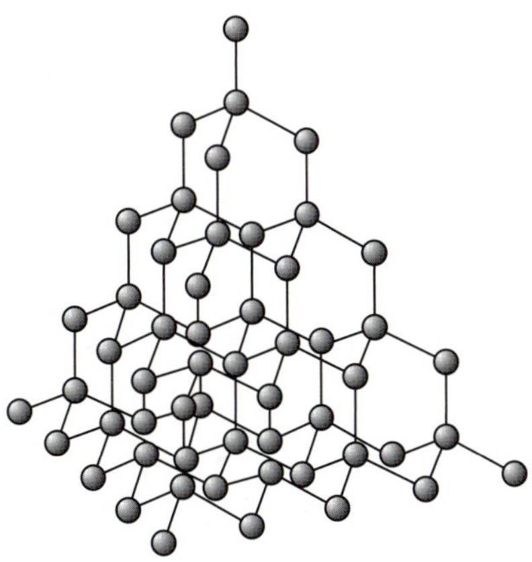

Figure 6.23 An 'open' model of the giant structure in diamond. Each black ball represents a carbon atom and each stick is a covalent bond.

In diamond, carbon atoms are joined to each other by strong covalent bonds. Inside the diamond structure (Figure 6.23), each carbon atom forms covalent bonds with four other carbon atoms. Check this for yourself in Figure 6.23. The strong covalent bonds extend through the whole diamond, forming a giant three-dimensional structure. A perfect diamond, without flaws or cracks, is a single giant molecule (macromolecule) with covalent bonds linking one carbon atom to the next.

Only a small number of atoms are shown in the model in Figure 6.23. In a real diamond, this arrangement of carbon atoms is extended billions and billions of times.

The properties and uses of diamond

- Hard. It is difficult to break the strong covalent bonds between carbon atoms in diamond. Another reason for diamond's hardness is that the atoms are not arranged in layers. So they cannot slide over one another like the atoms in metals. Most industrial uses of diamond depend on its hardness. Diamonds which are not good enough for jewellery are used in glass cutters, in diamond-studded saws and as abrasives for smoothing very hard materials.
- Very high melting point. Carbon atoms in diamond are linked together in the giant structure by very strong covalent bonds. This means that the atoms cannot vibrate fast enough to break away from their neighbours until the temperature is about 3800 °C.
- Non-conductor of electricity. Unlike metals, diamond has no free electrons. All the electrons in the outer shell of each carbon atom are held firmly in covalent bonds. There are no free electrons in diamond to form an electric current.

Graphite

Figure 6.24 shows a model of part of the structure of graphite. Notice that the carbon atoms are arranged in layers. Each layer contains billions and billions of carbon atoms arranged in hexagons. Each carbon atom is held in its layer by strong covalent bonds to three other carbon atoms. So, every layer is a giant covalent structure. The distance between carbon atoms in the same layer is only 0.14 nm, but the distance between the layers is 0.34 nm – more than twice as great.

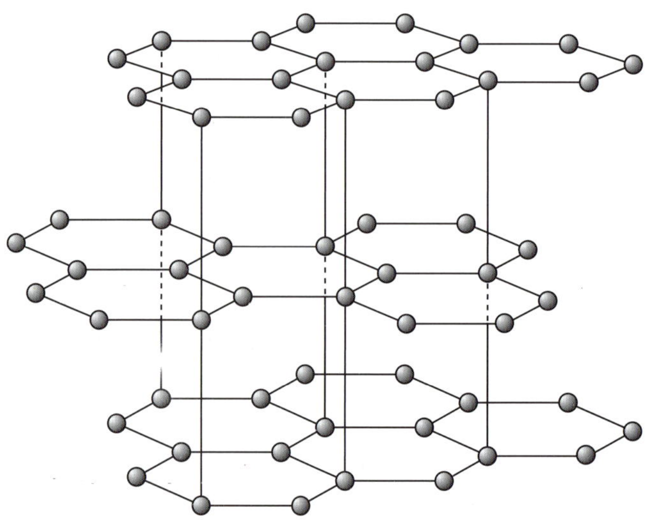

Figure 6.24 A model of the structure of graphite. Notice how graphite has layers of carbon atoms. Within the layers, the carbon atoms are arranged in hexagons

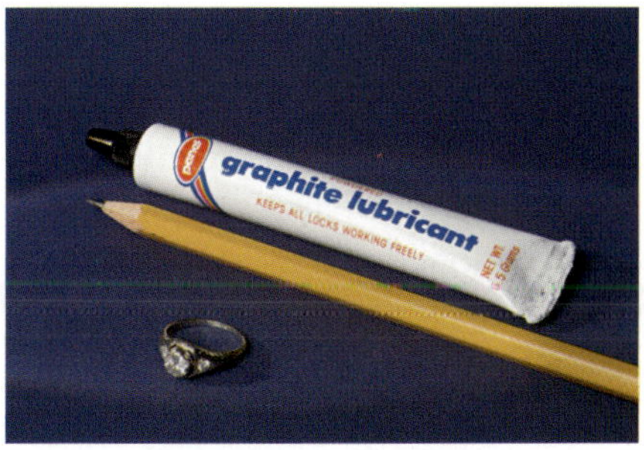

Figure 6.25 A tube of lubricating oil containing graphite. The layers in graphite slide over one another very easily. This makes graphite an excellent material to improve the lubricating action of oils.

Figure 6.26 Graphite fibres are used to reinforce the shafts of badminton rackets, golf clubs and even broken bones. The strong bonds between carbon atoms in layers of graphite mean that graphite fibres can be very strong.

The properties and uses of graphite

- Soft and slippery. In graphite, each carbon atom is linked by strong covalent bonds to three other atoms in its own layer. But, the layers are more than twice as far apart as carbon atoms in the same layer. This means that the forces between the layers are weak. If you rub graphite, it feels soft and slippery as the layers slide over each other and onto your fingers. This property has led to the use of graphite as the 'lead' in pencils and as a lubricant in engine oils.
- High melting point. Although the layers of graphite move over each other easily, it is difficult to break the strong covalent bonds between carbon atoms within one layer. Because of this, graphite does not melt until 3730 °C and it is used to make crucibles for hot molten metals.
- Conducts electricity and heat. Carbon atoms have four outer-shell electrons. In graphite, three of these electrons form covalent bonds with electrons from three other carbon atoms in the same layer. This leaves one unshared electron on each carbon atom. These unshared electrons are delocalised over the atoms in their layer. So, they allow graphite to conduct electricity and heat in a similar way to metals. Because of this property, graphite is used for electrodes in industry and as the positive terminal in dry cells.

18 a) Why is diamond called a 'giant molecule'?
b) Diamond is sometimes described as a three-dimensional giant structure and graphite as a two-dimensional giant structure. Why is this?

19 The largest natural diamond is the Cullinan diamond. This weighs about 600 g.
a) How many moles of carbon does it contain? (C = 12)
b) How many atoms of carbon does it contain? (1 mole of carbon is 6×10^{23} atoms.)

20 a) Make a table to show at least three similarities and three differences between diamond and graphite.
b) Why do diamond and graphite have some differences?

21 a) Why will a zip-fastener move more freely after being rubbed with a soft pencil?
b) Why is pencil a better alternative to oil?

22 Why is graphite better than oil for lubricating the moving parts of hot machinery?

6.6 Nanomaterials

Nanoparticles are manufactured particles with sizes measured in nanometres (nm).

Nanomaterials and nanotechnology belong to the twenty-first century. Very few people had heard of these terms before the year 2000. Since then, a wide range of materials have been developed and used in the form of **nanoparticles** between 1 and 100 nanometres (nm) in size. That's between one millionth and one ten thousandth of a millimetre in size.

Nanoparticles are groups of just a few hundred atoms. They include metals, carbon, plastics and polymers. Nanoparticles show different properties from the same material in bulk (large pieces) because of the precise way in which the atoms in them are arranged and because of their high surface area-to-volume ratio.

Figure 6.27 These polymer nanoparticles have been designed to carry drug molecules into the body. Just 100 nm to 500 nm across, they can pass across vein walls, and so the drug can be released into tissues in exactly the part of the body that needs treating.

Nanotechnology is already being used to manufacture products that take advantage of the ability to make layers of material just a few atoms thick or particles with a very large surface area per unit mass. Here are some of the current applications:

- One of the biggest developments for nanotechnology is in stain-resistant clothing. Fabrics can be coated with nano-sized polymer particles. Any liquid spilt on the fabric turns into 'beads' and rolls off without staining the fabric.
- Ultra-thin, yet extremely strong coatings of scratch-resistant polymers are now being used on lenses for spectacles, cameras and contact lenses. The coatings are so thin that the polymer material is transparent.
- New solar cells have been developed with nano-sized metal crystals on their surface. These have a vast surface area on which to collect the Sun's energy more efficiently.
- Ordinary tennis rackets are weakened by tiny gaps between the carbon fibres in their structure. These tiny gaps can be plugged and reinforced with nano-sized crystals of silicon dioxide.

- Nanoparticles have also led to important developments in catalysts because of their large surface area compared with bulk materials. These developments include the use of gold particles to oxidise poisonous carbon monoxide to carbon dioxide. The gold particles are totally inactive until they are less than about 8 nm in diameter. Their high surface area means you only need a tiny amount of gold – which is cheaper!

Future nanotechnology applications could include:

- smaller and more sensitive sensors in electronic devices and potentially smaller and faster computers and disc drives with layers of magnetic nanoparticles to increase data storage capacity;
- lighter yet stronger construction materials made from composite materials containing nanotubes. Carbon nanotubes are 10 times lighter than steel but 250 times stronger;
- 'smart' clothing with nano-sized sensors to measure pulse rate and temperature.

The future

Although nanomaterials open up exciting possibilities for new materials, there are concerns about the effects of nanomaterials when they get into the human body. Nanoparticles could be more reactive and so more toxic than larger masses of the same material. Although most areas of nanotechnology pose no risks, scientists agree that more research of the health risks of nanomaterials is urgent. They also suggest:

- Nanoparticles should be treated as 'new chemicals'.
- An independent scientific safety committee should approve new substances at the nano-scale before they are used in consumer products.
- Nanoparticles that have direct contact with our bodies such as those in some cosmetic and sunscreen creams are the most likely to cause long-term damage.
- There needs to be workplace regulations to protect workers in industry who are exposed to nanoparticles.

Activity – Nanomaterials and the future

1. Explain what is meant by nanoscience in no more than 25 words.
2. Scientific and technological developments offer different opportunities to different groups of people. Which groups of people stand to benefit most from the development of nanomaterials?
3. Describe three benefits to society from the development of nanomaterials.
4. Describe two potential risks from their development.
5. Should scientists or society make decisions about the development of nanomaterials?

If you would like more information on these issues, go to www.news.bbc.co.uk and search on 'nanomaterials' and 'nanotechnology'.

6.7 Giant ionic structures

> **Giant ionic lattices** form a regular structure of oppositely charged ions.

Ionic compounds are formed when metals react with non-metals. During these reactions, electrons are transferred from the metal to the non-metal forming positive metal ions and negative non-metal ions (see Section 5.6). For example, when calcium reacts with oxygen to form calcium oxide, two electrons are transferred from each calcium atom to each oxygen atom.

Ca	+	O	→	Ca^{2+}	O^{2-}
calcium atom		oxygen atom		calcium ion	oxide ion
				calcium oxide	

Ca	$\rightarrow Ca^{2+} + 2e^-$	Each Ca atom loses two electrons
$O + 2e^-$	$\rightarrow O^{2-}$	Each O atom gains two electrons

The structure and properties of ionic compounds

In ionic compounds, large numbers of positive and negative ions are packed together in a regular pattern. These **giant ionic lattices** containing billions of ions are further examples of giant structures.

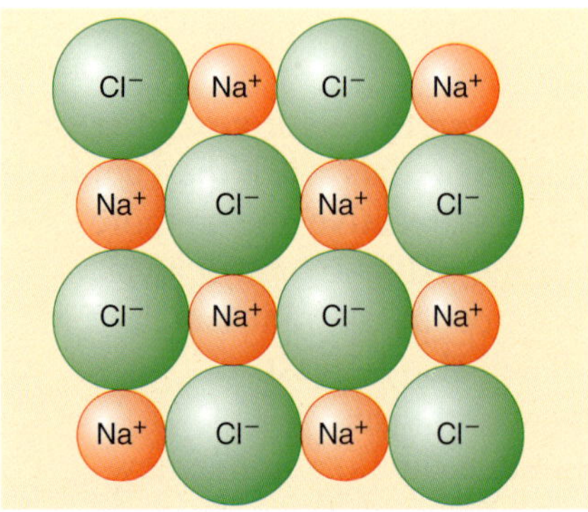

Figure 6.28 The arrangement of ions in one layer of a sodium chloride (salt) crystal

Figure 6.28 shows how the ions are arranged in one layer of sodium chloride (NaCl) and Figure 6.29 is a three-dimensional model of its structure. Notice that Na^+ ions are surrounded by Cl^- ions and that Cl^- ions are surrounded by Na^+ ions. This means that there are strong electrostatic forces in all directions in the lattice between oppositely charged ions. These forces of attraction between the oppositely charged ions are called ionic bonds (see Section 5.6).

Figure 6.29 A three-dimensional model of the structure of sodium chloride. The larger green balls represent Cl^- ions (A_r (Cl) = 35.5). The smaller red balls represent Na^+ ions (A_r (Na) = 23.0).

Strong ionic bonds hold the ions firmly together in ionic compounds. This explains why ionic compounds:

- are hard substances;
- have high melting points and high boiling points;
- do not conduct electricity when solid, because their ions cannot move away from fixed positions in the giant structure;
- conduct electricity when they are melted or dissolved in water because the charged ions are then free to move. Positive ions move towards the negative terminal and negative ions move towards the positive terminal and they carry the current through the liquid. The conduction of electricity by ionic compounds is discussed in more detail in Chapter 8.

The formulae of ionic compounds

The formulae of ionic compounds can be obtained by balancing the charges on positive and negative ions. For example, the formula of calcium chloride is $Ca^{2+}(Cl^-)_2$, or simply $CaCl_2$. Here, the two positive charges on one calcium ion (Ca^{2+}) are balanced by the single negative charges on two chloride ions (Cl^-).

Name of salt	Formula
Calcium nitrate	$Ca^{2+}(NO_3^-)_2$ or $Ca(NO_3)_2$
Zinc sulfate	$Zn^{2+}SO_4^{2-}$ or $ZnSO_4$
Magnesium carbonate	$Mg^{2+}CO_3^{2-}$ or $MgCO_3$
Potassium iodide	K^+I^- or KI
Iron(III) chloride	$Fe^{3+}(Cl^-)_3$ or $FeCl_3$
Copper(II) bromide	$Cu^{2+}(Br^-)_2$ or $CuBr_2$

Table 6.3 The names and formulae of some salts

The number of charges on an ion is a measure of its combining power or valency (Section 6.4). Na^+ has a combining power of 1, whereas Ca^{2+} has a combining power of 2. Na^+ can combine with only one Cl^- to form Na^+Cl^-, whereas Ca^{2+} can combine with two Cl^- ions to form $Ca^{2+}(Cl^-)_2$.

Elements such as iron, which have two different ions (Fe^{2+} and Fe^{3+}), have two valencies. So, iron can form two different compounds with chlorine – iron(II) chloride, $FeCl_2$, and iron(III) chloride, $FeCl_3$.

Table 6.3 shows the names and formulae of some other salts. Notice that the formula of calcium nitrate is $Ca(NO_3)_2$. The brackets around NO_3^- show that it is a single unit containing one nitrogen and three oxygen atoms with one negative charge. Thus, two NO_3^- ions balance one Ca^{2+} ion. Other ions, such as SO_4^{2-}, CO_3^{2-} and OH^-, should also be put in brackets when there are two or more of them in a formula.

23 Which of the following substances conduct electricity:
- a) when liquid;
- b) when solid?
  - i) diamond
  - ii) potassium chloride
  - iii) copper
  - iv) sulfur

24 Look carefully at Figures 6.28 and 6.29.
- a) How many Cl^- ions surround one Na^+ ion in one layer of the NaCl crystal?
- b) How many Cl^- ions surround one Na^+ ion in the three-dimensional crystal?
- c) How many Na^+ ions surround one Cl^- ion in the three-dimensional crystal?

25 Use the symbols and the charges on ions given in Section 6.7 and Table 6.3 to write formulae for the following compounds:
- a) iron(II) nitrate;
- b) sodium carbonate;
- c) iron(III) oxide;
- d) zinc chloride;
- e) magnesium sulfate;
- f) copper(I) bromide.

26 Sodium fluoride (NaF) and magnesium oxide (MgO) have the same crystal structure and similar distances between ions. The melting point of NaF is 992 °C but that of MgO is 2640 °C.
- a) Write the formula for sodium fluoride showing charges on the ions.
- b) Write the formula for magnesium oxide showing charges on the ions.
- c) Why is there such a big difference in the melting points of NaF and MgO?

Activity – Using models in science

Models are very important in science. They help us to think about the way substances behave and how things work. They also help us to test new ideas (hypotheses) and make predictions. The kinetic theory is a model that helps us to understand how the particles in solids, liquids and gases move and interact. Sometimes the models that scientists use are complex computer programs like those that help weather forecasters. In this chapter, we have been using models of the structures of different substances to help us understand their properties and uses.

Atomic models for giant metallic structures

You will need about 25 marbles or 25 polystyrene spheres for this activity. The marbles or polystyrene spheres represent atoms. Put three books flat on a bench so that they form a triangle around 10 atoms. Move the books carefully so that they enclose a layer of close-packed atoms like those in Figure 6.11.

Now add another layer of atoms on top of the first one. Then put further layers on top of this.

Look carefully at your structure, which represents a very good model for most metals.

1. How many atoms does an atom in the middle of the structure touch?
2. Why is this called a close-packed structure?
3. Why is this a giant structure?
4. How does this model help us to understand metals?

The structure that you have built for metals is sometimes described as a space-filling model because it shows all the space occupied by metal atoms.

Earlier in this chapter, we also used space-filling models to represent the structures of simple molecular substances in Figure 6.17.

These simple molecular substances can also be studied by using ball and stick models like that in Figure 6.23. Ball and stick models are useful because the 'sticks' show the bonds which hold the atoms together.

Building a ball and stick model for silicon dioxide

Silicon dioxide (silica, SiO_2) has a giant covalent structure (Figure 6.30). It can occur as large, beautiful crystals of quartz (Figure 6.3) or more often as impure gritty bits of sand.

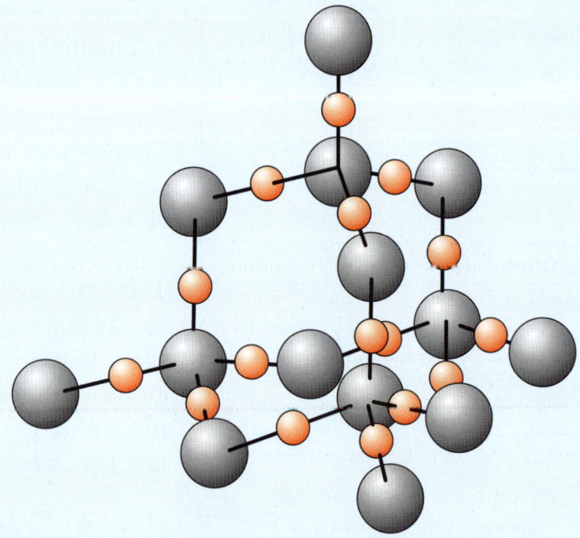

Figure 6.30 A ball and stick model of silicon dioxide, SiO_2

5. Use a ball and stick model kit to build a structure of silicon dioxide like that in Figure 6.30. Use black balls (normally carbon atoms) from the kit to represent silicon atoms and red balls to represent oxygen atoms.
   a) How many covalent bonds are formed by silicon atoms in the middle of your structure?
   b) How many covalent bonds are formed by oxygen atoms in your structure?
6. Explain why silicon dioxide:
   a) is hard;
   b) has a very high melting point;
   c) does not conduct electricity.

Silicon is the second most common element in the Earth's crust. Most rocks including sandstones and clays contain silicon, and the structures of these silicate rocks are based on that of silicon dioxide.

7. Why are models important in science?

Although models are usually helpful, it is important to remember that they are not real representations. For example, metal atoms are not really like marbles or polystyrene spheres and silicon dioxide doesn't have tiny balls and sticks.

Summary

- ✓ The structures of materials can be studied using X-rays.
- ✓ The regular arrangement of particles in a crystal is called a **lattice**.
- ✓ The structure and bonding of a substance determine its properties and these properties determine its uses.
- ✓ All substances are made up from only three kinds of particle – atoms, ions and molecules.
- ✓ These three particles result in four different types of solid structures – **giant metallic, giant ionic, giant covalent** and **simple molecular**.
- ✓ **Simple molecular substances** are small molecules with just a few atoms, compared with polymers or giant molecules.
- ✓ **Intermolecular forces** are weak forces between one molecule and another.
- ✓ The **combining power** or **valency** of an atom is the number of covalent bonds that it forms with other atoms.
- ✓ **Nanoparticles** are manufactured particles with sizes measured in nanometres (nm).
- ✓ The atoms in most metals are packed together as close as possible. This arrangement is called close packing.
- ✓ A **giant structure** is an arrangement of very large numbers (billions and billions) of atoms or ions held together by strong forces in a regular pattern.
- ✓ The particles, bonding, structure and properties of the four different solid structures are shown in Figure 6.31.

Type of structure	Particles in the structure	Type of substance	Structure	Bonding	Properties
Giant metallic	Atoms close-packed	Metals e.g. Na, Fe, Cu and alloys such as steel	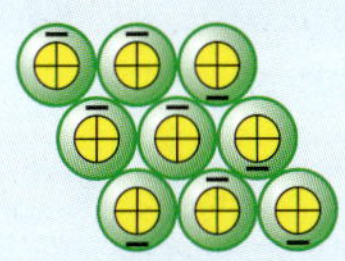	Atoms are held in a close packed giant structure by the attraction of positive ions for delocalised electrons.	• High melting points and boiling points • Conduct electricity • High density • Hard but malleable
Giant covalent (macro-molecular)	Very large molecules containing thousands or billions of atoms (giant molecules	A few non-metals (e.g. diamond, graphite) and some non-metal compounds (e.g. polythene, PVC, silicon dioxide (sand))	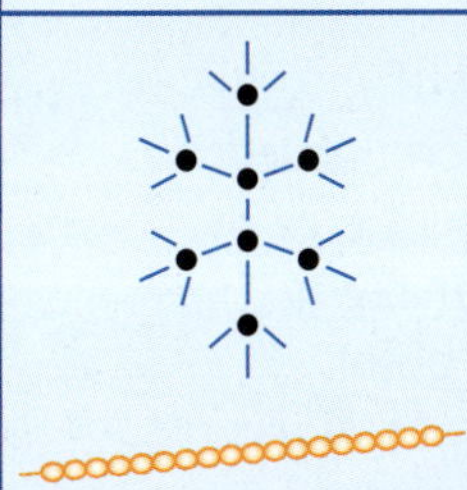	Large numbers of atoms are joined together by strong covalent bonds to give a giant 3D lattice or a very long, thin molecule.	• High melting points and boiling points • Do not conduct electricity (except graphite) • Hard but brittle (3D networks) or flexible polymers
Simple molecular	Small molecules containing a few atoms	Most non-metals and non-metal compounds e.g. O_2, I_2, H_2O, CO_2, sugar	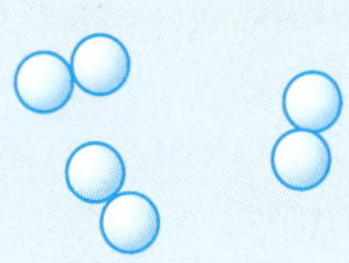	Atoms are held together in small molecules by strong covalent bonds. The bonds between molecules are weak.	• Low melting points and boiling points • Do not conduct electricity • Soft when solid
Giant ionic	ions	Metal / non-metal compounds e.g. Na^+Cl^-, $Ca^{2+}O^{2-}$, $Mg^{2+}(Cl^-)_2$	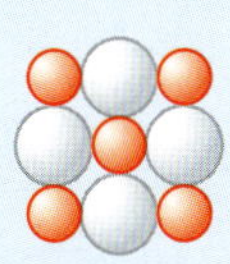	Positive and negative ions are held together by the attraction between their opposite charges – ionic bonds.	• High melting points and boiling points • Conduct electricity when melted or dissolved in water • Hard but brittle

Figure 6.31 The particles, structure, bonding and properties of the four different solid structures

EXAMQUESTIONS

1 Table 6.4 shows some properties of diamond and graphite.

Diamond	Graphite
Colourless crystals	Shiny black solid
Hardest natural substance	Soft and slippery
Does not conduct electricity	Conducts electricity

Table 6.4

a) Why would you expect diamond and graphite to have the same properties? *(1 mark)*
b) Why do diamond and graphite have different properties? *(1 mark)*
c) Explain why graphite is soft and slippery. *(2 marks)*
d) Explain why diamond does not conduct electricity. *(2 marks)*
e) Explain why graphite conducts electricity. *(3 marks)*

2 This question is about aluminium oxide and how it is formed from atoms of aluminium and oxygen.

a) Copy and complete the following sentences by choosing the most suitable words from the box below to fill in the blank spaces.

atoms covalent giant hard high
ionic ions low simple soft

Aluminium oxide is a substance with _____ bonding. It has a _____ structure composed of _____. Strong forces between particles in the structure of aluminium oxide make it very _____ with a _____ melting point. *(5 marks)*

b) The electron structure in an aluminium atom is 2, 8, 3 and the electron structure in an oxygen atom is 2, 6. Describe the changes in electron structure of the aluminium atoms and the oxygen atoms when aluminium oxide forms. *(4 marks)*

c) Explain why the formula of aluminium oxide is Al_2O_3. *(2 marks)*

3 Copy and complete Table 6.5 for methane and sodium chloride. *(5 marks)*

	Methane	Sodium chloride
Formula		NaCl
Particles in the substance	Molecules	
Appearance at room temperature		White solid
Type of bonds	Covalent	
One use		In cooking

Table 6.5

4 Substance Y melts at a high temperature and the liquid which forms conducts electricity.

a) Which of the following could Y be?
calcium chloride starch copper
polythene brass carbon disulfide *(3 marks)*

b) Explain your answers to part a). *(6 marks)*

5 a) Liquid and gaseous carbon dioxide at high pressure are used in fire extinguishers. When the extinguisher is used, carbon dioxide pours out and smothers the fire. Explain why carbon dioxide smothers and puts out fires. *(4 marks)*

b) Solid carbon dioxide is used for refrigerating ice-cream, soft fruit and meat. The solid carbon dioxide is called 'dry ice' or 'Dricold'. Why is 'dry ice' better than ordinary ice for refrigeration? *(2 marks)*

Chapter 7
How do we control the rate of chemical reactions and measure energy transfer?

At the end of this chapter you should:

- ✓ be able to use the state symbols (s), (l), (g) and (aq) in equations;
- ✓ understand why the yield in a chemical change is often not 100%;
- ✓ understand chemical calculations used with atomic mass numbers, including yield and atom economy, concentrations in solution, and reactions involving gas volumes;
- ✓ know that atom economy (atom utilisation) is important for sustainable development;
- ✓ be able to plot graphs of amount of products formed or reactants used over time in a reaction and interpret the graphs in terms of the rate of the reaction;
- ✓ know that the rate of a chemical reaction increases:
  - – if the temperature increases;
  - – if the concentration of dissolved reactants or pressure of gases increases;
  - – if solid reactants are in smaller pieces;
  - – if a catalyst is used;
- ✓ be able to use collision theory to model activation energy and explain how increased energy or increased collision frequency change the rates of reactions;
- ✓ understand the advantages and disadvantages of using catalysts in industrial processes;
- ✓ understand that energy can be transferred both to reactants and from reactants in a chemical change;
- ✓ know about exothermic and endothermic reactions;
- ✓ know that in a reversible reaction the products can react to reform the reactants, so the reaction goes both ways;
- ✓ understand about equilibrium and energy changes in a reversible reaction;
- ✓ be able to model the effects of changing the conditions of temperature and pressure on a given reaction or process;
- ✓ understand how the conditions used in the Haber process to manufacture ammonia are a compromise between yield, rate of reaction and cost;
- ✓ be able to evaluate the conditions used in industrial processes in terms of energy requirements.

Figure 7.1 Cooking involves many chemical changes. When you turn the oven on, some of the energy supplied starts chemical reactions. These chemical reactions change the flavour and texture of food – making potatoes soft and turning meat brown and tender. But if the temperature is too high, the reactions happen too fast and the meat is brown on the outside, and cold and uncooked inside. Being able to control the speed of reactions is important when making new materials in industry too.

7.1 How much useful product do chemists get from chemical changes?

State symbols

It makes equations much clearer if the states of the reactants and products are given. Usually solid, liquid and gas are shown by (s), (l) and (g) after the formula. If you see (aq) it means an aqueous solution was used in the reaction.

Figure 7.2 Ammonium chloride is made when ammonia reacts with hydrogen chloride.

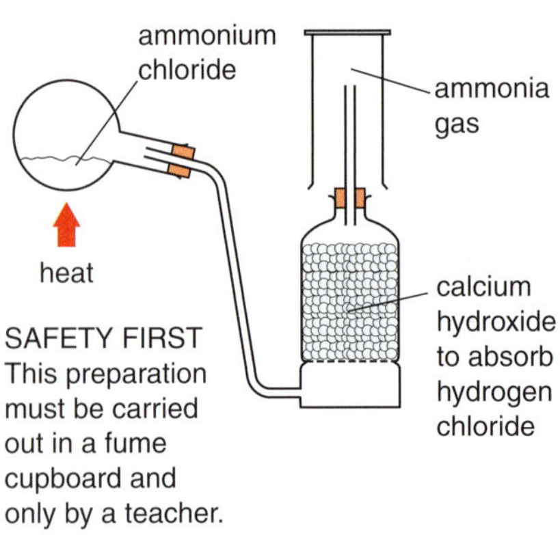

Figure 7.3 The reverse reaction: ammonium chloride decomposes making ammonia gas and hydrogen chloride. This is one way of making ammonia.

Chemical reactions are about change. A very general way of summing up a chemical reaction is shown below:

$$\text{reactants} \xrightarrow[\text{conditions}]{\text{in certain}} \text{products}$$

Chemical changes start with some 'reactants' as raw material and turn these into 'products'. A chemical reaction can make useful new materials such as nylon or ammonia, transfer stored energy such as in a combustion reaction, or it can be a useful process, such as when chlorine bleach makes a stained tea mug white again.

Many chemical reactions are **irreversible** – they do not easily go back to the reactants once the products are formed. For example:

$$\text{magnesium} + \text{oxygen} \rightarrow \text{magnesium oxide}$$
$$2Mg(s) + O_2(g) \rightarrow 2MgO(s)$$

Some chemical reactions go backwards and forwards easily, depending on the conditions. These are **reversible reactions**. An example is the reaction between the colourless gases ammonia and hydrogen chloride. At room temperature a white cloud of solid ammonium chloride forms:

$$\text{ammonia} + \text{hydrogen chloride} \rightarrow \text{ammonium chloride}$$
$$NH_3(g) + HCl(g) \rightarrow NH_4Cl(s)$$

When ammonium chloride is heated even gently, the compound decomposes and you get the ammonia and hydrogen chloride gases back.

$$\text{ammonium chloride} \rightarrow \text{ammonia} + \text{hydrogen chloride}$$
$$NH_4Cl(s) \rightarrow NH_3(g) + HCl(g)$$

Getting as much product as possible is important – the more product made, the greater the profit. Being able to control the speed of reactions is also important in industry, as time is money. If the reaction usually needs a high temperature or pressure, then equipment and fuel costs could be high. Reducing the amount of energy input can save money on fuel costs.

To be an effective scientist and to control chemical changes, you need to consider:

- how much of the reactants is turned into the useful product;
- how to make the change happen at the most cost-effective rate;
- how much energy needs to be transferred during the change.

Some chemical reactions are **reversible reactions**. This means the products can react to produce the original reactants. The equation can be represented by:

$$A + B \rightleftharpoons C + D$$

Many chemical reactions are **irreversible** – the products cannot be turned back into reactants.

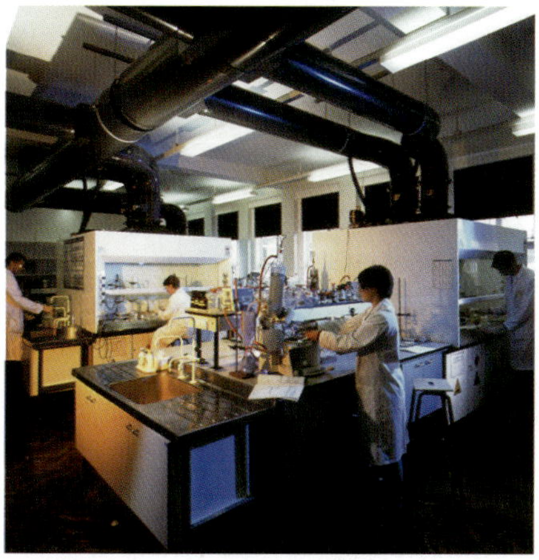

Figure 7.4 Pharmacists need to know exactly how much of a product they are making.

Actual yield is the amount of product obtained.

Theoretical yield is the maximum possible mass of pure product that could be obtained from the reaction.

Percentage yield is the amount in moles obtained of a specified product divided by the maximum amount in moles that could have been obtained if all the reactant had been converted to product. It is always expressed as a percentage.

Yield of a chemical reaction

The amount of product obtained is known as the **actual yield.** For example, the mass of iron formed by reducing iron oxide with carbon monoxide can be calculated from the total mass of reactants if you know the relative formula masses and the equation:

$$Fe_2O_3(s) + 3CO(g) \rightarrow 2Fe(l) + 3CO_2(g)$$

No atoms are gained or lost in a chemical reaction. The equation shows that the number of atoms of iron in the reactant (iron oxide) balances the number of atoms of iron in the product. The **theoretical yield** of a reaction assumes that all the reactants are turned into products and the products are successfully separated from the reaction mixture. However, chemists cannot always obtain the amount of product predicted from the equation and so the **percentage yield** is usually not 100%. Here are some possible reasons:

- The reactants may not be totally pure.
- Some of the product may get lost in the separation process.
- Not all of the reactants may react, or they may react in a different way than expected.
- With reversible reactions, some of the products may change back to reactants again.

Example

Slaked lime, or calcium hydroxide ($Ca(OH)_2$), is used as a weak alkali to neutralise acid soil. Slaked lime can be made by heating calcium carbonate to make calcium oxide, then reacting the calcium oxide with water.

❶ $CaCO_3(s) \xrightarrow{heat} CaO(s) + CO_2(g)$

calcium carbonate → calcium oxide (lime) + carbon dioxide

❷ $CaO(s) + H_2O(l) \rightarrow Ca(OH)_2(s)$

calcium oxide + water → calcium hydroxide

a) How much slaked lime can be theoretically be produced from 200 g of limestone or chalk (calcium carbonate)?

First, calculate the relative formula masses, M_r.

relative formula mass of $CaCO_3$ is $40 + 12 + (3 \times 16) = 100$ g

relative formula mass of $Ca(OH)_2$ is $40 + 2\,(16 + 1) = 74$ g

From the equation, 1 mole of calcium carbonate yields 1 mole of calcium hydroxide.

Using the relative formula masses for calcium carbonate and calcium hydroxide, 100 g of calcium carbonate gives 74 g of calcium hydroxide, so 200 g of calcium carbonate should give:

$$200\text{ g} \times \frac{74}{100} = 148\text{ g of calcium hydroxide}$$

Relative atomic masses

Ca = 40 O = 16
C = 12 H = 1

Chemical amounts are measured in moles. The symbol for the unit is **mol**.

Relative atomic masses

Na = 23 O = 16
H = 1 C = 12
Cl = 35.5

1. One mole of sodium hydroxide (NaOH) is reacted with hydrochloric acid according to the equation below.

   $$NaOH(aq) + HCl(aq) \rightarrow NaCl(aq) + H_2O(l)$$

   What is the theoretical amount of sodium chloride that can be produced?
2. One mole of methane was burned in air. Some sooty deposits were noticed. The carbon dioxide produced was absorbed by a chemical. The chemical gained 32 g in mass during the reaction.
   a) What was the percentage yield of carbon dioxide?
   b) Why was the percentage yield so low?

Atom economy (also called atom utilisation) refers to the proportion of atoms in the reactants that ends up in the useful product. Atom economy is calculated as the mass of atoms in the desired product divided by the mass of atoms of all the reactants, expressed as a percentage.

b) When the 148 g of slaked lime produced in this reaction was reacted with hydrochloric acid, it neutralised the equivalent of 3.30 moles of hydrochloric acid. What was the percentage yield of the conversion of calcium carbonate to calcium hydroxide?

The equation for the reaction is:

$Ca(OH)_2(s)$	+	$2HCl(aq)$	→	$CaCl_2(aq)$	+	$2H_2O(l)$
calcium hydroxide		hydrochloric acid		calcium chloride		water

From the equation, 1 mole of calcium hydroxide neutralises 2 moles of hydrochloric acid.

As 3.30 mol of acid were neutralised, then the solid added to the hydrochloric acid contained (3.30/2) = 1.65 moles of calcium hydroxide. What mass of reactant is this? Using the relative formula mass of calcium hydroxide:

$$1.65 \times 74\,g = 122\,g$$

From the answer to part a), the theoretical yield is 148 g. The actual percentage yield is therefore:

$$\text{percentage yield} = \frac{122\,g}{148\,g} \times 100\% = 82.4\%$$

Possible explanations for the yield being less than 100%:

1. The starting material (marble chips) contained some stone dust.
2. Some of the calcium hydroxide may be lost in the dissolving, filtering and drying processes.
3. The thermal decomposition was incomplete (not all the calcium carbonate decomposed).

Atom economy

The yield of a chemical reaction is the amount of desired product obtained. This calculation ignores how the product was obtained, for example what starting materials were used and the amount of unwanted products formed. Not all atoms of the reactants always end up in the required product. Sometimes by-products are formed. If you want information about the overall efficiency of a chemical reaction, you would calculate the **atom economy**.

Example

Glucose can be fermented to produce ethanol (this reaction is also used to make ethanol fuel from renewable plant resources):

glucose	$\xrightarrow{\text{yeast}}$	ethanol	+	carbon dioxide
$C_6H_{12}O_6(aq)$		$2C_2H_5OH(aq)$		$2CO_2(g)$

If all the sugar really did turn to alcohol in this reaction, the atom economy would be 100%. But some sugar turns to carbon dioxide.

We can calculate the atom economy for this way of making ethanol.

relative formula mass of glucose = $(6 \times 12) + (12 \times 1) + 6 \times 16) = 180\,g$

relative formula mass of ethanol = $(2 \times 12) + (6 \times 1) + (16) = 48\,g$

From the equation, 1 mole of glucose produces 2 moles of ethanol.

$$\text{atom economy} = \frac{\text{mass of atoms in required product}}{\text{total mass of atoms in reactants}} \times 100\%$$

$$= \frac{2 \times 48\,g}{180\,g} \times 100\% = 53.3\%$$

Nearly half the sugar is 'wasted' in this process. Not all of the reactant atoms end up in molecules of ethanol – some carbon and oxygen atoms are released as carbon dioxide.

In the 1960s, Boots made the anti-inflammatory drug ibuprofen in a six-step reaction that has an atom economy of just 40%. When the patent expired, another company developed a new method. This has three stages and produces far less waste, as more of the reactant atoms end up in the required product.

Atom economy and sustainability – green chemistry

Some reactions where there are several stages and several by-products score low on atom utilisation. Other direct combination or decomposition reactions score highly because there are fewer by-products.

Chemists in the pharmaceutical industry now look for alternative ways to make the same product with a good yield and a higher atom economy. This is more efficient and minimises waste.

A system is **sustainable** if it meets present needs without compromising those of future generations. For example, a reaction will be more sustainable if we can reduce the amount of resources used, including energy.

High atom economy reactions may be more **sustainable**, since they use fewer resources and reduce the amount of waste material that has to be disposed of. It's better to produce less waste in the first place, than to treat waste afterwards to remove even harmless by-products. This reduces energy used in waste processing.

There are other environmental issues to consider in industrial chemistry. For example, how much energy is used in the process, including that needed to separate the products? Does the reaction use hazardous substances (such as organic solvents) and does it produce by-products that are toxic to human health and the environment? Or, can the starting materials be made from renewable resources?

3 Aniline ($C_6H_5NH_2$) is an important chemical used to make synthetic dyes. Aniline can be prepared in two ways. In the first method, nitrobenzene ($C_6H_5NO_2$) reacts with iron to produce aniline and iron oxide. In the second method, a catalyst speeds up the conversion of nitrobenzene to aniline, and water is the only by-product.

a) Explain why the atom economy is higher for the second process.
b) Explain why most aniline is produced using the catalyst method.

Relative atomic masses

Na = 23 Ti = 48
O = 16 Mg = 24

4 The following reactions can be used to reduce titanium oxide to titanium metal.

$TiO_2(s)$	+	$4Na(s)$	→	$2Na_2O(s)$	+	$Ti(s)$
$TiO_2(s)$	+	$2Mg(s)$	→	$2MgO(s)$	+	$Ti(s)$
titanium dioxide		sodium or magnesium metal		sodium or magnesium oxide		titanium metal

a) Calculate the atom economy of reducing titanium oxide to titanium using:
  i) sodium metal;
  ii) magnesium metal.
b) Which is a better process?

7.2 How do we measure the rate of a chemical change?

Chemists need to control how fast a chemical change happens when they make new materials.

The **rate of reaction** is the speed at which a reaction takes place. It can be measured as the rate of formation of a product or the rate of removal of a reactant.

How can you measure a rate of reaction?

A 'rate' is a speed. You calculate a rate as a measured quantity divided by time taken. For example, your pulse rate is the number of heart beats in 1 minute.

Measuring the time taken for a reaction is straightforward. Use a clock, or a calendar for very slow reactions.

Figure 7.5 The reactants are used up very quickly – an explosion is a fast reaction.

Figure 7.6 Sometimes you have to wait a long time to see the products form in a chemical reaction – rusting is a slow reaction.

Figure 7.7 When cooking an egg you can control the outcome carefully by controlling the temperature and how long you let the reaction continue.

The quantity you measure in a chemical change can be:

- mass lost (if the reaction produces a gas);
- time for all the solid reactants to be used up;
- amount of unreacted solid left at any time;
- temperature change produced (if energy is given out);
- change in colour;
- change in transparency of a solution; or
- change in viscosity (thickness of flow).

In the school laboratory, we usually measure rates of reaction by the amount of reactant used up or the amount of product formed:

$$\text{rate of reaction} = \frac{\text{amount of reactant used up}}{\text{time taken}}$$

or

$$\text{rate of reaction} = \frac{\text{amount of product formed}}{\text{time taken}}$$

For example, when magnesium reacts with acid, hydrogen gas is formed. How could the rate of reaction be measured?

$$\underset{\text{magnesium}}{Mg(s)} + \underset{\text{sulfuric acid}}{H_2SO_4(aq)} \rightarrow \underset{\text{magnesium sulfate}}{MgSO_4(aq)} + \underset{\text{hydrogen}}{H_2(g)}$$

You could measure the volume of gas collected, or if the gas was allowed to escape, you could measure the mass of the flask at regular intervals (see Figures 7.8 and 7.9).

Graphs of rates of reaction follow the same rules as the distance–time graphs you have studied. A steep graph line shows a fast reaction. A flat graph line shows the reaction has stopped.

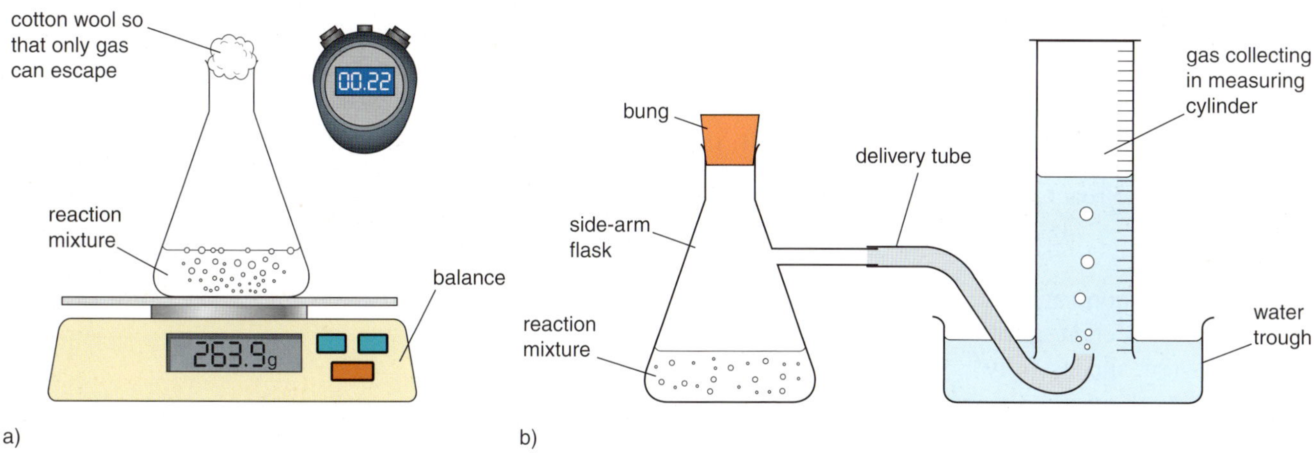

Figure 7.8 The rate of a reaction that produces a gas can be measured by a) the mass lost as the gas escapes, or b) by collecting the gas produced.

Figure 7.9 a) The rate of a reaction can be measured by recording the change in mass over time. When the graph levels off, one of the reactants has been used up and the reaction stops. **b)** This graph shows the volume of gas formed over time. The rate of reaction is highest when the gradient is steepest.

7.3 What makes a reaction happen, and how can we control it?

A collision model for chemical reactions

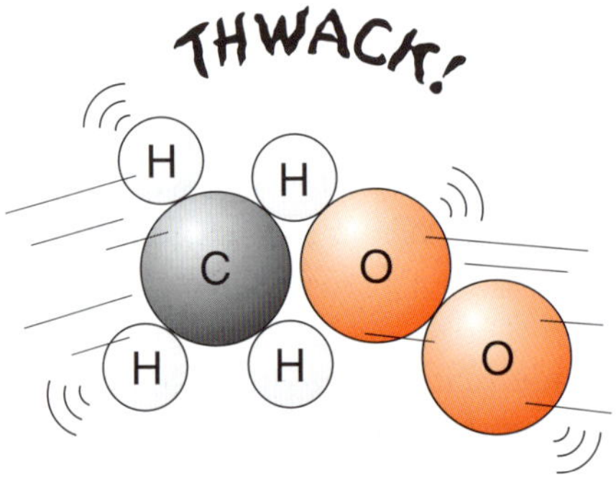

Figure 7.10 When two molecules meet, they only react if the collision transfers a large amount of energy.

The **activation energy** is the minimum energy needed if molecules are to react when they collide.

Effective collisions are collisions between atoms or molecules that successfully transfer enough energy for the atoms or molecules to react together.

For a chemical change to happen, the groups of atoms reacting have to collide. A model is a simplified picture that scientists construct to fit observed data to a theory. Observations of reactions show that the reaction is usually not over instantaneously. The collision model says that molecules only react if the collision is hard enough for energy to be transferred to break bonds between atoms. The minimum energy required to allow the reaction to happen is called the **activation energy**.

The collision model can be summarised as follows:

- Particles can only react if they collide with each other.
- For particles to meet, some of the particles have to be a liquid or a gas so they are moving about.
- In solids, only the particles on the surface can react.
- Not all collisions result in a reaction. There has to be enough energy transferred as the particles collide together to make the reaction happen. These are the **effective collisions**.

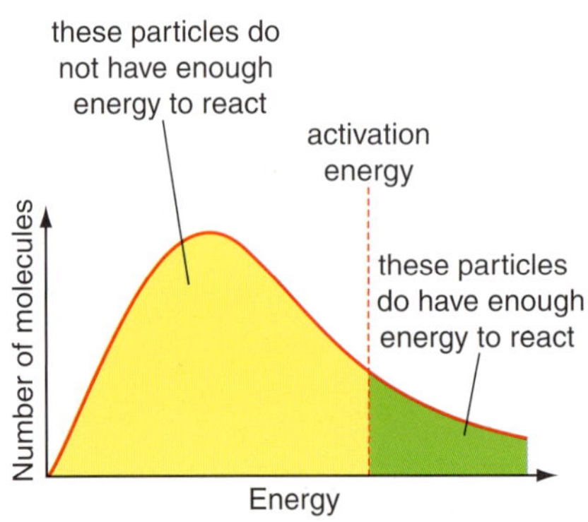

Figure 7.11 How much energy different particles have.

Figure 7.12 Reaction time is very important in cooking. There are several factors that change the rate of cooking reactions. The cook has to control the reactions so the parts of the meal are all ready at the same time.

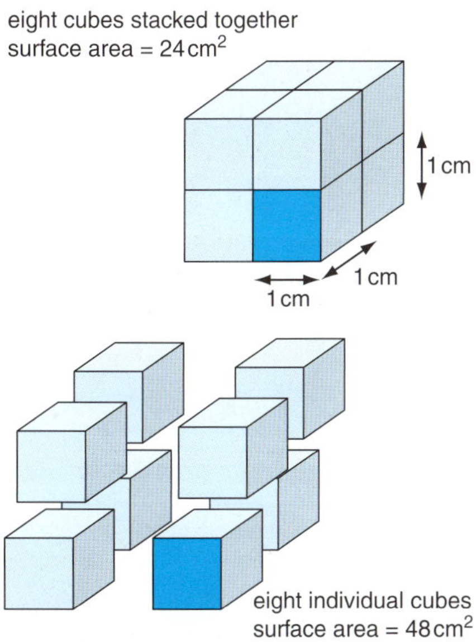

Figure 7.13 Making the pieces of reactant smaller increases the surface area and the number of particles exposed on the surface.

> **6** Use the collision model to explain why temperature has a large effect on rates of reaction.

> **5** Explain why not all collisions between reactants result in a chemical change.

Making reactions go faster

Two things can happen that cause a faster reaction (increase the rate):

- increase the number of collisions;
- make the collisions have more energy.

You already know that increased temperature causes a faster reaction (increases the rate). Other factors that can increase the number of collisions or increase the number of effective collisions are concentration, pressure, particle size and presence of a catalyst.

The collision model explains how these factors increase the number or energy of collisions.

- Increasing the temperature of the reactants makes the particles move about faster so they collide more often. The collisions are also faster with greater kinetic energy. Both increase the number of effective collisions.
- Increasing the concentration means there is a greater number of particles in a certain volume of a solution. The particles are crowded more closely together, so there are more collisions.
- Increasing the pressure of a reacting gas is like increasing the concentration of a solution; there are more collisions.
- If a solid reactant is cut up into more pieces then there are more reactant particles on the surface area that are exposed and able to react.

Predicting changes in rates of reaction

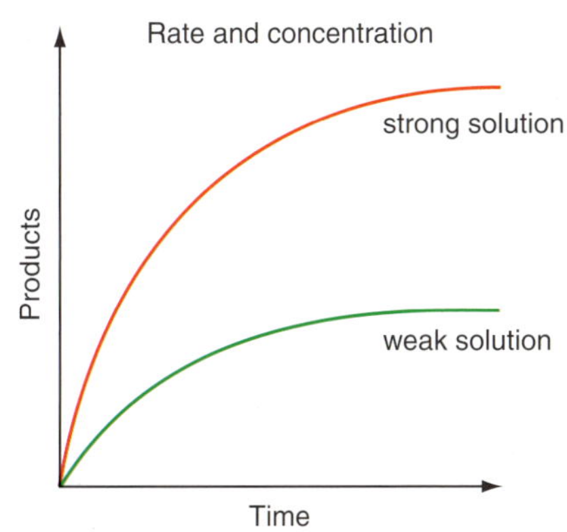

Figure 7.14 If a reactant in a solution is diluted to half the concentration this would halve the number of collisions in a certain time.

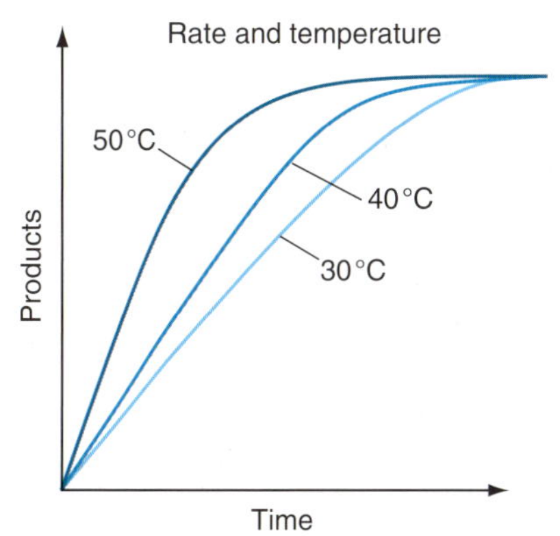

Figure 7.15 Each time the solution becomes 10 °C hotter the rate roughly doubles (this is a very approximate rule of thumb).

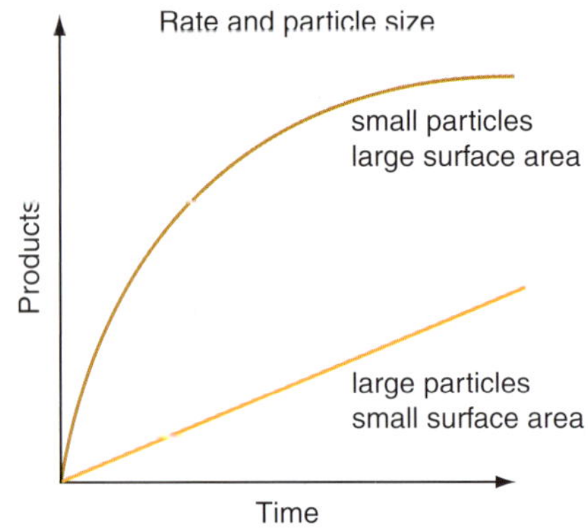

Figure 7.16 If more surface area is exposed then the reaction rate increases.

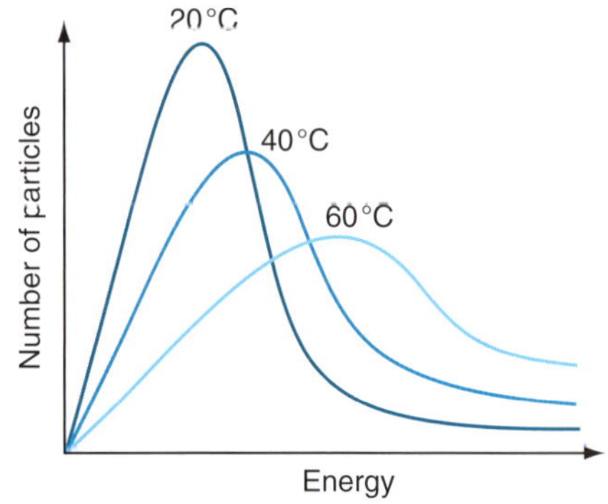

Figure 7.17 In a group of moving particles, the graph shows that for a higher temperature, the average energy is increased.

Figure 7.18 In a test tube of acid at 20 °C not all the particles have the same energy – some are moving faster than others. Only the faster acid particles are moving fast enough when they collide with the marble chip to react and produce carbon dioxide gas. At a higher temperature many more of the acid particles have enough energy.

A thinking model for collision theory – blind mice and rice crispy bar

This is a thinking model for magnesium reacting with hydrochloric acid. The acid particles (the mice) react with the magnesium (rice crispy bar) and gradually the magnesium is used up (the rice crispy bar is eaten).

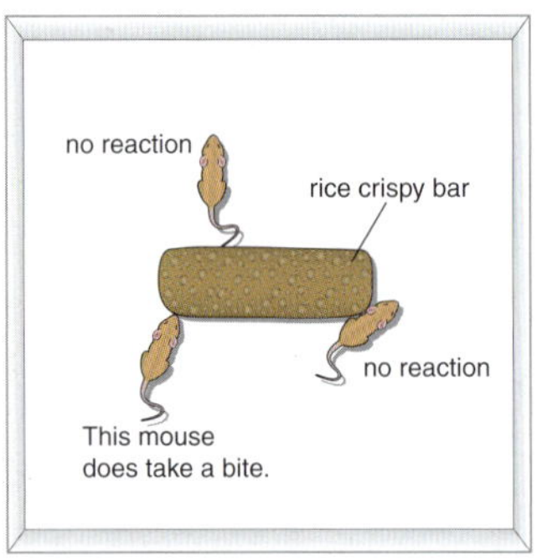

Figure 7.19 The acid particles (mice) will react with the magnesium (bar) only if they collide directly with it.

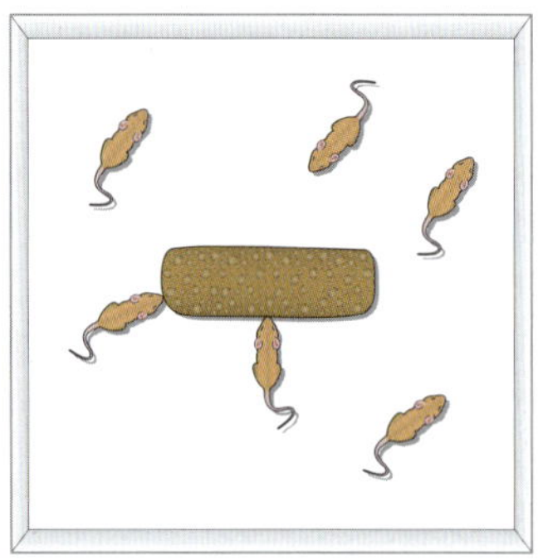

Figure 7.20 Slow-moving mice (low temperature) take all day to find and eat the rice crispy bar (slow reaction).

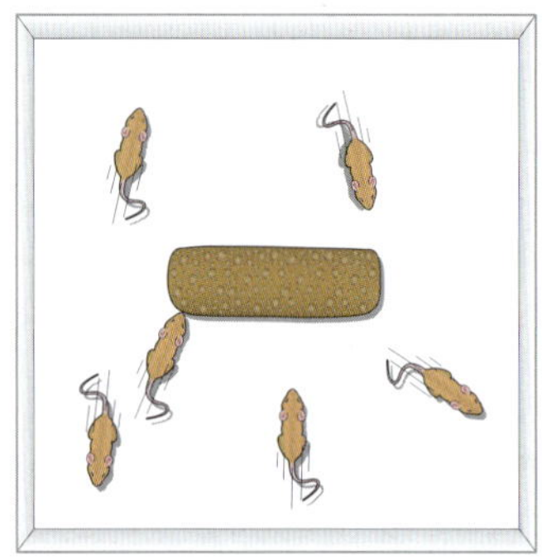

Figure 7.21 Fast scurrying mice (higher temperature) eat the bar up much more quickly (faster reaction).

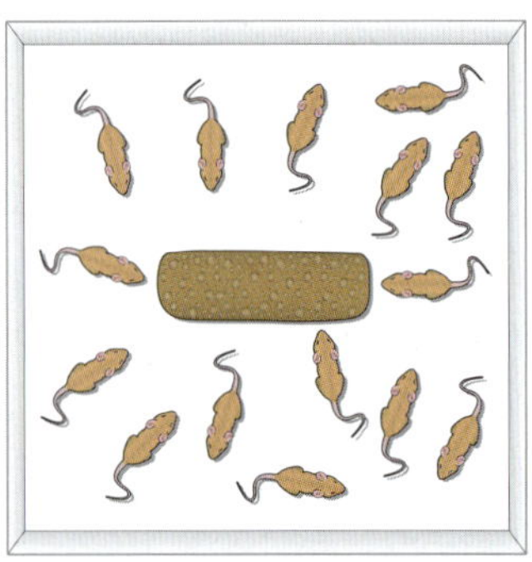

Figure 7.22 Lots more mice in the same space (higher concentration) eat the bar more quickly than a small number of mice.

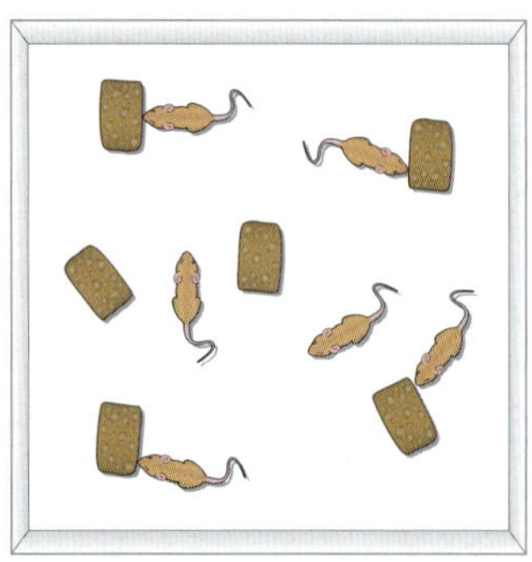

Figure 7.23 Even with a few mice, if the rice crispy bar is cut up into pieces it's more likely the mice will bump into a piece.

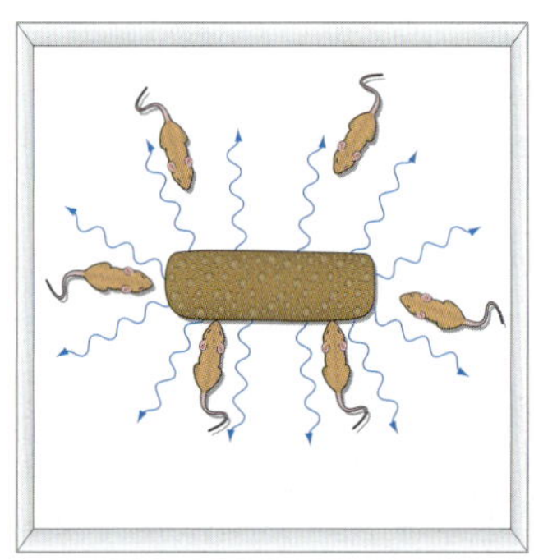

Figure 7.24 Explaining catalysts with this thinking model is difficult. But if a vibration attracted the mice to the rice crispy bar, then it would get eaten much more quickly (faster reaction).

Figure 7.25 Cooking potatoes is a chemical change that sometimes takes ages and sometimes only a minute or two. The cooking process breaks down the strong cell walls, making the food easier to digest. Cooking also releases the starch from inside the cells.

The mice are not clever. For a mouse to take a bite out of the rice crispy bar it has to bump its nose into the bar first (this is like an effective collision needing the correct orientation of particles). If the mouse just brushes past the bar (unsuccessful collision) then no rice crispies get eaten.

7. Explain why chips that are deep-fried in oil cook in 8 minutes, but boiling potatoes takes about 20 minutes.
8. If you cut the potatoes up smaller they cook faster. Crisps only take 20–30 seconds to deep fry. Explain why this is so.
9. Explain why crinkle cut chips cook faster than straight chips.

Catalysts

Catalysts speed up or catalyse the rate of chemical reactions but are not used up in the reaction. This is why the formula for the catalyst does not appear in the equation for the reaction.

Enzymes are called biological catalysts (see Chapter 3, p. 35 for more details).

A **catalyst** is a material that speeds up the rate of a chemical change, without it being used up itself. The same amount of catalyst will be present after the reaction has finished.

10. Name two catalysts that make hydrogen peroxide decompose more quickly.
11. Write a word equation and a balanced symbol equation for the decomposition of hydrogen peroxide.
12. When 1.0 mole of hydrogen peroxide H_2O_2 decomposes it forms 0.5 mole of oxygen.
    a) What is the mass of 1.0 moles of hydrogen peroxide?
    b) What is the mass of 0.5 moles of oxygen molecules?
13. Suggest how you could measure the rate of a reaction to decompose hydrogen peroxide with a manganese(IV) oxide catalyst.
14. Sketch the graph that you would plot of your results, and show the point at which the reaction stops.
15. What mass of oxygen should be released by the end of the experiment? Suggest a possible reason why less gas than this might be collected.

Figure 7.26 Hydrogen peroxide is found in highlight kits and permanent hair dyes. It doesn't just bleach – it also releases oxygen, which combines with the dye molecules and helps them deposit colour.

a)

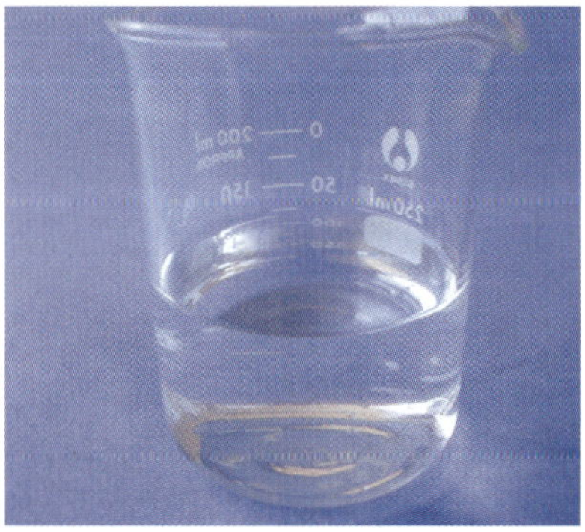

b)

c)

Figure 7.27 a) Hydrogen peroxide (H_2O_2) decomposes very slowly at room temperature to form water and oxygen. Adding a catalyst such as b) manganese(IV) oxide or c) peroxidase (an enzyme found in raw liver) makes the decomposition reaction much faster.

Catalysts are used to increase the rate of reaction of some important industrial processes. Without the catalyst, the reaction would happen only very slowly, or would have to be carried out at a higher temperature. One disadvantage of using catalysts is that the catalyst needs to be separated from the product after the reaction. This is easy if the catalyst is a solid and the reactants are gases, but could be difficult if both the catalyst and reactants are liquids.

Different catalysts speed up different reactions, so each catalyst has only one use. Researchers have to test new catalysts for new industrial processes.

Reactants	Catalyst	Product	Notes
Nitrogen and hydrogen	Iron mesh to give large surface area	Ammonia	Haber process, manufacture of ammonia for fertilisers
Sulfur dioxide and oxygen	Granules of vanadium pentoxide	Sulfur trioxide	Contact process, manufacture of sulfuric acid
Hydrogen and unsaturated fats or oils	Fine nickel particles	Margarine	Nickel catalyses breakdown of carbon double bonds to make saturated fat, which is solid. People are eating less saturated fat, so this process is becoming less important
Carbon monoxide and nitrogen oxides in cars (catalytic converters in exhaust systems)	Platinum and rhodium on a honeycomb metal support to increase surface area	Carbon dioxide and nitrogen (less polluting gases)	Catalyst is ruined if lead in the fuel gets on its surface
Ethene and steam	Phosphoric acid absorbed on to silica (sand)	Ethanol	Very low yield reaction; gases are recycled to avoid waste
Cracking of hydrocarbons	Zeolite crystals	Shorter chain hydrocarbons	The rate of cracking and the formation of diesel and petrol strongly depend on the presence of a catalyst
Ammonia and oxygen	Platinum mesh	Nitrogen pentoxide	Used to make nitric acid for fertilisers and explosives

Table 7.1 Industrial reactions and catalysts

16 Use Table 7.1 to describe three examples that show the importance of a large surface area when using a catalyst.

17 Describe a problem that can arise that reduces the effectiveness of catalysts. Explain how you would overcome this problem.

18 Catalysts are used in industrial processes to reduce costs.
a) Name two industrial processes where catalysts are used.
b) Suggest how catalysts can reduce energy costs in industrial processes, and explain how this might work.
c) Suggest how catalysts can increase the rate of industrial chemical reactions and explain how this might work.

19 Some catalysts are supported on an inert substance so they stay in one place. Other catalysts are mixed up with the reacting mixture.
a) Give one example of a catalyst from Table 7.1 that is supported on an inert substance.
b) Margarine has nickel particles in it when it is manufactured. What has to happen to these nickel particles before the margarine can be sold?
c) What does this processing do to the cost of making margarine?

Activity – Is there a cost-effective amount of a catalyst?

Lyubov investigated the question above as part of her GCSE practical work. She chose the decomposition reaction of hydrogen peroxide (H_2O_2) catalysed by manganese(IV) oxide.

$$2H_2O_2(aq) \xrightarrow{MnO_2} 2H_2O(l) + O_2(g)$$

She used 60 cm^3 of 2 volume hydrogen peroxide solution in all her tests. All the tests were carried out at room temperature and atmospheric pressure. She used similar apparatus each time.

Lyubov eventually produced this table of results (Table 7.2).

She needs to analyse the data to reach a conclusion.

Hydrogen peroxide solutions do not have their concentration shown on them as molarity (molar concentration). They have an indication of how much oxygen you can get from a certain volume of the solution.

For example 100 cm^3 of '20 volume' hydrogen peroxide produces 100 $cm^3 \times 20 = 2000$ cm^3 of oxygen gas.

Grams of catalyst used	0 g	5 g	10 g	15 g	20 g	25 g
Time in seconds	**Total volume of oxygen gas released in cm^3**					
0	0	0	0	0	0	0
10	0	5	12	20	22	24
20	0	10	20	37	40	43
30	0	15	30	55	57	60
40	1	20	39	72	74	76
50	1	25	47	86	87	88
70	1	35	65	110	110	110
100	2	48	90	115	115	115
150	2	70	118	120	120	120
200	2	92	120	120	120	120

Table 7.2

1. Materials such as platinum are used as catalysts in several chemical processes. Explain why it is important to be cost-effective in the use of catalysts.
2. List and draw the apparatus that Lyubov could have used to carry out this investigation.
3. Copy and complete Table 7.3 to summarise how Lyubov dealt with the many possible factors that would affect this investigation.

Factor	Type of variable	Range chosen	Controlled by Lyubov
Type of catalyst used		Manganese(IV) oxide	
Temperature and pressure			
Concentration of peroxide solution		2.0 volume solution	yes
Amount of catalyst			
Volume of oxygen given off			

Table 7.3

4. a) What is the maximum amount of oxygen gas produced in this experiment?
   b) What is the longest time measured?
   c) Use these answers to produce an *x*-axis scale (time) and a *y*-axis scale (oxygen gas given off) for a set of graphs.
5. Plot a line graph for each set of results. Plot them all on the same axes on one piece of graph paper.
6. Write a conclusion answering the question in the title. Suggest a quantitative answer for this set of reaction conditions.

7.4 Calculating concentrations of reactants in solution

In a well-mixed solution the solute particles are spread out evenly through the whole mixture. The solvent chemists use most often is water. We refer to solutions in water as aqueous solutions.

Chemicals are easy to handle in solutions. They are easy to measure, pour, heat and mix.

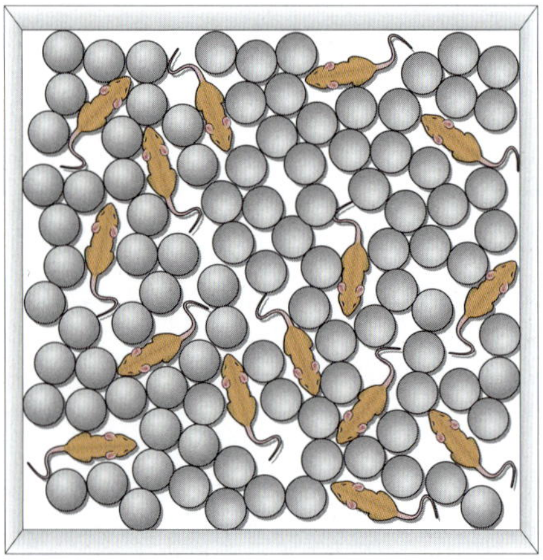

Figure 7.28 The mice represent the acid particles. The ping-pong sized balls are the water molecules. In a very concentrated solution, there would be many more mice (acid particles) in the same volume of solution.

Using the mice model

As can be seen from Figures 7.19–7.23, the **concentration** of a solution is how many reactant particles there are in each unit of volume. Figure 7.28 shows the 'mice thinking model' for solutions.

Concentrations in moles per cubic decimetre

Moles per cubic decimetre (mol/dm^3) is the unit of solute concentration in solutions. Remember that 1 mole of a compound always contains 6 × 10^{23} particles (see Section 5.2). The relative formula mass in grams (i.e. one mole) of every compound also contains the same number of atoms.

The **concentration** is the quantity of a chemical dissolved in each unit of volume. Gas and liquid concentrations are expressed in moles per cubic decimetre (mol/dm^3).

Always dissolve the solute in less solvent than is needed, then make the total volume up to the correct total volume. Dissolving a solvent can sometimes add volume and sometimes makes the total volume reduce.

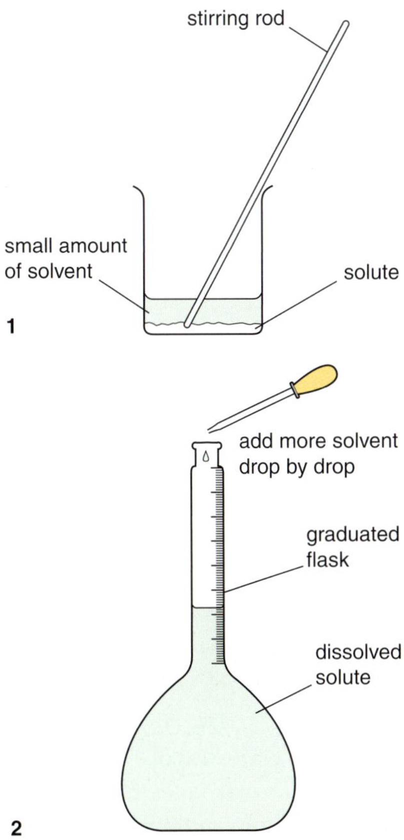

Figure 7.29 Making a solution with an accurately known concentration

A decimetre is 10 cm, so 1 dm^3 is 1000 cm^3. If you dissolve 1 mole of a solute and make the solution up to 1000 cm^3 (1 dm^3) in volume, then you will have 1000 cm^3 (1 dm^3) of 1.0 mol/dm^3 solution. Sometimes this is called a 1.0 molar solution.

Molarity and calculations

Example

100 cm^3 of waste water from a bottling factory was analysed and found to have 0.4 g of sodium hydroxide in it. Sodium hydroxide is an alkali and is used in cleaning solutions. The alkali in the waste water needs to be neutralised with hydrochloric acid.

NaOH(aq)	+	HCl(aq)	→	NaCl(aq)	+	H_2O(l)
sodium hydroxide		hydrochloric acid		sodium chloride		water

From the equation, 1 mole of hydrochloric acid neutralises 1 mole of sodium hydroxide.

relative formula mass of sodium hydroxide
= relative atomic masses of Na, O and H
= 23 + 16 + 1 = 40 g

so there is 40 g of sodium hydroxide in 1 mole.

Therefore in a 100 cm^3 sample of waste water there is:

$$\frac{0.4\,\text{g}}{40\,\text{g/mol}} = 0.01 \text{ moles of sodium hydroxide}$$

A chemist at the bottling factory therefore needs 0.01 moles of hydrochloric acid to neutralise this sample.

You could use:

- a small amount of concentrated acid; or
- a large amount of dilute acid.

It is important to get exactly the right amount of hydrochloric acid solution to neutralise the alkaline sodium hydroxide. So it is very important to be able to measure the volumes and concentrations of solutions accurately.

When the waste water has been treated it is neither acid nor alkali. The neutral, slightly salty water can be released into the environment if there are no other pollutants in it.

Equal volumes of solutions of the same molar concentration (units = mol/dm^3) contain the same number of moles of solute, so they contain the same number of particles. So 25 cm^3 of 0.5 mol/dm^3 glucose ($C_6H_{12}O_6$) solution contains the same number of molecules as 25 cm^3 of 0.5 mol/dm^3 ammonia (NH_3) solution. Because each glucose molecule is big and heavy and each ammonia molecule is small and light, the glucose solution contains a bigger mass of solute, but the same number of particles.

20 Calculate the number of moles of solute in these solutions:

a) 1000 cm^3 of 0.5 mol/dm^3 potassium hydroxide solution;
b) 25 cm^3 of 1.0 mol/dm^3 potassium hydroxide solution;
c) 100 cm^3 of 0.1 mol/dm^3 sodium chloride solution;
d) 10 cm^3 of 6 mol/dm^3 copper sulfate solution;
e) 3 dm^3 of 0.01 mol/dm^3 copper sulfate solution.

21 Sulfuric acid reacts with solid magnesium oxide and is neutralised. Excess magnesium oxide remains undissolved and sinks to the bottom.

MgO	+	H_2SO_4	→	$MgSO_4$	+	H_2O
magnesium oxide		sulfuric acid		magnesium sulfate		solution water

How much magnesium oxide would exactly neutralise 250 cm^3 of 0.5 mol/dm^3 sulfuric acid?

22 Potassium hydroxide reacts with sulfuric acid.

KOH	+	H_2SO_4	→	K_2SO_4	+	H_2O
potassium hydroxide		sulfuric acid		potassium sulfate		solution water

How much potassium hydroxide solution is required to exactly neutralise 250 cm^3 of 0.5 mol/dm^3 sulfuric acid?

23 a) A detergent works has quantities of sulfuric acid in its waste water. Explain how it could treat this water to make it environmentally safe.
b) Explain why magnesium oxide is a better chemical to use for this purpose than potassium hydroxide solution.

Particles, moles and gases

The **molar volume of a gas** is the volume of 1 mole of a gas at a fixed temperature and pressure. At normal temperature and pressure this volume is 24.0 dm^3 (24 000 cm^3).

Liquids are easy to handle and the volume of aqueous solutions does not change on heating. Gases are another matter. They are easy to compress and expand a lot on heating. One fact makes handling gases easy: No matter what gas you have, one mole of the gas takes up the same volume at normal temperature and pressure. This is the **molar volume of a gas.**

For example, in the combustion of methane:

CH_4	+	$2O_2$	→	CO_2	+	$2H_2O$
methane		oxygen		carbon dioxide		water vapour

One molecule of methane reacts completely with two molecules of oxygen. Since the same volume of gases at the same temperature and pressure would contain the same number of molecules, to get twice as many oxygen molecules the volume of oxygen that reacts must be twice the volume of methane. Therefore 100 cm^3 of methane reacts completely with 200 cm^3 of oxygen.

Figure 7.30 A gas phase reaction

Convention
'Normal temperature and pressure' for measuring gas volumes is 20 °C and normal atmospheric pressure. You need a standard, because gases expand when they are heated and when pressure is reduced.

24 a) Draw a particle picture to represent a certain volume of methane. Draw a box with six methane molecules in it.
b) Draw a particle picture to represent the number of oxygen molecules needed to react with the methane. Draw a box twice the size and put the right number of oxygen atoms in it.
c) What do you notice about the spacing between the atoms in the two boxes you have drawn?

7.5 Energy change in reactions

Many chemical changes transfer energy to the surroundings. Usually the energy heats up the surroundings. Sometimes the energy is transferred as light (glow sticks) or sound (explosions). These energy changes are called **exothermic reactions**. Combustion is an example of an exothermic reaction between a fuel and oxygen in the air.

Here is an example of an exothermic change you can try in the laboratory. During neutralisation, energy is given out when the new bonds are formed and this causes the solution to be heated.

Mix 25 cm^3 of acid solution with 25 cm^3 of alkali solution

Temperature before mixing: 20 °C   Temperature after mixing: 29 °C

Not all chemical reactions cause a temperature increase. Some chemical changes cool down the reactants and their surroundings. To do this the reaction takes in energy from the surroundings and transfers it to the reactants. This is called an **endothermic reaction**. Thermal decomposition is an endothermic reaction, as the energy must be transferred to the reactant before it breaks down.

An **exothermic reaction** is a chemical change where energy is transferred to the surroundings, often causing heating.

An **endothermic reaction** is a chemical change where energy has to be absorbed from the surroundings, often as a heat transfer that causes cooling of the surroundings.

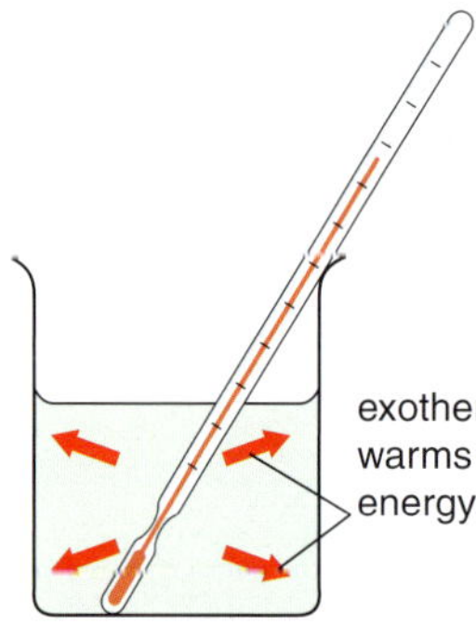

Figure 7.31 An exothermic reaction transfers energy to the surroundings.

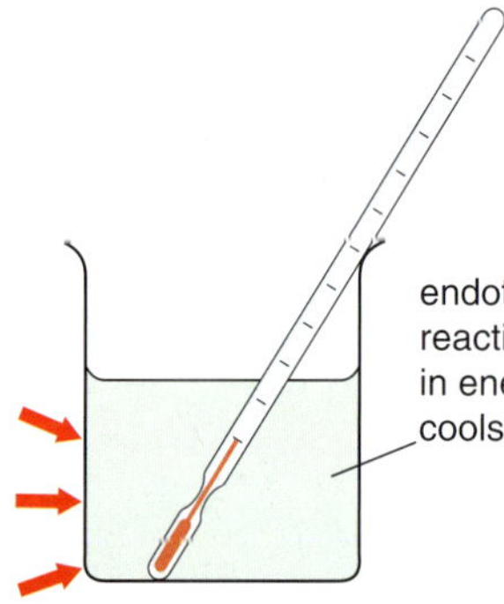

Figure 7.32 An endothermic reaction absorbs energy from the surroundings.

Here is an example of an endothermic change you can try in the laboratory. When sodium thiocyanate and barium hydroxide dissolve in water, this causes cooling.

Mix 4 g sodium thiocyanate and 8 g barium hydroxide in 100 cm^3 of water

Temperature before mixing: 20 °C   Temperature after mixing: 6 °C

Figure 7.33 A self-warming can of coffee heats the coffee with an exothermic reaction. Press the bulb on the bottom of the can and wait 2 minutes. Water reacts with anhydrous calcium oxide in a sealed compartment inside the can. The reaction gives out energy. This energy is transferred to the coffee, causing it to heat up.

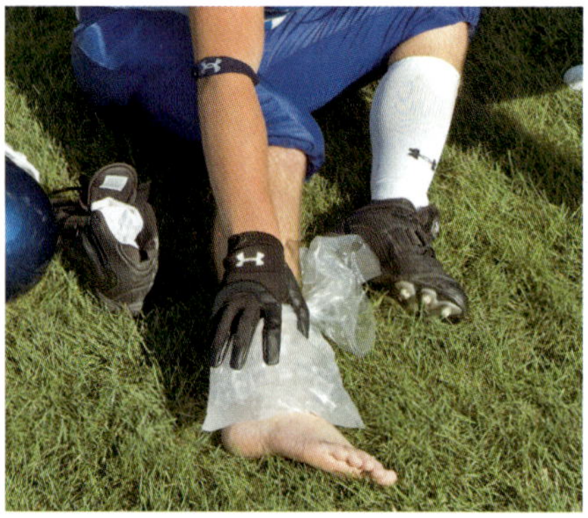

Figure 7.34 Twist a cold pack and it gets cold enough to numb the pain of a sports injury. Injuries such as sprains or bruises hurt because of the swelling; cold helps to reduce swelling. The chemicals combine to take in energy, so the pack gets cold.

Figure 7.35 Glow sticks contain luminol, a chemical that gives out light energy when it reacts with another liquid in the glow stick.

25 When would 'self-heating coffee' be useful?

26 The can is heated by the reaction between calcium oxide and water. The only product of this reaction is calcium hydroxide. Write a word equation for the reaction.

27 What type of injuries are treated with cold packs?

28 Complete Table 7.4.

Chemical change	Endothermic or exothermic?
Acid–alkali reaction	
Methane burning in a Bunsen burner	
Sodium reacting with water	
Calcium carbonate decomposing to calcium oxide and carbon dioxide	
Making aluminium metal	
Luminol reacting	

Table 7.4

Energy changes in a reaction that goes both ways

Figure 7.36 Testing for water. Filter paper is soaked in copper sulfate solution and dried in a hot oven. When the paper comes in contact with water, the anhydrous copper sulfate turns blue.

Figure 7.37 Hydrated (blue) copper sulfate crystals (left) have a formula of $CuSO_4.5H_2O$. They can be turned into anhydrous copper sulfate (right) on heating. Anhydrous copper sulfate has a slight tinge of colour due to water absorbed from the air.

When blue crystals of hydrated copper sulfate are heated, water vapour is given off and anhydrous copper sulfate is formed. The reaction is reversible, depending on how much water is present. The blue copper sulfate reforms when water is added to anhydrous copper sulfate. This colour change can be used as a test for water (Figure 7.36).

$$CuSO_4.5H_2O(s) \underset{\text{exothermic}}{\overset{\text{endothermic}}{\rightleftharpoons}} CuSO_4(s) + 5H_2O(g)$$

hydrated copper sulfate (blue) ⇌ anhydrous copper sulfate (white) + water

❷❾ Describe a procedure to test a few drops of a mystery colourless liquid, to see if it is water.

The thermal decomposition of hydrated copper sulfate is endothermic as heat is absorbed. The reverse reaction is exothermic. When 5 g of anhydrous copper sulfate are dissolved in 50 g of water the temperature rises by 10 °C.

In a reversible reaction if the forward reaction is endothermic, then the reverse reaction is exothermic. Exactly the same amount of energy is transferred in each case.

7.6 Equilibrium in reversible reactions

When a reversible reaction occurs in a closed system, the reactants and products cannot escape. The amount of reactants and products reaches a balance, or **equilibrium**. At equilibrium, the rates of the forward and reverse reactions are the same, so as much product is being made in the forward direction as there are reactants being used up in the reverse direction.

Equilibrium is a state of balance in a reversible reaction. The amounts of each chemical do not change, because the reactions occur at exactly the same rate in each direction. **Dynamic equilibrium** means that the reactions are still continuing.

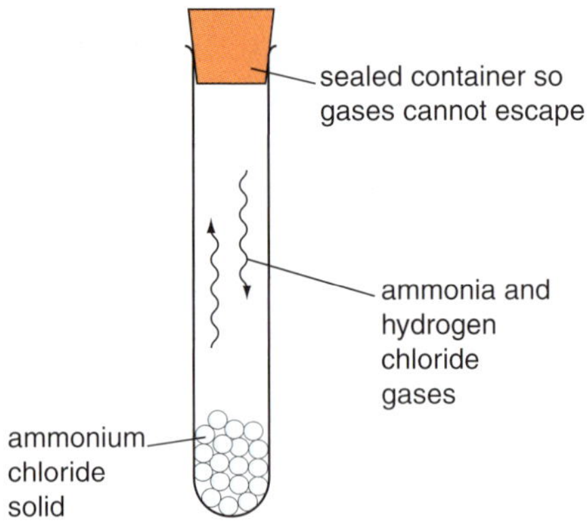

Figure 7.38 A reversible reaction in a closed system soon reaches a fixed amount of reactants and products at equilibrium.

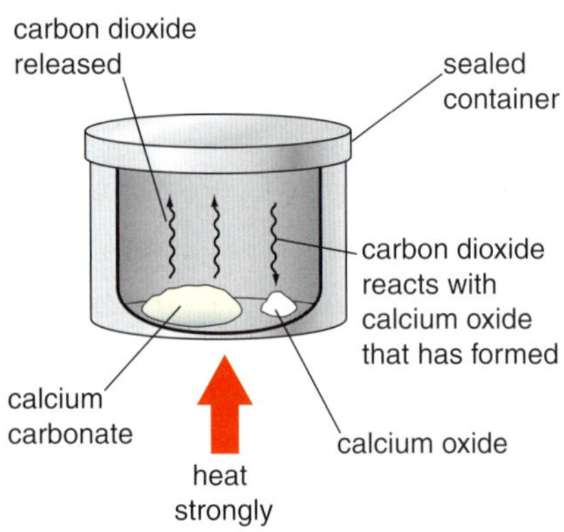

Figure 7.39 In a closed system, when calcium carbonate is heated strongly both decomposition and formation of calcium carbonate can occur.

Temperature in °C	Pressure of CO_2 in Pa $\times 10^2$
700	19
800	250
850	474
900	790

Table 7.5

The reactions don't stop – the particles keep swapping from reactants to products and back, but these effects balance out at equilibrium. This is called **dynamic equilibrium**.

The relative amounts of each reacting substance at equilibrium depend on the reaction conditions, such as temperature and pressure or the concentration of reactants. If you change the reaction conditions then you will change the equilibrium mixture. This affects the yield of products. If the forward reaction is faster this will result in more products being formed. A faster reverse reaction turns more of the mixture back into the original reactants.

Example

In a sealed container of solid ammonium chloride, some of the space above the solid contains molecules of ammonia and hydrogen chloride gases.

$$NH_3(g) + HCl(g) \rightleftharpoons NH_4Cl(s)$$

At room temperature, the equilibrium mixture is mainly ammonium chloride. Heating the container increases the rate of decomposition of ammonium chloride, so there will be a greater concentration of ammonia and hydrogen chloride.

The reaction to decompose calcium carbonate is endothermic.

$$CaCO_3 \rightleftharpoons CaO + CO_2$$

The amount of carbon dioxide in the mixture can be shown by the pressure exerted by the carbon dioxide inside the container. The greater the pressure, the more molecules of carbon dioxide are present (Table 7.5).

30 Draw simple particle pictures of the equilibrium mixture at 700 °C and 900 °C.

31 What is the effect of increasing the temperature on the equilibrium mixture?

32 If the closed system were heated to 900 °C and allowed to cool, describe what would happen inside the glass vessel as the mixture cooled.

33 If the reactants were heated to 900 °C with the bung removed so gases could escape, describe what the difference would be as the mixture cooled.

34 When calcium oxide and carbon dioxide react to form calcium carbonate, is this reaction endothermic or exothermic?

7.7 The Haber process

Figure 7.40 Fritz Haber is known for making ammonia from its elements. He was born in Prussia in 1868. Haber won a Nobel prize for his work.

Ammonia compounds are used to make fertilisers. In the first part of the twentieth century, population growth and the demand for more fertilisers meant the world demand for ammonia exceeded the existing supply. The largest natural source of ammonia was a huge guano (bird dung) deposit in Chile. This 380 km long deposit was fast disappearing.

Just before the First World War, Fritz Haber invented a process to manufacture ammonia without using guano. Ammonia is also used to make the explosives for shells and bullets. Haber's invention allowed Germany to fight the First World War even though it was cut off from Chile. Haber was also involved in directing the first poison gas (chlorine) attacks against Allied troops, resulting in 10 000 deaths.

Although ammonia and its exploitation had the ability both to sustain life and destroy it, Haber did not have either reason specifically in mind when performing his research.

In 1909 Karl Bosch developed a large-scale catalytic process for making ammonia from the process Haber invented. The reactants (the elements, hydrogen and nitrogen gas) are easy to obtain and inexpensive:

- hydrogen from natural gas (methane, CH_4) or from cracking other hydrocarbons;
- nitrogen obtained from the air.

In the 1930s when Jewish academics were persecuted, Haber realised his strong patriotism could not outweigh his Jewish heritage. Because of his service to his country in the First World War, his life was not actually threatened, but he realised that it was time to emigrate. He was offered a position at Cambridge and he left Germany in 1933.

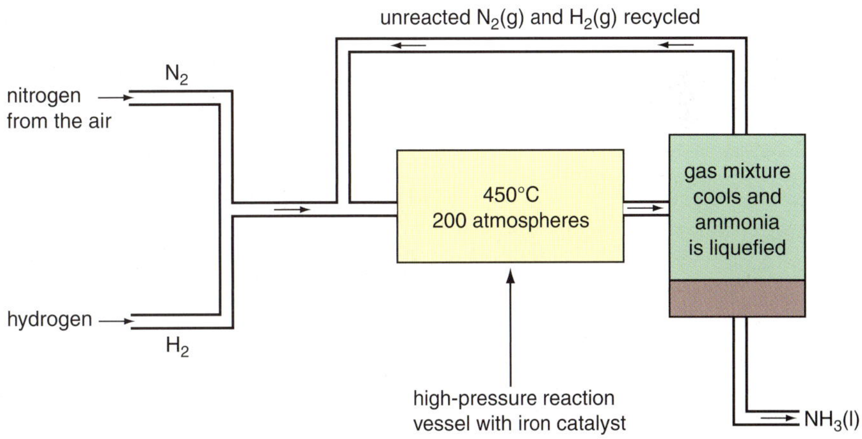

Figure 7.41 Flow diagram for the Haber process. Not all the hydrogen and nitrogen react. The remaining gases are recycled.

An iron catalyst is used to speed up the reaction, so that ammonia can be produced quickly.

$N_2(g)$	+	$3H_2(g)$	⇌	$2NH_3(g)$
nitrogen		hydrogen		ammonia

The forward reaction is exothermic and the reverse reaction is endothermic.

This is an important industrial process, and chemists want the yield to be reasonable.

Equilibrium conditions – maximising the yield

For a reversible reaction in equilibrium conditions, **Le Chatelier's principle** states that: 'The equilibrium position will respond to oppose a change in the reaction conditions.'

As mentioned in Section 7.6, different reaction conditions shift the equilibrium mixture (the proportions of reactants and products) one way or another. A rule to predict the change in equilibrium mixture is **Le Chatelier's principle**.

For the Haber process equilibrium conditions this means that if you increase the pressure, the equilibrium mixture changes to oppose the change – to reduce the pressure.

In the Haber process when you turn hydrogen and nitrogen molecules into ammonia molecules, then four molecules are replaced by two molecules. When 2 moles of gas are produced from 4 moles of gas the pressure reduces. This decreases the rate of the reverse reaction. The equilibrium position therefore shifts and more ammonia is produced.

- If there are more molecules on the reactants side of the balanced symbol equation, an increase in pressure produces more product.
- If there are more molecules on the product side of the balanced symbol equation, an increase in pressure produces less product.

Pressures of 200 times normal atmospheric pressure are used in the Haber process.

Changing the temperature conditions also changes the equilibrium. The forward reaction is exothermic. If chemists increase the temperature it makes it harder for the forward reaction to give out heat, so the yield of the forward reaction decreases. Less ammonia is produced.

- If the temperature is raised, the yield from the exothermic reaction decreases and the yield from the endothermic reaction increases.
- If the temperature is lowered, the yield from the endothermic reaction decreases and the yield from the exothermic reaction increases.

Cooler temperatures would help increase the yield in the Haber process as it would be easier to transfer energy to cooler surroundings.

Why are optimum conditions not used?

A graph of possible yield against temperature and pressure conditions is shown in Figure 7.42. At very high pressures and lower temperatures the yield is higher. However, a temperature of 450 °C and a pressure of 200 atmospheres is used, giving a yield of about 15%. Even though these conditions may not be those that give the highest yield, they ensure that less extra energy is used.

- Very high pressure reactors are expensive and require lots of energy input, which is a wasteful use of energy.
- A low temperature leads to a very slow forward reaction that could take days. This is wasteful as it is expensive to run the plant.

There is also a compromise between high yield and high rate of reaction.

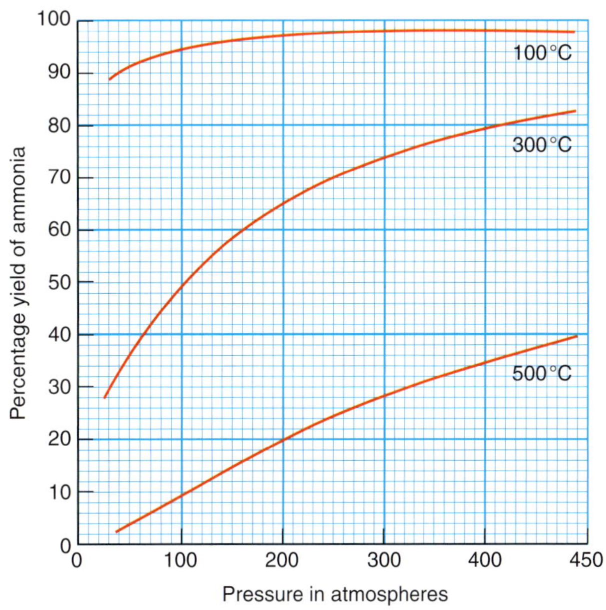

Figure 7.42 The percentage yield of ammonia at equilibrium for the Haber process at different temperatures and pressures

35 Look at Figure 7.42. Use this information to explain the effect of increasing the temperature on the yield of ammonia from the Haber process.

36 Explain the effect of increasing the pressure on the yield in the Haber process:
a) at 500 °C;
b) at 100 °C.

37 a) Why is the Haber process not carried out at 100 °C?
b) Why is the Haber process not carried out at the highest possible pressure?

38 The Haber process has a continuous flow of reactants through the reaction chamber rather than batches of reactants. Explain:
a) why this has an advantage regarding the amount of reactants used;
b) how the product (ammonia) is separated from the flow of reactants.

39 Describe the benefits for society of the discovery of the Haber process. Explain why the benefits must be balanced against the need for sustainable use of resources.

Industrial chemistry and sustainable development

Scientific principles, such as that of Le Chatelier and the atom economy principles, are useful in determining the most efficient conditions. The atom economy of the Haber process is 100% since there are no by-products (see Section 7.1). In sustainable development terms, atom economy is more important than the yield since all parts of the starting material are used and there are no waste products.

It is important for sustainable development to run industrial processes at conditions of low energy waste. Running processes sustainably may also require:

- the use of catalysts to reduce energy costs by carrying out the reaction at a lower temperature;
- new technology to recycle unreacted materials that could be reused;
- new technology to turn unwanted by-products (waste) into useful products;
- new reactions with higher atom economy to reduce volume of waste and conserve resources.

The Haber process is run as a continuous reaction. This has benefits:

- The unused reactants can constantly be recycled. This is an efficient use of materials.
- The ammonia can be easily extracted from the mixture. It liquefies more easily. This is efficient use of energy and materials.

However, even with the use of a catalyst the Haber process has an enormous energy consumption, due to the high temperature of the reaction. Energy is also needed to extract nitrogen from the air.

Summary

- ✓ Chemical reactions do not always turn all the reactants into products so the **yield** is never 100%.
- ✓ In **reversible** reactions the products can react to form the original reactants, depending on the conditions.
- ✓ **Percentage yield** = mass of product obtained / theoretical mass possible.
- ✓ **Atom economy** = the mass of atoms in the desired product divided by the mass of atoms of all the reactants, expressed as a percentage.
- ✓ A high atom economy helps the **sustainability** of chemical processes.
- ✓ The rate of a reaction can be measured as the amount of product formed divided by how long it takes, or the amount of reactant used up divided by the time taken.
- ✓ Concentrations of solutions are given in moles per cubic decimetre (**mol/dm^3**).
- ✓ One mole of any gas occupies the same volume – 24 dm^3 – at normal temperature and pressure.
- ✓ Reactions occur when reacting particles collide with more than the **activation energy**.
- ✓ The frequency and energy of collisions can be used to explain how factors affect reaction rate.
- ✓ **Catalysts** speed up the rate of a reaction but are not used up. Each reaction needs a specific catalyst.
- ✓ **Exothermic** reactions give out energy; **endothermic** reactions take in energy.
- ✓ In a closed system, a reversible reaction reaches a stable **equilibrium** between reactants and products.
- ✓ The **Haber process** turns nitrogen and hydrogen into ammonia using an iron catalyst, high pressure and moderate temperatures.
- ✓ **Le Chatelier's principle** can be used to make predictions about the effect of changing conditions on equilibrium. Low temperature favours (increases the yield of) exothermic reactions; high temperature favours endothermic reactions. High pressures favour gas phase reactions where the number of molecules reduces. The effect of these factors on yield, together with reaction rates, are considered when planning the conditions for industrial processes.
- ✓ Industrial processes should choose sustainable methods that minimise energy requirements and material waste. Improved processes could also recycle unreacted materials, use renewable starting materials and discover ways of converting waste to useful by-products.

EXAMQUESTIONS

1 Ethanoic acid is used to make plastics and the synthetic fibre rayon. Before 1970, most ethanoic acid was made by heating butane in air with a catalyst:

$$\underset{\text{butane}}{2C_4H_{10}} + \underset{\text{oxygen}}{5O_2} \rightarrow \underset{\text{ethanoic acid}}{4CH_3COOH} + \underset{\text{water}}{2H_2O}$$

Several side products may also form, including butanone and formic acid. Formic acid is toxic.

a) Suggest one reason why the yield of ethanoic acid is never 100%. *(1 mark)*

Most ethanoic acid is now made from reacting methanol with carbon monoxide in the presence of a catalyst.

$$\underset{\text{methanol}}{CH_3OH} + \underset{\text{carbon monoxide}}{CO} \rightleftharpoons \underset{\text{ethanoic acid}}{CH_3COOH}$$

b) Calculate the atom economy of this reaction. *(3 marks)*

c) Explain why you think this would be greater than the atom economy of the first reaction. *(2 marks)*

Methanol and butane are both obtained from natural gas, but methanol is cheaper to obtain than butane. Methanol can also be obtained from wood or sewage.

d) Explain why making ethanoic acid from methanol is more sustainable than making ethanoic acid from butane. *(3 marks)*

2 Two clear solutions, X and Y, are mixed in a conical flask. They gradually go cloudy until a cross under the conical flask can no longer be seen. The time for the cross to disappear is measured for different temperatures of the reacting solutions.

Temperature in °C	22	27	35	43	50	58
Time taken in seconds	327	260	198	194	118	100

Table 7.6

a) Draw a line graph of the data. Use temperature as the *x*-axis (from 20 °C to 60 °C) and time as the *y*-axis (from 0 to 360 seconds). *(6 marks)*

b) Identify the one anomalous result. *(1 mark)*

c) Use your graph to find how long it takes for the cross to become obscured at 30 °C. *(2 marks)*

d) Use collision theory to explain the shape of the graph. *(5 marks)*

3 In the Contact process, sulfur dioxide is turned into sulfur trioxide. This is reacted with water to make sulfuric acid. Vanadium pentoxide is used as the catalyst.

exothermic reaction

$$\underset{\text{sulfur dioxide}}{2SO_2(g)} + \underset{\text{oxygen}}{O_2(g)} \rightleftharpoons \underset{\text{sulfur trioxide}}{2SO_3(g)}$$

a) What is the purpose of the catalyst? *(2 marks)*

b) Why is no extra catalyst added in the flow diagram? *(2 marks)*

c) Use Le Chatelier's principle to explain:

i) the effect of pressure on the equilibrium mixture; *(2 marks)*

ii) the effect of temperature on the equilibrium mixture; *(2 marks)*

iii) the effect of removing the sulfur trioxide from the equilibrium mixture. *(2 marks)*

d) Explain how the best use is made of energy in the process. *(2 marks)*

e) Suggest why it is important to make the best use of energy and materials in an industrial process. *(2 marks)*

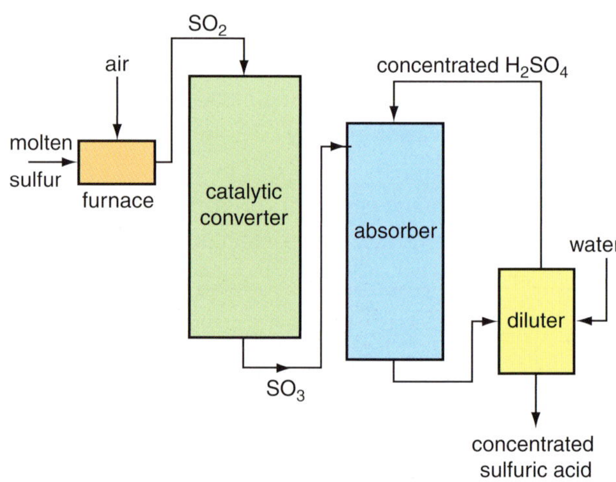

Figure 7.43 Flow diagram for making sulfuric acid

Chapter 8
How can we use ions in solutions?

At the end of this chapter you should:

- ✓ know that when an ionic substance is melted or dissolved in water, the ions are free to move about within the liquid or solution;
- ✓ know that salt solutions can be crystallised to produce solid salt;
- ✓ know about the uses of precipitation reactions;
- ✓ understand about acids, bases and neutralisation;
- ✓ know how to predict what salt is produced in a reaction;
- ✓ know how ammonium salts are produced and their use as fertilisers;
- ✓ be able to choose methods to make a named salt;
- ✓ be able to explain electrolysis of ionic liquids to break down compounds into elements;
- ✓ be able to use half equations for the reactions occurring at the electrodes;
- ✓ understand oxidation and reduction in electrolysis;
- ✓ know if there is a mixture of ions, the products formed depend on the reactivity of the elements involved;
- ✓ understand the electrolysis of sodium chloride solution produces important substances for the chemical industry;
- ✓ know copper can be purified by electrolysis.

Figure 8.1 Common salt – it's used for more than chips. It's a raw material for many useful products. Salt is used to make bleach, soap, washing soda, caustic soda (sodium hydroxide), water softeners, chlorine, PVC, baking soda, the enema sodium phosphate, and glass. Salt is also used for preserving meat (and Egyptian mummies), making freezing mixtures, dyeing and to remove traces of water from aviation fuel after it is purified. Every cell of your body contains salt, a total of 250 g per person. Salt in body fluids is essential for muscle action – too little and you get cramp. For many of these uses and products, a solution of salt is needed. If salt did not dissolve, none of these uses would be possible.

8.1 What are ions – and what does melting and dissolving do to ions?

Ions (charged particles) can form when atoms react. They can be made from a single atom (e.g. a magnesium ion, Mg^{2+}) or from a group of atoms (e.g. a nitrate ion, NO_3^-). Pure ionic substances are all solids at room temperature. There are strong electrostatic bonds holding the ions in a giant lattice. (Ionic bonds are discussed in Section 5.6 and giant ionic structures in Section 6.7.)

When an ionically bonded substance melts, the ions are free to move in the liquid. Ions can also be freed from the lattice by dissolving in water. When soluble ionic solids are put into water, the water molecules can get in between the particles and separate them.

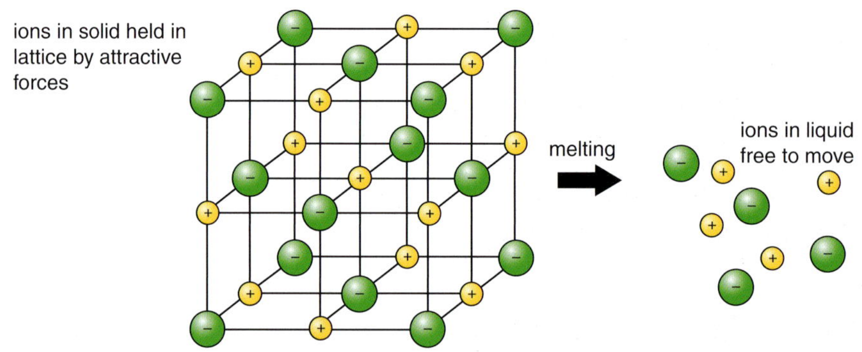

Figure 8.2 Melting an ionic compound means the ions are free to move.

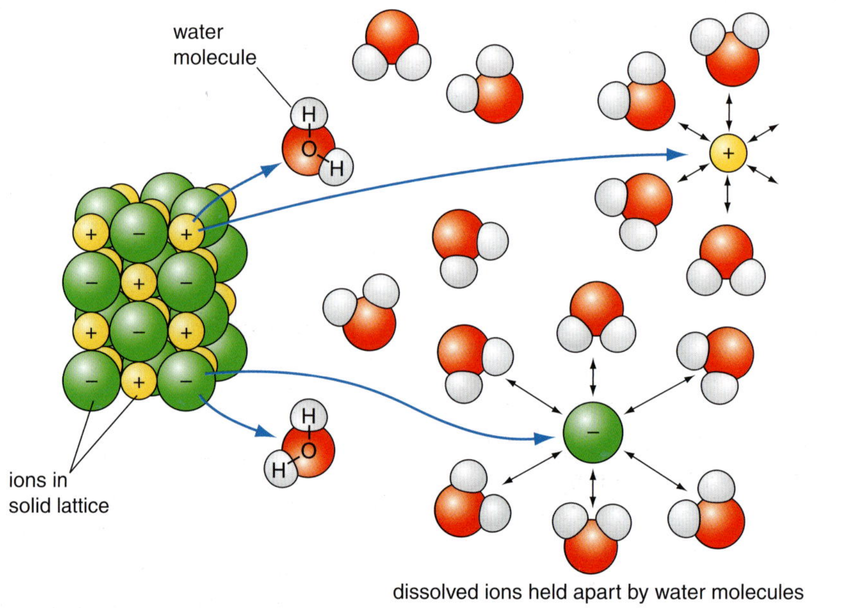

Figure 8.3 A model for a solution of an ionic substance. In a solution of an ionic compound the positive and negative ions are free to move about separately, kept apart by water molecules round the ions. There are equal numbers of positive and negative charges.

A solid, liquid or gas dissolved in a solvent is a **solution**.

A **solvent** is a substance (usually a liquid) that dissolves another substance to form a solution.

A **precipitation reaction is** a reaction that produces an insoluble solid from solutions. The solid produced is called a precipitate.

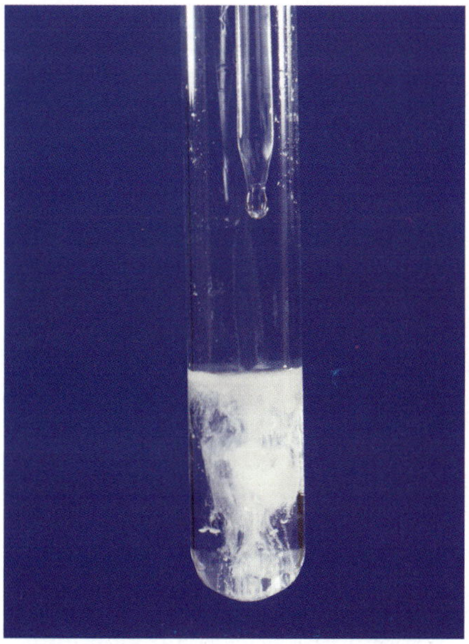

Figure 8.4 The colourless solutions in the pipette and test tube are two separate mixtures, one of barium and chloride ions and the other of sodium and sulfate ions. When the solutions are mixed, the barium and sulfate ions react together to form a white precipitate.

Precipitation reactions are used in forensic analysis to test if certain dissolved ions are present in a sample, for example those in poisons or explosives residues. Barium chloride solution is used as a test for dissolved sulfate ions.

Crystallisation

If the water or other **solvent** in the **solution** is allowed to evaporate, the solution becomes more concentrated. When this happens there may not be enough water to hold the ions in solution. The positive and negative ions join back together to form a solid. If the solvent evaporates slowly, the ionic solid forms as large regular crystals as each ion takes its place in an extended giant structure lattice (see Section 6.1).

Precipitation

If two solutions are mixed and one pair of ions reacts to form an insoluble substance as a solid, this is called **precipitating** out. For example:

$BaCl_2(aq)$	+	$Na_2SO_4(aq)$	→	$BaSO_4(s)$	+	$2NaCl(aq)$
barium chloride		sodium sulfate		barium sulfate		sodium chlorate
(solution)		(solution)		(solid)		(solution)

The solid barium sulfate precipitates out (Figure 8.4), leaving the sodium ions and chloride ions still in solution (remember, (aq) means aqueous or in solution). These ions are called 'spectator ions' because they do not take part in the reaction.

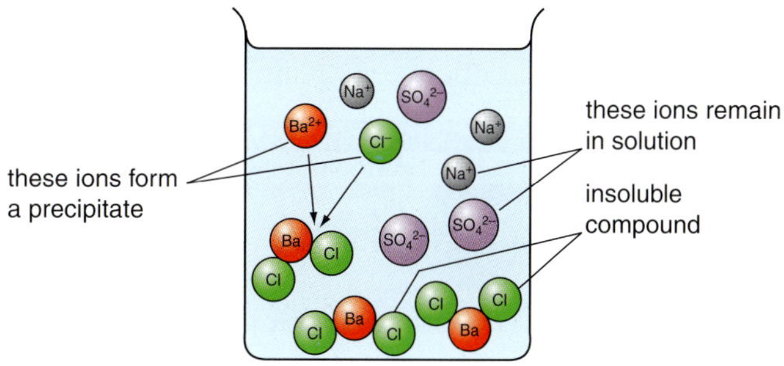

Figure 8.5 When two ionic solutions are mixed, one pair of ions forms a solid precipitate that can be removed from the solution, but the other ions remain in solution.

Uses of precipitation reactions

Precipitation can be used to remove selected ions from solution. The solution is mixed with another solution containing ions that form an insoluble precipitate with the unwanted ions.

Iron and some other metal ions in drinking water are not harmful to human health but can be a nuisance. Dissolved metal ions form brown stains on sinks, and darken cups when combined with tannin in tea. They also discolour vegetables during cooking. These ions can be removed in waste water treatment plants by adding a lime (calcium hydroxide) solution. The hydroxide ions react with the metal ions in solution to form insoluble iron hydroxide. Filters remove the precipitated particles.

A **salt** is a ionic compound. Most salts are made up of positively charged metal ions and negatively charged non-metal ions. Salts form when an acid neutralises an alkali.

The same precipitation reaction can be used to remove soluble metals from mine discharges and industrial effluent. Dissolved heavy metals such as cadmium and lead are precipitated out as metal hydroxides when the effluent is mixed with calcium hydroxide.

Phosphate fertilisers can contaminate rivers and groundwater and cause eutrophication by excess weed growth. Adding a metal **salt** (such as aluminium sulfate) to the waste water precipitates out the phosphate.

1. Use the data from page 86 to write the formulae of:
   a) sodium nitrate;
   b) aluminium chloride;
   c) magnesium sulfate;
   d) ammonium carbonate;
   e) calcium hydroxide.
2. Explain why a dissolved metal ion can form a solid when you mix a colourless sample solution with another colourless solution.
3. Draw a diagram to represent ions and molecules in a solution of magnesium chloride ($MgCl_2$).
4. Use the idea of ions and lattices to explain why large crystals of sodium chloride take a long time to dissolve.
5. Table 8.1 gives some data on solutions and precipitates.

Solutions mixed	Colour of precipitate
Silver nitrate and sodium chloride	White precipitate
Silver nitrate and calcium chloride	White precipitate

Table 8.1

What is the white precipitate in each case? Explain your answers.

8.2 How do acids and alkalis react?

An **acid** is a substance that produces H^+ ions to make an acidic solution with a pH less than 7.

An **alkali** is a substance that releases OH^- ions to make an alkaline solution with a pH greater than 7.

Oxygen is very reactive. It oxidises both metal and non-metal elements. Some non-metal oxides are acids if they dissolve in water. Metal oxides are alkalis if they dissolve in water. That's where many acid and alkali solutions come from.

Acid solutions all contain hydrogen ions. Hydrogen ions (H^+) are the acid ions. **Alkali** solutions all contain hydroxide ions (OH^-). These are the alkali ions.

When an acid or alkali dissolves in water, the substance splits up to make hydrogen ions or hydroxide ions. The other dissolved ion formed is a 'spectator ion'.

$$HCl(aq) \rightarrow H^+(aq) + Cl^-(aq)$$

$$NaOH(aq) \rightarrow Na^+(aq) + OH^-(aq)$$

All acids react in similar ways. This is because only the hydrogen ion in the acid reacts. The alkali reactions of the hydroxide ion are all the same for a similar reason. The spectator ions take no part in acid or alkali reactions.

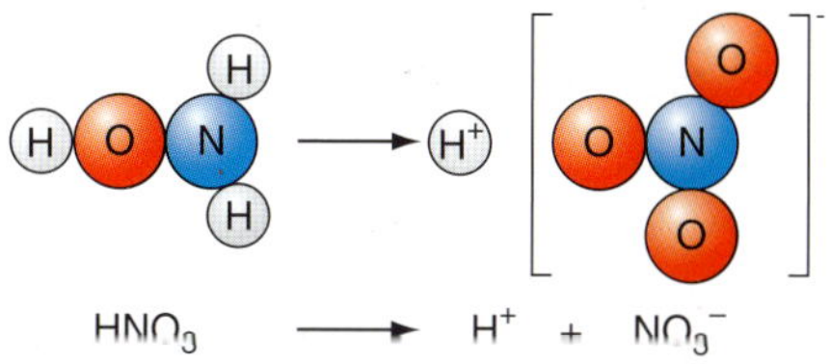

Figure 8.6 Nitric acid HNO_3 splits into H^+ (hydrogen ions) and NO_3^- (nitrate ions).

Explaining neutralisation

In a neutralisation reaction between an acid and an alkali, hydrogen ions react with hydroxide ions to produce water:

$$H^+(aq) + OH^-(aq) \rightarrow H_2O(l)$$

The spectator ions stay dissolved in the solution.

Example

$H^+(aq)$ and $NO_3^-(aq)$ + $Na^+(aq)$ and $OH^-(aq)$ → $Na^+(aq)$ and $NO_3^-(aq)$ + H_2O

nitric acid + sodium hydroxide → sodium nitrate (dissolved) + water

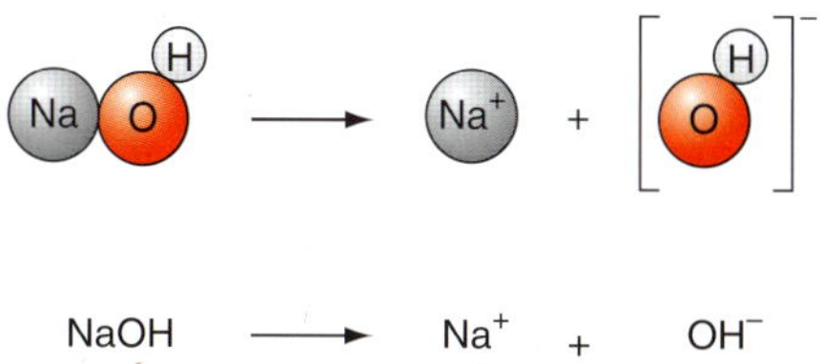

Figure 8.7 Sodium hydroxide NaOH splits into Na^+ (sodium ions) and OH^- (hydroxide ions).

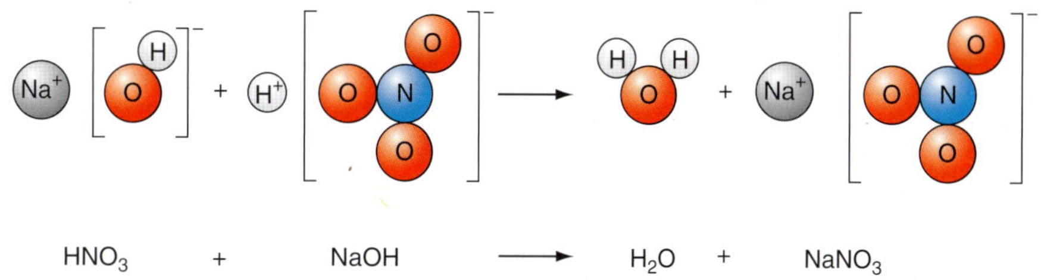

Figure 8.8 A neutralisation reaction. When sodium hydroxide (an alkali) reacts with nitric acid the H+ and OH^- ions react to form water, but the Na^+ and NO_3^- ions stay dissolved.

Note that:

- If we remove the spectator ions from the picture, then all neutralisation equations become basically the same:

  $$H^+(aq) + OH^-(aq) = H_2O(l)$$

  This means there is really only one change happening in any acid/alkali reaction – hydrogen ions join with hydroxide ions to make water molecules.
- The spectator ions are left over. They form the salt in the reaction.

pH scale

The pH scale used to measure the acidity or alkalinity of a solution is a measure of hydrogen ion concentration.

- pH 7 is the value for neutral solutions (1 in every 10^7 water molecules has split to make an H^+ ion);
- pH 1 is strong acid (1 water molecule in 10 is has split to make an H^+ ion)
- pH 14 is a strong alkali (very low concentration of H^+ ions).

8.3 How can we make different salts by neutralisation?

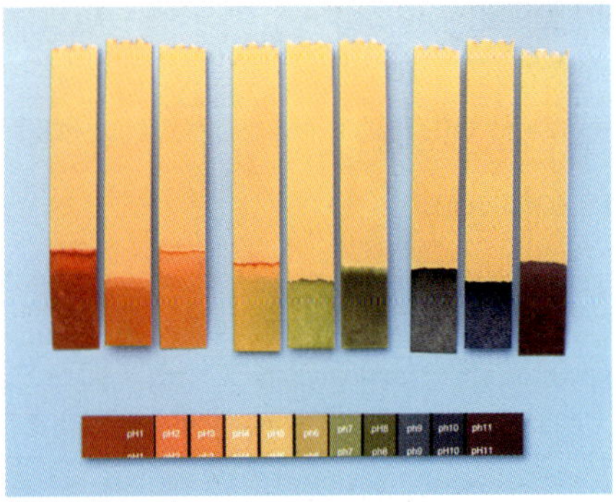

Figure 8.9 Universal indicator is a mixture of substances that reacts to the pH of a solution by turning different colours. This range of colours matches the pH scale.

Acid or alkali	Salt made
Nitric acid	Nitrates
Hydrochloric acid	Chlorides
Sulfuric acid	Sulfates
Ethanoic acid	Ethanoates
Sodium hydroxide	Sodium salts
Potassium hydroxide	Potassium salts
Ammonia solution (alkali)	Ammonium salts

Table 8.2

When acids are neutralised the spectator ions are left as ions in solution. If all the water is evaporated, just the solid salt is left behind. An acid plus an alkali forms a salt plus water. The acid and alkali used determine the type of salt made (Table 8.2).

Using indicators to prepare a salt

As acid and alkali solutions are usually both colourless, when we are making a salt we need to take a measurement to find when the solution is exactly neutral. In a neutral solution only the dissolved salt will be present, and no excess acid or alkali.

You could use a pH meter to test when the solution is neutral. You could also add the acid or alkali solution a little at a time and check the pH after each addition by dropping a sample onto indicator paper. Another method is to leave the indicator in the reaction flask as the solutions are mixed. The indicator is removed before crystallising the salt, by adding two spatulas of charcoal and heating. The charcoal absorbs the indicator and can be filtered off, leaving a colourless solution.

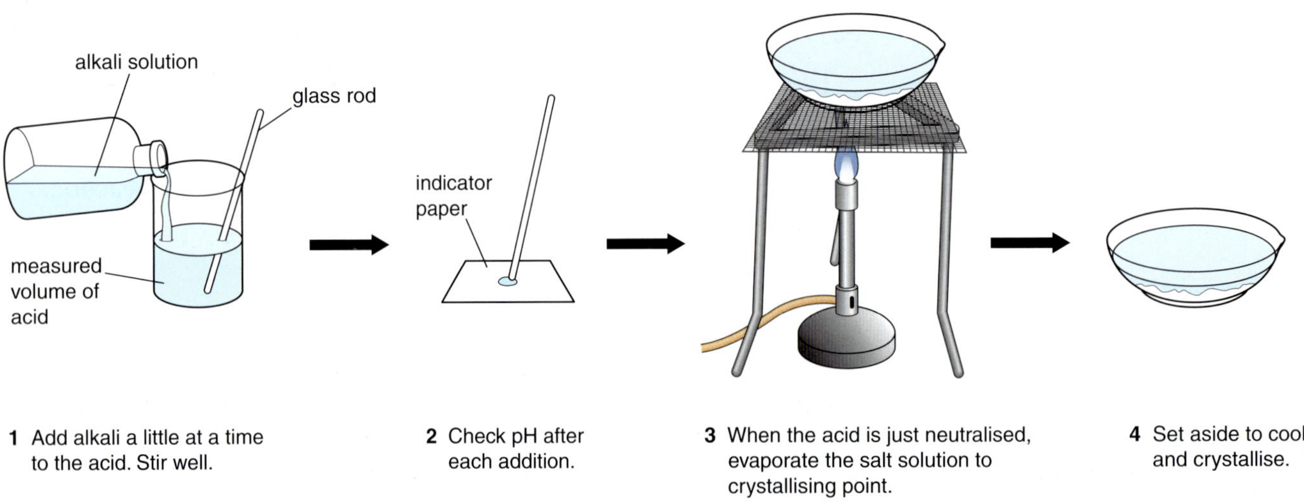

Figure 8.10 Preparing a pure soluble salt by neutralisation

Figure 8.11 Measuring the volume of acid accurately for a neutralisation reaction

Ammonia

Ammonia (NH_3) is a very smelly gas. It is very soluble in water – 1 dm^3 of water dissolves 1500 dm^3 of ammonia gas. When it dissolves in water, some ammonia molecules separate to form an ammonium ion (NH_4^+) and a hydroxide ion to give an alkaline solution.

Ammonium salts are important constituents of fertilisers. The ammonia provides the source of nitrogen for plants to make proteins.

6 a) What substances dissolve in water to produce acids?
b) What substances dissolve in water to produce alkalis?

7 a) 'Only the hydrogen ion matters in an acid reaction.' Explain what is meant by this statement.
b) What is the corresponding ion in an alkali reaction?
c) What new molecule is produced in neutralisation?
d) What is meant by a 'spectator ion'?

8 Copy and complete Table 8.3.

Name of acid	Name of alkali	Name of salt	Formula of salt
Sulfuric acid	Sodium hydroxide		
Hydrochloric acid		Lithium chloride	
		Calcium nitrate	
			$MgCl_2$
			NH_4NO_3

Table 8.3

9 Draw a flowchart for a method to produce clean, dry salt crystals by neutralising sulfuric acid with potassium hydroxide solution, using Universal indicator.

8.4 What other ways are there of making salts?

A **base** is a compound that will neutralise an acid by forming water molecules as one of the products.

Alkalis are a particular sort of chemical **base**. Don't confuse the chemical word 'base' with all the other meanings of the word base, for example in sports, in apparatus, in mountain climbing, in 'back to base, and so on. In chemistry, a base is a metal oxide or hydroxide. If a base reacts with water to form a hydroxide solution, it is an alkali, but some bases are insoluble.

Figure 8.12 Copper oxide dissolves in hydrochloric acid to give a blue solution of copper chloride. Unreacted copper oxide has settled to the bottom.

Acid plus insoluble base forms a soluble salt

$2(H^+$ and $Cl^-)(aq)$	+	$CuO(s)$	$\rightarrow$	$(Cu^{2+}$ and $2Cl^-)(aq)$	+	$H_2O(l)$
hydrochloric acid		copper oxide		copper chloride		water

To prepare copper chloride, add copper oxide to hydrochloric acid until no more will react. The oxygen in the oxide forms hydroxide ions, which neutralise the hydrogen ions in the acid to form water. The 'spectator ions' are left in solution to make copper chloride. Once all the acid is neutralised, filter off the remaining (excess) copper oxide. Then heat the mixture gently for a few minutes. This evaporates the copper chloride solution until it starts to crystallise out.

Many metal carbonates react in a similar way to metal oxides, carbon dioxide is an additional product as the carbonate reacts

$2(H^+$ and $Cl^-)(aq)$	+	$MgCO_3(s)$	$\rightarrow$	$(Mg^{2+}$ and $2Cl^-)(aq)$	+	$H_2O(l)$	+	$CO_2(g)$
hydrochloric acid		magnesium carbonate		magnesium chloride		water		carbon dioxide

A **displacement reaction** is a reaction where a more reactive metal displaces a less reactive one from a solution of its compound.

Acid plus metal forms a soluble salt plus hydrogen

Many reactive metals also form salts when added to acids. The reaction is a **displacement reaction**, not a neutralisation reaction. The reaction does not work for the less reactive metals such as copper or gold, and the reaction does not work for certain acids such as nitric acid.

Reactivity series for metals

Potassium
Sodium
Lithium
Calcium
Magnesium
Aluminium
Zinc
Iron
Lead
Hydrogen
Copper
Silver
Gold

Only the metals above hydrogen in the reactivity series react with an acid to make a salt. Aluminium does not make salts with acids since a hard aluminium oxide layer forms on the surface of aluminium and this resists acid attack.

To make a salt from a metal plus an acid, add an excess of metal. Leave the reaction for a length of time – don't heat, since hydrogen gas forms an explosive mixture with air. Once the reaction has finished you can filter off the unreacted metal to leave a salt solution.

For example, you can make zinc sulfate by adding zinc to sulfuric acid:

$Zn(s)$	+	$(H_2SO_4)(aq)$	$\rightarrow$	$ZnSO_4(aq)$	+	$H_2(g)$
zinc metal		sulfuric acid		zinc sulfate		hydrogen gas

Figure 8.13 Soluble zinc sulfate is formed when zinc reacts with sulfuric acid. The fizz is hydrogen being released.

Insoluble salts

In Section 8.1 you saw that when two ionic solutions are mixed a precipitate can form. The precipitate is an insoluble salt and can be filtered off. The solid is washed with pure water to remove any residual salt solution, and dried to give the pure dry insoluble salt.

10. What is the difference between a base and an alkali?

11. Magnesium chloride could be made by reacting magnesium granules with hydrochloric acid.
   a) What safety precautions do you need to take?
   b) Why would this method not work for copper chloride?
   c) Write a step-by-step report of making magnesium chloride crystals by this method, detailing what you would expect to see at each stage.

12. a) Explain how you would know a certain volume of sulfuric acid had been completely neutralised by copper carbonate.
   b) What salt is made in this reaction?
   c) Write a balanced symbol equation for the reaction.

13. Write a step-by-step plan for making salt crystals from zinc oxide powder and nitric acid.

8.5 Electrolysis

Figure 8.14 Electrolysis does many jobs in science. These batteries are used in a chemical factory to electrolyse brine.

When an ionic substance is molten or dissolved in water, the ions are free to move about. In **electrolysis** an electric circuit is connected to the liquid and the ions move towards the **electrodes** that have the opposite charge. Chemical changes take place at the electrodes as the ions gain electrons at the cathode and ions lose electrons at the anode. The energy transferred by the electricity can reform elements from ions and can break down a compound back into its elements.

Electrolysis is the process of splitting up a chemical compound into its elements by passing an electric current through the molten or aqueous solution containing ions (the **electrolyte**).

The **electrode** is the physical connection between an electric circuit and another material. It is usually made from a material that won't corrode such as a carbon rod or platinum foil.

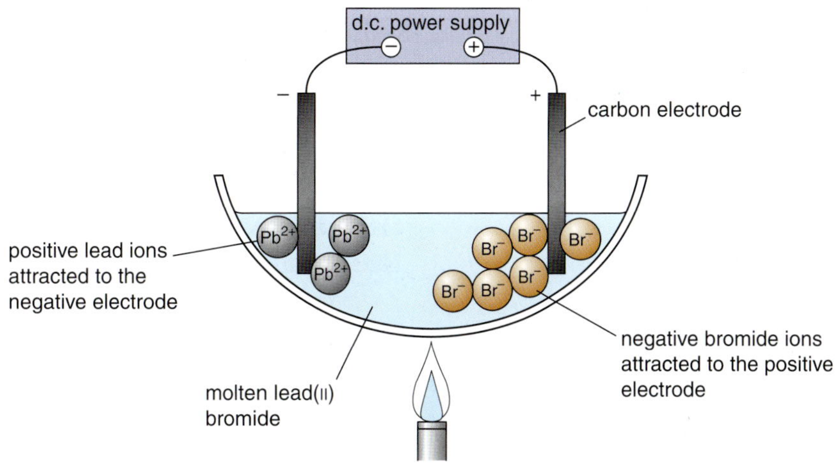

Figure 8.15 Lead bromide can be broken up into its elements, lead metal and bromine gas, by electrolysis.

Let us look at the electrolysis of molten lead(II) bromide.

Lead ions (Pb^{2+}) are attracted to the **cathode** (negative electrode). The lead ions gain electrons so they become lead metal again:

$$Pb^{2+} + 2e^- \rightarrow Pb$$

lead ions + 2 electrons → lead metal (neutral)

The **cathode** is the negative electrode in a solution and attracts positive ions.

The **anode** is the positive electrode in a solution and attracts negative ions.

Bromide ions (Br^-) are attracted to the **anode** (positive electrode). Electrons are pulled away from the bromide ions to turn them into atoms again, so they become bromine as an element:

$$2Br^- \quad 2e^- \quad \rightarrow Br_2$$

bromide ions − 2 electrons → bromine gas (neutral)

If a salt can exist in a molten state, then it can be decomposed into its elements like this. Electrolysis forms the basis of the production of most reactive metals, such as sodium and aluminium, from their molten metal ores.

Electrolysis equations

A **half equation** describes what reaction takes place at one of the electrodes in an electrolysis cell. This is only half the total process because another, different, reaction takes place at the other electrode.

The equations for the processes at the electrodes are called **half equations** because each equation represents only one of the two processes that make up the overall electrolysis reaction. The pairs of half equations must obey the same rules. Each half equation must be balanced in terms of atoms, show complete compounds as the product, and the loss and gain of electrons in each pair must match.

When oxygen reacts with a metal and oxidises it, the oxygen atoms remove electrons from the metal to make negatively charged oxide ions. The metal becomes a positively charged ion. When any other non-metal reacts with a metal, electrons are also transferred from the metal to the non-metal. This process is also called **oxidation**.

Reduction with carbon or hydrogen is the reverse process. The carbon pulls the oxygen away from the less reactive metal ion and gives the electrons back, so the ion becomes a metal atom again.

We can define oxidation and reduction as follows:

Oxidation Is Loss (of electrons)
Reduction Is Gain (of electrons)

This gives us the mnemonic OIL RIG.

In electrolysis, the anode takes electrons away – so the anode oxidises materials. The cathode gives electrons to materials – so the cathode reduces them.

Electrolysis of solutions

For salt solutions containing simple ions, the situation is similar to that for molten simple compounds. The ions in solution are attracted to the electrode with the opposite charge, where they are turned into atoms of the element. Negatively charged ions (e.g. Cl^-) lose electrons (oxidation) and positively charged ions (e.g. Cu^{2+}) gain electrons (reduction). However, the presence of water in a solution means that a different substance can be produced at the electrode.

Hydrogen ions (H^+) in the water gain electrons at the cathode to form molecules of hydrogen gas (H_2). For example, when sodium chloride solution is electrolysed, hydrogen is formed at the cathode. The negative ion from the salt (Cl^-) loses electrons at the anode to form molecules of chlorine gas (Cl_2). The positive ion from the salt (Na^+) stays in solution. Hydroxide ions (OH^-) from the water also stay in solution. This means the original sodium chloride solution forms three products: hydrogen, chlorine and sodium hydroxide solution.

The reactions at the electrodes are:

anode: $2Cl^- \rightarrow Cl_2 + 2e^-$

cathode: $2H^+ + 2e^- \rightarrow H_2$

Mixtures of ions in solution

In solutions containing a mixture of ions, the products formed depend on the reactivity of the elements. If a mixture of positive metal ions is present, then the ion of the element with the lowest reactivity will form an atom first (the reactivity series for metals is given in Section 8.4, page 148). For example, in a mixture of magnesium chloride and hydrochloric acid, hydrogen is produced, not magnesium. In a mixture of iron sulfate and copper sulfate, copper is produced, not iron.

The negative ions in salt solutions are usually simple halide ions (e.g. Cl^-, Br^-). The reactivity series for the halogens determines what product forms in electrolysis of solutions with a mixture of halide ions. For example, in a mixed solution of sodium bromide and sodium chloride, bromine is less reactive so bromine gas is produced at the anode. It then dissolves in the solution.

14 Explain what these terms mean.
a) electrolyte;
b) electrolysis;
c) anode;
d) cathode.

15 a) Write a plan for a procedure to turn copper chloride crystals back into copper metal and chlorine using electrolysis.
b) What safety precautions should you take?
c) Draw a diagram of the apparatus you would use.

16 Copy and complete Table 8.4.

Liquid being electrolysed	Product at cathode	Product at anode
Molten lead bromide		
Molten sodium oxide		
Copper nitrate solution		
Potassium iodide solution		
A mixture of sodium iodide solution and copper chloride solution		

Table 8.4

8.6 Uses of electrolysis

Electrolysis of water

Pure water is a very poor conductor. If a little acid is added to the water then it will conduct electricity – acidified water can be electrolysed. This reaction breaks down water into hydrogen and oxygen gases. It's the basis of making hydrogen used in fuel cells for electric vehicles.

cathode: $4H^+(aq) + 4e^- \rightarrow 2H_2(g)$

anode: $4OH^-(aq) - 4e^- \rightarrow O_2(g) + H_2O(l)$

Making aluminium metal

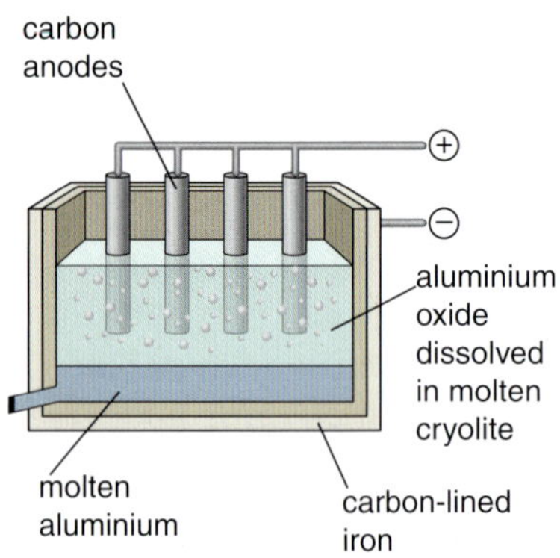

Figure 8.16 Aluminium oxide is decomposed by electrolysis in this industrial plant. The molten aluminium is siphoned out of the bottom of the cell.

Aluminium is too high in the reactivity series to extract it from its ore using carbon reduction. Most reactive metals are produced by electrolysis of a molten metal compound.

Aluminium metal is produced by the electrolysis of molten aluminium oxide (obtained from bauxite ore). The aluminium oxide has a very high melting point and is dissolved in molten sodium aluminium fluoride (cryolite) to make it melt at a lower temperature. Only aluminium and no sodium is produced because sodium is higher in the reactivity series. The half equations are:

cathode: $4Al^{3+} + 12e^- \rightarrow 4Al(l)$

anode: $6O^{2-} - 12e^- \rightarrow 3O_2(g)$

Purification of copper metal by electrolysis

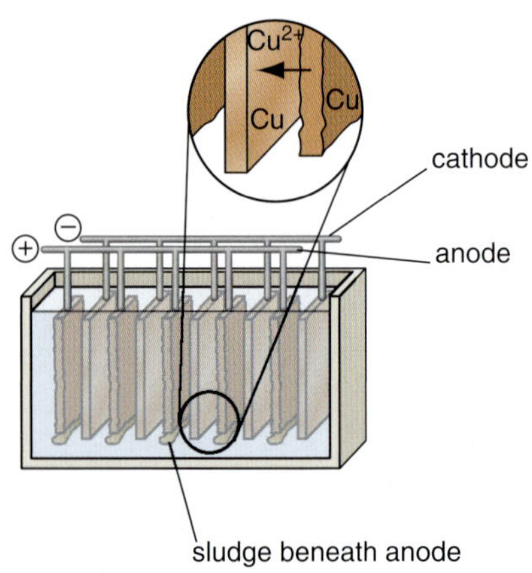

Figure 8.17 The impure copper anode dissolves away and pure copper is deposited on the cathode

Copper ore is reduced to copper metal by smelting with carbon. However, the metal obtained contains many impurities (lead, nickel, zinc, gold, silver) that reduce its electrical conductivity. The impure copper is purified by electrolysis.

Large impure slabs of copper are used as anodes and pure sheets of copper are used as cathodes. The electrolyte is acidified copper sulfate solution, which remains unchanged overall. During electrolysis copper from the impure anode is reduced to copper ions and these ions are transferred into solution. The positive copper ions are attracted to the cathode, where they are reduced. Copper atoms are deposited on the cathode. As the impure anode crumbles away, all the impurities collect at the bottom of the cell as sludge. This anode sludge can be reprocessed to recover precious metals.

anode: $Cu(s) - 2e^- \rightarrow Cu^{2+}(aq)$

cathode: $Cu^{2+}(aq) + 2e^- \rightarrow Cu(s)$

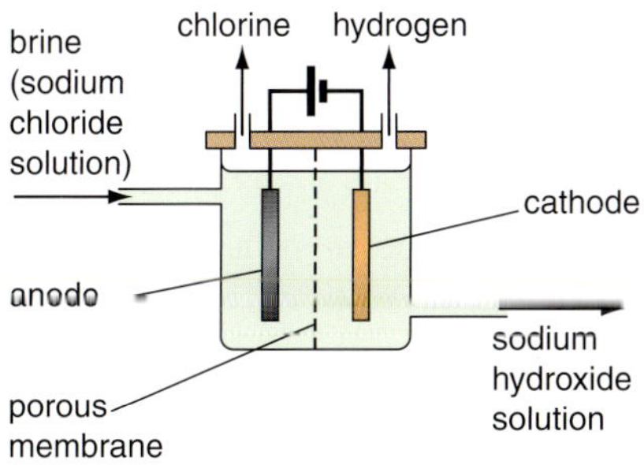

Figure 8.18 The membrane cell, part of a Chloralkali plant

Electrolysis of sodium chloride solution

The electrolysis of concentrated brine (salt solution) to produce chlorine, hydrogen and sodium hydroxide (see page 151) is used for the industrial production of chlorine and sodium hydroxide, an alkali known as caustic soda. These chemicals have many industrial uses (see page 141). Hydrogen gas is a by-product of the process.

Sodium chloride solution is electrolysed in a membrane cell that separates the anode chamber from the cathode chamber. This is called Chloralkali electrolysis. A porous membrane divides the electrolytic cell and allows only sodium ions to pass through it. Hydroxide ions cannot pass through the membrane to the anode.

17 a) Name three products that can be made from the electrolysis of sodium chloride solution
b) Write half ionic equations for the reactions at the anode and cathode of the membrane cell.

18 a) What is the name of the aluminium ore from which aluminium oxide is obtained for electrolysis?
b) For what purpose is cryolite used?
c) Explain why no sodium metal is produced, even though sodium ions are present.
d) Use your knowledge of the reactivity series for metals to predict three metals other than aluminium that cannot be reduced by carbon and so must be made by electrolysis.

19 a) Calculate the atom economy for the electrolysis of molten aluminium oxide.
b) Electrical energy is needed for electrolysis. What other costs are involved in the manufacturing of aluminium?
c) Explain why electrolysis of molten aluminium oxide adds to carbon dioxide emissions and could contribute to global warming.
d) Explain why producing aluminium by electrolysis is not as sustainable as recycling aluminium.

Summary

- ✓ Ions are free to move within a molten ionic compound or an ionic solution.
- ✓ Evaporation of a salt solution **crystallises** the solid salt.
- ✓ Ions dissolved in ionic solutions can form an insoluble **precipitate** when two solutions are mixed. Forming a precipitate is useful to remove unwanted ions from a solution.
- ✓ Acid solutions contain **hydrogen ions** (H^+); alkalis contain **hydroxide ions** (OH^-).
- ✓ Metal oxides and hydroxides are **bases**, and form alkalis if they are soluble in water.
- ✓ **Neutralisation** of an acid with an alkali produces water molecules.
- ✓ There are several types of substances that will neutralise acids and form a **salt**:

  acid + alkali → salt + water
  acid + metal oxide (base) → salt + water
  acid + reactive metal → salt + hydrogen

- ✓ Ammonium salts produced by adding acid to ammonia solution are important as fertilisers.
- ✓ Liquids containing ions conduct electricity.

✓ When electricity passes through liquids there are chemical changes at the electrodes. The ions are **oxidised** (lose electrons) or **reduced** (gain electrons).

✓ Positive ions (such as metal ions) are attracted to the **cathode**, while non-metal negative ions are attracted to the **anode**. The reactions at the electrodes can be described using **half equations.**

✓ Electrolysis is an important industrial process. It can be used to:
- produce hydrogen fuel;
- extract aluminium and other reactive metals from their ores;
- purify copper metal for electrical use;
- obtain chlorine and sodium hydroxide from the electrolysis of rock salt (sodium chloride).

EXAMQUESTIONS

1 Briefly suggest the chemicals needed for making each of the salts in Table 8.5 below. Credit will be given for the variety of starting chemicals used.

Name of salt	Function	Formula
a) Washing soda	Prevents scum from soap	Na_2CO_3
b) Epsom salts	Help digestive system	$MgSO_4$
c) Moss killer for lawns	Gardening aid	$FeSO_4$
e) Road salt	Preventing water freezing	NaCl
f) Fish tank cleaner	Stops growth of fungi	$CuCl_2$

Table 8.5

(16 marks)

2 Making salts is about neutralising acids. How would you make sure that all the acid had been exactly neutralised in each of these reactions?

a) an acid plus insoluble metal carbonate reaction *(2 marks)*
b) an acid plus metal oxide reaction *(2 marks)*
c) an acid plus alkali reaction. *(2 marks)*

3 Write balanced half ionic equations for the electrolysis of these liquids.

a) acidified water (H_2O) *(2 marks)*
b) molten zinc chloride ($ZnCl_2$) *(2 marks)*
c) concentrated sodium chloride solution (NaCl)(aq) *(2 marks)*
d) dilute copper sulfate solution ($CuSO_4$). *(2 marks)*

4 Oxidation is loss. Reduction is gain.

a) Explain how the oxidation of a metal fits in with the definition of oxidation above. *(4 marks)*
b) How can this principle for defining oxidation and reduction can be applied to electrolysis? *(4 marks)*

5 The apparatus in the diagram is used in industry to purify copper. The anode and cathode are made out of copper and the electrolyte is copper sulfate solution.

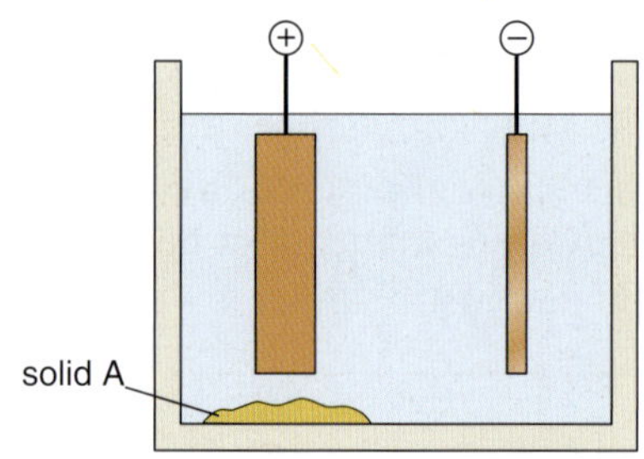

Figure 8.19

a) Explain why the anode is made of a large block of impure copper. *(2 marks)*
b) Explain why the cathode is made of a thin sheet of pure copper. *(2 marks)*
c) What is the difference in properties of pure and impure copper? *(1 mark)*
d) What is the solid A that accumulates below the anode? *(2 marks)*
e) What are the main differences between this process and the electrolysis of copper sulfate solution with carbon electrodes that would be carried out in a laboratory? *(4 marks)*

Chapter 9
How can we describe and change the way things move?

At the end of this chapter you should:

- ✓ be able to describe the movement of a body using a distance–time graph or velocity–time graph;
- ✓ know that the slope (gradient) of a distance–time graph represents speed;
- ✓ know that the slope (gradient) of a velocity–time graph represents acceleration;
- ✓ know that the area under a velocity–time graph represents distance travelled;
- ✓ understand that if the resultant force acting on a body is not zero, the body accelerates;
- ✓ know that a falling body initially accelerates due to the force of gravity but reaches a terminal velocity when the resultant force is zero;
- ✓ be able to describe factors that affect the stopping distance of a vehicle;
- ✓ understand that when a force transfers energy to, or from, a body, work is done;
- ✓ know that the kinetic energy of a body depends on both its mass and its speed;
- ✓ know that momentum is conserved in any collision or explosion, provided no external forces act on the colliding or exploding bodies;
- ✓ be able to use and rearrange equations for acceleration, work done, kinetic energy and momentum;
- ✓ appreciate that safety features are often explained using the idea of momentum.

Figure 9.1 In an accident, the crumple zones, seat belt and air bag are all designed to increase the time it takes for you to slow down and stop. This makes the forces on you smaller. The smaller the force, the greater the chance of avoiding serious injury.

9.1 What's the difference between speed, velocity and acceleration?

Figure 9.2 The average speed of a snail is just 0.0005 m/s. How far would a snail go in one hour?

Speed and velocity

If you travel at a fast speed, it takes less time to finish a journey than when you travel at a slow speed. Some passenger trains are so fast they can travel 92 metres in just one second. This is a speed of 92 metres per second (92 m/s) and is the average speed of the train. During a one-hour journey the train will sometimes go faster and sometimes slower.

When you go somewhere it's not just speed that is important – direction also counts. Figure 9.3 shows two routes that Stacey can take to school.

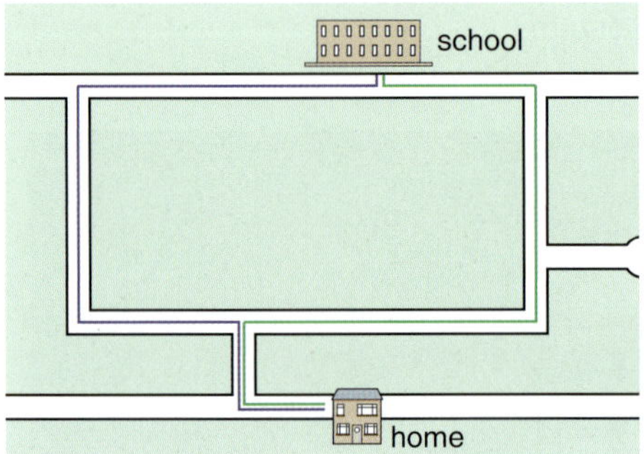

Figure 9.3 Stacey's routes to school

The two routes are the same distance and take Stacey the same time. This means that Stacey goes at the same speed on both routes. But the two routes involve travelling in different directions and each time Stacey changes direction her **velocity** changes. This is because velocity includes speed and direction.

To give the velocity of a body, you need to give both its speed and its direction. Direction can be shown in different ways. You can use:

- an arrow;
- a compass direction;
- a + or − sign.

The **velocity** of a body is its speed in a given direction.

In Figure 9.4 the two joggers are moving at the same speed but have different velocities.

Figure 9.4 Where you end up depends on your speed and direction

The **acceleration** of an object is the rate at which its velocity changes.

Figure 9.5 Olympic runners accelerating off the blocks

1. A falcon hovering in the sky sees its prey and dives downwards. The falcon reaches a velocity of 9 m/s in just 1.5 s. Calculate its acceleration.
2. A motorbike decelerates from 20 m/s to rest (0 m/s) in 4 seconds. Calculate the deceleration of the motorbike.
3. A cyclist accelerates from rest at 0.9 m/s^2 for 8 seconds. Calculate the final velocity of the cyclist.
4. A high-speed train travelling at 36 m/s accelerates at 0.2 m/s^2. How many seconds will it take the train to reach 50 m/s?
5. Explain the following statement: 'A model train running at a constant speed around a circular track is accelerating.'

Acceleration

Something is accelerating when its velocity is changing. The bigger the change in velocity, or the shorter the time it takes, the larger the **acceleration**.

Acceleration can be calculated using this equation:

$$\text{acceleration (m/s}^2) = \frac{\text{change in velocity (m/s)}}{\text{time taken for change (s)}}$$

When bodies move in a straight line, 'change in velocity' and 'change in speed' are the same thing.

If velocity is measured in metres per second and time in seconds, the unit of acceleration is metres per second per second, which is usually written as m/s^2.

Example

At the start of a 100 metre race, an Olympic runner accelerates to 12 m/s in 2 seconds. What is the acceleration of the runner?

starting velocity = 0 m/s

final velocity = 12 m/s

time taken = 2 s

$$\text{acceleration} = \frac{\text{change in velocity}}{\text{time taken}} = \frac{12 - 0}{2} = 6\ \text{m/s}^2$$

Deceleration

A body that is slowing down is decelerating. The body has a negative acceleration. Putting the brakes on makes a car decelerate and slow down. If it decelerates at 3 m/s^2, then its velocity goes down by 3 m/s every second.

Figure 9.6 On landing, a jet fighter uses its brakes and a parachute to produce a large deceleration.

9.2 Using graphs to describe the motion of a body

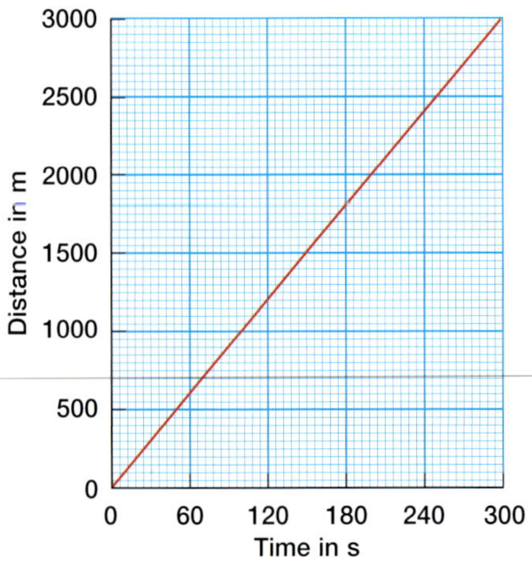

Figure 9.7 A distance–time graph for a short car journey

Distance–time graphs

A **distance–time graph** can be used to describe and work out the speed of a body.

Figure 9.7 shows the distance–time graph for a short car journey.

The car is travelling the same distance, 600 metres, every minute. So the car is moving at a steady speed of 10 metres per second (m/s). This is the same as the slope (gradient) of the line.

When a distance–time graph gives a straight line the body is moving at a constant (or zero) speed. Calculating the slope (gradient) of the line gives the value of the speed.

The slope of a **distance–time graph** gives the speed of a body.

Steve and his horse Rocket take part in a long distance ride. Figure 9.8 shows the distance–time graph for the ride. The graph has been divided into three parts.

- Part A – Steve and Rocket move at a constant speed. They travel 16 kilometres in 2 hours. The slope of the line equals 8 km/h, the same as their average speed.
- Part B – Steve and Rocket have stopped to take a rest. The distance moved does not change and the slope of the line is zero.
- Part C – Steve and Rocket move at a steady speed. They travel 24 kilometres in 2 hours. The slope of the line is 12 km/h. This means their speed was the greatest during this part of the ride.

When a body is stationary (not moving), the line on a distance–time graph is horizontal.

A steeper slope means a faster speed.

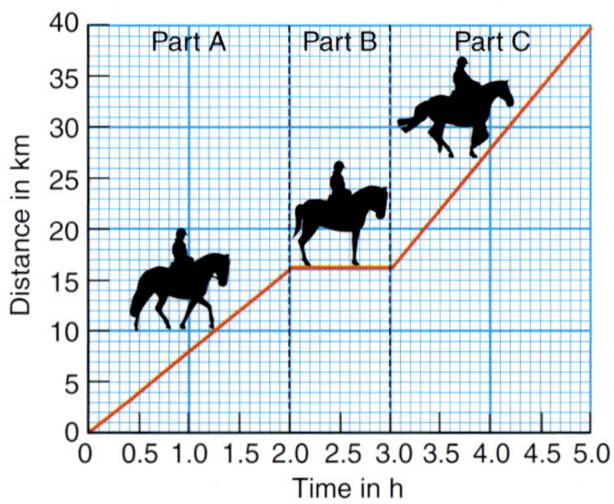

Figure 9.8 Distance–time graph for a horse ride

❻ Curtis cycles to school.
Figure 9.9 shows the distance–time graph for his journey.

a) How long did Curtis stop at the traffic lights?
b) During which part of the journey was Curtis cycling the fastest?

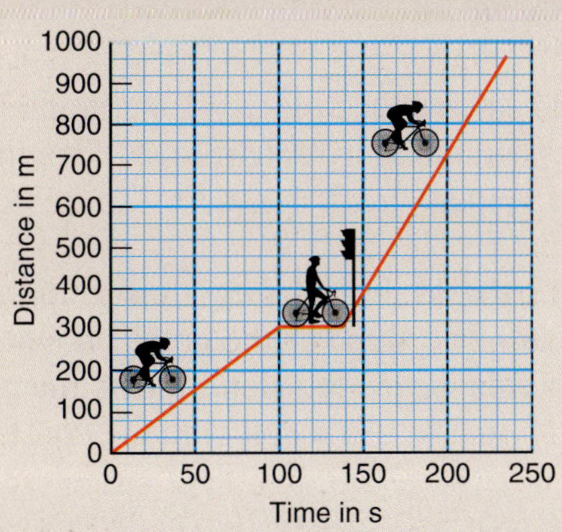

Figure 9.9

❼ As Sue and Steve walk down the high street they stop and look in two shop windows. Figure 9.10 shows the distance–time graph for their walk.

a) How long did they spend looking in the windows?
b) How far apart were the two shops they looked in?
c) Between which two times did they walk the slowest? Calculate this speed.
d) Calculate Sue and Steve's average speed as they walked along the high street.

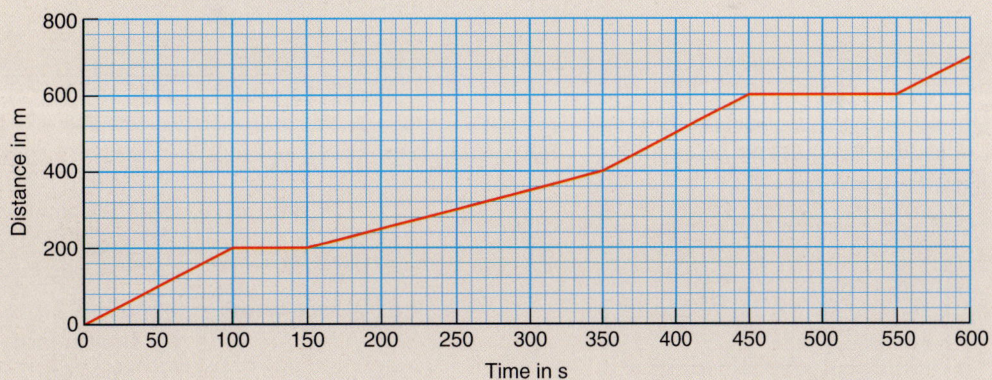

Figure 9.10

Velocity–time graphs

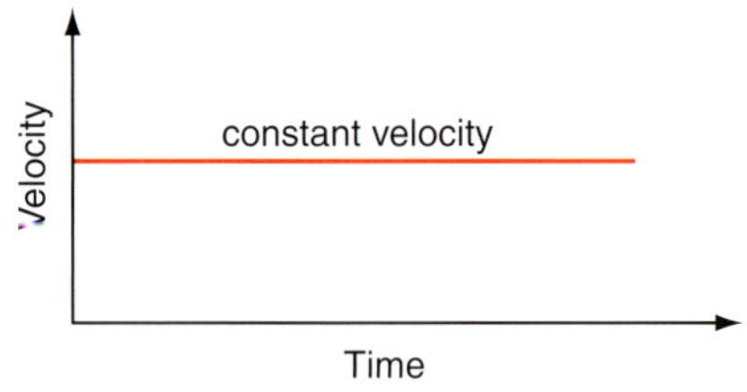

Figure 9.11 The velocity–time graph for something moving with a constant velocity is a horizontal line.

A velocity–time graph can be used to describe the velocity and acceleration of a body. Although these graphs may look very similar to distance–time graphs, they mean different things. Always look at the axes.

Figure 9.11 shows the velocity–time graph for a car moving at a constant speed along a straight road. This means the car is moving with a constant velocity.

The **slope** (gradient) of a velocity–time graph gives the acceleration of a body.

Figure 9.12 shows the velocity–time graph for a car accelerating along a straight road. The slope of the graph shows how quickly the velocity is changing. This means the slope shows the acceleration of the car. A straight line means the acceleration is constant.

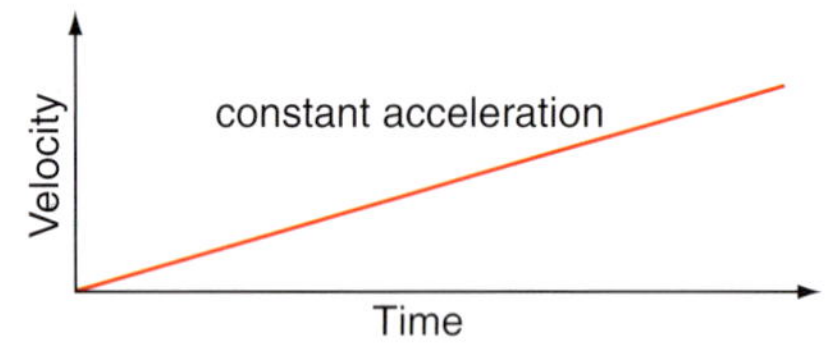

Figure 9.12 The slope of a velocity–time graph gives acceleration. A steeper slope means a greater acceleration.

How far does a body travel when it accelerates?

Figure 9.13 shows Ravi's velocity as he cycles downhill on a straight road. How far does Ravi cycle in 10 seconds?

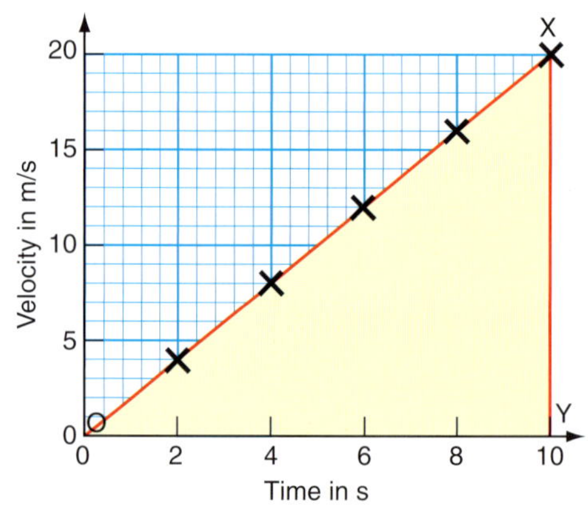

Figure 9.13 The straight line means that Ravi has a constant acceleration.

The area below the graph line in a velocity–time graph represents distance travelled.

distance = average velocity × time

average velocity = ½ × 20

So, the distance cycled = (½ × 20) × 10 = 100 m
= ½ × final velocity × time
= ½ × XY × OY
= shaded area below the graph line

Example

Figure 9.14 shows the velocity–time graph for a lift moving between two floors in a hotel. The graph has been divided into two parts.

- Part A – The velocity is increasing at a constant rate; the lift has a constant acceleration.
- Part B – The velocity is decreasing at a constant rate (negative slope); the lift has a constant deceleration.

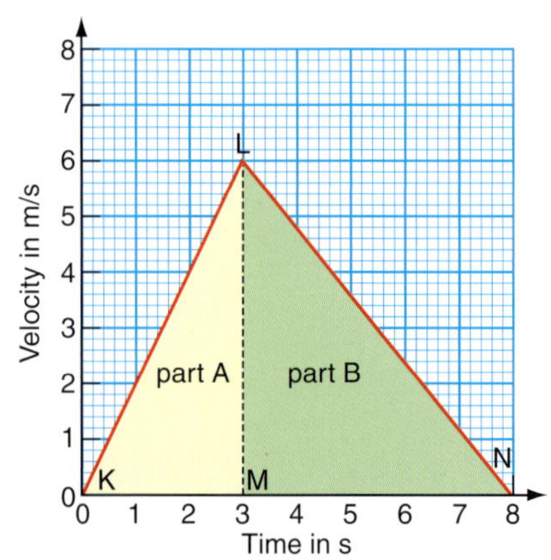

Figure 9.14 Velocity–time graph for a lift

To find the acceleration of the lift in part A we work out the slope of the graph line.

$$\text{slope} = \frac{LM}{KM} = \frac{6}{3} = 2\,\text{m/s}^2$$

You should be able to use the same method to show that the deceleration of the lift in part B is 1.2 m/s^2.

To find the distance the lift moves while it is accelerating, we work out the area of part A.

$$\text{area} = ½ \times 6 \times 3 = 9\,\text{m}$$

You should be able to use the same method to show that the distance between the two floors in the hotel is 24 m.

8. Figure 9.16 shows the velocity–time graph for a cheetah.
   a) Calculate the acceleration of the cheetah.
   b) Calculate the distance travelled by the cheetah in 10 seconds.

Figure 9.15

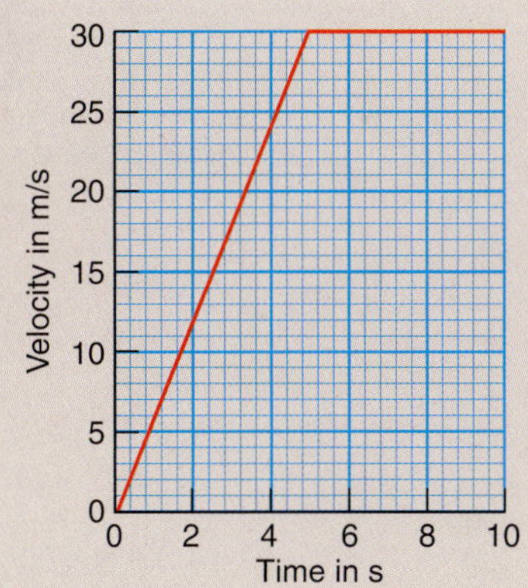

Figure 9.16

9. A train pulls out from Maidenhead station and accelerates at a constant rate, reaching a velocity of 25 m/s after 90 seconds. The train then travels at this speed for 180 seconds, at which point the brakes are applied and the train comes to a stop at Taplow station 60 seconds later.
   Draw a velocity–time graph for the train and use it to calculate:
   a) the acceleration of the train;
   b) the distance between Maidenhead and Taplow stations.

10. Table 9.1 gives some data for a speed skier travelling in a straight line down a steep slope.

Time in s	0	2	4	6	8	10	12	14
Velocity in m/s	0	12	24	32	38	40	40	40

Table 9.1

   a) Draw a velocity–time graph for the skier.
   b) Calculate the acceleration of the skier during the first 4 seconds.
   c) What is the acceleration of the skier during the last 4 seconds?

9.3 How do forces affect the movement of a body?

Figure 9.17 When you push on the trolley it pushes equally hard on you.

Forces have size and direction. We use an arrow to show the direction of a force. The length of the arrow represents the size of the force.

To make a supermarket trolley move is simple. You push and the trolley moves forward. You pull and the trolley moves backwards. But whatever the direction of the force you exert, the trolley always exerts an equal sized force in the opposite direction on you. This is because forces always come in pairs. You just can't have one force without another.

Whenever two bodies interact, the forces they exert on each other are always equal in size and opposite in direction.

But the two forces always act on different bodies; this is why they do not cancel out.

11 Josh knows that when he kicks a ball into the air the force of gravity pulls the ball back down. Since forces come in pairs, he thinks that as the ball is pulled down by the Earth, the ball should pull the Earth up. But he has never noticed this. Explain why.

What happens when more than one force acts on the same body?

Each diagram in Figure 9.18 shows two forces. But only one force is shown acting on each different body. This would be unusual. In most situations there will always be more than one force acting on a single body.

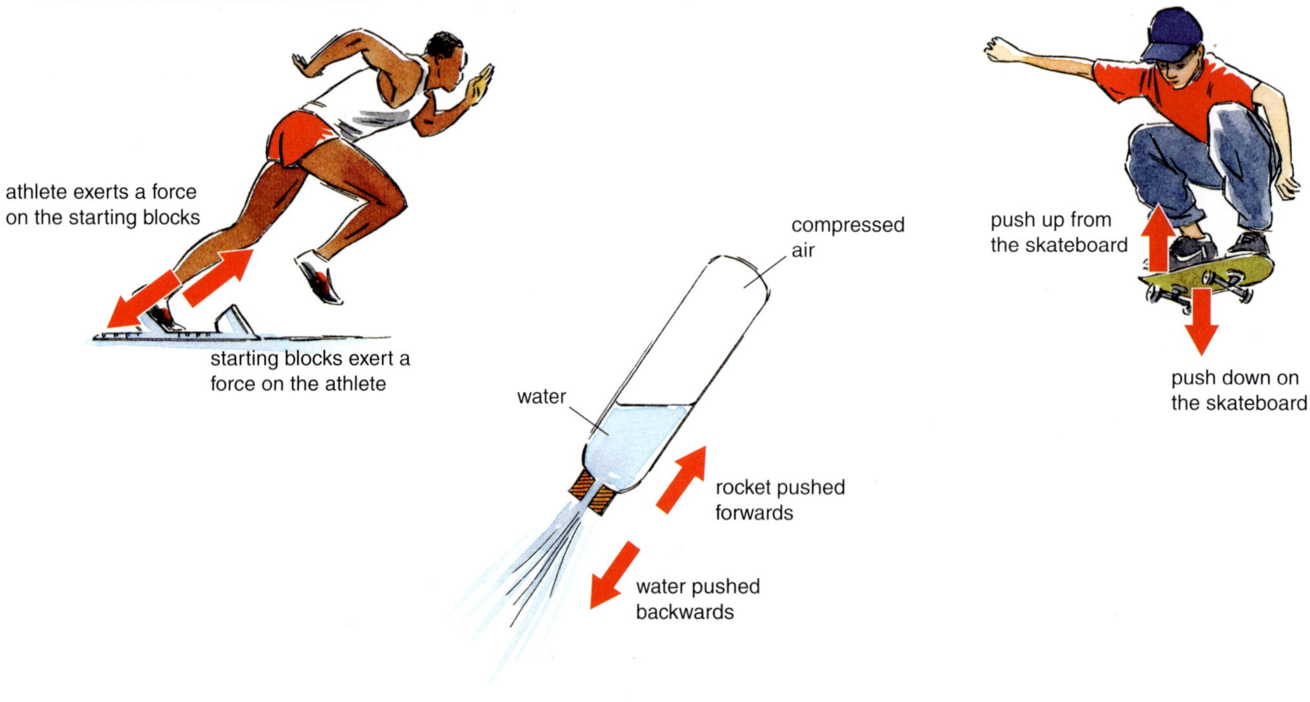

Figure 9.18 Some examples of interacting bodies

The **resultant force** is a single force that has the same effect on a body as all the original forces acting together.

To find out what happens to a body when more than one force acts on it we imagine all the individual forces being replaced by a single force that has the same effect. This single force is called the resultant force. The size and direction of the **resultant force** determines how or even if the body moves.

These forces acting on a body	give this resultant force
2 N ← □ → 2 N	□ 0 N (zero)
2 N → □ → 3 N	□ → 5 N
2 N ← □ → 3 N	□ → 1 N

Table 9.2 Two forces acting in the same direction add to give the resultant force. Two forces acting in opposite directions subtract to give the resultant force.

⓬ Tom and Sam are pulling on the opposite ends of a rope. Tom pulls with a force of 70 N and Sam pulls with a force of 100 N.

a) What is their resultant force?

b) Jim now joins in pulling the rope. The new resultant force is zero. What force does Jim pull with and does he help Tom or Sam?

What happens when the forces are balanced?

Figure 9.19 shows the forces acting on a toy bird. The weight of the toy causes the spring to stretch. The spring stretches until the upward force in the spring (tension) equals the downward weight of the toy. The forces are now **balanced**. In effect the forces have cancelled each other out. So, the resultant force is zero and the toy is stationary (not moving).

If the resultant force on a body is zero, the movement of the body does not change. If the body is stationary, it remains stationary. But what if the body is moving? If the forces are balanced so that the resultant force is zero, the body keeps moving at the same speed and in the same direction.

If the resultant force acting on a body is zero, the forces are **balanced** and the body does not accelerate. It remains at rest or continues at the same speed and in the same direction.

Figure 9.20 shows the forward and backward forces acting on a cyclist. The cyclist is riding along a straight road, keeping the same constant speed. This means that there is no change in the movement of the cyclist. So the two forces must be balanced giving a resultant force of zero.

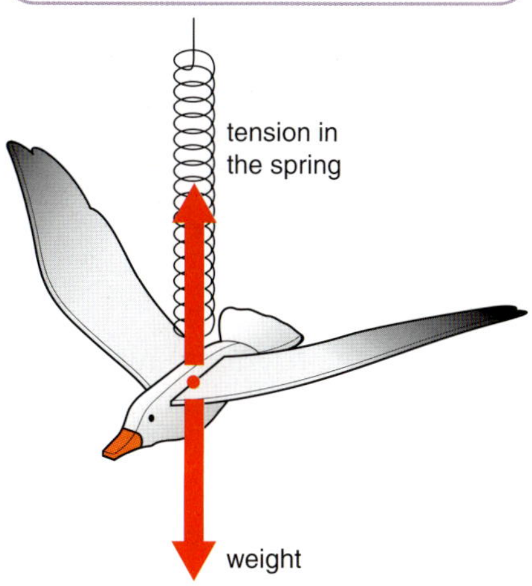

Figure 9.19 When the toy bird is stationary, the resultant force on the toy is zero.

Figure 9.20 The resultant force on a cyclist with a constant velocity is zero.

What happens when the forces are unbalanced?

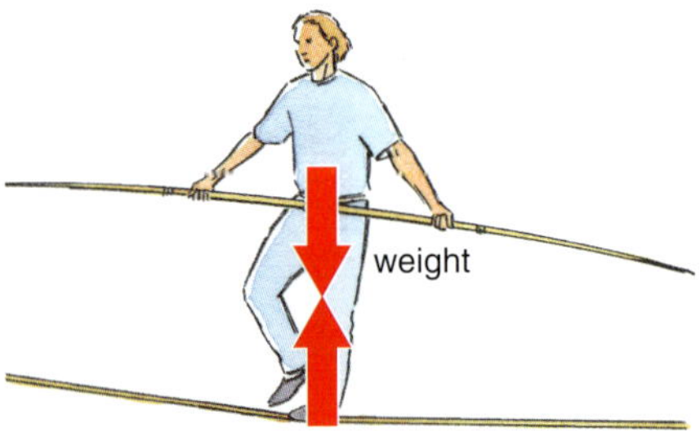

Figure 9.21 The tight rope walker would have problems if the forces did not balance.

In a tug of war, when both teams pull equally hard, the resultant force is zero and the rope does not move. But when one team starts to pull with a larger force the rope moves. The resultant force is no longer zero. The rope and both teams start to move in the direction of the resultant force.

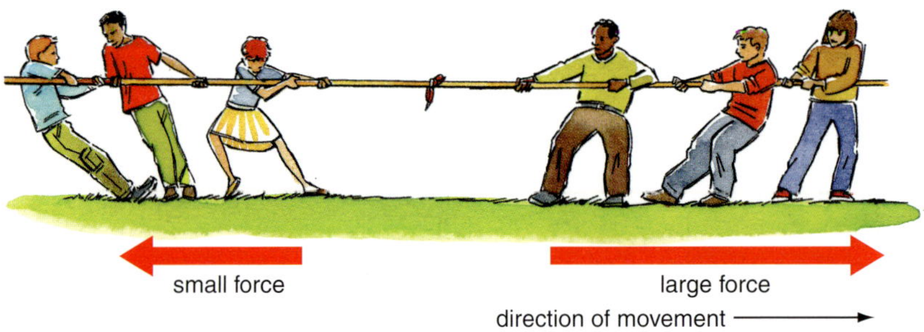

Figure 9.22 When forces are unbalanced, the resultant force is not zero.

If the resultant force acting on a body is not zero, the forces are **unbalanced** and so the body changes speed.

When the forces acting on a body are **unbalanced**, the resultant force changes the velocity of the body. Since velocity involves both speed and direction, a resultant force can make a body speed up, slow down or change direction.

An engine produces the driving force needed to move a car forwards. If the car is stationary pushing the accelerator pedal produces a resultant force forwards. The car then accelerates in the direction of the resultant force.

Air resistance (or drag) is a force of friction. The direction of air resistance is always opposite to the direction of the moving object.

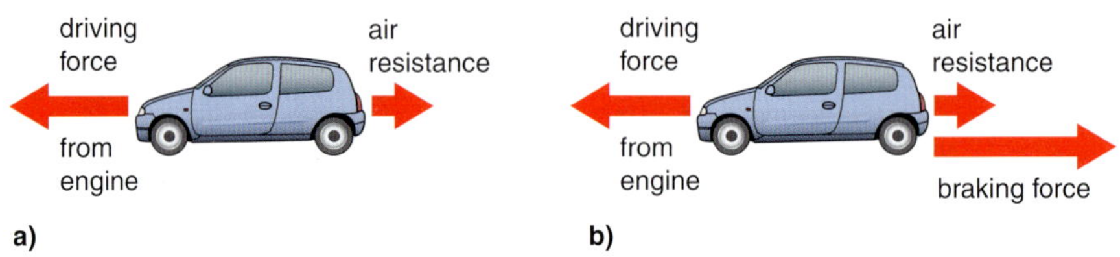

Figure 9.23 a) The car accelerates in the direction of the resultant force. b) The car decelerates in the direction of the resultant force.

When the resultant force on a stationary or moving body is not zero, the body accelerates in the direction of the resultant force.

If the car engine stops or the driver puts the brakes on, the car decelerates (slows down). This happens because the frictional forces backwards are now larger than the force forwards. The resultant force is in the opposite direction to the way the car is moving.

When a body is moving in the opposite direction to the resultant force, it decelerates.

⑬ Look at the forces acting on a moving boat.

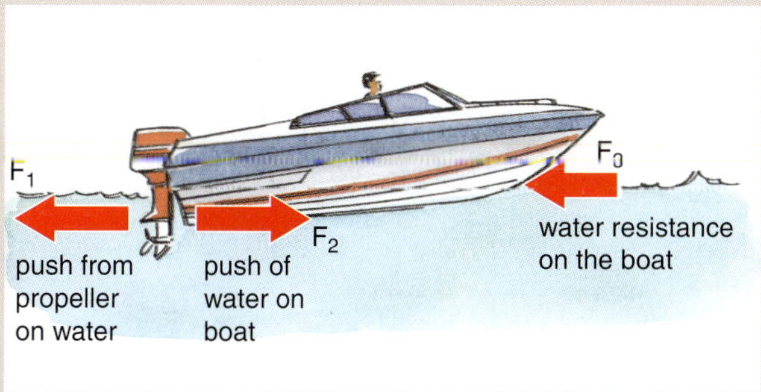

Figure 9.24

a) Which two forces are always equal? Explain the reason for your choice
b) Describe the motion of the boat when:
   i) $F_2 = F_3$;
   ii) F_2 is larger than F_3.

⑭ Four forces act on a submerged submarine.

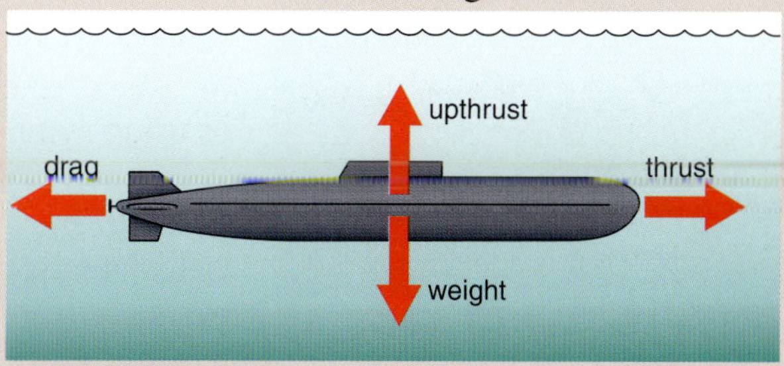

Figure 9.25

a) The submarine is cruising with a constant velocity and at a constant depth. Write down the connection between weight and upthrust; drag and thrust.
b) Explain what happens if the weight of the submarine is increased by filling the buoyancy tanks with water.

Force, mass and acceleration

Figure 9.26 The acceleration of the car depends on the resultant force applied to the car.

If you have ever tried to push a broken down car you will know that it is not easy. If you are the only person pushing, the car accelerates and moves slowly. The more people that push, the greater the resultant force on the car and the greater the acceleration.

The greater the resultant force on a body, the greater the acceleration of the body.

Common sense would tell us that it is much more difficult to give a van the same acceleration as a car. A much larger force is needed. This is because the mass of the van is far bigger than the mass of the car. Pushing a larger and larger mass with the same force gives a smaller and smaller acceleration.

The bigger the mass of a body, the bigger the resultant force needed to make it accelerate.

Figure 9.27 A large resultant force acting on the small mass of the drag car gives it massive acceleration.

Figure 9.28 More force is needed to give a van the same acceleration as a car.

Figure 9.29 A huge force is needed to accelerate this mass.

The force needed to accelerate a mass can be calculated using this equation:

resultant force (newton, N)	=	mass (kilogram, kg)	×	acceleration (metre/second², m/s²)

or using symbols $F = m \times a$

Example

Calculate the resultant force needed to give a 2 kg ball an acceleration of 6 m/s^2.

$F = m \times a$

$F = 2 \times 6 = 12\,\text{N}$

9.4 Does a falling body keep on accelerating?

A falling body speeds up or accelerates because of the force of gravity. Gravity is a force of attraction. A ball thrown into the air is pulled back to the ground by gravity. As the ball falls downwards, gravity makes it accelerate. On Earth, if there were no frictional forces (air resistance), the ball would accelerate at 10 m/s^2. This means that the velocity of a falling object increases by 10 m/s every second – it keeps accelerating.

In a vacuum, there is no air resistance so gravity is the only force acting on the body and all falling objects accelerate at the same rate, 10 m/s^2.

15 The part of the space shuttle which returns to Earth is called the orbiter. It has a mass of 78 000 kg and lands at a speed of 100 m/s. After touchdown it takes 50 s to decelerate and come to a halt.
  a) Calculate the deceleration of the orbiter.
  b) Calculate the force needed to bring the orbiter to a halt.

16 Gurpal is cycling along a flat road when he stops pedalling. Gurpal's speed drops from 8 m/s to 5 m/s in 6 s.
  a) Calculate Gurpal's deceleration.
  b) The mass of Gurpal and his bicycle is 90 kg. Calculate the resistance force slowing Gurpal down.

17 Explain why the acceleration of a car is reduced when it tows a caravan.

18 Explain why a canoeist slows down when they stop paddling.

Activity – Investigating the acceleration of a falling body

Liam has read about Galileo's famous experiment with falling bodies. Galileo believed that gravity makes all falling bodies accelerate at the same rate. Most people at the time did not believe Galileo. To show that his idea was right, Galileo is supposed to have dropped a small iron ball and a large iron ball from the top of the Leaning Tower of Pisa, in Italy. The two objects are said to have hit the ground at virtually, but not quite, the same time.

1 Most people expected the large iron ball to hit the ground first, and it did. Why did people expect different bodies to fall at different rates?

2 Explain why this result on its own would not disprove Galileo's idea.

Figure 9.30 Galileo planned his famous experiment at the leaning tower of Pisa to test if all falling objects accelerate at the same rate.

Liam decided to investigate the acceleration of falling bodies, to see if Galileo's prediction was right. The apparatus Liam used is shown in Figure 9.31.

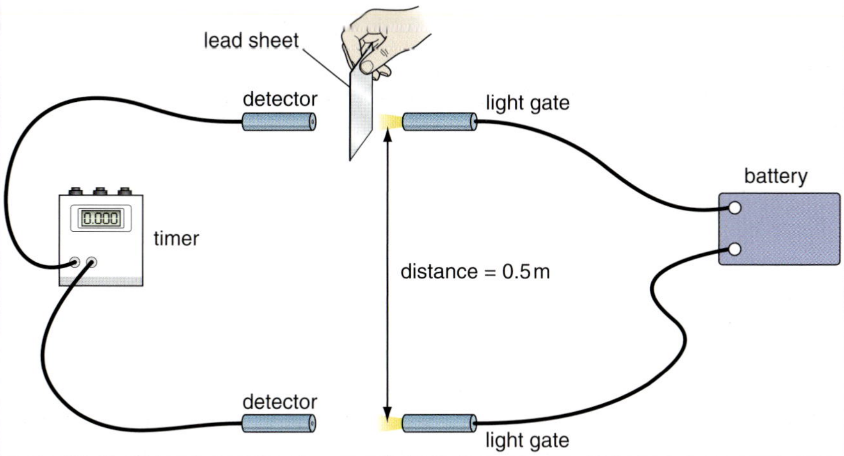

Figure 9.31 The apparatus used by Liam to measure the acceleration of a falling body

Liam started with a small sheet of lead. As soon as he let go, the sheet passed through the top light gate and the electronic timer started. The timer stopped when the sheet passed through the bottom light gate. Liam repeated this four times. The four timer readings are written in Table 9.3.

Result	Time in s
1	0.326
2	0.330
3	0.465
4	0.319

Table 9.3

❸ Why did Liam repeat the time measurement?

❹ Liam left out the third result when he calculated the mean (average) time. Why do you think he did this?

❺ What was the mean time calculated by Liam?

❻ Use the following equation to calculate the acceleration of the lead sheet:

$$\text{acceleration} = \frac{2 \times \text{distance the body falls}}{(\text{mean time taken})^2}$$

By increasing the distance between the light gates Liam was able to get enough information to draw the graph shown in Figure 9.32.

❼ The gradient of the graph line equals the acceleration of the falling lead sheet.
  a) Measure and record the gradient of the line.
  b) Why is the value obtained by measuring the gradient likely to be more accurate than the value worked out by averaging?

❽ When Liam measured the acceleration of a falling polystyrene ball, he got a value considerably less than the value for the lead sheet. Why do think this was?

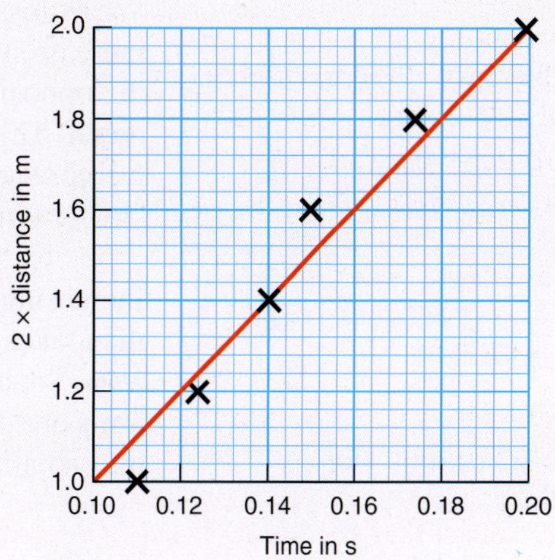

Figure 9.32 The graph drawn using Liam's results

What happens when frictional forces act against gravity?

Usually air resistance does act on a falling body. It has the effect of reducing the resultant force on the body.

Joss is a sky-diver. She understands how important air resistance is in keeping her alive. At the moment when Joss jumps from a plane the only force acting on her is her weight. So she starts to accelerate downwards, as shown in the first part of Figure 9.33.

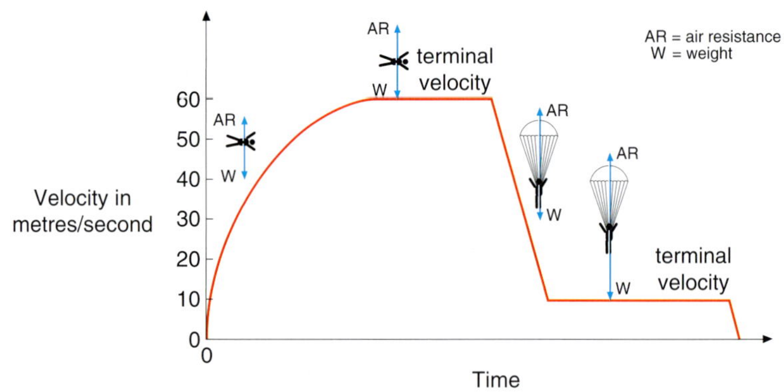

Figure 9.33 The velocity–time graph of a sky-diver

As soon as Joss starts to fall, air resistance begins to act upwards on her. Since her weight is bigger than the air resistance, she still accelerates towards the ground, but her acceleration decreases (the slope of the graph decreases).

Terminal velocity is the constant velocity reached by a moving body when the resultant force acting on it (in the direction it is moving) is zero.

As Joss's speed increases, air resistance increases until it equals her weight. At this point the resultant force on Joss is zero and she stops accelerating. But she doesn't stop falling! She carries on falling but at a constant speed. The velocity–time graph is a straight line. Joss is falling at her **terminal velocity**.

When Joss opens her parachute, the increased surface area causes an increase in the air resistance. This produces a resultant force upwards – the opposite direction to her motion – and so Joss decelerates and slows down. This reduces air resistance so that once again the two forces, weight and air resistance, become balanced. Joss then falls with a new, slower terminal velocity until she lands safely on the ground.

Increasing the surface area of an object increases the air resistance. It then takes less time for the forces to balance to give a resultant force of zero. So, a sky-diver wearing loose clothing and spreading out their arms and legs has a lower terminal velocity than a sky-diver curled up into a ball.

⓳ The sky-diver in Figure 9.34 is falling at her terminal velocity. Explain why curling up into a ball makes her fall faster and increase her terminal velocity.

⓴ The velocity–time graph drawn in Figure 9.33 is for a sky-diver weighing 600 N.

a) How big is the air resistance force when the sky-diver is falling at their terminal velocity? Explain the reason for your answer.

b) Estimate the size of the air resistance force when the sky-diver first opens the parachute. Explain the reason for your answer.

c) After landing the sky-diver stands still on the ground. Explain why the resultant force on the sky-diver is zero.

Figure 9.34

Figure 9.35 The hull of a hydrofoil lifts out of the water. This reduces the water resistance allowing the hydrofoil to accelerate to a higher velocity.

Substances that flow are **fluids**. Liquids and gases are both fluids.

It's not just sky-divers that have a terminal velocity. All objects falling or moving through a **fluid** have a terminal velocity.

If you have ever paddled a canoe you will know that no matter how hard you paddle, you cannot keep increasing your speed. To start with your speed increases, but as you go faster the water resistance force also increases. Eventually the forwards force you produce and the water resistance will be equal. The resultant force is zero and you have reached your terminal velocity.

Activity – Investigating terminal velocity

Figure 9.36 shows a simple model parachute made from a sheet of plastic. When dropped, the plasticine figure soon reaches its terminal velocity.

❶ Plan an experiment to find out if the terminal velocity of the plasticine figure depends on the area of the parachute.

❷ What measurements would you take?

❸ How will you know that the plasticine figure has reached its terminal velocity?

❹ Which one of the following is the independent variable in this experiment?

- distance the parachute falls
- area of the parachute
- weight of the plasticine figure
- time taken to fall

❺ What are the control variables in this experiment?

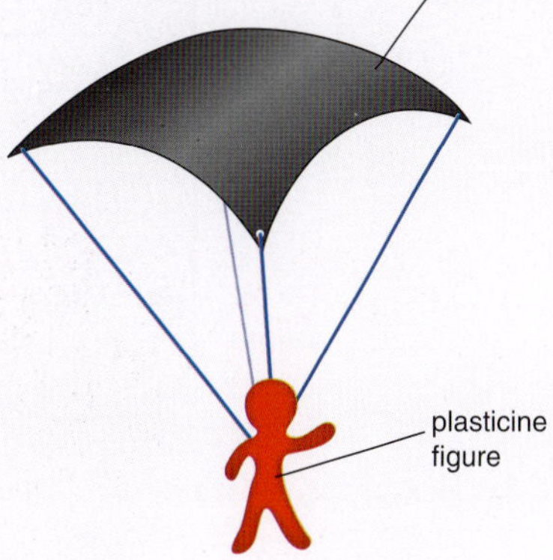

Figure 9.36

Figure 9.37 To measure your weight the bathroom scales must measure in newtons.

Mass and weight

If you want to know your weight, you will probably stand on some bathroom scales.

But the units on your bathroom scales are mass units – not weight units. The bathroom scales give a number in kilograms and mass is measured in kilograms, not weight.

Weight is a force, so like all forces it is measured in newtons. Weight is the force which **gravity** exerts on a mass.

More mass does mean more weight, because there is more mass for the force of gravity to pull on. On Earth, gravity pulls on every one kilogram of mass with a force of about 10 newtons. This is called the gravitational field strength (g).

$$g = 10\text{ N/kg}$$

Sakhib, who has a mass of 50 kilograms, will weigh:

$$50 \times 10 = 500\text{ newtons}$$

You can use this equation to calculate the weight of an object:

$$\underset{\text{(newton, N)}}{\text{weight}} = \underset{\text{(kilogram, kg)}}{\text{mass}} \times \underset{\text{(newton/kilogram, N/kg)}}{\text{gravitational field strength}}$$

21 Explain why a ball-bearing falling through oil has a much lower terminal velocity than an identical ball-bearing falling through the air.

22 Kathy, Jon and Cary go on a diet. Table 9.4 shows the mass of each person at the start and end of the month.

Person	Mass at start of the month in kg	Mass at end of the month in kg
Kathy	72.0	70.5
Jon	115.0	110.0
Cary	68.0	66.0

Table 9.4

How much weight did each person lose in 1 month?

23 When he was asked his weight, Gorese said it was 45 kg. Why is Gorese wrong?

9.5 Stopping safely

The **thinking distance** is how far a vehicle travels during the driver's reaction time, before the brakes are applied.

The **braking distance** is how far a vehicle travels before stopping, once the brakes have been applied.

Stopping Distance = Thinking Distance + Braking Distance

Friction forces decelerate a moving car and bring it to a stop. In an emergency, for example a child running out in front of a car, the driver must apply the brakes as soon as possible. But the average driver has a reaction time of about three-quarters of a second. This is the time taken by the driver to react and move their foot from the accelerator pedal to the brake pedal. During this time the car carries on moving at a steady speed. The distance the car moves during the reaction time is called the **thinking distance**. Once the brakes have been applied the car slows down and comes to a stop. The distance the car moves once the brakes are put on is called the **braking distance**.

The total **stopping distance** of a vehicle is made up of the two parts: the thinking distance and the **braking distance**.

Figure 9.38 Thinking distance + braking distance = stopping distance

Speed affects both the thinking distance and the braking distance. Figure 9.39 shows the stopping distances for a typical car at different speeds. The force applied by the brakes is the same for each of the speeds.

As the vehicle goes faster, a greater braking force is needed to make the vehicle stop in the same distance. But beware – too great a braking force can make a vehicle skid.

The stopping distances given in Figure 9.39 are average values for a family car in good conditions on a dry road. Under different conditions the actual stopping distance can be much longer.

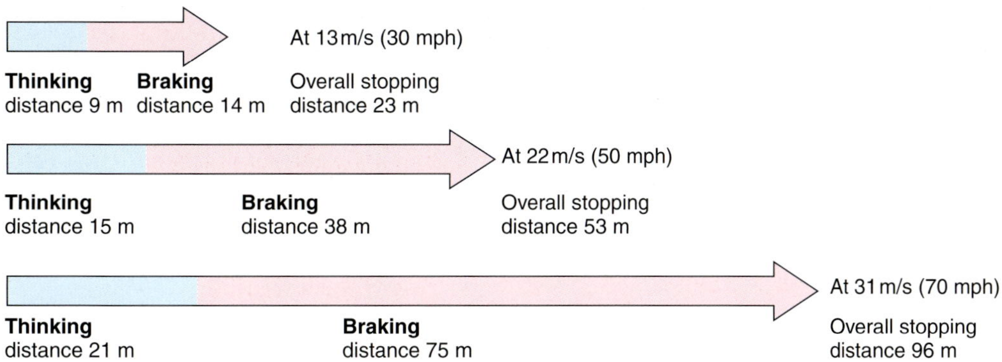

Figure 9.39 For a certain size braking force, the faster the vehicle the greater the stopping distance.

The driver's reactions may be slower than usual. The slower the reaction time, the longer the thinking distance. A driver's reactions are much slower if they:

- have been drinking alcohol;
- have been taking certain types of drug;
- are tired;
- are talking on a mobile phone.

Braking distance can be affected by several factors as well as speed:

- weather conditions – in wet or icy conditions the friction between the car tyres and road is reduced. This increases the braking distance.
- the vehicle being poorly maintained – worn brakes or worn tyres increase the braking distance.
- the road surface – a rough surface increases the friction between the road and the tyres, reducing the braking distance. You may have noticed that high-friction surfaces are often used on the approaches to busy junctions and roundabouts.

24 Explain the effect on the stopping distance of a car when there is ice on the road.

25 Drivers should leave a gap between their vehicle and the one in front. A learner driver said to his instructor, 'If I go twice as fast, I should leave a gap twice as big.' Explain why the learner driver is wrong.

26 A road safety advert had the slogan, 'Only a fool breaks the 2 second rule'. This means that at whatever speed vehicles are being driven, there should be at least a 2 second gap between them.

Copy out Table 9.5. Use the information in Figure 9.39 to complete the table.

Speed in m/s	Distanced travelled in 2 s in m	Stopping distance in m
13	26	
22		53
31		

Table 9.5

a) Is a '2 second gap' between cars long enough to stop safely? Give a reason for your answer.
b) Under what conditions would you advise motorists to leave a larger gap than 2 seconds?

27 A policeman caught driving at 160 mph (72 m/s) was found not guilty of dangerous driving. The court was told that the policeman was a trained advanced driver practising his skills.

Do you think that high-speed driving can ever be justified? Give reasons for your answer.

28 Table 9.6 gives the thinking distance and braking distance for a car at different speeds.

Speed in m/s	0	9	13	18	26	36	52
Thinking distance in m	0	6	9	12	18	24	36
Braking distance in m	0	6	14	24	56	96	224

Table 9.6

a) Plot a graph of thinking distance against speed.
b) What pattern links thinking distance and speed?
c) Plot a graph of braking distance against speed.
d) What pattern links braking distance and speed?
e) Use the graphs to find the stopping distance for a car travelling at 72 m/s. (Hint: Extend the graph lines assuming they continue to follow the same pattern. Remember, this is called extrapolating the graph.)

9.6 Are you working?

What is work?

Ask anyone what they think work is and you are likely to get a lot of different answers. But the answers usually involve doing something, maybe mowing the lawn, or lifting a box, or even writing an essay.

Figure 9.40 A machine like this crane can do more work than a human.

Work is done when a force makes something move. Work is measured in joules.

In science, **work** has a very specific meaning. Work is done whenever a force makes a body move. A force that causes a body to move is doing work. The bigger the force and the further the force makes the body move, the more work is done.

Work, like energy, is measured in joules (J).

The work done in moving a body can be calculated using the equation:

$$\underset{\text{(joule, J)}}{\text{work done}} = \underset{\text{(newton, N)}}{\text{force applied}} \times \underset{\text{(metre, m)}}{\text{distance moved in the direction of the force}}$$

This means that for a force to do work it must make something move. No matter how big the force, if it doesn't make something move it hasn't done any work.

Example

Calculate the work done by a weightlifter when lifting a weight of 750 N to a height of 2.4 m.

$$\begin{aligned}\text{work done} &= \text{force} \times \text{distance moved}\\ &= 750 \times 2.4 = 1800\ \text{J}\end{aligned}$$

29 The Falkirk Wheel is the first ever rotating boat lift. It lifts 600 000 kg of water plus boat through a height of 35 metres.
a) Calculate the weight that the Falkirk Wheel is able to lift.
b) Calculate the work done by the Wheel in one rotation.

Figure 9.41 The Falkirk Wheel in action

Figure 9.42 To lift its own body weight and the rider over the fence, the horse must exert a large force and do a lot of work.

Work and energy

It's not easy for a horse to lift itself and the rider over a fence. It needs a large force and a lot of energy. When they are off the ground the horse and rider have gained gravitational potential energy. Since energy is conserved, this energy must have come from somewhere. In this case some of the chemical energy in the horse's muscles has been transferred to the gravitational potential energy of the horse and rider.

Richard works on a building site. One of his jobs is to move sand in a wheelbarrow. When he starts pushing the wheelbarrow, it moves, so work is being done. When it moves, the wheelbarrow gains kinetic energy. This energy has been transferred from Richard. Some of the chemical energy in Richard's muscles has been transferred into the kinetic energy of the wheelbarrow and sand.

Figure 9.43 Pushing the wheelbarrow involves transferring energy.

Whenever a force makes a body move, work is done and energy must be transferred.

In fact work and energy are linked by the equation:

$$\text{work done} = \text{energy transferred}$$

So if Richard does 1000 J of work to move the wheelbarrow and sand, 1000 J of energy must be transferred.

To keep the wheelbarrow moving at a constant speed Richard must keep pushing with a constant force. This is because there are frictional forces trying to stop the wheelbarrow from moving.

Imagine pushing a heavy crate across the floor. It's hard work! As you push, friction acts with an equal force but in the opposite direction to your push. Since the resultant force on the crate is zero the crate moves across the floor at a constant velocity. Although you are doing work, the kinetic

Figure 9.44 When friction tries to stop the movement between two surfaces, energy is transformed into heat.

energy of the crate is not changing. The work you do is against the frictional forces that are trying to stop the crate moving. Where the crate rubs against the floor both the crate and the floor get a little hotter. Chemical energy from your muscles has been transformed into heat.

When work is done against frictional forces, energy is mainly transformed into heat.

Example

Ahmed uses a force of 225 N to drag a heavy box 5 m across a rough floor at a steady speed. Calculate the work done against friction.

$$\text{work done} = \text{force} \times \text{distance moved}$$
$$= 225 \times 5$$
$$= 1125\,\text{J}$$

30 Copy and complete Table 9.7.

Task	Force applied	Distance moved	Work done
Opening a door	12 N	0.8 m	
Pushing a loaded trolley		80 m	2000 J
Lifting a suitcase	180 N		288 J
Stretching a spring	30 N	5 cm	

Table 9.7

31 Explain why falling over and sliding on an artificial astroturf pitch can burn you.

32 Ray, a survival expert, can light a fire by rubbing two pieces of wood together. Why does this work?

33 Figure 9.45 shows Matthew pulling a heavy sack up a ramp. The ramp is a simple machine that makes the job of lifting the sack easier to do. Explain why the energy transferred to the sack is less than the work done pulling the sack up the ramp.

Figure 9.45

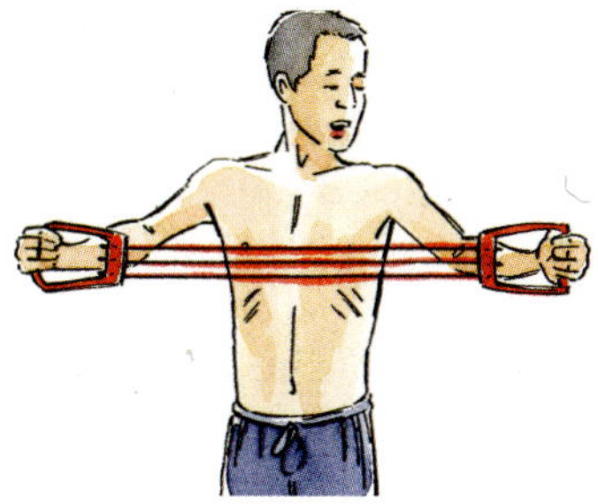

Figure 9.46 Using a chest expander involves doing work and transferring energy.

Elastic potential energy is the energy stored in an elastic object when work is done to change its shape.

Elastic potential energy

Some objects break easily – a small force is all that is needed to cause permanent damage. If you apply a force to an elastic object it may change shape, but not permanently. When the force is taken away the object goes back to the way it was.

Imagine bending a ruler. As long as the force is not too big, the ruler pings back into shape when the force is removed.

To stretch, squash, twist or bend an elastic object work must be done and energy transferred. The energy stored in an elastic object when work is done to change its shape is called **elastic potential energy**. In Figure 9.46, chemical energy from the person's muscles is transformed into elastic potential energy and stored in the stretched springs. The stored elastic potential energy has the potential to do work.

Figure 9.47 A bungee rope is designed to stretch. The jumper accelerates until the rope becomes tight. The rope then starts to stretch as work is done on the rope. Energy is transferred from the jumper to the rope and the jumper slows down. Some work is also done against air resistance, so some of the jumper's energy is transformed into heat. This is just as well, or the bungee jumper would bounce up and down forever.

Work and kinetic energy

Whenever a force makes a body move, work is done and energy is transferred.

Moving bodies have kinetic energy. The kinetic energy of a body increases when a force makes it speed up and decreases when it slows down.

Kinetic energy is not just to do with the speed of a body; it is also to do with the mass of the body. A lorry with a large mass moving at 20 m/s has more kinetic energy than a car with a small mass moving at 20 m/s. So, the kinetic energy of a moving body depends on:

- its mass;
- its speed.

The kinetic energy of a moving body can be calculated using the equation:

$$\underset{\text{(joule, J)}}{\text{kinetic energy}} = \tfrac{1}{2} \times \underset{\text{(kilogram, kg)}}{\text{mass}} \times \underset{\text{((metre/second)}^2\text{, (m/s)}^2\text{)}}{\text{speed}^2}$$

Example

A jogger of mass 60 kg runs at 3 m/s. What is the kinetic energy of the jogger?

$$\text{kinetic energy} = \tfrac{1}{2} \times \text{mass} \times \text{speed}^2$$
$$= \tfrac{1}{2} \times 60 \times 3 \times 3 = 270\text{ J}$$

Braking distance, braking force and kinetic energy

Brakes are used to stop a moving vehicle. The work done by the braking force reduces the vehicle's kinetic energy causing the vehicle to slow down and stop. The kinetic energy is transformed into heat. This is why friction brakes always get hot.

We saw in Section 9.5 that braking distance depends on speed. The greater the speed the longer the braking distance. But they do not increase in direct proportion, i.e. doubling the speed does not double the braking distance. In fact doubling the speed increases the braking distance four times. Why is this?

To stop a vehicle it must lose all of its kinetic energy. The equation for kinetic energy shows us that kinetic energy depends on speed squared. So, doubling a vehicle's speed increases its kinetic energy four times. If the same braking force is applied but four times as much energy must be transferred, then the vehicle must travel four times further.

You should be able to work out what happens to the braking distance if the speed of a vehicle increases three times.

34 Calculate the kinetic energy of:
   a) a motorbike of mass 350 kg travelling at 20 m/s;
   b) a 14 kg baby crawling at 0.5 m/s;
   c) a 6 kg cat walking at 60 cm/s;
   d) a 50 g bird flying at 40 m/s.

35 A ball thrown at 40 m/s has 160 J of kinetic energy. Calculate the mass of the ball.

36 Jake is puzzled. The brakes on his car are not working as well as when he drives the car to work on his own. Explain why this is.

Figure 9.48

Kinetic energy also depends on mass. A lorry with a mass ten times the mass of a car must transfer ten times more kinetic energy to stop than a car travelling at the same speed. So, although lorries have powerful brakes, they still take longer to stop than a car because they have a greater mass.

In Section 9.5 we saw that road conditions affect braking distance. For example if the road is icy braking distances increase. The ice reduces the friction between the tyres and the road. To avoid skidding the driver must use a small braking force. But to transfer the same amount of kinetic energy using only half the braking force would double the braking distance.

9.7 What is momentum?

Momentum is the mass of a body multiplied by the velocity of the body.

A moving body has kinetic energy and **momentum**. The greater the mass of the body and the faster it moves, the more kinetic energy and momentum it has. Momentum can be a really useful concept in calculations about collisions or explosions – more about these later.

The momentum, mass and velocity of a body are linked by the equation:

momentum	=	mass	×	velocity
(kilogram metre/second, kg m/s)		(kilogram, kg)		(metre/second, m/s)

There is no short name for the unit of momentum, but you can remember it as the unit of mass (kilogram) multiplied by the unit of velocity (metre/second).

Just like velocity, momentum has a size and a direction. The momentum of a body is always in the same direction as the velocity of the body. If two bodies move in opposite directions, one has a positive momentum and the other negative momentum.

37 Calculate the momentum of:
a) a 60 kg cyclist peddling at 8 m/s;
b) a football of mass 0.4 kg moving at 7 m/s;
c) a bullet of mass 5 g moving at 250 m/s;
d) a 500 kg pony galloping at 16 m/s.

38 A racing car moving at 85 m/s has a momentum of 42 500 kg m/s. Calculate the mass of the racing car.

39 A 1800 kg elephant has a momentum of 10 800 kg m/s. Calculate the velocity of the elephant.

Example

A lorry and a car are travelling in opposite directions. Use the data in the box to calculate the momentum of each vehicle.

Figure 9.49

Lorry	**Car**
mass = 9000 kg velocity = 14 m/s → momentum = mass × velocity = 9000 × 14 = 126 000 kg m/s momentum of the lorry = +126 000 kg m/s	mass = 900 kg velocity = 25 m/s ← momentum = mass × velocity = 900 × 25 = 22 500 kg m/s momentum of the car = −22 500 kg m/s

Since the momentum of the lorry moving to the right has been given as positive, the momentum of the car moving to the left must be given as negative.

How do unbalanced forces affect momentum?

Figure 9.50 A tennis player 'follows through' to give the ball more momentum.

When a resultant force acts on a body, the body accelerates. This means that the velocity of the body changes. If velocity changes, so does momentum. So, a resultant force acting on a body causes a change in momentum.

The size of the resultant force and the change in momentum that occurs are linked by the equation:

$$\text{force} = \frac{\text{change in momentum}}{\text{time taken for the change}}$$

where the force is in newtons (N), time in second (s) and change in momentum is in kilogram metre/second (kg m/s).

A small force acting for a long time can cause the same change in momentum as a large force acting for a small time.

Figure 9.51

In lots of sports that involve hitting a ball, the players 'follow through'. In tennis the 'follow through' means that the racquet does not stop the moment it hits the ball. The racquet continues, for a short time, to move with the ball. This action increases the time that the force acts on the ball, which increases the change in momentum of the ball. So the ball gains more speed.

Example

Figure 9.51 shows a golfer about to hit a golf ball of mass 0.045 kg. When the golf club hits the ball it is in contact for 0.001 s and exerts a force of 3600 N on the ball. Calculate the velocity that the ball has when it leaves the club.

$$\begin{aligned}\text{change in momentum} &= \text{force} \times \text{time}\\ &= 3600 \times 0.001 = 3.6\ \text{kg m/s}\end{aligned}$$

As the ball started off stationary, its initial momentum = 0. Therefore:

$$\text{change in momentum} = \text{mass} \times \text{final velocity}$$

$$\begin{aligned}\text{final velocity} &= \frac{\text{change in momentum}}{\text{mass}}\\ &= \frac{3.6}{0.045}\\ &= 80\ \text{m/s}\end{aligned}$$

40 During a crash test, a car of mass 840 kg is driven into a wall at 5 m/s. The car slows down and stops in 1.5 seconds. Calculate the force on the car during the collision.

Figure 9.52 A cricketer draws his hands back to reduce the force on the ball and the force on his hands.

41 Rafael hits a stationary hockey ball of mass 0.5 kg with a horizontal force of 80 N. The ball leaves Rafael's hockey stick at 12 m/s.
   a) Calculate the momentum of the hockey ball immediately after being hit.
   b) State the change in momentum of the ball.
   c) Calculate the time Rafael's hockey stick was in contact with the ball.

42 A ball and a lump of plasticine of equal mass are thrown at a wall. The ball is in contact with the wall for 0.05 s, then bounces back. The plasticine hits the wall and stops in 0.05 s. It does not bounce back. Explain why the ball exerts a larger force on the wall than the plasticine.

Momentum and saving lives

When two bodies collide, each exerts a force on the other. These forces are equal in size but opposite in direction. The change in momentum of each body is equal in size, but opposite in direction. The longer the time of contact, the smaller is the force needed to change the momentum. This is the principle behind many different types of devices aimed at saving lives during collisions.

Figure 9.53 Horse rider wearing a helmet and body protector

If you ride a bicycle or go horse riding you should always wear a helmet. Often horse riders also wear a body protector. A helmet and body protector work in the same way. If you fall off your bicycle and hit your head, the padding inside the helmet starts to crush. If you fall off a horse, the padding inside the body protector starts to crush. In both cases the time taken for your body to stop moving increases and the force which could cause an injury is reduced.

The surface of a child's play area needs to be tough but it also needs to be flexible. This is so that if a child falls, the surface squashes a little. The child will slow down more gradually than if it fell on a hard surface. This reduces the force on the child and so reduces the risk of injury.

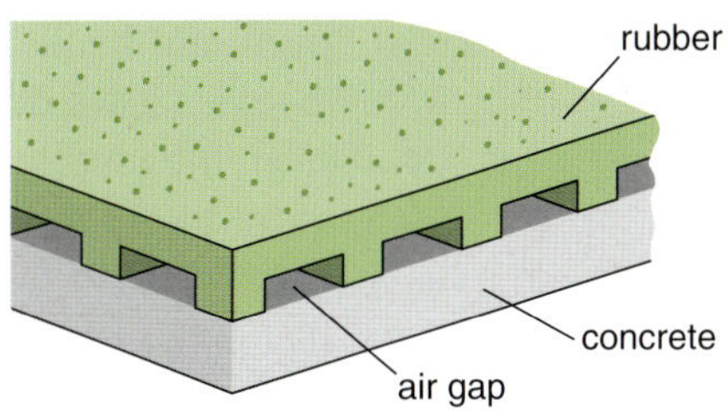

Figure 9.54 A safe surface for a children's area can be made from rubber tiles.

43 Explain the reason for each of the following.

Figure 9.55 This trainer has a gas-filled heel.

Figure 9.56 A climbing rope is designed to stretch a little.

Figure 9.57 The goalkeeper kit is well padded.

Activity – Safety surfaces

Rakesh has bought a children's slide and swing. Before putting them in his garden he wants to put down a safety surface. The chart in Figure 9.58 shows some data Rakesh found from a manufacturer. The data gives the average height a child can fall onto different surfaces without serious injury.

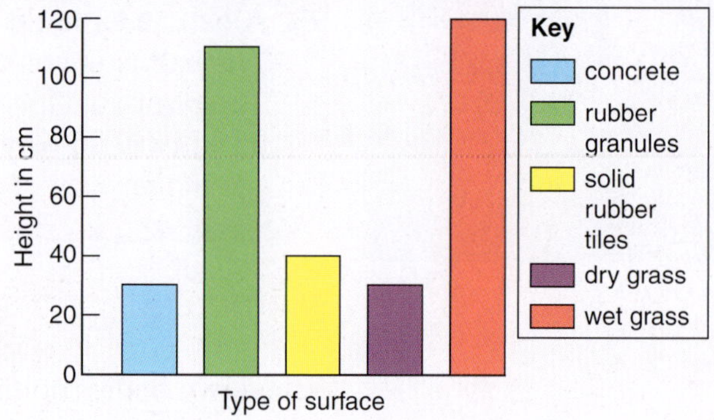

Figure 9.58

1. Are these categoric or continuous variables?
   a) the height the child falls;
   b) the type of surface.
2. The data presented in Figure 9.58 were obtained using a dummy fitted with electronic sensors. Rakesh thinks this makes the data more valid. Do you agree? Explain the reason for your answer.
3. Which type of surface would you recommend Rakesh to use? Explain the reason for your choice.

Car safety

Car design is not all about performance and looks – it is just as much about safety.

A modern car, even in a minor accident is easily damaged. But this is part of the safety design. The car is designed with 'crumple zones' at the front and back. In a collision the crumple zones crush. As they crush, the car slows down and stops gradually. The longer it takes the car to stop, the smaller the force exerted by the car on the occupants and the more likely you are to survive the accident without serious injury.

If you are in a car that suddenly slows down, you keep moving forwards until a force acts to reduce your momentum. Without a seat belt this force may be provided by the impact between your head and the windscreen, often a large and lethal force.

Figure 9.59 This car has been in a serious collision but the important part, where the passengers and driver sit, is undamaged.

Figure 9.60 A seat belt can save a life!

A seat belt is not rigid. In a crash it is designed to stretch slightly. This is very important as it increases the time taken for your momentum to be reduced to zero. So both the force on your body and the risk of injury are reduced.

44 In a crash it takes about 0.04 s for an air bag to inflate. A fraction of a second later the driver's head hits the air bag. The bag, which has tiny holes in it, will start to deflate as the force of impact pushes some of the gas out (Figure 9.61).

a) What happens to the movement of the driver's head when it hits the air bag?
b) Why is it important for an air bag to deflate?
c) Explain how the air bag reduces the risk of serious injury to the driver's head.

Figure 9.61

45 John is driving his car at 15 m/s when it is in a collision. John's seat belt slows him down and stops him moving in 0.12 s.

a) Taking John's mass to be 70 kg, calculate:
   i) John's momentum before the collision;
   ii) the change in John's momentum;
   iii) the average (mean) force exerted by the seat belt on John.
b) Explain why seat belts need to be very strong.

46 Explain why it would not be a good idea to make cars from thick, rigid steel.

Activity – Investigating the idea of a crumple zone

To investigate the idea of a crumple zone Tracy used the apparatus shown in Figure 9.62. In a collision Tracy expects the trolley and test material to behave in the same way as a car with a crumple zone.

1. Write down one more way that Tracy made this investigation a fair test.
2. Suggest another way that Tracy could have produced a constant force on the trolley.

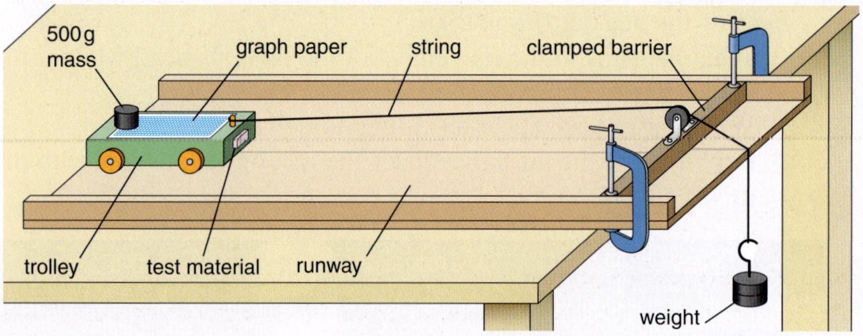

Reminder In a fair test, only the independent variable affects the dependent variable.

Figure 9.62 Using a trolley and test material to model a car with a crumple zone

A constant force was applied to the trolley by a falling weight. When the trolley hit the barrier it decelerated and stopped. The 500 g mass on top of the trolley slid forwards until it also stopped. Tracy marked the graph paper to show how far the 500 g mass moved. Tracy tested five different types of material for the crumple zone, each of the same area and thickness.

Because a constant force was applied, the trolley always accelerated to hit the barrier at the same speed. This was one factor that made the investigation a fair test.

3. In Tracy's investigation, what was:
   a) the independent variable;
   b) the dependent variable?
4. What sort of variable was the 'type of material' used in Tracy's investigation?

Figure 9.63 shows two sets of data obtained using different accelerating forces.

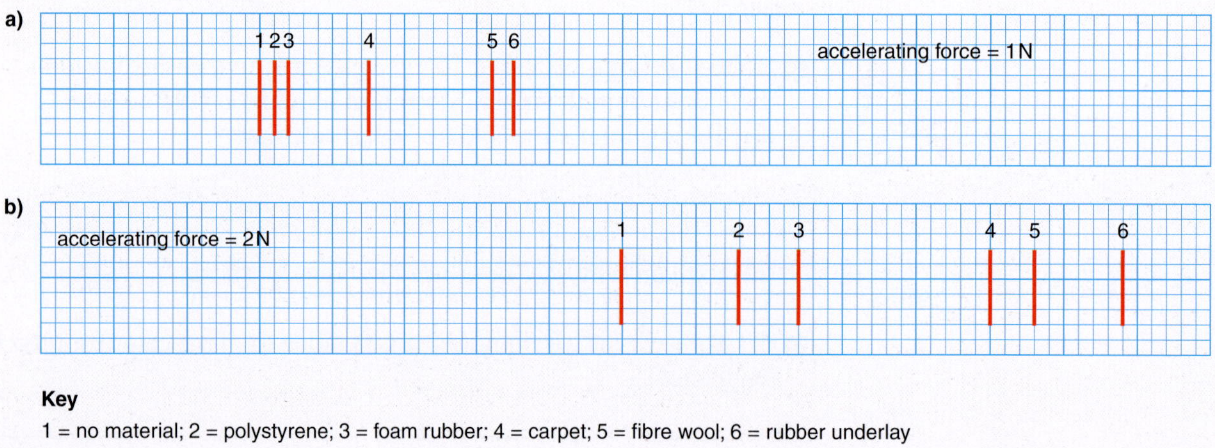

Figure 9.63 a) Stopping distance using an accelerating force of 1 N **b)** Stopping distance using an accelerating force of 2 N

❺ Which accelerating force gave the biggest range of results?

Remember The range refers to the maximum and minimum values used or recorded.

❻ Draw a bar chart for each set of data.

❼ Why is it more appropriate to draw a bar chart than a line graph?

In her analysis of the investigation Tracy has written:

'Crumple zones do reduce the force on a colliding body by increasing the time taken to stop. Of the five materials that I tested the best was rubber underlay.'

❽ Do both sets of data support Tracy's analysis? Explain the reasons for your answer.

Collisions and explosions

In any collision or explosion, the momentum after the collision or explosion in a particular direction is the same as the momentum in that direction before the collision or explosion.

total momentum after a collision or explosion = total momentum before a collision or explosion

Momentum is **conserved** in a collision. The total momentum before a collision is the same as the total momentum after the collision.

The total momentum is unchanged by the collision or explosion. It doesn't go up and it doesn't go down. The total momentum is **conserved**. This is always true, provided no external forces act on the colliding or exploding bodies.

Figure 9.64 Understanding forces and momentum can make the difference between winning and losing a game of snooker.

Look at the white snooker ball in Figure 9.65. It is moving with velocity *v* directly towards a red snooker ball. Before they collide, the red ball is not moving. The red ball has zero momentum.

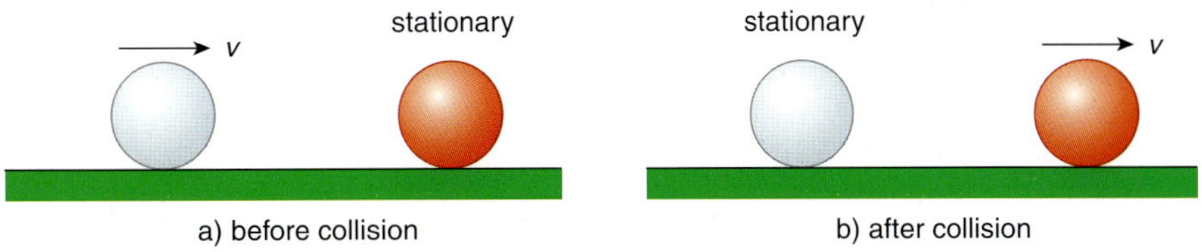

Figure 9.65

During the collision, an equal size force acts on each ball, but in opposite directions. The forces also act for the same time. This means that the momentum of each ball changes by the same amount. (Remember, force × time = change in momentum.)

After the collision, the white ball will be stationary. The white ball has zero momentum. The red ball will move with a velocity *v* in the same direction as the white ball was moving. The total momentum after the collision is the same as the total momentum before the collision.

Although momentum has been transferred from the white ball to the red ball, the total momentum has been conserved.

Figure 9.66 The launch of a rocket

An explosion is the opposite of a collision. Instead of moving together, bodies move apart. But as in a collision, the total momentum of the bodies involved in an explosion remains constant. In an explosion momentum is conserved.

The principle of momentum conservation is used in the launch of a space rocket. Before the launch the total momentum of the rocket and fuel is zero. After lift-off the total momentum must still be zero. The downward momentum of the hot exhaust gases must be equal to the upward momentum of the rocket.

47 A 2 kg trolley, moving at 3 m/s, collides with and sticks to a stationary 1 kg trolley. Calculate:
   a) the total momentum before the collision;
   b) the speed of the two trolleys after the collision.

48 Explain how the speed of a rocket moving through space can be increased.

49 Explain why, when you step ashore from a rowing boat, the boat moves backwards.

50 Jackie and Jasmin are on roller blades. They stand facing each other, and then give each other a gentle push. Figure 9.67 shows what happens next.
   a) Explain why both Jackie and Jasmin roll backwards.
   b) What is the total momentum before they push each other?
   c) Calculate Jackie's momentum immediately after the push.
   d) Calculate Jasmin's velocity immediately after the push.

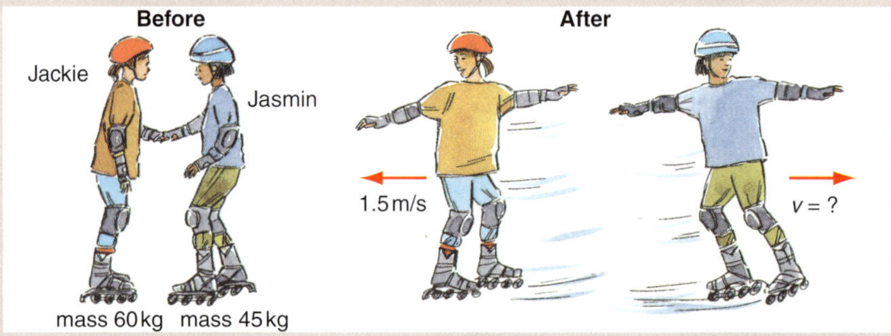

Figure 9.67

Summary

- ✓ **Velocity** is the speed of a body in a given direction.
- ✓ **Acceleration** is the rate at which the velocity of a body changes.
- ✓ **Distance–time graphs** and velocity–time graphs can be used to show the motion of a body.
- ✓ The slope (gradient) of a distance–time graph gives the speed of a body.
- ✓ The **slope** (gradient) of a velocity–time graph gives the acceleration of a body.
- ✓ The area under a velocity–time graph line represents distance travelled.
- ✓ Two interacting bodies exert forces on each other that are always equal in size and opposite in direction.
- ✓ The **resultant force** is a single force that has the same effect on a body as all the original forces acting together.
- ✓ When the resultant force on a body is zero, the movement of the body does not change because the forces are **balanced**. When the resultant force acting on a body are not zero, the forces are **unbalanced** and so the body changes speed.
- ✓ **Air resistance** (or drag) is a force of friction. The direction of air resistance is always opposite to the direction of the moving object.

- ✓ When the resultant force on a body is not zero the body accelerates.
- ✓ The greater the resultant force, the greater the acceleration of the body.
- ✓ The bigger the mass of a body, the bigger the resultant force needed to make it accelerate. Force and mass are linked by:

  resultant force (N) = mass (kg) × acceleration (m/s^2)
- ✓ **Gravity** is a force of attraction that acts between all bodies.
- ✓ When the resultant force on a falling body is zero the body falls at its **terminal velocity**.
- ✓ When a vehicle travels at a steady speed the frictional forces balance the driving force.
- ✓ **Stopping distance** = **thinking distance** + **braking distance**.
- ✓ The stopping distance of a vehicle depends on the braking force, the driver's reaction time, the condition of the road and the vehicle, weather conditions, the speed and the mass of the vehicle.
- ✓ Whenever a force makes a body move, **work** is done and energy is transferred.
- ✓ When work is done against frictional forces, energy is transformed into heat.
- ✓ The faster a body moves through a **fluid**, the greater the frictional forces.
- ✓ **Elastic potential energy** is the energy stored when work has been done to change the shape of a body.
- ✓ Kinetic energy is the energy of moving bodies.
- ✓ **Momentum** is defined by the equation:

  momentum (kg m/s) = mass (kg) × velocity (m/s)
- ✓ A resultant force acting on a body causes a change in momentum.
- ✓ In any collision or explosion, the total momentum is **conserved**, provided no external forces act.

EXAMQUESTIONS

1. Bill and Veneeta took part in a sponsored run. The distance–time graph for Bill's run is shown in Figure 9.68. Veneeta did not start the run until 500 seconds after Bill. She completed the whole run at a constant speed in 3000 seconds.
   a) During which part of the race was Bill running the fastest? *(1 mark)*
   b) Copy the distance–time graph for Bill's run. Draw on the same axes a distance–time graph for Veneeta's run. *(2 marks)*
   c) How far had Bill run when Veneeta overtook him? *(1 mark)*

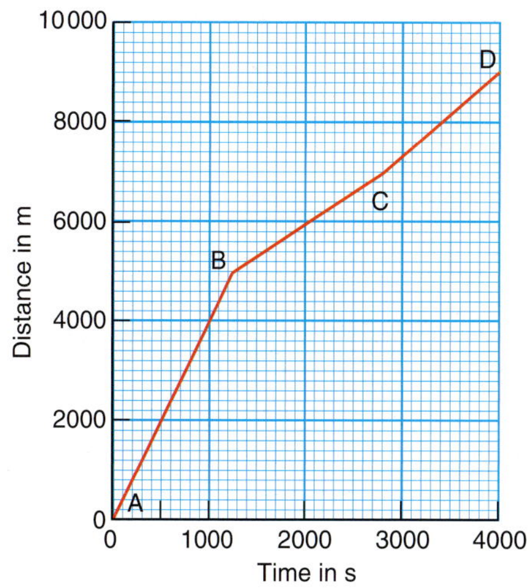

Figure 9.68

EXAMQUESTIONS

❷ Figure 9.69 shows a space rocket lifting off from the launch pad.

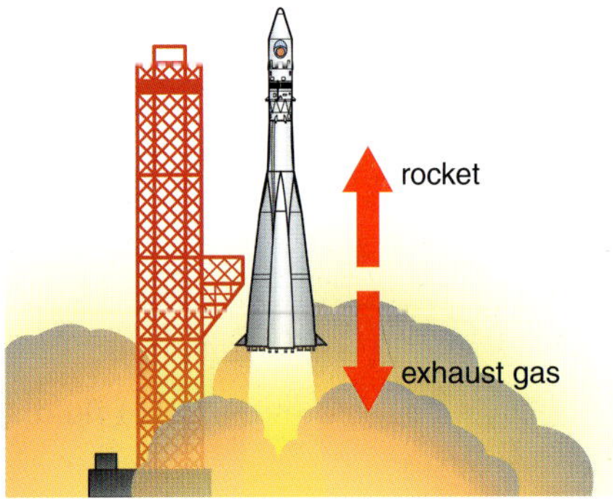

Figure 9.69

a) Use the idea of momentum to explain why the rocket moves off the launch pad. *(3 marks)*

b) To achieve lift-off, a rocket ejects 2500 kg of exhaust gases every second at a speed of 3500 m/s. The mass of the rocket and fuel at launch is 40 000 kg.

  i) Calculate the thrust force produced by the rocket. *(3 marks)*

  ii) Calculate the initial acceleration of the rocket. (Ignore the weight of the rocket and fuel.) *(2 marks)*

c) During the first 10 seconds of flight the rocket maintains the same thrust force. Explain why the acceleration of the rocket increases. *(2 marks)*

❸ Amrita has investigated how different forces stretch a spring. The results of her investigation are given in Table 9.8.

Force in N	Length of spring in cm	Extension of spring in cm
0	5.0	0.0
2	7.5	2.5
4	10.0	
6	11.0	
8	15.0	
10	17.5	12.5

Table 9.8

a) Copy and complete Table 9.8. *(1 mark)*

b) Plot a graph of force against extension. *(3 marks)*

c) Amrita has one anomalous result. What would you expect this result to be? *(1 mark)*

d) What length would the spring be were a 3 N force used? *(1 mark)*

e) Calculate the mean force exerted on the spring during the investigation. *(1 mark)*

f) Calculate the work done to extend the spring 12.5 cm *(2 marks)*

g) What is the maximum elastic potential energy stored in the spring? *(1 mark)*

Chapter 10
What is static electricity and how is it used?

At the end of this chapter you should:

- ✓ know that some insulating materials become electrically charged when they are rubbed against each other;
- ✓ understand that electrons are transferred from one material to another when materials become charged by friction;
- ✓ understand that the material that gains electrons becomes negatively charged and the material that loses electrons becomes positively charged;
- ✓ know that objects with the same type of charge repel one another and objects with different types of charge attract;
- ✓ understand that an electric current is a flow of charge;
- ✓ understand that a spark may jump across a gap between a charged body and a nearby earthed conductor if the charge on the body becomes high enough;
- ✓ appreciate that static charges are useful in photocopiers, smoke precipitators and electrostatic paint spray guns;
- ✓ appreciate that static electricity is dangerous in some situations;
- ✓ understand how electrostatic charge can be discharged safely.

Figure 10.1 A flash of lightning is a gigantic spark. Billions and billions of electrons shoot from the bottom of the cloud to Earth. So much heat is produced that it causes a flash of light and the air expands rapidly, causing a clap of thunder.

10.1 What is static electricity?

Static electricity is the formation of stationary positive and negative electric charges on materials when they are rubbed together or move over each other.
The materials become positive or negative and are described as electrically **charged**.

People often call static electricity just 'static' for short. 'Static' results in lightning flashes (Figure 10.1), it makes your hair stand on end and it makes dust stick to TV screens. The word 'static' is normally used to mean 'stationary' and **static electricity** results when materials have stationary charges.

Invisible electrostatic forces

Try this simple experiment. Comb your hair briskly with a plastic comb and then use the comb to pick up tiny pieces of paper. (It only works if your hair is dry and not gelled.) When you comb your hair, the comb becomes **charged** (Figure 10.2), and the charged comb can pick up bits of paper because of electrostatic forces.

Figure 10.2 A plastic comb gets charged when you comb your hair briskly.

You may have noticed some other effects of electric charges.

- When you take off a shirt or top, it tends to cling to your body or your vest.
- A balloon can stick to a wall and possibly the ceiling after you have rubbed it against your sweatshirt or fleece.

These effects show that when certain materials are rubbed against each other or move over each other, they become electrically charged. People sometimes say the materials have 'static electricity' on them. This is how electric charges were first discovered.

Where do the charges come from?

When certain materials are rubbed against each other, friction causes negatively charged electrons to move off one material onto the other – off hair onto the comb, off your body and onto your shirt or top, off your fleece and onto a balloon.

When you comb your hair briskly, the comb removes electrons from some atoms in your hair (Figure 10.2). The comb now has more electrons than protons so it has an overall negative charge. Your hair has lost the electrons. It now has more protons than electrons and so it has an equal positive charge. If you bring the negatively charged comb close to a tiny bit of paper, it repels negative electrons from the area of the paper nearest to it (Figure 10.3a). This part of the paper therefore becomes positive. It is attracted to the comb because objects with different charges **attract**. If the paper is small enough, it can be picked up with the comb (Figure 10.3b).

Have you noticed that your hair sometimes stands up when it is combed – but probably not as much as the hair in Figure 10.2? This is more likely to happen if your hair is clean and dry. It happens because each hair becomes positively charged, and objects with the same charges **repel**.

When electrically charged objects are close together, they exert electrostatic forces on each other:

- objects with the same type of charge **repel** each other;
- objects with opposite (different) charges **attract** each other.

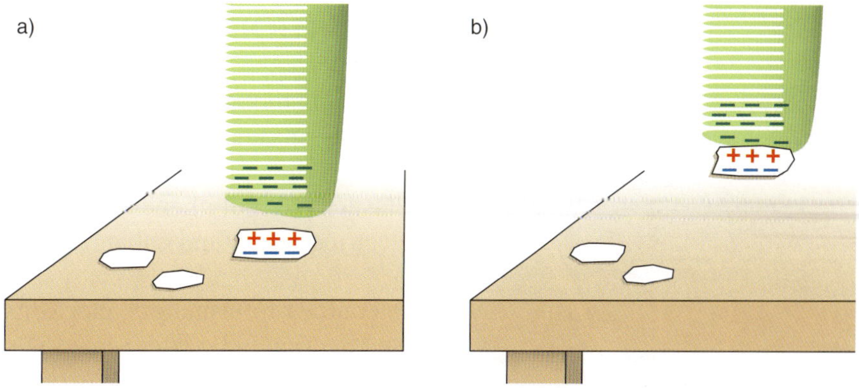

Figure 10.3 A charged comb can pick up bits of paper.

❶ Copy and complete the following sentences using words from the box below.

charge	electrons	friction	neutrons	negative
positive	protons	rubbed	static	transfer

When a polythene rod is _____ with a cloth, the cloth loses _____ to the rod, so the rod gets a _____ charge. The cloth has more _____ than electrons, so it has a _____ charge. This _____ of electrons is caused by _____.

❷ When certain materials are rubbed against each other, electrons move from one material to the other, but protons and neutrons never move. Why is this?

❸ When a Perspex rod is rubbed with a cloth, the Perspex rod becomes positively charged. Explain how the rod gets its charge.

❹ Look at Figure 10.4. The dome on which the boy is resting his hand has a large negative charge and the boy is standing on a rubber mat.

a) What is the charge on the boy's hand?
b) What is the charge on the boy's hair?
c) Why is the boy's hair sticking out?
d) Why is he standing on a rubber mat?

Figure 10.4 A hair-raising experience!

❺ Figure 10.5 shows two identical lightweight plastic balls attached to the same hook by nylon threads. The balls are charged.

a) What can you say about the charges on the balls?
b) Copy Figure 10.5 and show the forces acting on each ball.

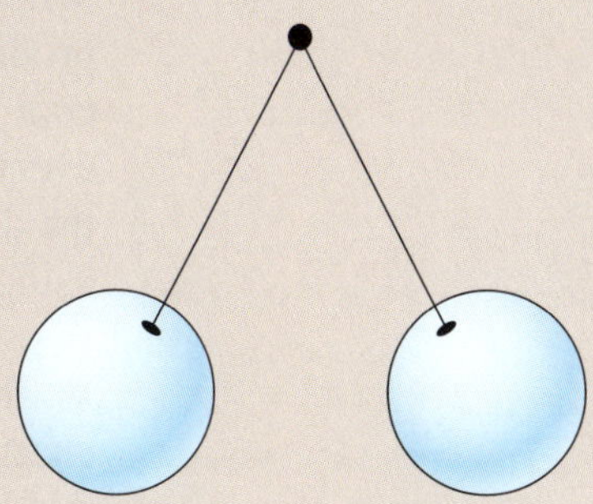

Figure 10.5

10.2 Insulators and conductors

Figure 10.6 Plastics like polythene and PVC are good insulators. They are used to insulate electrical wires and cables.

Insulators are substances that can hold their charge. Electrons cannot flow through them, so they cannot conduct an electric current.

Conductors are substances through which electrons flow easily, so they conduct an electric current.

Materials like plastic, hair, rubber and paper can hold their charge. The charges on them are 'static' (stationary) and electrons do not flow through them. Because of this, these materials are called **insulators**. Plastics like polythene and polyvinylchloride (PVC) are used to insulate electrical wires and cables (Figure 10.6).

In contrast to insulators, electrons flow easily through metals and alloys (see Section 6.3). These materials are described as **conductors**. The flow of negative charges (i.e. electrons) forms an electric current. An electric current can also be carried by ions, which can have either positive or negative charges (see Section 8.5).

Table 10.1 shows good conductors, poor conductors and insulators. The best conductors are metals because they contain outer shell, delocalised electrons that are free to move. The outer electrons in insulators are held tightly in covalent bonds.

Conductors			Insulators
Good	Moderate	Poor	
• Metals, e.g. copper, aluminium, iron • Alloys, e.g. steel, brass	• Carbon (graphite) • Silicon	• Water • Humans	• Plastics, e.g. polythene, PVC • Rubber • Wood • Air

Table 10.1 Some important conductors and insulators

10.3 How do we use static electricity?

Static electricity is important in the working of smoke precipitators, photocopiers and paint spray guns.

Smoke precipitators

When coal is burnt in power stations and factories, a lot of smoke is produced. The smoke consists of tiny particles of soot and ash. A large coal-burning power station can produce up to 40 tonnes of soot and ash every hour. It is important to remove this soot and ash before it gets into the air and causes pollution. In power stations, this is usually done by using an electrostatic smoke precipitator (Figure 10.7).

As the smoke goes up the chimney, it passes through a negatively charged metal grid. The smoke particles pick up electrons from the grid and become negatively charged themselves. The grid now repels the negative smoke particles towards the chimney lining. Here they are attracted by large positively charged collecting plates. The smoke

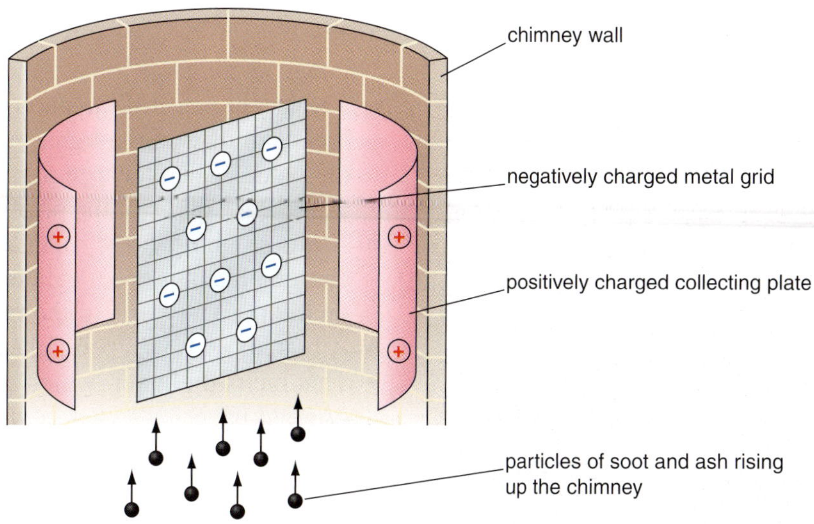

Figure 10.7 An electrostatic smoke precipitator

particles lose their charge on the collecting plates, then fall and collect together (precipitate) at the bottom of the chimney.

Photocopiers

Some substances can act as photoconductors. This means that they conduct electricity in the light, but not in the dark.

- In a photocopier, there is a metal roller coated with a thin layer of photoconductor (Figure 10.8). At the start of the copying process, this photoconducting layer is given a positive charge.

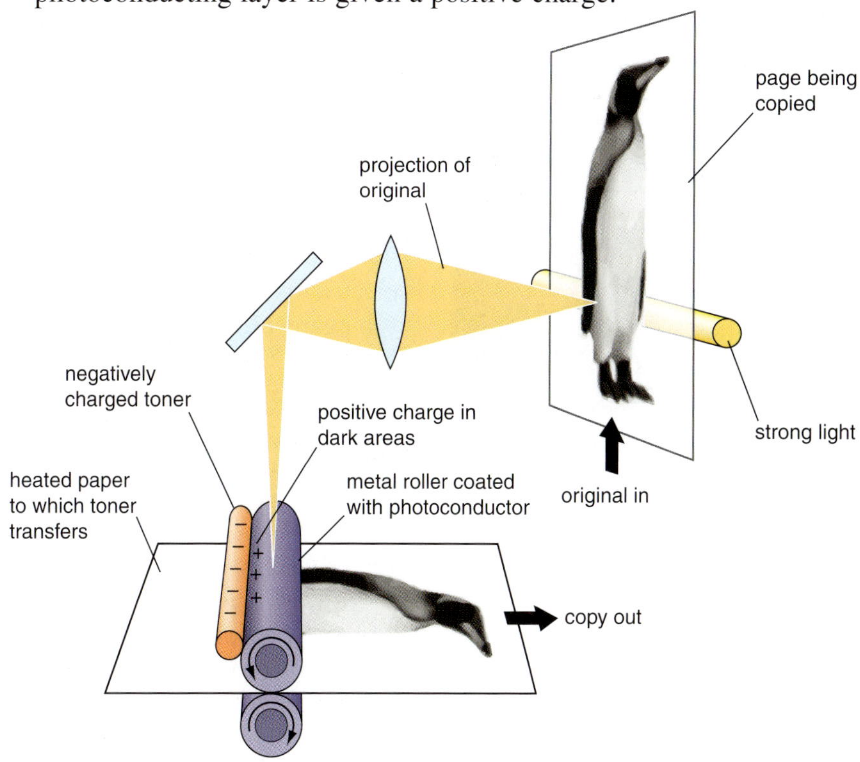

Figure 10.8 The photocopying process

- The page to be copied is then lit with a strong light. This allows an image of the page to be projected onto the charged photoconductor. The bright areas of the photoconductor now lose their charge because it can conduct in the light, but the dark areas keep their charge. So, the places where charge remains on the photoconductor are the same as the dark parts on the page being copied.
- At the same time, the roller moves near a supply of negatively charged black powder called toner. The toner is attracted to and sticks on the positive parts of the photoconductor.
- A blank sheet of paper is then heated and pressed against the roller.
- This melts the toner, which sticks to the paper making a copy of the original page.

6 From the list in the box below, name:
a) one metal;
b) one alloy;
c) two non-metals;
d) two good conductors;
e) one (moderate) semi-conductor;
f) two insulators.

brass graphite sulfur titanium wood

7 An electrostatic paint spray gun like the one in Figure 10.9 produces a fine spray of positively charged droplets.
a) How does the charge on the droplets help to keep the spray fine and evenly spread?
b) Why is less paint needed if the car bodywork has an opposite charge to the paint?
c) Why is an opposite charge on the car bodywork beneficial to the workman?
d) Why is the workman wearing protective head gear?

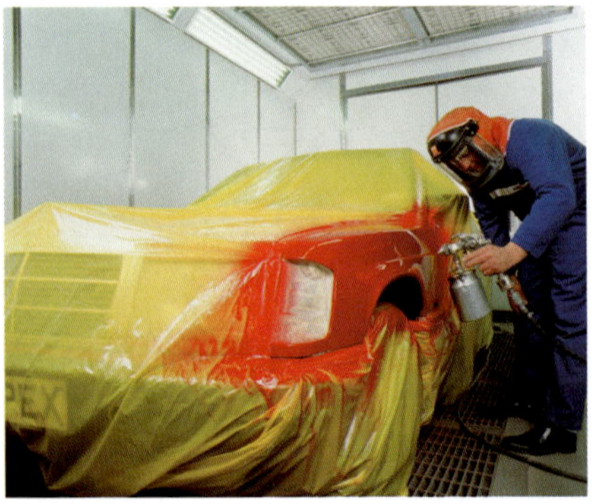

Figure 10.9 A workman re-spraying parts of a car using an electrostatic paint spray gun

Activity – 'Static' in pipes

Industrial liquids and powders, like flour and custard powder, can be moved from one place to another through pipes. As the liquids and powders flow along a pipe, static electricity is generated. The static electricity is produced by friction as particles in the liquid or powder rub against the wall of the pipe and against one another. Voltages as high as 1000 volts can be produced. These high voltages can result in sparks and start a fire as many of the powders will burn.

Ellie and Jake set up the apparatus in Figure 10.10 to study this problem of 'static' in pipes. They used different sizes of polystyrene beads.

1 The polystyrene beads become negatively charged as they flow down the pipe.
a) What charge will the pipe have?
b) What charge will the can and electroscope have when the polystyrene beads start to fill the can?

2 Why does the leaf move to an angle with the vertical part of the metal T-piece as soon as the electroscope is charged?

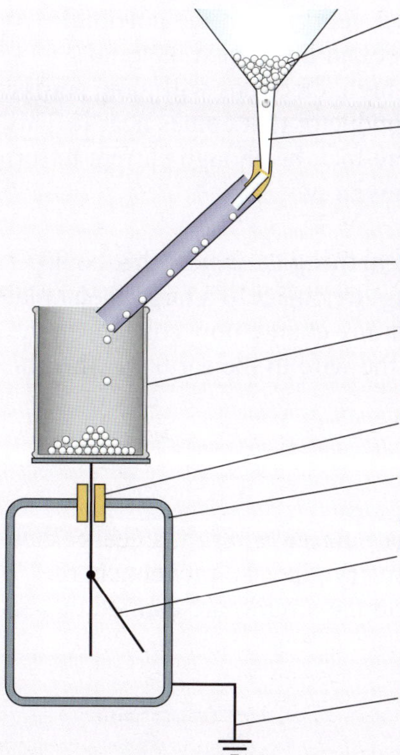

Figure 10.10 Investigating the electrostatic charges developed when polystyrene beads flow down a pipe

Type of beads used	Estimated angle of thin metal leaf with vertical
Small	15°
Smaller	25°
Very small	45°

Table 10.2

3. Ellie and Jake poured 50 cm^3 of small beads down the pipe and then estimated the deflection of the thin metal leaf. Then they repeated their experiment, first with 50 cm^3 of smaller beads and finally with 50 cm^3 of very small beads (Figure 10.10).

Their results are shown in Table 10.2.

a) Copy and complete the following sentences.
   i) As the deflection of the metal leaf increases, the charge on the electroscope _______.
   ii) As the polystyrene beads decrease in size, the charge on the electroscope _______.
b) Explain why very small beads cause greater deflection of the metal leaf than small beads.

4. In some industries such as flour milling, very large charges can build up as the powdery flour passes along the pipes. How do you think the problem can be overcome? (Hint: How can you get rid of charges?)
5. How do you think the following will affect the charge on the electroscope? Explain your answers.
   a) Making the pipe longer.
   b) Increasing the speed of the beads down the pipe.
6. State three variables that Ellie and Jake controlled to make sure their investigation was fair.
7. How could Ellie and Jake's results be made more reliable?
8. Ellie suspects that Jake has measured the angle inaccurately. How could human error like this be reduced in their investigation?
9. What would you do to get more precise, more quantifiable information about the effect of bead size on the charge on the electroscope?

10.4 What are the dangers of static electricity?

Earthing involves connecting a charged body to a metal spike or plate in the ground so that it is discharged, and its potential (voltage) remains close to zero.

As the electrostatic charge on an object gets greater, the potential difference (voltage) between the object and uncharged materials increases. If the voltage becomes too high, electrons will jump across the gap between the object and any conductor that comes near it. This is an electric current. In some cases, there may be enough current to form a spark. Even a small spark can be dangerous.

The problem is usually overcome by **earthing** the object that could become charged. This involves joining the object to a large metal plate in the ground by a conducting wire. If any charge now collects on the object, it just flows harmlessly along the wire to the earth and the object is discharged (loses its charge).

Fuel in pipes

When tankers deliver fuel to petrol stations and aircraft, a charge can build up as fuel flows through the delivery pipe. To prevent charge building up, the petrol storage tank and the aircraft are earthed (Figure 10.11).

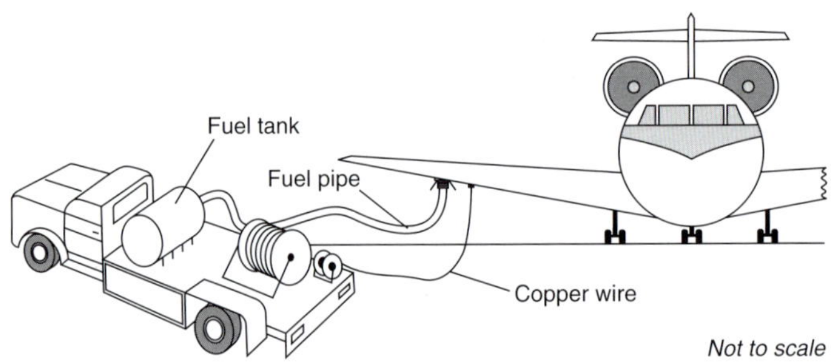

Figure 10.11 An aircraft being refuelled

8 Figure 10.11 shows an aircraft being refuelled.
a) Explain how electrostatic charge can build up on the fuel pipe and on the aircraft during refuelling.
b) Why is the build-up of charge on the aircraft dangerous?
c) In order to prevent charge building up, a copper cable is connected between the aircraft and the tanker. Why does this prevent charge building up? (Hint: The fuel pipe is also connected to the tanker.)

Conducting 'tails' for cars

Cars are sometimes fitted with conducting 'tails' that touch the ground. This prevents any build-up of charge on the car. As the car moves over the ground and through the air, electrons are transferred from the ground to the car. Discharging reduces the risk of unpleasant sparks when you get out of the car or of a fire caused by sparks when the car is being refuelled.

Aircraft tyres

When an aircraft lands, there is enormous friction between its tyres and the runway. To reduce the build-up of charge, aircraft tyres are made of special rubber that conducts electricity. Any charge that forms on the tyres should then flow straight to earth (Figure 10.12).

Figure 10.12 When an aircraft lands, friction between the tyres and the runway is so great that sparks can fly and the tyres begin to smoke.

Activity – Lightning strikes!

Figure 10.13 shows what happens when lightning strikes the lightning conductor on a church spire.

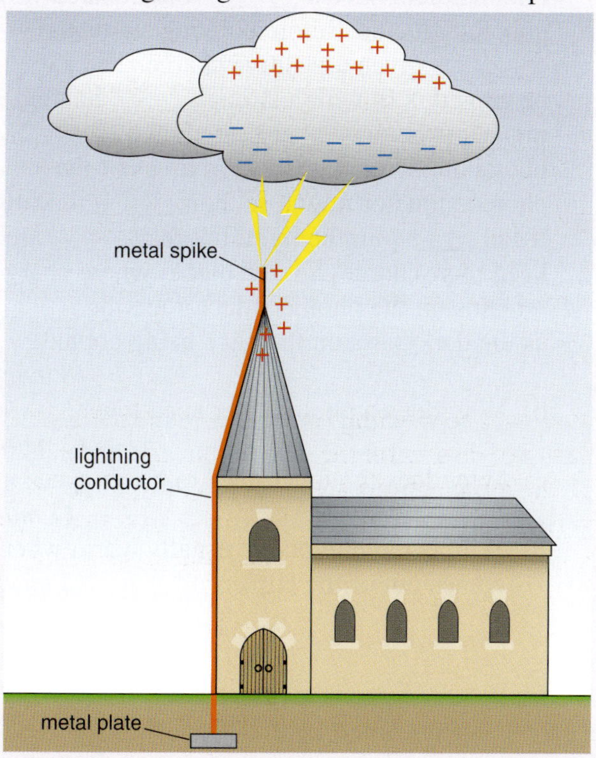

Figure 10.13 Lightning strikes the lightning conductor on a church spire.

❶ Copy and complete the following explanation using the terms in the box.

cloud	convection currents	copper	earth
electrons	energy	flash of light	ground
frictional forces	negative	positive	spire

Large heavy thunderclouds are filled with water vapour and ice crystals moving around in strong _______. As these move around, _______ cause charge to build up and the bottom of the thundercloud has a large _______ charge.

The lightning conductor on the church spire consists of a thick _______ strip down the outside of the building. This is connected to a metal spike at the top of the _______ and a large metal plate in the _______. When the thundercloud passes overhead, the charge on the cloud repels _______ and the top of the lightning conductor becomes _______. If the charge on the cloud is large enough, electrons jump across the gap from the _______ to the spike. In some cases, so much _______ is lost by the electrons that a _______ is produced. Fortunately, the electrons can flow down the conductor to _______ without damaging the church.

❷ Explain why the lightning conductor on the church is:

a) fixed to the ground;
b) made of metal;
c) attached to the highest point on the church.

Summary

- ✓ **Static electricity** results when materials have stationary charges.
- ✓ When certain insulating materials are rubbed against each other, friction causes electrons to move off one material onto the other.
- ✓ The material gaining electrons becomes negatively **charged** and the material losing electrons is left with an equal positive charge.
- ✓ Two bodies (objects) with the same charge **repel** each other and two bodies with different (opposite) charges **attract**.
- ✓ **Insulators** are substances that can hold their charge. Electrons cannot flow through them, so they cannot conduct an electric current.
- ✓ **Conductors** are substances through which electrons flow easily, so they conduct an electric current.
- ✓ An **electric current** is a flow of charge. The charge may be carried by electrons or by ions.
- ✓ Electrostatic charges are important in the working of smoke precipitators, photocopiers and paint spray guns.
- ✓ Static electricity can be dangerous. If the electrostatic charge on an object creates a large potential difference in voltage, a spark may jump across the gap between the charged object and any earthed conductor. This movement of charge is an electric current.
- ✓ The dangers of static electricity and sparking can usually be overcome by **earthing**.

EXAMQUESTIONS

1 What is:

a) an electric current; *(2 marks)*
b) a conductor, *(1 mark)*
c) an insulator; *(1 mark)*
d) a photoconductor? *(2 marks)*

2 Clingfilm is thin plastic material made of polythene. When clingfilm is peeled off a roll, it tends to stick to itself. Why do you think this happens? *(3 marks)*

3 a) This question is about photocopiers. Copy and complete the following passage using words from the box below.

bright charge conduct dark light
metal photoconductor same

Photocopiers have a ______ roller coated with photoconductor. Before copying starts, the ______ is given a positive charge. The page to be copied is lit with a strong ______ and an image of the page is projected onto the photoconductor. The ______ areas of the photoconductor now lose their ______ because it can ______ in the light, but the ______ areas keep their charge. So, the places where charge remains on the photoconductor are the ______ as the dark parts on the page being copied. *(8 marks)*

b) Why does a photocopier need toner? *(2 marks)*

c) Why does the toner need to be charged? *(1 mark)*

d) Why is the photocopy usually warm when it comes out of the copier? *(2 marks)*

Chapter 11
What affects the current in an electric circuit?

At the end of this chapter you should:

- ✓ be able to interpret and draw circuit diagrams using standard symbols;
- ✓ recognise the current–potential difference graph for a resistor at constant temperature, a filament lamp and a diode;
- ✓ be able to use the equation:
  potential difference = current × resistance
- ✓ know that the current through a component depends on the resistance of the component;
- ✓ recognise errors in the wiring of a three-pin plug;
- ✓ be able to determine the period and frequency of an electricity supply from the oscilloscope trace it produces;
- ✓ understand the difference between direct current (d.c.) and alternating current (a.c.);
- ✓ be able to explain how mains electricity can be used safely;
- ✓ understand that an electric current is a flow of charge;
- ✓ know that the rate at which energy is transformed in a device is called the power.

Figure 11.1 The first Blackpool Illuminations, held in 1879, had just eight electric arc lamps. Today's illuminations having one million lamps connected by more than 320 kilometres of cables and wiring, stretch out over a distance of 10 kilometres. If one light bulb 'blew', would all the lights go out?

11.1 Circuits – starting out

A **component** is a part of an electric circuit.

Remember that current is a flow of electric charge (see Section 10.2). For a current to flow through any **component** in a circuit, there must be a potential difference across the component. This means the circuit must include an energy supply and the circuit must be complete.

Each component in a circuit has a standard symbol. Rather than drawing a complicated picture, symbols are used to draw circuit diagrams. This makes life much easier for us and for electricians.

Figure 11.2 shows the symbols you need to know, with the names of the components they represent.

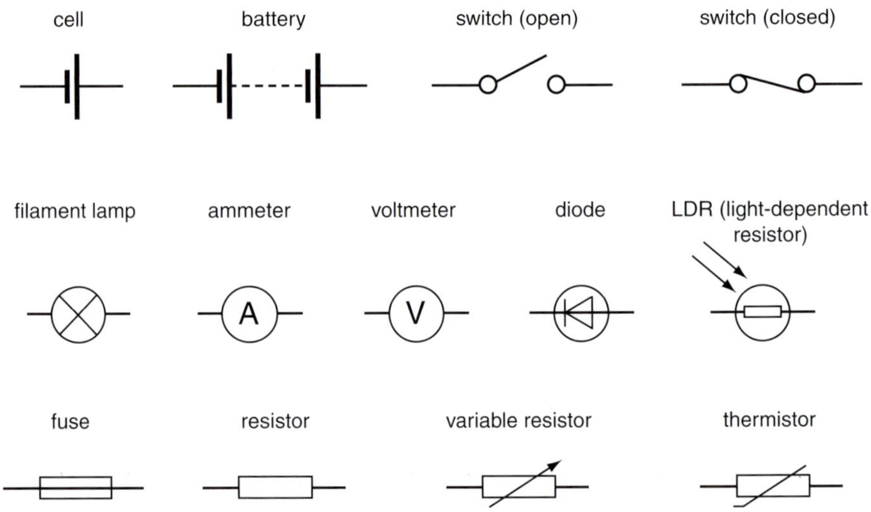

Figure 11.2 Using standard symbols for components makes a circuit easier to understand.

In a **series** circuit there is only one path for current to follow.

Potential difference (or p.d.) is often called voltage. A potential difference causes current to flow.

In a **parallel** circuit each branch is independent of the others. There could be a break in one part of a parallel circuit and the other parts would still have a complete loop for current to flow.

The current in a circuit is measured with an ammeter connected in **series**. This is so that the current flowing around the circuit also flows through the ammeter.

The **potential difference** is measured with a voltmeter connected in **parallel** across a component. Potential difference (or p.d. for short) is measured in volts.

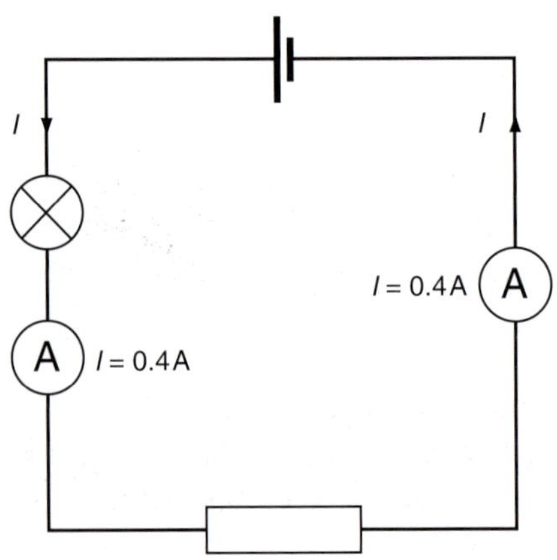

Figure 11.3 The same current flows through components joined in series.

How are series circuits different from parallel circuits?

A series circuit is a single pathway for an electric current through a set of wires and components. A parallel circuit gives more than one pathway for the electric current.

Components joined in series follow each other in one complete loop. The current has only one path it can take. So the same current must flow through each component and wire in the circuit.

A **cell** uses chemical reactions to produce a potential difference across its two terminals. A **battery** is a number of cells connected together.

Figure 11.4 A 12 V car battery is six 2 V cells joined together.

The ammeters in Figure 11.3 show the same reading. This is because the current is the same at all points in a series circuit.

Cells and batteries

If you call one **cell** on its own a battery then you are wrong. A **battery** is a number of cells joined together. A cell or battery provides charges with energy that can be transformed into other types of energy as the charges flow around the circuit.

Potential difference – cells in series

For cells joined in series, the total potential difference is worked out by adding the separate potential differences together. This only works if the cells are joined together correctly, positive (+) to negative (−).

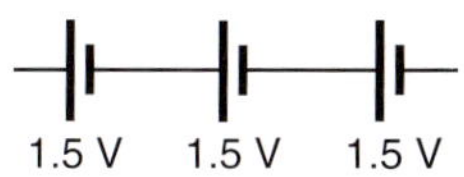

Figure 11.5 The cells are joined correctly. The separate potential differences add to give 4.5 V.

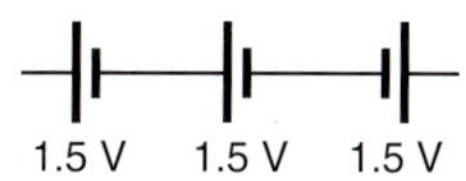

Figure 11.6 One cell is the wrong way round. The p.d. of this cell cancels out the p.d. of one of the other cells. The total p.d. is only 1.5 V.

1. Calculate the potential difference of each cell combination shown in Figure 11.7.

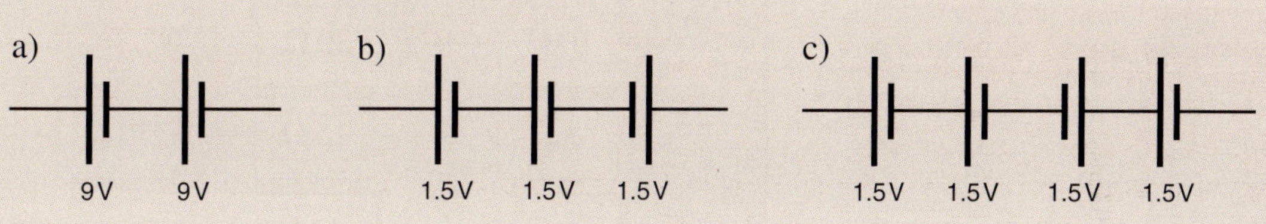

Figure 11.7

11.2 What does resistance mean?

Resistance is measured in ohms (Ω). The resistance (*R*) of a component is defined as potential difference (*V*) across it divided by the current (*I*) through it.

All components resist the flow of an electric current through them. The more easily a current flows through a component, the less **resistance** the component has. A high resistance component lets only a small current flow.

Some components change their resistance in response to the environment (more about this later). Resistance changes can be useful in electronics. For the same potential difference across a component, changing the resistance changes the current in the circuit: the greater the resistance, the smaller the current.

Figure 11.8 These resistors can be used to control the value of current in a circuit, for example to limit the current in a sensitive electrical component.

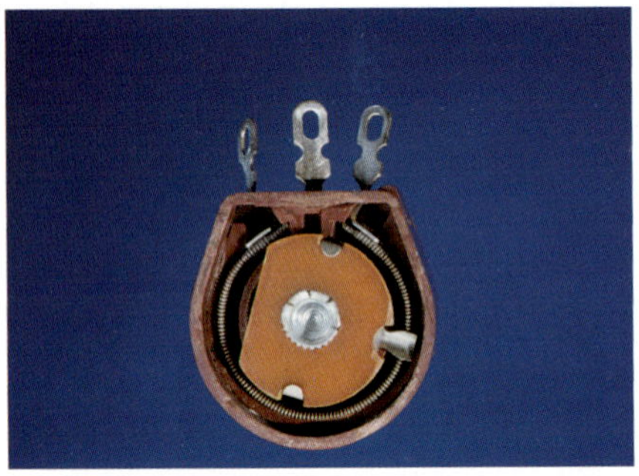

Figure 11.10 The resistance of a variable resistor is changed by moving a sliding contact. The variable resistor can be used to control the current and change the potential difference across a component.

Adding resistors in series

Adding more lamps to a circuit (Figure 11.9) makes the current go down, which means the resistance of the circuit has gone up.

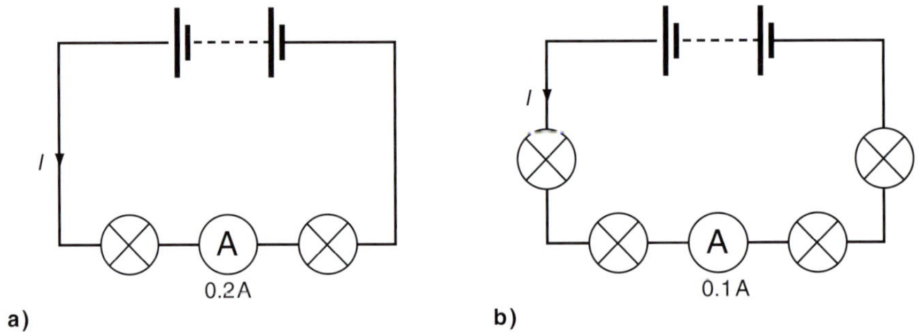

Figure 11.9 Adding components to a series circuit increases the resistance of the circuit.

The total resistance of a series circuit is the sum of the individual resistances.

Example

total resistance = 5 + 10 = 15 ohms (Ω)

2 Work out the total resistance of the following arrangements.

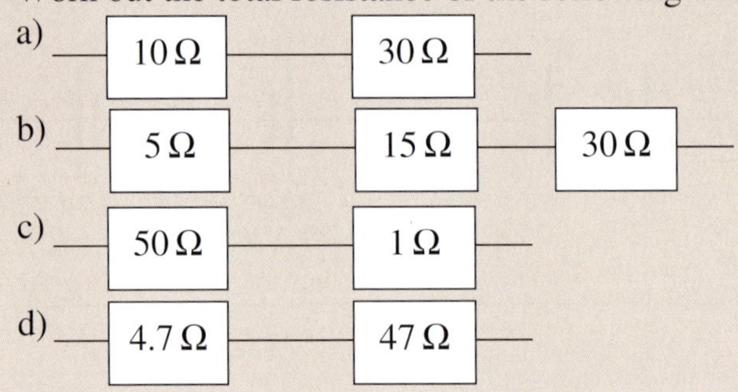

Linking potential difference, current and resistance

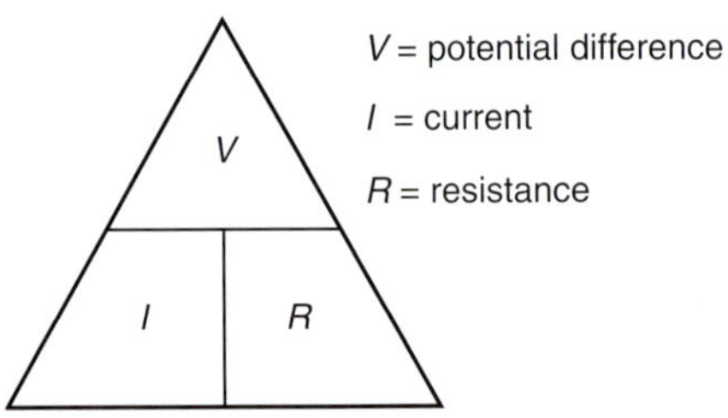

Figure 11.11 Equation triangle for potential difference, current and resistance

The potential difference across a component, the current through a component and the resistance of a component are linked by the equation:

potential difference (volt, V) = **current** (ampere, A) × **resistance** (ohm, Ω)

You might find the equation easier to use if you remember it like the triangle shown in Figure 11.11.

If you put your finger over the '*R*' in the triangle, the equation becomes:

$$R = \frac{V}{I}$$

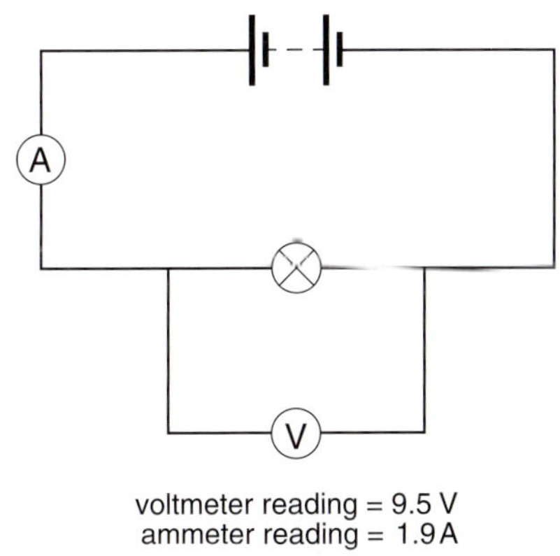

Figure 11.12 Knowing the current and potential difference allows the resistance to be calculated.

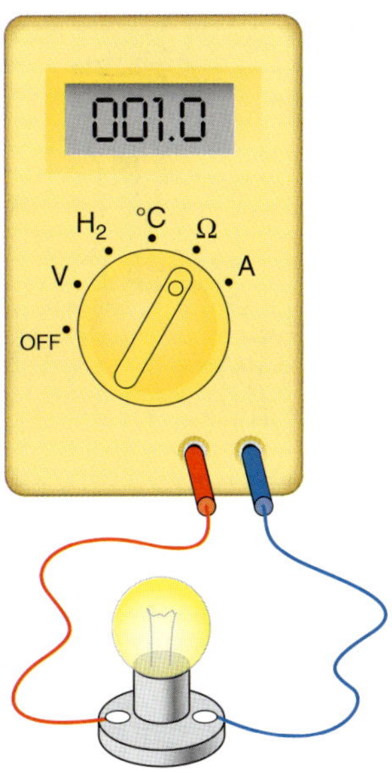

Figure 11.13 The resistance of the lamp, or any other component, can be measured directly using an ohmmeter. The resistance is small because the lamp is cold.

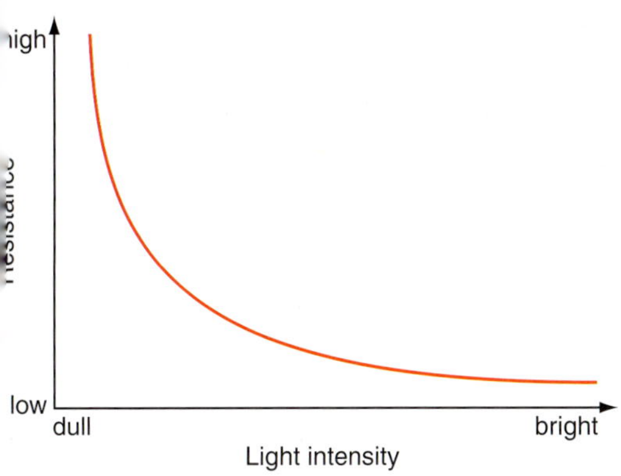

Figure 11.14 The resistance of an LDR changes with light intensity.

You can do the same thing to find the equation for '*I*' and the equation for '*V*'.

Example

A 24 Ω resistor has a potential difference of 12 V across it. What current flows through the resistor?

If you are not sure how to get the equation for '*I*', use the equation triangle in Figure 11.11. Put your finger over the '*I*'. This shows that '*V*' is above '*R*'. So, the equation is:

$$I = \frac{V}{R} = \frac{12}{24} = 0.5\text{ A}$$

❸ Copy and complete Table 11.1

Device	Potential difference across device in V	Current through device in A	Resistance of device in Ω
Resistor		0.5	20
Lamp	12	3	
Kettle	230	10	
Motor	415		83
Iron	230		57.5

Table 11.1

How is the resistance of a component measured?

The equation above shows that resistance is defined as $R = V/I$. The circuit drawn in Figure 11.12 shows how the resistance of a component can be found by measuring the current flowing through (I) and potential difference (V) across a component. In this case the component is a lamp.

The resistance of the lamp is calculated using the equation:

$$R = \frac{V}{I} = \frac{9.5}{1.9} = 5\ \Omega$$

The resistance of many components is not fixed – it can change. For example, a lamp has a higher resistance when it is hot than when it is cold (more about this in Section 11.3).

Two special types of resistor

The resistance of a **light-dependent resistor (LDR)** changes as the intensity (brightness) of light shining on it changes. Table 11.2 shows that the resistance goes down as the intensity of the light goes up.

Light level	Resistance (ohms)
Dark	1 000 000
Bright	2 000

Table 11.2 Resistance of an LDR

A **light-dependent resistor (LDR)** is a component in an electric circuit whose resistance decreases as the intensity of light falling on it increases.

A **thermistor** is a component in an electric circuit whose resistance decreases as the temperature increases.

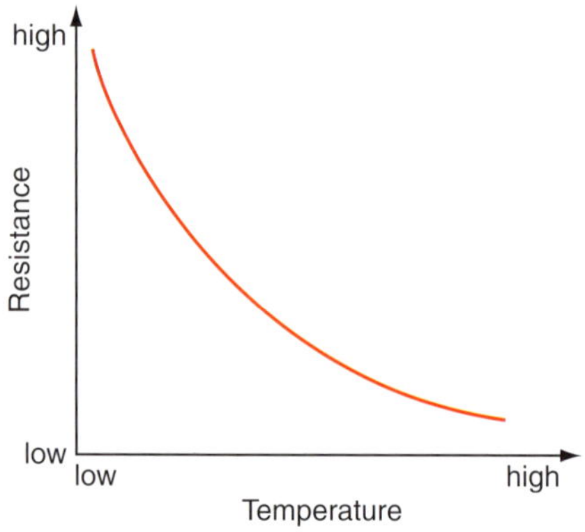

Figure 11.15 The resistance of a thermistor changes with temperature.

The LDR can be used as a sensor in light-operated circuits, such as security lighting. The change in resistance of LDRs is used in digital cameras to control the total amount of light that enters the camera.

The resistance of a **thermistor** changes with temperature. As the temperature of the thermistor rises the resistance decreases.

A thermistor can be used as the sensor in a temperature-operated circuit, such as a fire alarm. Some electronic thermometers use a thermistor to detect changes in temperature.

Figure 11.16 The change in the resistance of a thermistor can be used to switch on other electrical circuits automatically.

❹ Figure 11.17 shows a thermistor in series with a high-power lamp and positioned close to it.

a) Explain why the lamp only shines dimly when the switch is closed.

b) Explain why the lamp gets slowly brighter.

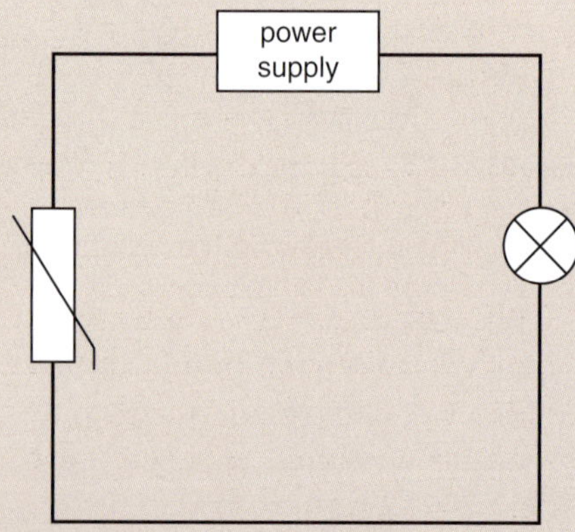

Figure 11.17

❺ Ramesh is using the ammeter in Figure 11.18 as a simple light intensity meter.

a) Explain why the reading on the ammeter changes when the light intensity changes.

b) Sketch a graph to show how the ammeter reading changes with light intensity.

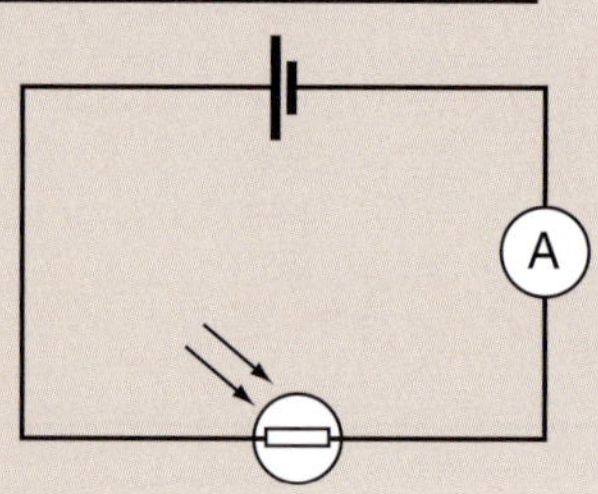

Figure 11.18

Activity – Misti designs an oven thermometer

Misti has designed the circuit shown in Figure 11.19 to replace the broken temperature display on her oven. The thermistor, which Misti is using as a temperature sensor, goes inside the oven. The rest of the circuit is outside the oven.

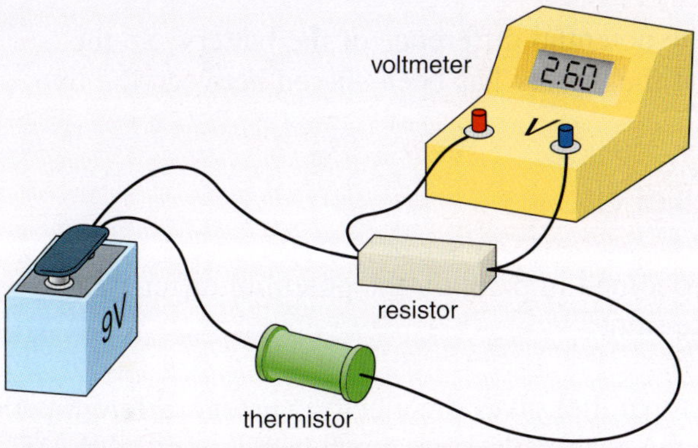

Figure 11.19 Misti's design for an oven thermometer

1. Draw a circuit diagram of Misti's oven thermometer design.
2. Explain why the voltmeter reading changes as the oven temperature changes.

Before using her oven thermometer Misti must **calibrate** it. She does this by putting the thermistor in a beaker of water and heating the water. She recorded different water temperatures and the reading on the voltmeter at those temperatures. Misti then drew the calibration graph shown in Figure 11.20.

> **Calibrate** means to make a standard scale between two fixed points so that you can give a value to a measured quantity. Testing a measuring device to check its accuracy is also called calibration.

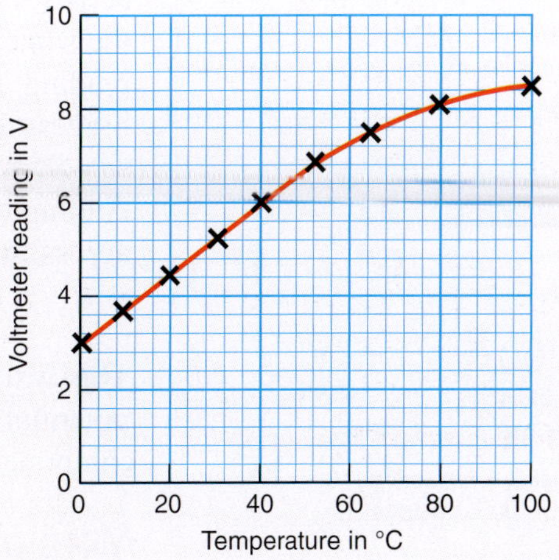

Figure 11.20 Misti's calibration graph

3. Explain how Misti can use the calibration graph to convert voltmeter readings into temperature values.
4. When Misti tried her thermometer in her oven she obtained voltmeter readings that varied between 7.5 V and 8.0 V. What range of temperatures does this give for the oven?
5. Suggest why the voltmeter reading was not constant.
6. Misti realises there is a problem with her design. It cannot be used to measure high oven temperatures.
   Why can this design not measure temperatures above 100 °C?

More about components in series

The current through components joined in series is the same. But the potential difference across the components may be different. The potential differences are the same only if the components have the same resistance.

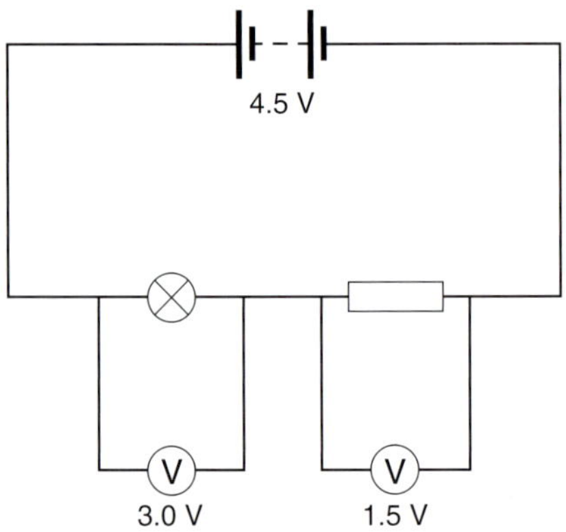

Figure 11.21 The potential difference across a component depends on the resistance of the component.

The potential differences across the components in a series circuit add to give the potential difference of the power supply.

6 Calculate the reading on the voltmeter shown in Figure 11.22.

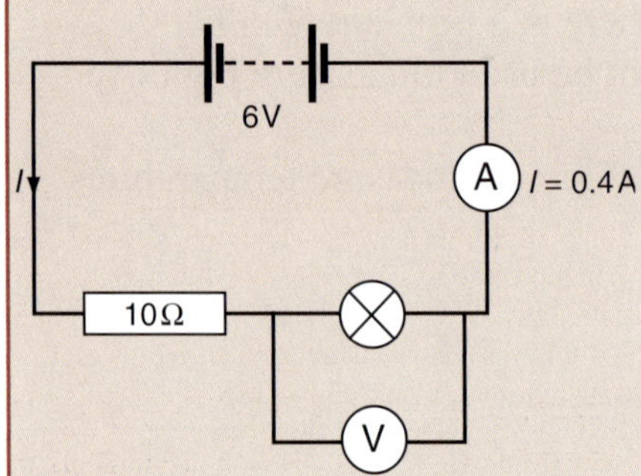

Figure 11.22

The voltmeters in Figure 11.21 are measuring the potential difference across the lamp and the resistor. The lamp and the resistor cannot have the same resistance as the voltmeters are giving different readings. The reading across the lamp is the biggest, so the lamp must have the biggest resistance.

Adding the two voltmeter readings gives the total potential difference across the circuit components. In this case:

total potential difference = 3.0 + 1.5 = 4.5 V

This is the same as the potential difference of the battery. So the potential difference of the battery has been shared between the two components.

More about parallel circuits

When components are joined in parallel, the potential difference across each component is the same.

Joining components in parallel gives the electric current different paths. Some current goes down each path. How much current goes through each component depends on the resistance of the component. The one with the biggest resistance has the smallest current flowing through it.

In Figure 11.23 half the total current flows through each lamp. So the resistance of the lamps must be the same because the current has split into two equal parts. The current joins back together where the parallel paths meet.

In a parallel circuit, the total current flowing through the whole circuit is the sum of the currents flowing through the separate components where the current has split (Figure 11.24).

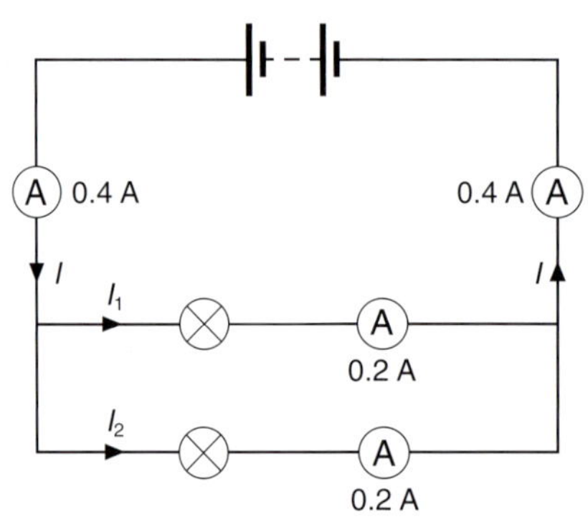

Figure 11.23 The current in a parallel circuit divides between the different paths.

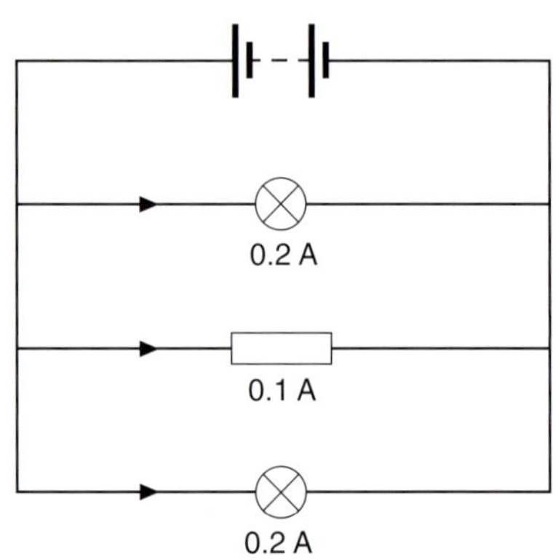

Figure 11.24 Total current = 0.2 + 0.1 + 0.2 = 0.5 A

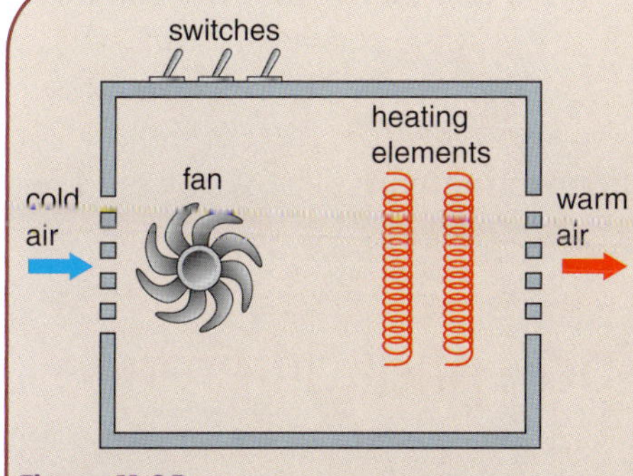

Figure 11.25

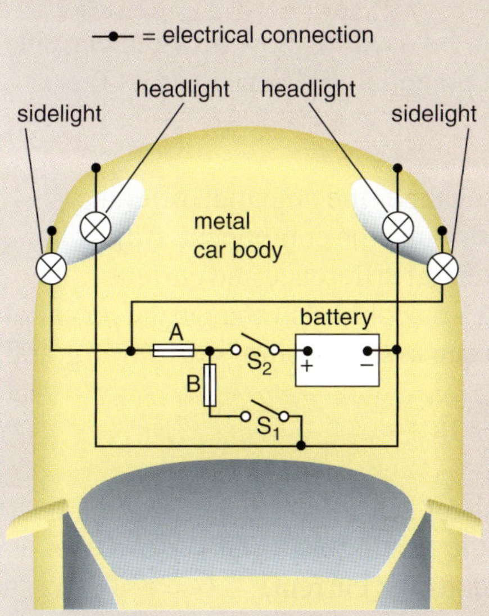

Figure 11.26

7 Figure 11.25 shows a simplified picture of the inside of a small fan heater. The electrical wiring is not shown.
Draw, using circuit symbols, a diagram to show how the heating elements, fan and switches would be connected together. It is essential that:
a) when connected to the mains and switched on the fan comes on;
b) both heating elements can be switched on independently;
c) on hot days the heater can be used as a fan.

8 Figure 11.26 shows a simplified circuit diagram for the front lights of a car. The metal car body acts like a wire in the circuit.
a) Which lights would not work if fuse A melted?
b) Which switch operates the headlights?
c) Can the sidelights be switched on without the headlights? Give a reason for your answer.
d) If one headlight breaks, will the other one still work? Give a reason for your answer.
e) How would this circuit need to be changed if the car had a plastic body?

Appliance	Working current in A
Computer	1
Hairdryer	4
Television	2
Stereo	1
Heater	10

Table 11.3 The current drawn from the supply by an appliance depends on its power rating.

Overloaded circuits

An adaptor lets you plug more than one appliance into a single mains socket. The appliances are in parallel. So the total current taken from the socket is the sum of the currents flowing through each appliance.

If the computer, stereo and television are plugged into the adaptor:

$$\text{total current} = 1 + 1 + 2 = 4\,\text{A}$$

This is not yet a problem. Up to 13 amps can safely flow through the wire connecting the socket to the mains electricity supply.

Figure 11.27 Overloaded circuits can cause fires.

However, plugging the hairdryer, television and heater into the adaptor could cause a big problem.

total current = 4 + 2 + 10 = 16 A

The total current is too large for the connecting wire. The wire could get so hot it causes a fire.

11.3 What does a current–potential difference graph show?

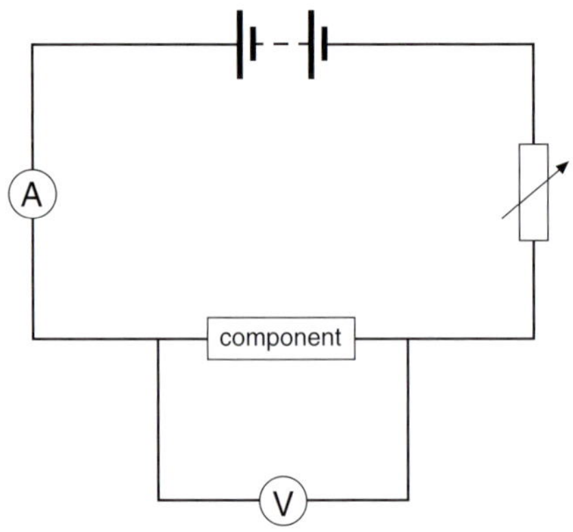

Figure 11.28 A circuit used to investigate the relationship between current and potential difference

The circuit shown in Figure 11.28 can be used to show how the current through a component depends on the potential difference across the component.

If you adjust the variable resistor, this changes the potential difference across the component and the current through the component. Adjusting the variable resistor allows a set of potential difference and current readings to be taken for a component. (You could also change the potential difference by adding more cells.) You can use the readings to draw a graph.

When the component is a resistor

As long as the temperature of the resistor stays the same, the graph is always a straight line going through the origin (0, 0). This shows that as the potential difference increases so does the current.

If you connect the resistor the other way round this does not change its resistance. The graph is still a straight line.

A metal wire has a constant resistance, but only if the temperature of the wire stays the same.

9 Copy Figure 11.29. Label the line A. Draw a second graph line for a resistor with a higher value than A. Label the second line B.

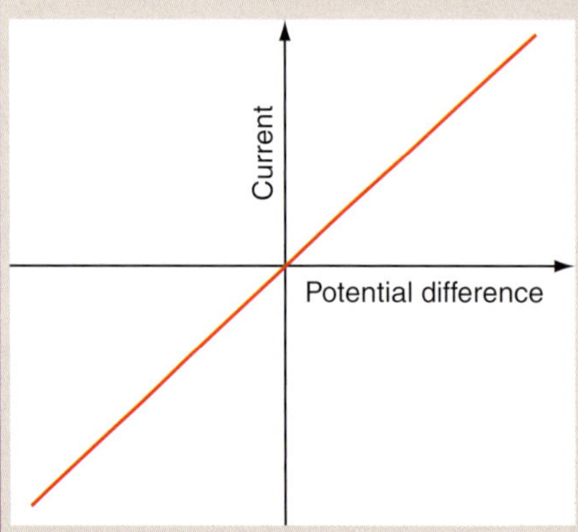

Figure 11.29 Complete current–potential difference graph for a resistor

When the component is a filament lamp

A filament lamp uses a very hot wire (filament) to give out light.

As the potential difference across the lamp increases, the light gets brighter. The light is brighter because more electrical energy is being transformed into light – and heat too. As the filament gets hotter its resistance increases. As a result of the higher resistance, the current does not increase in the same proportion as the potential difference (Figure 11.30). The resistance of a filament lamp is not constant – it depends on the potential difference.

Connecting the lamp the other way round makes no difference to the way the resistance of the lamp changes. The resistance always goes up when the temperature of the filament goes up.

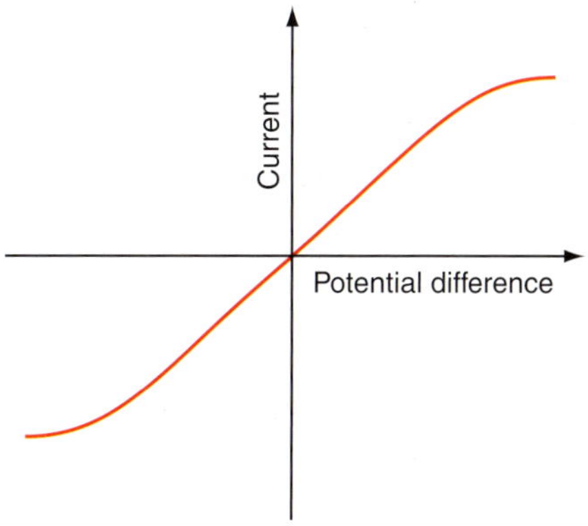

Figure 11.30 Current–potential difference graph for a filament lamp

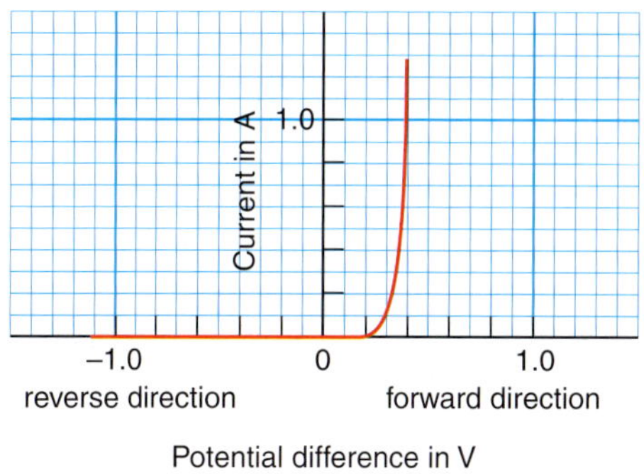

Figure 11.31 Current–potential difference graph for a diode

When the component is a diode

A **diode** is a device that allows current to flow in one direction only, since the diode has a very high resistance in the reverse direction.

The pattern for a **diode** is different from both a resistor and a filament lamp (Figure 11.31). The resistance of a diode does depend on which way round it is connected in a circuit.

Diodes only let current flow in one direction (called the forward direction). In the reverse direction diodes have a very high resistance so no current flows.

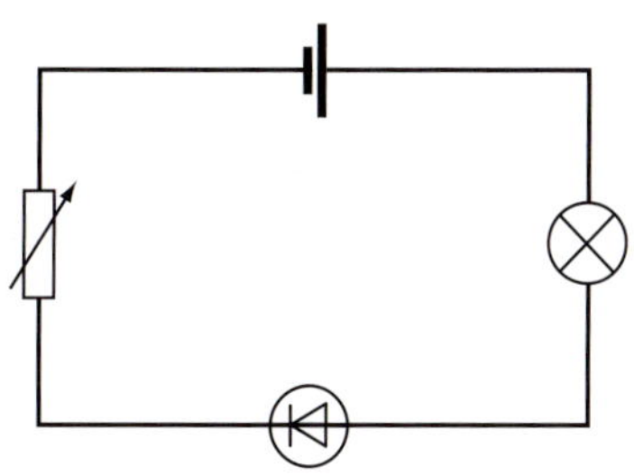

a)

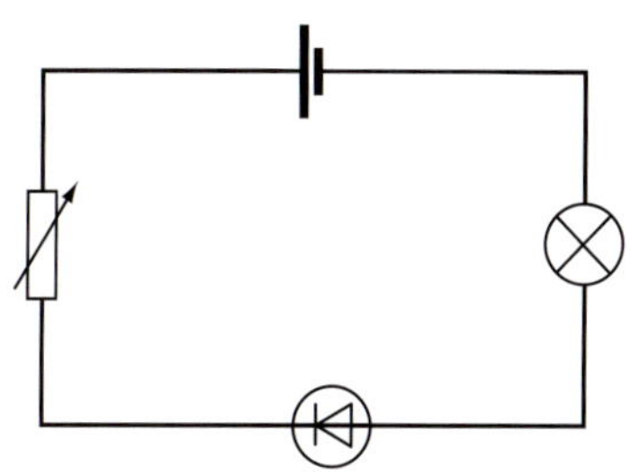

b)

Figure 11.32 **a)** Lamp is on. **b)** Lamp is off.

Activity – QTC (Quantum Tunnelling Composite)

Invented in 1997 by David Lussey, QTC is an amazing material, and as materials go it is very new. In one form it looks just like a piece of black rubber. But, unlike rubber, when you squash it its electrical resistance falls as it changes from an insulator to a conductor.

The range of potential applications for QTC is huge – from toys to textile switches, robotic sensors to space travel.

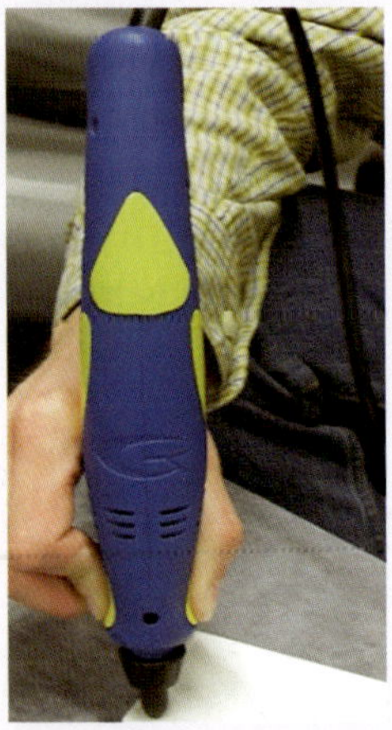

Figure 11.33 The outside casing of this prototype drill contains QTC. Squeezing the drill controls its speed.

Figure 11.34 QTC textile switches can be incorporated into 'smart' clothing and bags. Tapping the switches controls your mobile phone and MP3 player. They are even used in space suits.

1. Use the internet to investigate at least five different applications for QTC. Start your search by looking at the website www.peratech.co.uk. Write a few sentences about each application.
2. Which application that you have written about do you think will benefit people most? Give reasons for your choice.

Josh designed a simple experiment to check out what he had read about QTC. The apparatus he used is shown in Figure 11.35. Josh used various weights to squeeze the QTC, which was sandwiched between two metal plates. For each new weight Josh waited 20 seconds before taking the ohmmeter reading. He did this because he had noticed that the reading often changed rapidly in the first few seconds. Even after 20 seconds the reading still changed, but more slowly. For each weight Josh recorded a range of resistance values. These are shown in Figure 11.36.

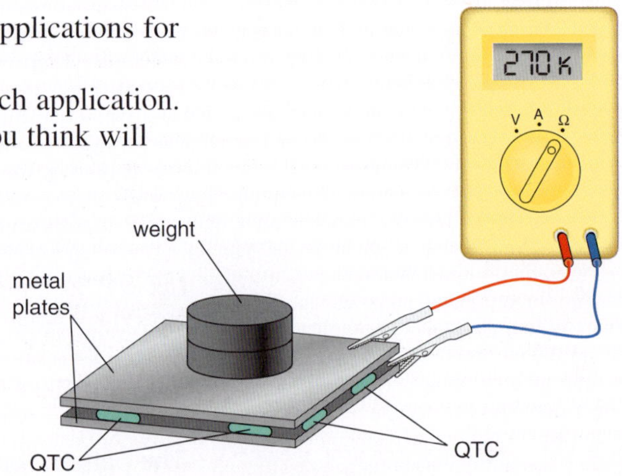

Figure 11.35 Measuring the resistance of QTC with an ohmmeter

3. With a weight of 20 N Josh measured the resistance as 10 Ω. Why has Josh not plotted this value on his results chart?
4. Josh added another weight to the QTC 'sandwich'. The reading on the ohmmeter was a fairly steady 3 Ω. How many newtons do you think this weight was? Give a reason for your answer.
5. Josh noticed that there is no overlap between the resistance values produced by two different weights. State with a reason whether this means that QTC could be used as a reliable way to tell one weight from a different one.

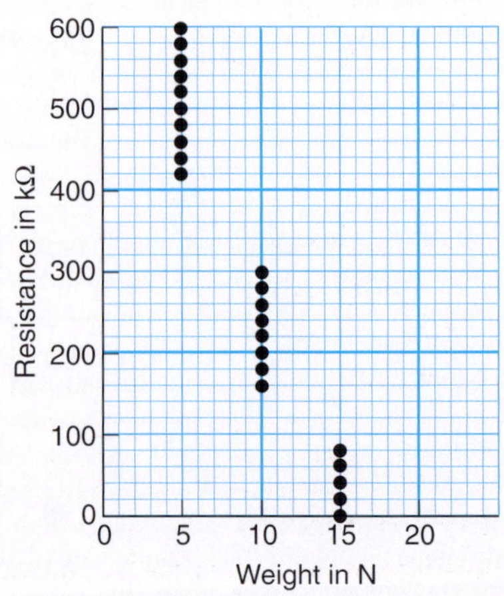

Figure 11.36 For each weight the QTC has a range of resistance.

11.4 What is the difference between direct current and alternating current?

Direct current (d.c.) is electric current that flows in the same direction all the time.

A **cathode ray oscilloscope (CRO)** is a device that displays how a potential difference varies over time.

A **direct current (d.c.)** always flows in the same direction around a circuit. It is shown in circuit diagrams by an arrow, usually labelled *I*, going from the positive terminal to the negative terminal of the power supply. (This is called the conventional current.) Cells and batteries produce a constant direct current (d.c.)

You can use a **cathode ray oscilloscope (CRO)** to show that the potential difference of a d.c. supply is constant. The display or 'trace' on the CRO screen shows the potential difference in volts across the supply. In Figure 11.37 connecting a cell to the input terminals has made the line on the CRO jump up above the middle line. Connecting the cell the other way around would make the line jump down. The bigger the potential difference of the cell, the further the line jumps. The CRO therefore gives us a way of comparing the potential differences of different d.c. supplies.

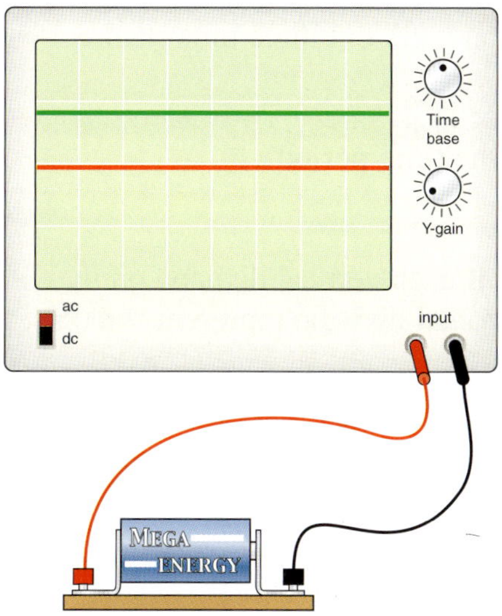

Figure 11.37 The line (trace) on the CRO shows that the cell produces a constant potential difference. The zero value is shown as a red line.

Alternating current is like having a cell in a circuit but you keep turning the cell around. First the current goes one way, then it goes back again. The current flows backwards and forwards as the terminals of the power supply change from positive to negative. But a.c. changes direction faster and more often than you could turn the cell around.

An alternating current (a.c.) is one that is constantly reversing its direction. The number of times the current changes direction in one second gives the **frequency** of the supply.

Alternating current (a.c.) is electric current that continually changes its direction.

The **frequency** of an a.c. current is the number of cycles per second, or how many times per second the electric current reverses its direction.

Comparing CRO traces for two different a.c. supplies

Figure 11.38 shows the CRO traces for two a.c. supplies. The controls on the oscilloscope were the same for both supplies. Each time the trace changes from above to below (or from below to above) the red zero line, the current in the circuit changes direction.

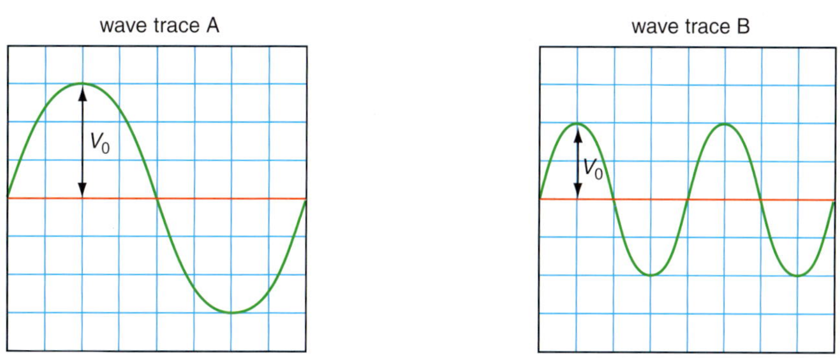

Figure 11.38 The two a.c. supplies have a different frequency and peak potential difference (V_0).

10 Explain the difference between an alternating current and a direct current.

11 Figure 11.39 shows the CRO traces for different a.c. supplies.

a) Which of the supplies has the:
   i) largest peak voltage;
   ii) highest frequency;
   iii) lowest frequency;
   iv) smallest peak voltage?

b) Each horizontal division on the CRO screen represents 0.002 s. Calculate the frequency of each trace.

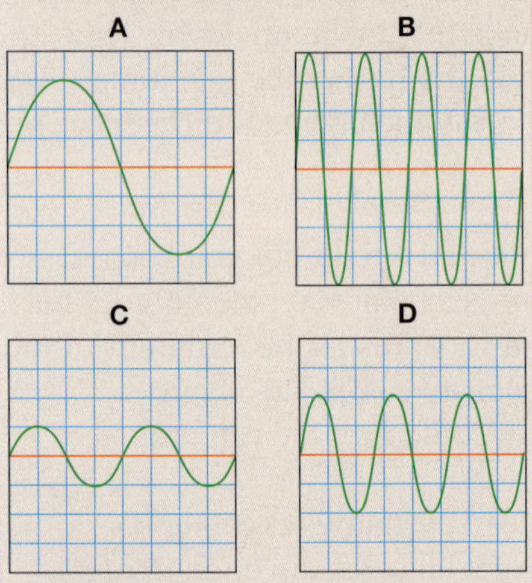

Figure 11.39

The **time period** is the time taken for a.c. current to complete one cycle and reverse its direction. Time period is related to frequency.

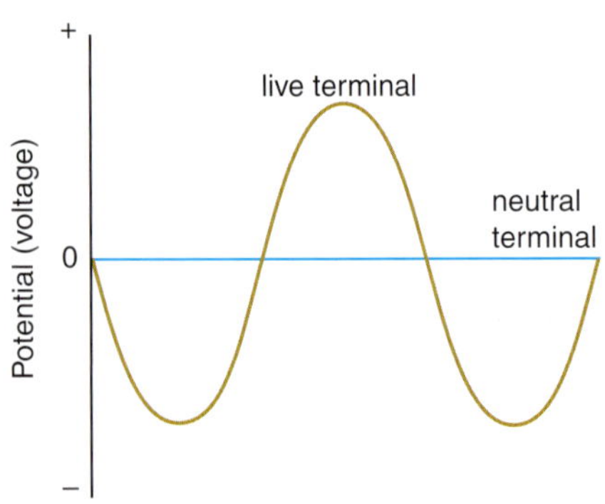

Figure 11.40 The alternating potential at the live terminal makes the current flow backwards and forwards (a.c.).

Trace A is 1½ times taller than trace B. So the peak potential difference (V_0) of supply A is 1½ times bigger than that of supply B.

The CRO trace for supply B shows twice as many waves as supply A. This means the potential difference (and current) of supply B changes direction twice as often as the potential difference (and current) of supply A. So the frequency of supply B is twice the frequency of supply A.

Using the measurements from a CRO trace for an a.c. supply

The screen of a CRO is like a graph. The vertical and horizontal divisions have a scale. Each vertical division represents a certain number of volts. Each horizontal division represents a certain length of time. When you know the scale you can work out three important quantities:

- peak (maximum) potential difference (V_0);
- time to complete one cycle (called the **time period**);
- frequency of the supply.

Look back at trace A in Figure 11.38. If each vertical division on the CRO represents 2 volts and each horizontal division represents 0.005 seconds, then:

$$\text{peak potential difference} = 3 \text{ divisions} \times 2 \text{ volts per division} = 6\,\text{V}$$

$$\text{time period} = 8 \text{ divisions} \times 0.005 = 0.04\,\text{s}$$

$$\text{frequency} = \frac{1}{\text{time period}} = \frac{1}{0.04} = 25\,\text{Hz}$$

The mains electricity supply

The UK mains electricity is an a.c. supply of frequency 50 Hz. This means the current flows one way, then back again, 50 times in each second.

The mains electricity supply cable to a house has two wires – a live wire and a neutral wire. The current comes into the house on one wire and returns on the other.

Electricity is supplied through the live wire. The potential (voltage) at the live terminal alternates between positive and negative with respect to the neutral wire with a mean (average) potential of 230 V. The live wire is a dangerous wire.

The neutral wire is kept at a potential (voltage) close to zero. This is done by connecting it to a huge metal plate in the earth at the local electricity sub-station.

11.5 How can the mains electricity supply be used safely?

Many electric appliances are designed to work from the mains electricity supply. Most of these appliances are connected to the mains using a cable and three-pin plug. Both the cable and plug are designed to make the appliance safe to use.

Inside the cable are either two or three copper wires (the inner cores). Copper is used because it is a good electrical conductor. A layer of plastic covers each wire and another layer forms the outside of the cable. Plastic is used because it is a good insulator and is flexible.

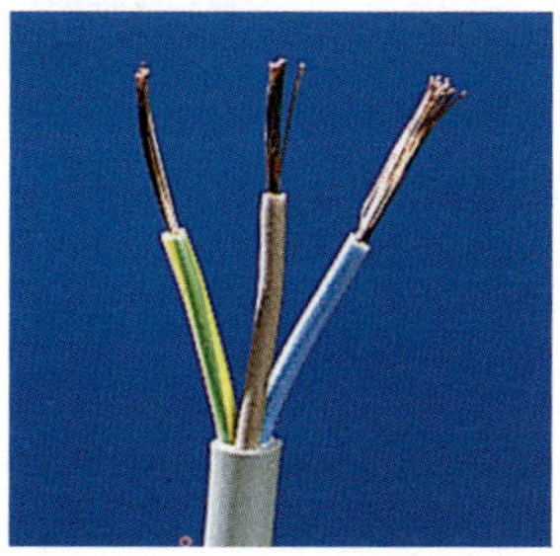

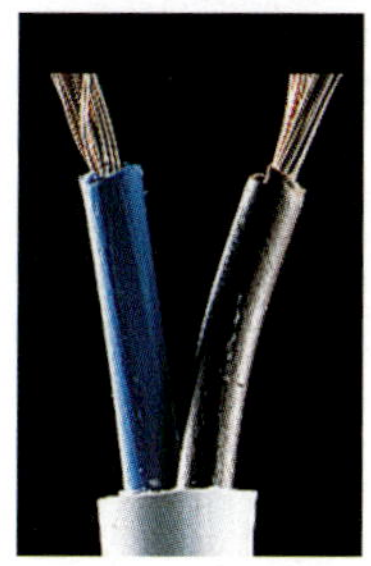

Figure 11.41 Three-core and two-core cables

Figure 11.42 The outside of a three-pin plug and its wall socket

The outside case of the plug is made of plastic or rubber. These materials are used because they are good electrical insulators.

Pushing the plug into a socket joins the three brass pins of the plug to the terminals of the socket. Brass is used for the pins because brass is a good electrical conductor.

Inside the plug there is a cable grip and a fuse. The cable grip is there to hold the cable firmly in place. If the cable is pulled the cable grip stops the copper wires inside the plug being pulled loose.

Fuses

A **fuse** is a thin piece of wire that lets a current of up to a certain value flow through it. Above this value the fuse overheats and melt. We often say that the fuse has 'blown'.

The fuse joins the live pin to the live wire inside the plug. If a fault causes the fuse to melt the live wire is disconnected. This protects the appliance from taking a current that might damage it or cause its wiring to overheat and start a fire.

A **fuse** is a thin wire that is designed to melt and break a circuit when the current through it exceeds the fuse's rating.

Most plugs are fitted with a 3 A or 13 A fuse. Appliances like table lamps and TVs take small currents (well below 3 A), so they should have plugs with 3 A fuses. Kettles, irons and hairdryers usually take currents greater than 3 A, so they should have plugs with a 13 A fuse.

Figure 11.43 Electricity is useful but also dangerous. Many household fires are caused by electrical faults.

Connecting an appliance to a three-pin plug

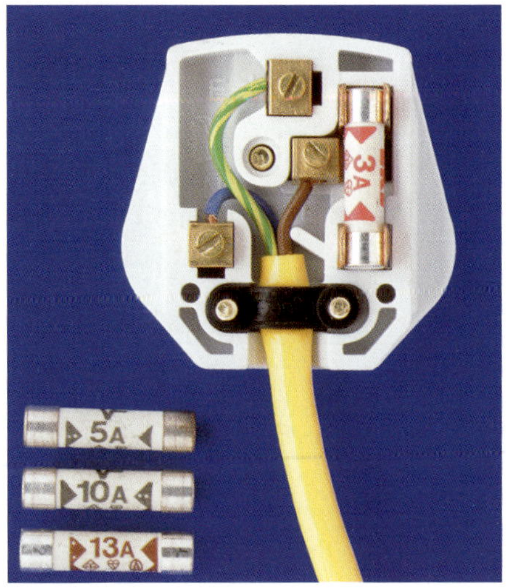

Figure 11.44 A correctly wired three-pin plug:
- The brown wire (live wire) is joined to the fuse, which is joined to the live pin;
- The blue wire (neutral wire) is joined to the neutral pin;
- The green/yellow wire (earth wire) is joined to the earth pin.

All new electrical appliances come with a plug already fitted. But at some time you may need to fit a new plug to an older appliance. When you do this you must connect the correct wire from the appliance to the correct pin in the plug. The wires are colour coded to help you connect them in the right place.

12 An electric coffee maker takes a current of 2 A from the mains supply. Explain why the plug of the coffee maker should not be fitted with a 13 A fuse.

13 Why would it be dangerous to connect the fuse inside a plug to the neutral wire rather than the live wire?

14 Say why each of the plugs drawn in Figure 11.45 is not safe to use.

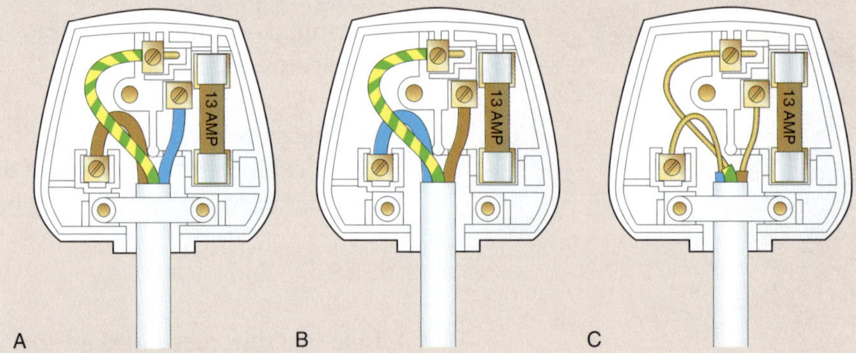

Figure 11.45

Circuit breakers

The mains supply to a house starts at a consumer unit. Often this is called the 'fuse box'. In the consumer unit are several separate fuses. Each fuse leads to a different circuit supplying electricity to a different part of the house.

Many consumer units now contain **circuit breakers** rather than fuses. The circuit breaker is a fast acting switch that automatically turns off

A **circuit breaker** is a resettable fuse.

('trips') when the current through it goes above a set value. Having mended the fault that caused the current to rise you press a button to reset the circuit breaker.

Figure 11.46 A RCCB plugged into a socket ready for use

A second type of circuit breaker, a **residual current circuit breaker (RCCB)**, should be used with certain types of appliance, particularly those used outside. It is a circuit breaker that disconnects the circuit when it detects current leaking out of the circuit to earth due to a fault.

A RCCB works by detecting any difference between the currents in the live and neutral wires of the supply cable. If everything is working properly the two currents are the same. If something happens to make the current in the wires different, the RCCB automatically switches the circuit off.

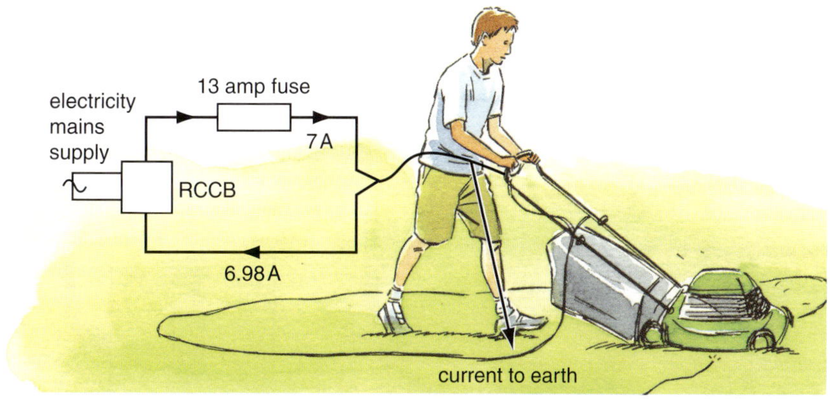

Figure 11.47 Using a RCCB saves Vince from a nasty experience.

⑮ Give two ways that a circuit breaker is a better safety device than a fuse.

⑯ Why should electric hedge trimmers always be plugged into a RCCB?

For extra safety Vince plugs his lawn mower into a RCCB. Just as well, because Vince has been careless and cut into the cable insulation. This causes a current to flow through Vince to earth. This means the currents in the live and neutral wires are now different. The RCCB detects this difference and rapidly switches the circuit off saving Vince from a very nasty electric shock.

Earthing

Any electrical appliance with an outside metal case is usually earthed. Figure 11.48 shows an electric toaster. It has been earthed by joining the earth wire from the three-core cable to the metal casing. If while it's switched on, a fault causes the live wire to touch the metal case, a large current flows from the live wire to the earth wire. This large current in the circuit causes the fuse to melt, which switches the toaster off.

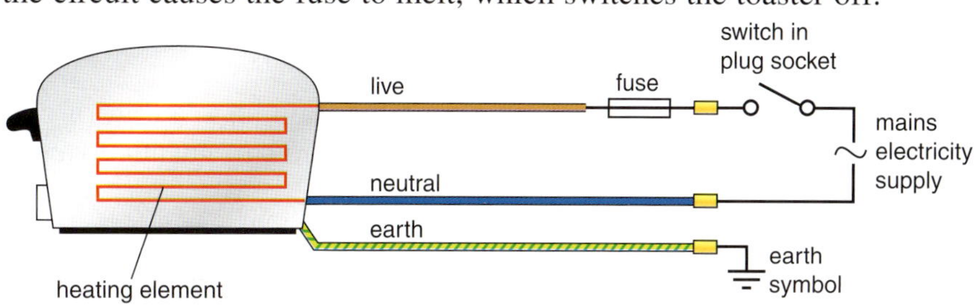

Figure 11.48 The earth wire is an important safety feature of appliances with outer metal parts.

Without the earth wire the toaster would become live. Anyone who touches the metal case would get an electric shock as the current flows through them to earth.

Activity – Using electricity safely

We use electrical appliances and gadgets to make our lives more comfortable and enjoyable. Yet electricity is dangerous, it can and does kill. We not only run the risk of electrocution, but also the risk of fires caused by electrical faults.

Write a short, lively article for a gadget or fashion magazine. The article should start by saying why the discovery of electricity was so important to individuals and society. It should go on to warn readers about the potential risks of using electricity and also give advice on how to reduce these risks.

17 The pictures drawn in Figure 11.49 show electricity being used dangerously. Explain the danger in each picture.

Figure 11.49

18 Zafran leans against his washing machine. Unfortunately the live wire inside the machine has become loose and is touching the metal casing. Explain how the earth wire, which is correctly connected, protects Zafran from a serious electric shock.

11.6 What links current, charge, energy and power?

Current and charge

An electric current is a flow of charge. In a metal wire, an electric current is a flow of negatively charged electrons.

The amount of charge transferred by a circuit depends on two factors:
- the size of the current;
- how long the circuit is switched on.

1 **coulomb** is the charge that passes a point when a current of 1 **ampere** flows for 1 second.

Charge is measured in **coulombs** (C) and current is measured in **amperes** or **amps** (A). The link between charge and current is given by the equation:

$$\underset{\text{(coulomb, C)}}{\text{charge}} = \underset{\text{(ampere, A)}}{\text{current}} \times \underset{\text{(second, s)}}{\text{time}}$$

⓳ A horse got an electric shock from touching an electrified fence. Calculate how much charge passed through the horse if a current of 0.020 A flowed for 0.1 s.

Example

To boil water a current of 10 A flows through the heating element of an electric kettle for 2 minutes. How much charge passes through the heating element?

$$\begin{aligned}\text{charge} &= \text{current} \times \text{time}\\ &= 10 \times 120\\ &= 1200 \text{ coulombs}\end{aligned}$$

Energy and charge

In any circuit, the battery or mains supply is an energy source that provides energy to charges. Energy is transformed into other sorts of energy as the charges flow around the circuit.

How much total energy is transformed by a component in a circuit depends on two factors:

- the potential difference across the component;
- how much charge flows through the component.

The link between charge, energy transformed and potential difference is given by the equation:

$$\underset{\text{(joule, J)}}{\text{energy transformed}} = \underset{\text{(volt, V)}}{\text{potential difference}} \times \underset{\text{(coulomb, C)}}{\text{charge}}$$

This equation also applies to the electrical energy transferred from a power supply to an appliance.

Power and energy

Sometimes knowing how quickly energy is transferred or transformed is as important or more important than knowing how much energy is transferred or transformed.

Power is the rate at which a device transforms energy, in J/s or W.

For example, an electric kettle transfers heat energy to the water inside the kettle. But if the transfer takes a long time the water warms up slowly. To know how quickly the water warms up you need to know how much energy the kettle transfers to the water every second. What you need to know is the **power** of the kettle.

$$\text{power (watt, W)} = \frac{\text{energy transferred (joule, J)}}{\text{time (second, s)}}$$

A kettle with a high power rating of 2000 W (2 kW) transfers 2000 joules of electrical energy every second. This is a rapid transfer, so the kettle heats the water quickly.

If you put all three equations in this section together you end up with a fourth equation. This is the equation for electrical power.

$$\text{power (watt, W)} = \text{current (ampere, A)} \times \text{potential difference (volt, V)}$$

Most appliances have their power and the p.d. of the supply they need printed on them. From this you can work out the current they use and the fuse they need.

Activity – Using the information on an information plate

All electrical appliances used at home have an information plate somewhere on the outside. Find the information plates on three different types of appliance.

1. For each appliance write down the technical information from the plate.
2. Calculate the normal operating current of each appliance.
3. Suggest the correct fuse rating to use with each appliance.

20 Table 11.4 shows how long it takes three different electric kettles to boil some water. The starting temperature of the water in each kettle is the same.

Kettle	Mass of water in the kettle	Time to boil the water
X	1.0 kg	4 minutes
Y	500 g	2½ minutes
Z	1.2 kg	4 minutes

Table 11.4

Assuming the kettles are equally efficient, which one has the highest power? Explain your choice.

21 Calculate the power rating in watts of:
a) a car starter motor operating from a 12 V supply, taking a 100 A current;
b) a torch bulb operating from a 4.5 V supply, taking a 0.3 A current;
c) a pocket calculator operating from a 3 V supply, taking a 0.0001 A current.

22 A 24 W set of Christmas lights has 20 identical lamps in series worked from a 120 V supply. Calculate:
a) the current through each lamp;
b) the potential difference across one lamp;
c) the resistance of the lighting circuit.

23 A 12 V battery drives a motor taking a current of 2 A for 20 seconds. Calculate the electrical energy transferred to the motor.

24 Usually a 3 A or 13 A fuse is fitted to the plug of a 230 V household appliance.
a) Calculate the current each of the appliances in Table 11.5 draws from the mains.
b) State the correct fuse to use with each appliance.

Appliance	Power rating
Microwave	750 W
Oven	2.5 kW
Toaster	350 W
Radio	15 W

Table 11.5

25 Figure 11.50 shows the circuit diagram for a 'flame effect' electric fire.

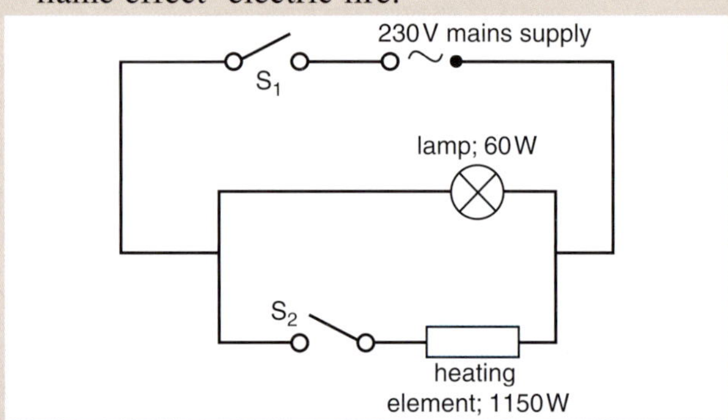

Figure 11.50

a) Explain why you cannot switch only the heating element on.
b) With both switches closed calculate:
   i) the current taken by the heating element;
   ii) the current taken by the lamp (give your answer to the nearest whole number);
   iii) the total current taken from the supply;
   iv) the resistance of the heating element.
c) What size fuse should be fitted to the fire, 3 A or 13 A? Give a reason for your choice.

Summary

✓ A **component** is a part of an electric circuit.

✓ **Potential difference** (or p.d.) is often called voltage. A potential difference causes current to flow.

✓ A **cell** uses chemical reactions to produce a potential difference across its two terminals. A **battery** is a number of cells connected together.

✓ The **resistance** of a component in ohms is defined as the potential difference across it divided by the current through it.

✓ The **resistance** of a **light-dependent resistor (LDR)** goes down as the intensity of the light goes up.

✓ The resistance of a **thermistor** increases as its temperature decreases.

✓ A resistor at constant temperature has a constant resistance – the current is directly proportional to the potential difference.

✓ The resistance of a filament lamp increases as the temperature of the filament increases.

✓ **Calibrate** means to make a standard scale between two fixed points so that you can give a value to a measured quantity. Testing a measuring device to check its accuracy is also called calibration.

✓ A **diode** lets current flow in only one direction.

✓ For components joined in **series:**
- the same current flows through each component;
- the total resistance is the sum of the individual resistances;
- the potential differences across the components add to give the potential difference of the power supply.

✓ For components joined in **parallel:**
- the potential difference across each component is the same;
- the total current flowing through the whole circuit is the sum of the currents flowing through the separate components;

✓ **Direct current (d.c.)** flows in one direction only but **alternating current (a.c.)** changes direction.

✓ In the UK the mains supply is at 230 V a.c. with a **frequency** of 50 hertz.

✓ Traces on a **cathode ray oscilloscope (CRO)** can be used to compare potential differences of a.c. and d.c. supplies and to determine the frequency of an a.c. supply.

✓ The **time period** is the time taken for a.c. current to complete one cycle and reverse its direction. Time period is related to frequency.

✓ A correctly wired three-pin plug contains a **fuse** and earth wire.

✓ A **circuit breaker** is a resettable fuse. A **residual current circuit breaker** (**RCCB**) is a circuit breaker that disconnects the circuit when it detects current leaking out of the circuit to earth due to a fault.

✓ Any appliance with a metal case should be earthed.

✓ 1 **coulomb** is the charge that passes a point when a current of 1 **ampere** flows for 1 second.

✓ Important equations that you should be able to use:

$$\text{potential difference} = \text{current} \times \text{resistance}$$
$$\text{charge} = \text{current} \times \text{time}$$
$$\text{energy transformed} = \text{potential difference} \times \text{charge}$$
$$\text{power} = \frac{\text{energy transferred}}{\text{time}}$$
$$\text{power} = \text{current} \times \text{potential difference}$$

EXAMQUESTIONS

1 Tasmin wants to find out how the current through component 'X' varies with potential difference. To do this she sets up the circuit shown in Figure 11.51. Tasmin's one set of results are recorded in Table 11.6.

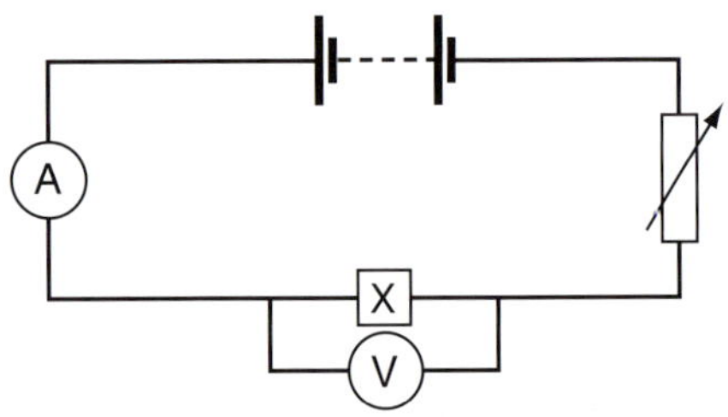

Figure 11.51 The circuit set up by Tasmin

Potential difference in V	0.0	3.0	5.0	7.0	9.0	11.0
Current in A	0.0	1.0	1.4	1.7	1.9	2.1

Table 11.6 Tasmin's results

a) i) What did Tasmin do to vary the potential difference across component 'X'? *(1 mark)*
ii) What range of potential difference values did Tasmin use? *(1 mark)*
iii) Suggest why Tasmin should have included some values of potential difference below 3 volts. *(1 mark)*

b) i) Plot a graph of potential difference (horizontal axis) against current (vertical axis). *(3 marks)*
ii) Use your graph to calculate the resistance of component 'X' when the potential difference is 10 V. *(3 marks)*

c) What is component 'X'? Explain the reason for your answer. *(2 marks)*

Figure 11.52 Sulaman investigates heating

2 Figure 11.52 shows Sulaman using a 12 V heater to warm a block of metal. He is using a joulemeter to measure the energy transferred to the heater.

Before starting the experiment Sulaman reset the joulemeter to zero. After switching on and leaving for 5 minutes the reading was 7200.

a) i) Calculate the energy transferred each second to the heater. *(1 mark)*
ii) State the power of the heater. *(1 mark)*

b) Calculate the charge that flowed through the heater in 5 minutes. Give the unit for your calculated answer. *(3 marks)*

c) Calculate the current, in amps, through the heater during the 5 minutes. *(2 marks)*

d) Sulaman correctly calculated that the temperature of the metal block should go up by 18 °C. But, when he measured the temperature he found it had increased by only 15 °C. Give **two** reasons why the temperature of the block did not increase by 18 °C. *(2 marks)*

3 The ammeters in Figure 11.53 are identical.

a) i) What are the readings on the ammeters A_1 and A_2? *(2 marks)*
ii) Is the resistance of 'K', bigger, smaller or equal to 30 Ω? Give a reason for your choice of answer. *(2 marks)*

b) i) Calculate the reading on the voltmeter. *(2 marks)*
ii) State the potential difference of the power supply? Give a reason for your choice of value. *(2 marks)*

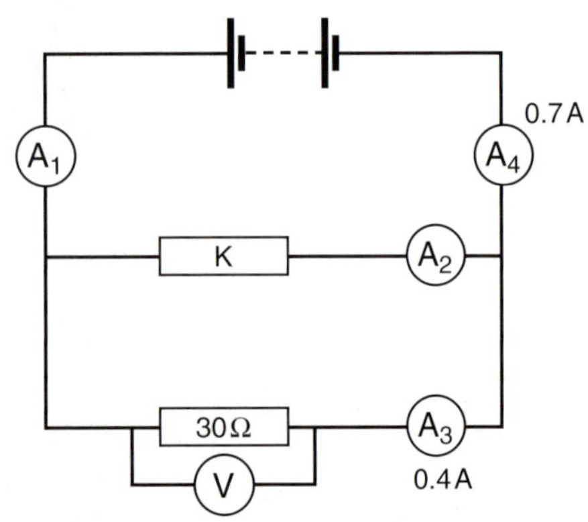

Figure 11.53

Chapter 12
What happens during radioactive decay, nuclear fission and nuclear fusion?

At the end of this chapter you should:

- ✓ be able to explain from the experimental evidence why the nuclear model of atomic structure replaced the 'plum pudding' model;
- ✓ know the relative masses and relative charges of protons, neutrons and electrons;
- ✓ know that atoms have a very small nucleus containing protons and neutrons surrounded by a much larger region of empty space in which there are electrons;
- ✓ understand how atoms can lose or gain electrons to form ions;
- ✓ know that alpha, beta and gamma radiations are emitted when the nuclei of radioactive substances decay;
- ✓ understand the changes in atomic number and mass number as a result of alpha and beta decay;
- ✓ know what causes background radiation;
- ✓ know that nuclear fission releases large amounts of energy which can be used in nuclear reactors to generate electricity;
- ✓ understand that the neutrons released by nuclear fission can start a chain reaction;
- ✓ know that nuclear fusion involves the joining together of two nuclei with the release of vast amounts of energy.

Figure 12.1 A small nuclear reactor on board this submarine provides sufficient energy for it to remain submerged in the ocean for months or even years without refuelling. The energy comes from the break-up (fission) of uranium nuclei. The heat and light emitted from stars also comes from nuclear processes. In this case, the energy comes from the joining together (fusion) of hydrogen nuclei.

12.1 Where do radioactivity and atomic energy come from?

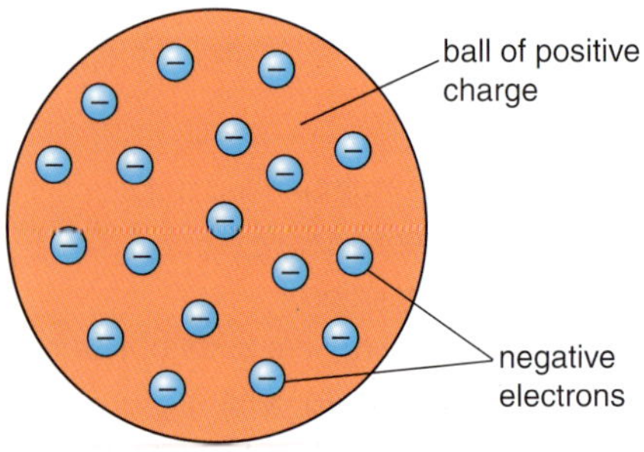

Figure 12.2 Thomson's 'plum pudding' model for the structure of atoms

Radioactive substances such as uranium give out (emit) energy naturally. When radioactivity was discovered in 1896, no one could explain where this energy came from. Marie Curie soon discovered that the intensity of the radiation emitted depended only on the amount of uranium in her sample. Nothing she did to the uranium – such as heating it up – affected the rays. This, she said 'shows that radioactivity is an atomic property'.

What do we know about the structure of atoms?

In 1897, J. J. Thomson discovered tiny negative particles that were about 2000 times lighter than hydrogen atoms. He called these particles electrons. When Thomson put very high voltages across terminals made of different metals in different gases, the particles that he obtained all had the same mass and charge. This led him to suggest that all substances and all atoms must contain electrons (see Section 5.1).

Thomson knew that atoms had no electrical charge overall. So, the rest of the atom must have a positive charge to balance the negative charge of the electrons.

In Thomson's **'plum pudding' model**, each atom was thought to be a positively charged sphere with electrons embedded in it.

In 1904, Thomson suggested a model for the structure of atoms. This became known as the **'plum pudding' model** of atomic structure. Thomson suggested that atoms were tiny balls of positive material with electrons embedded in it, like currants scattered throughout a cake, or chocolate chips in a chocolate chip cookie (Figure 12.2).

Activity – Rutherford and his colleagues find the positive nucleus

In 1898, Ernest Rutherford showed that there were at least two types of radiation given out by radioactive materials. He called these alpha 'rays' and beta 'rays'.

At this time, Rutherford and his colleagues didn't know exactly what alpha rays were. But, they did know that alpha rays contained particles. These alpha particles were small, heavy and positively charged. Rutherford and his colleagues used the alpha particles from radioactive substances as tiny 'bullets' to fire at atoms.

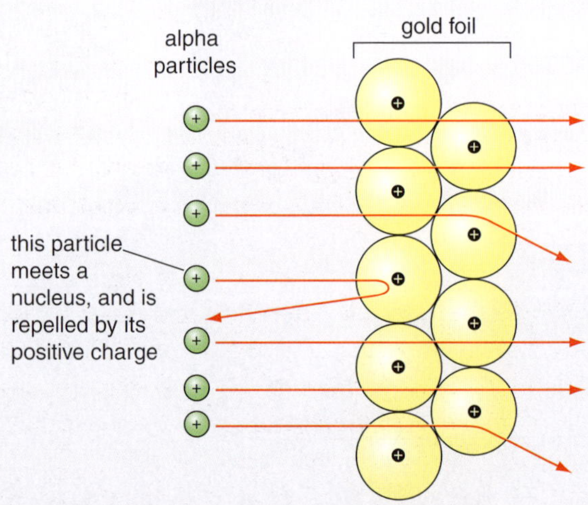

Figure 12.3 When positive alpha particles are directed at a very thin sheet of gold foil, they emerge at different angles. Most pass straight through the foil, some are deflected and a few appear to rebound from the foil.

In 1909, Rutherford designed an experiment in which his colleagues Hans Geiger and Ernest Marsden directed narrow beams of positive alpha particles at very thin gold foil only a few atoms thick (Figure 12.3). They expected the particles to pass straight through the foil or to be deflected slightly.

The results showed that:
- most of the alpha particles went straight through the foil;
- some of the alpha particles were scattered or deflected by the foil;
- a few alpha particles rebounded from the foil.

1. Why did most of the alpha particles pass straight through the foil? (Hint: Most of an atom is empty space.)
2. What conclusions can you draw about the size of any positive and negative particles in the gold atoms if most alpha particles pass straight through the foil?
3. Why were some alpha particles deflected? (Remember that alpha particles are positive.)
4. How did these results cast doubts on Thomson's plum pudding model for atomic structure?
5. Why did a few alpha particles seem to rebound from the foil? (Hint: What will happen if an alpha particle approaches another positive charge head-on?)
6. In 1911, Rutherford interpreted these results and put forward a new model for the structure of atoms. How do you think Rutherford described atoms?

Rutherford's nuclear model

Rutherford summarised the results of Geiger and Marsden's experiment by saying that atoms have a very small positive nucleus surrounded by a much larger region of empty space in which electrons orbit the nucleus like planets orbiting the Sun (Figure 12.4).

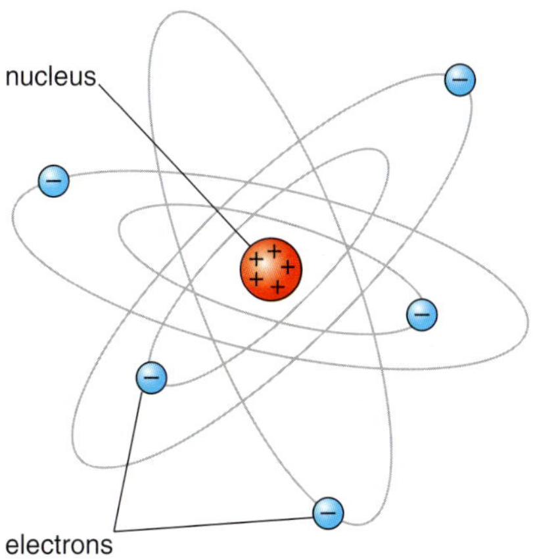

Figure 12.4 Rutherford's nuclear model for the structure of atoms. Rutherford pictured atoms as miniature solar systems with electrons orbiting the nucleus like planets around the Sun.

> In Rutherford's **nuclear model**, each atom was thought to have a very small positively charged nucleus surrounded by electrons.

Rutherford's model of atomic structure was called the **nuclear model**. His nuclear model quickly replaced Thomson's plum pudding model and is still the basic model of atomic structure that we use today.

Through the work of Thomson, Rutherford and their colleagues we now know that:
- the positive charge of the nucleus is due to positive particles called protons;
- protons are about 2000 times heavier than electrons;
- electrons have a relative charge of −1 and protons have a relative charge of +1;
- atoms have equal numbers of protons and electrons, so that atoms have no overall electrical charge;
- the nuclei of atoms contain neutrons as well as protons. Neutrons have no charge and their mass is the same as that of protons (see Section 5.1).

All atoms are made up from protons, neutrons and electrons. These particles are sometimes called sub-atomic particles. Their relative masses and relative electric charges are summarised in Table 12.1.

Particle	Relative mass	Relative charge
Proton	1	+1
Neutron	1	0
Electron	$\frac{1}{2000}$	−1

Table 12.1 The relative masses and relative charges of protons, neutrons and electrons

12.2 Atoms of different elements

The **atomic number** is the number of protons in an atom.

The **mass number** is the total number of protons plus neutrons in an atom.

Atoms of different elements have different numbers of protons. Hydrogen atoms are the only atoms with one proton. Helium atoms are the only atoms with two protons, lithium atoms are the only atoms with three protons, and so on. This means that the number of protons in an atom tells you straight away which element it is. Scientists call this number the **atomic number**. So, hydrogen has an atomic number of one, helium has an atomic number of two and so on.

The atomic number of an atom can tell you which element it is, but it cannot tell you its mass. The mass of an atom depends on the total number of protons and neutrons in its nucleus. Scientists call this number the **mass number** of an atom.

mass number = 63

Cu

atomic number = 29

Figure 12.5 We can write the symbol $^{63}_{29}Cu$ to show the mass number and atomic number for a copper nucleus.

Hydrogen atoms (with one proton and no neutrons) have a mass number of 1, lithium atoms (with three protons and four neutrons) have a mass number of 7 and copper atoms (with 29 protons and 34 neutrons) have a mass number of 63.

All the atoms of a particular element have the same atomic number and therefore the same number of protons. But they don't all have the same number of neutrons. These atoms of the same element with different numbers of neutrons and therefore different mass numbers are called **isotopes** (see also Section 5.2).

Isotopes are atoms of an element with the same atomic number, but different mass numbers.

From atoms to ions

When gamma rays and fast moving beta particles (electrons) hit atoms, they sometimes cause the atoms to become ions. These ionising radiations have so much energy that they can remove outer electrons from the atoms to form positively charged particles called ions (Figure 12.6).

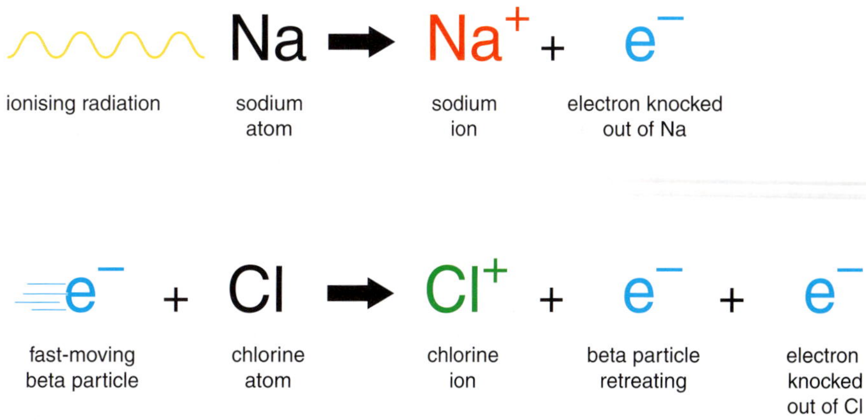

Figure 12.6 The formation of ions when sodium and chlorine atoms are hit by ionising radiations

1 Copy and complete the following sentences.

Uranium has two isotopes. Each isotope has 92 protons and _____ electrons and therefore an _____ number of 92. But one of these isotopes has 143 neutrons and the other has 146 neutrons. Their mass numbers are therefore _____ and _____. They are sometimes called uranium-235 and _____.

2 Copy and complete Table 12.2 using words from the box below.

atomic chemical neutrons physical protons

Isotopes have the <u>same:</u>	Isotopes have <u>different:</u>
• number of _____ • number of electrons • _____ number • _____ properties	• numbers of _____ • _____ properties

Table 12.2

3 Because there are different isotopes, chlorine gas can exist as $^{35}_{17}Cl_2$ and $^{37}_{17}Cl_2$. These two forms have the same chemical properties but different physical properties.

a) Which particles determine the chemical properties of substances – protons, neutrons or electrons?

b) Why do $^{35}_{17}Cl_2$ and $^{37}_{17}Cl_2$ have the same chemical properties?

c) Why do $^{35}_{17}Cl_2$ and $^{37}_{17}Cl_2$ have different boiling points?

d) Which has the higher boiling point, $^{35}_{17}Cl_2$ or $^{37}_{17}Cl_2$?

4 How many protons, neutrons and electrons are there in:

a) $^{19}_{9}F$ and $^{19}_{9}F^-$;

b) $^{27}_{13}Al$ and $^{27}_{13}Al^{3+}$?

12.3 What causes background radiation?

Background radiation is the nuclear radiation that is present all around us. It comes mainly from natural sources.

Nuclear radiation is all around us. This is because there are naturally occurring radioactive elements in low concentrations in many materials. There is also nuclear radiation from space and from medical examinations, such as X-rays. This **background radiation** gives all living things a dose of nuclear radiation. Fortunately, the level of background radiation is normally low and this is not a health risk for

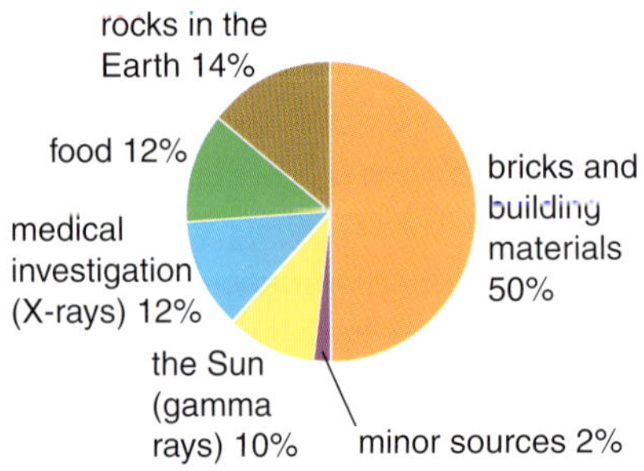

Figure 12.7 The main sources of background radiation in the UK

most people. However, people who work with radioactive materials, such as radiographers and radiotherapists, must take special precautions to reduce their exposure to nuclear radiations.

Figure 12.7 shows the main sources of background radiation for people living in the UK.

- Various rocks in the Earth, particularly granite, contain small percentages of radioactive uranium and thorium. As these elements decay they emit radioactive radon gas, which can accumulate to dangerous levels in confined spaces.
- Bricks and other building materials also give off radiations, because they are produced from rocks and clay in the Earth's crust.
- Our food contains traces of radioactive materials.
- The Sun and other stars in the Universe emit gamma radiation, some of which reaches the Earth.
- X-rays used for diagnosis by doctors and dentists are ionising radiations.

12.4 What happens during radioactive decay?

Radioactive decay is the random emission of radiation from the unstable nuclei of radioactive atoms as alpha particles, beta particles and gamma rays.

Alpha particles are helium nuclei, ${}^{4}_{2}He^{2+}$.

Beta particles are electrons with negligible (almost zero) mass and a charge of −1, so they are written as ${}^{0}_{-1}e$.

Gamma rays are very penetrating electromagnetic rays.

Radioactive materials emit ionising radiation all the time. During **radioactive decay**, the unstable nuclei of radioactive atoms break up. The break-up is random. When the nuclei break up, they emit **alpha particles**, **beta particles** and **gamma rays**. But what exactly happens during these radioactive decay processes?

Alpha decay

Unstable isotopes with atomic numbers above 83 often decay (break up) by losing an alpha particle. This is called alpha decay. Isotopes that break up by alpha decay include radium-226, uranium-238 and plutonium-238. These isotopes tend to decay because their nuclei are just too heavy – they contain lots of protons and neutrons. Their nuclei become more stable by losing mass in the form of an alpha particle.

For example, when an atom of ${}^{226}_{88}Ra$ loses an alpha particle, it loses two protons and two neutrons from its nucleus. The atom left behind has a mass number of 222 (four less than ${}^{226}_{88}Ra$) and an atomic number of 86 (two less than ${}^{226}_{88}Ra$).

All atoms of atomic number 86 are those of radon, Rn. So we can summarise the alpha decay of radium-226 in a nuclear equation as:

$${}^{226}_{88}Ra \rightarrow {}^{222}_{86}Rn + {}^{4}_{2}He$$

Beta decay

Radioactive isotopes with atomic numbers below 83 tend to undergo beta decay by losing an electron ($_{-1}^{0}e$). During beta decay, a neutron in the nucleus splits up into a proton and an electron. The proton stays in the nucleus, but the electron is ejected as a beta particle. Thus, the mass number of the remaining nucleus stays the same, but its atomic number increases by one (Table 12.3).

For example, when carbon-14 ($_{6}^{14}C$) loses a beta particle ($_{-1}^{0}e$), the product nucleus has an atomic number one more than $_{6}^{14}C$. This is $_{7}^{14}N$. The nuclear equation for the process is

$$_{6}^{14}C \rightarrow {}_{7}^{14}N + {}_{-1}^{0}e$$

The nuclei left behind after radioactive decay are called decay products.

	Alpha decay	Beta decay
Isotopes involved	Atomic number > 83	Atomic number < 83
Particle lost	$_{2}^{4}He^{2+}$	$_{-1}^{0}e$
Change in mass number	-4	0
Change in atomic number	-2	$+1$

Table 12.3 Comparing alpha decay and beta decay. In both cases, the atomic number changes so one element is converted to another element.

Remember that:
- Nuclear equations only show changes in the nuclei of radioactive elements. They do not involve electrons in the shells of the atom.
- The electrons ejected in beta decay come from the nucleus and not, as you might expect, from the shells of the decaying atoms.
- The total mass and total charge of the decay products are the same as those of the initial nucleus.

5 Uranium 238 ($_{92}^{238}U$) decays by losing an alpha particle to form thorium (Th).
a) What is the mass number of the thorium produced?
b) What is the atomic number of the thorium?
c) Write a nuclear equation for the decay process.

6 Write nuclear equations for the beta decay of:
a) $_{19}^{43}K$ to calcium;
b) $_{11}^{24}Na$ to magnesium.

7 Explain the following terms:
a) radioactivity;
b) nuclear reaction;
c) alpha decay.

12.5 Nuclear fission and atomic energy

Chemical reactions and nuclear reactions

Chemical reactions involve changes in the electrons in the outer parts of atoms (Section 5.6). During chemical reactions, electrons are either:
- transferred from one atom to another; or
- shared between two atoms.

Nuclear reactions, on the other hand, involve changes to nuclei in the centre of atoms. During nuclear reactions, one element is converted to another element by:
- radioactive decay;
- nuclear fission; or
- nuclear fusion.

Activity – From Dalton to the atom smashers

Figure 12.8 John Dalton was born in Cumbria in 1766. For most of his life, he was a teacher in Manchester. John Dalton put forward his atomic theory in 1807.

Dalton's ideas about atoms are still helpful to scientists. But modern knowledge about elements and atomic structure has shown that some of his ideas were incorrect. Dalton said that:

- all matter is made up of tiny particles, called atoms;
- atoms cannot be made;
- atoms cannot be broken apart;
- all the atoms of one element are exactly alike;
- atoms of one element are different from those of all other elements.

The first scientists to convert one element into another were Rutherford and his colleagues in the 1920s. They turned sodium into magnesium and aluminium into silicon. In 1940, chemists in the USA managed to make (synthesise) new elements from uranium, the heaviest natural element. They did this by bombarding heavy elements like uranium with neutrons. For example, neptunium-239 and plutonium-239 were obtained by bombarding uranium-238 with neutrons.

1. We now know that matter is composed of smaller particles than atoms. What are these smaller particles called?
2. Atoms of new elements were first made by chemists in the 1940s.
   a) Name two elements synthesised by chemists.
   b) Where do these synthesised elements lie in the Periodic Table?
   c) Why do you think that neutrons were better 'bullets' than protons and alpha particles for synthesising new elements?
3. a) What type of element breaks apart naturally?
   b) What happens when elements break apart?
4. a) What name is given to atoms of the same element which are not exactly alike?
   b) How do these atoms differ?
5. How do atoms of one particular element always differ in atomic structure from those of all other elements?
6. In 1938, German scientists discovered that bombarding uranium-235 with neutrons could produce enormous amounts of energy. This process split uranium atoms in two and was called atomic fission.
   What were the consequences of the discovery of atomic fission, or 'splitting the atom'?

Nuclear fission

Nuclear fission is the splitting of an atomic nucleus, resulting in the release of large amounts of energy.

In 1938, the German scientist, Otto Hahn, discovered that enormous amounts of energy could be obtained from **nuclear fission**. His discovery happened almost by chance. Hahn and his colleagues were trying to make a new element by bombarding uranium with neutrons. Instead of producing just one new element with a slightly different atomic number, the neutrons caused the uranium nuclei to break up violently, forming two smaller nuclei. More neutrons were also released plus vast quantities of energy (Figure 12.10).

Figure 12.9 Lise Meitner was born in Austria and worked with Otto Hahn in Germany for several years. Lise was Jewish and had to flee from Germany in 1938. It was Hahn who first split the atom, but Lise Meitner who explained the process and gave it the name nuclear fission.

> A **chain reaction** occurs when the neutrons released by splitting one nucleus go on to split more nuclei. The reaction needs no further input.

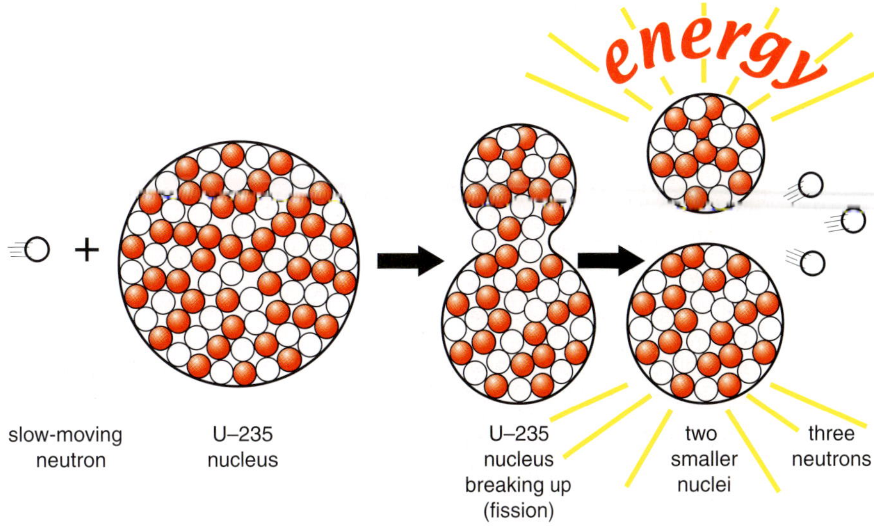

Figure 12.10 Fission of a nucleus of uranium-235

Nuclear fission differs from radioactive decay in two important ways.

- Nuclear fission does not happen spontaneously like radioactive decay. It only happens when unstable nuclei like uranium-235 absorb neutrons.
- Nuclear fission involves the break-up of one large nucleus into two fragments of roughly the same size. During radioactive decay, the products are one large fragment and one very small fragment (either an alpha particle or a beta particle).

Natural uranium contains two isotopes, $^{235}_{92}U$ and $^{238}_{92}U$. Only 0.7% is uranium-235. Experiments show that only uranium-235 takes part in nuclear fission. This has led scientists to realise that if natural uranium is enriched with more uranium-235, the neutrons released during fission can go on to split more uranium nuclei and start a **chain reaction**.

In an atomic bomb, the fission of enriched U-235 atoms releases three neutrons. These three neutrons collide with three more U-235 atoms, releasing nine neutrons; these nine release 27, then 81, and so on. Each time, more and more energy is produced in an uncontrolled reaction resulting in vast amounts of energy.

In a nuclear reactor, a lower concentration of U-235 is used to produce a controlled chain reaction. In this case, only one of the three neutrons released at each fission goes on to cause another fission and a steady chain reaction occurs.

Activity – How do nuclear reactors work?

Figure 12.11 shows a simplified diagram of a gas-cooled nuclear reactor. At the centre of the reactor, rods of 'enriched' uranium containing 3% of uranium-235 are stacked inside a large block of graphite. Neutrons released by the fission of uranium-235 are slowed down by collision with carbon atoms in the graphite. A slow-moving neutron splits a nucleus more easily.

The energy released by nuclear fission in the fuel

rods heats up the reactor. The temperature of the reactor is controlled by moveable rods of boron that absorb neutrons. A controlled chain reaction can be obtained by carefully adjusting these neutron-absorbing rods. Heat is produced steadily and taken away by carbon dioxide circulating through the reactor. The heat is used to turn water into steam, which drives a turbine to generate electricity.

Reactors have also been developed that use plutonium-239 as the fuel in place of uranium-235. Plutonium-239 can use fast neutrons, unlike uranium-235, which undergoes fission more readily with slow neutrons. This means that a plutonium reactor does not need a graphite block to slow down neutrons. These reactors are called fast reactors. The first atomic power station to use a fast reactor for generating electricity was built at Dounreay in Scotland.

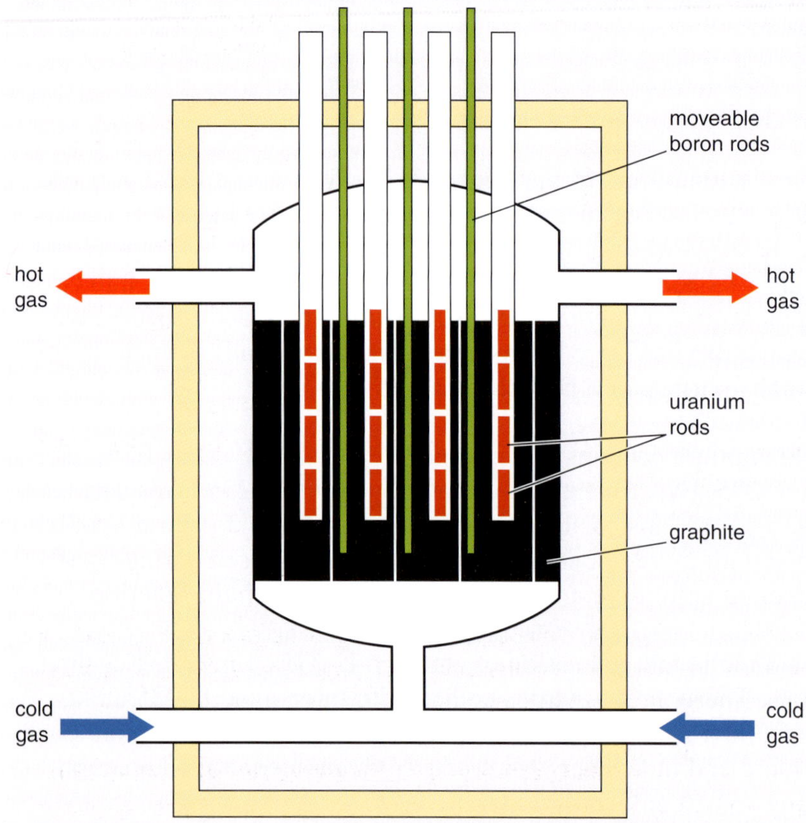

Figure 12.11 A simplified diagram of a gas-cooled nuclear reactor

1. Why are the uranium rods sunk in graphite?
2. How do the boron rods control the temperature of the reactor?
3. What should a technician do if the reactor core suddenly gets too hot?
4. Why is the reactor inside thick concrete?
5. How is the energy from nuclear fission converted into electricity?
6. Which two fissionable isotopes are used in nuclear reactors?
7. Why is the symbol for a neutron, $^{1}_{0}n$?
8. What numbers should replace the letters **A**–**E** in the following equation for the possible fission of uranium-235?

$$^{1}_{\mathbf{A}}n + ^{\mathbf{B}}_{92}U \rightarrow ^{\mathbf{C}}_{56}Ba + ^{88}_{\mathbf{D}}Kr + \mathbf{E}\,^{1}_{0}n$$

9. Draw a labelled diagram to show:
   a) how a controlled, steady chain reaction can occur in a nuclear reactor;
   b) how an uncontrolled explosive chain reaction can occur in an atomic bomb.

12.6 Nuclear fusion

Nuclear fusion is the joining together of two atomic nuclei, resulting in the release of large amounts of energy.

The energy that is released by our Sun and other stars comes from **nuclear fusion**. Fusion means 'joining together'. During nuclear fusion, two nuclei are joined together to form just one larger nucleus and energy is released.

Temperatures get to about 15 000 000 K (fifteen million kelvin) at the centre of the Sun. At these temperatures, the nuclei of atoms are stripped of their electrons. The nuclei collide at high speed with each other and with individual protons and neutrons. Some of the collisions result in fusion. The particles stick together to form larger nuclei. One of the major fusion processes in stars involves hydrogen nuclei fusing to form helium (Figure 12.12).

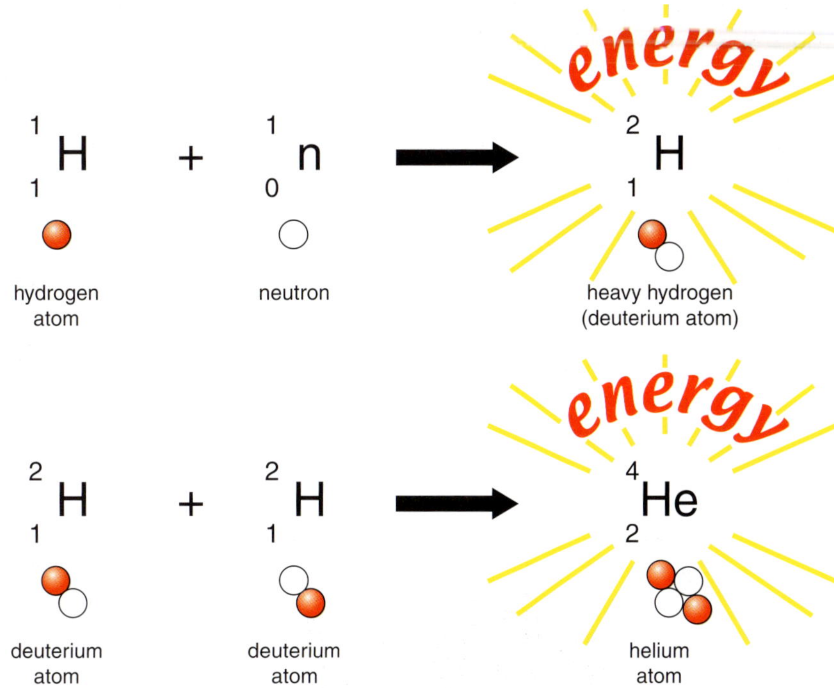

Figure 12.12 The fusion processes which produce helium from hydrogen inside a star

Summary

- ✓ Experiments by Rutherford and his colleagues led to the idea that atoms have a tiny positive nucleus containing protons and neutrons surrounded by a much larger region of empty space in which there are electrons.
- ✓ This idea became known as the '**nuclear model**' of atomic structure, which rapidly replaced the '**plum pudding model**' suggested by Thomson.
- ✓ All the atoms of a particular element have the same number of protons. The number of protons in an atom is known as the **atomic number**.
- ✓ The total number of protons + neutrons in an atom is known as the **mass number**.
- ✓ **Isotopes** are atoms of an element with the same atomic number, but different mass numbers.
- ✓ The main sources of **background radiation** in the UK are rocks in the Earth, bricks, building materials, our food, the Sun and medical uses.
- ✓ **Radioactive decay** is the random emission of radiation from the unstable nuclei of radioactive atoms as alpha particles, beta particles and gamma rays.

  Alpha particles are helium nuclei, $^4_2He^{2+}$.
  Beta particles are electrons.
  Gamma rays are very penetrating electromagnetic rays.
- ✓ During alpha decay, the mass number of a nucleus decreases by four and its atomic number decreases by two.
- ✓ During beta decay, the mass number of a nucleus remains unchanged, but the atomic number increases by one.

- ✓ During **nuclear fission**, a nucleus first absorbs a neutron and then splits into two smaller nuclei releasing two or three neutrons and large amounts of energy. The neutrons released in the process can start a **chain reaction**.
- ✓ There are two fissionable nuclei in common use in nuclear reactors – uranium-235 and plutonium-239.
- ✓ During **nuclear fusion**, two nuclei join together to form one larger nucleus, releasing vast amounts of energy.

EXAMQUESTIONS

1 a) Some patients who suffer from cancer are given an injection of boron, which is absorbed by cancer cells. The cancerous tissue is then irradiated with neutrons. After this, the reaction which occurs is:

$$^{11}_{5}B \rightarrow {}^{7}_{x}Li + {}^{y}_{z}He$$

Copy the equation and write numbers in place of x, y and z. *(3 marks)*

b) What is the special name for this type of reaction? *(1 mark)*

c) Why do the lithium and helium nuclei repel each other? *(1 mark)*

d) Why can this treatment kill cancer cells? *(1 mark)*

2 Copy and complete the following sentences.

In a nuclear reactor, the fuel rods are made of ______ 'enriched' with about 3% of uranium-235. For ______ to occur, the uranium-235 atoms must first absorb a ______. The process releases energy in a controlled ______ reaction and can be used to generate ______. Some reactors use ______ as the fissionable material in place of uranium-235. *(6 marks)*

3 In Geiger and Marsden's experiment, about one in every 10 000 alpha particles appeared to bounce back from the gold foil.

Explain how you think the number of alpha particles bouncing back would change if:

a) thicker gold foil was used; *(2 marks)*

b) aluminium foil of the same thickness was used. *(3 marks)*

4 a) What is nuclear fission? Say what happens and what is produced. *(5 marks)*

b) State one way in which nuclear fission is similar to radioactive decay. *(1 mark)*

c) State two ways in which nuclear fission is different from radioactive decay. *(2 marks)*

d) What numbers or symbols replace the letters A–E in the following nuclear equation?

$$^{A}_{92}B \rightarrow {}^{234}_{C}Th + {}^{D}_{2}E$$ *(5 marks)*

5 Many people are concerned about our use of nuclear energy. Their worries can be summed up in three words 'cost, disposal and security'.

a) Suggest two major costs involved in providing electricity from nuclear energy. *(2 marks)*

b) Explain the concerns that people have about 'disposal' *(2 marks)*

c) What are people's concerns about security? *(1 mark)*

d) Suggest two benefits or advantages of using nuclear energy to generate electricity. *(2 marks)*

Data sheet

1. Reactivity series of metals

Potassium	most reactive
Sodium	↑
Calcium	
Magnesium	
Aluminium	
Carbon	
Zinc	
Iron	
Tin	
Lead	
Hydrogen	
Copper	
Silver	
Gold	↓
Platinum	least reactive

(elements in italics, though non–metals, have been included for comparison)

2. Formulae of some common ions

Positive ions

Name	Formula
Hydrogen	H^+
Sodium	Na^+
Silver	Ag^+
Potassium	K^+
Lithium	Li^+
Ammonium	NH_4^+
Barium	Ba^{2+}
Calcium	Ca^{2+}
Copper(II)	Cu^{2+}
Magnesium	Mg^{2+}
Zinc	Zn^{2+}
Lead	Pb^{2+}
Iron(II)	Fe^{2+}
Iron(III)	Fe^{3+}
Aluminium	Al^{3+}

Negative ions

Name	Formula
Chloride	Cl^-
Bromide	Br^-
Fluoride	F^-
Iodide	I^-
Hydroxide	OH^-
Nitrate	NO_3^-
Oxide	O^{2-}
Sulfide	S^{2-}
Sulfate	SO_4^{2-}
Carbonate	CO_3^{2-}

1	2											3	4	5	6	7	0
							1 H hydrogen 1										4 He helium 2
7 Li lithium 3	9 Be beryllium 4											11 B boron 5	12 C carbon 6	14 N nitrogen 7	16 O oxygen 8	19 F fluorine 9	20 Ne neon 10
23 Na sodium 11	24 Mg magnesium 12											27 Al aluminium 13	28 Si silicon 14	31 P phosphorus 15	32 S sulfur 16	35.5 Cl chlorine 17	40 Ar argon 18
39 K potassium 19	40 Ca calcium 20	45 Sc scandium 21	48 Ti titanium 22	51 V vanadium 23	52 Cr chromium 24	55 Mn manganese 25	56 Fe iron 26	59 Co cobalt 27	59 Ni nickel 28	63.5 Cu copper 29	64 Zn zinc 30	70 Ga gallium 31	73 Ge germanium 32	75 As arsenic 33	79 Se selenium 34	80 Br bromine 35	84 Kr krypton 36
85 Rb rubidium 37	88 Sr strontium 38	89 Y yttrium 39	91 Zr zirconium 40	93 Nb niobium 41	96 Mo molybdenum 42	Tc technetium 43	101 Ru ruthenium 44	103 Rh rhodium 45	106 Pd palladium 46	108 Ag silver 47	112 Cd cadmium 48	115 In indium 49	119 Sn tin 50	122 Sb antimony 51	128 Te tellurium 52	127 I iodine 53	131 Xe xenon 54
133 Cs caesium 55	137 Ba barium 56	139 La lanthanum 57	178 Hf hafnium 72	181 Ta tantalum 73	184 W tungsten 74	186 Re rhenium 75	190 Os osmium 76	192 Ir iridium 77	195 Pt platinum 78	197 Au gold 79	201 Hg mercury 80	204 Tl thallium 81	207 Pb lead 82	209 Bi bismuth 83	[209] Po polonium 84	[210] At astatine 85	[222] Rn radon 86
[223] Fr francium 87	[226] Ra radium 88	[227] Ac* actinium 89	[261] Rf rutherfordium 104	[262] Db dubnium 105	[266] Sg seaborgium 106	[264] Bh bohrium 107	[277] Hs hassium 108	[268] Mt meitnerium 109	[271] Ds darmstadtium 110	[272] Rg roentgenium 111	Elements with atomic numbers 112–116 have been reported but not fully authenticated						

Key

relative atomic mass
atomic symbol
atomic name
proton number

*The Lanthanides (atomic numbers 58–71) and the Actinides (atomic numbers 90–103) have been omitted.

Cu and **Cl** have not been rounded to the nearest whole number.

Index